Scottish Highlanders
and Native Americans

Scottish Highlanders and Native Americans

Indigenous Education in the
Eighteenth-Century Atlantic World

Margaret Connell Szasz

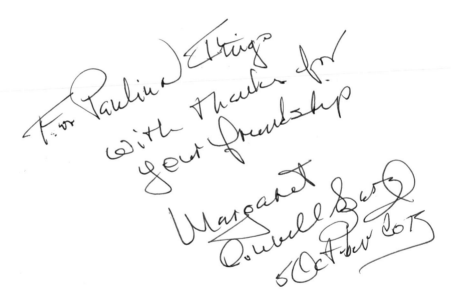

University of Oklahoma Press : Norman

Also by Margaret Connell Szasz

Education and the American Indian: The Road to Self-Determination, 1928–1973 (Albuquerque, 1974)

Education and the American Indian: The Road to Self-Determination since 1928, 2nd. ed. (Albuquerque, 1977)

First Congregational Church of Albuquerque, New Mexico, A Centennial History: 1880–1980 (Albuquerque, 1980)

Indian Education in the American Colonies, 1607–1783 (Albuquerque, 1988; Lincoln, 2007)

(ed.) *Between Indian and White Worlds: The Cultural Broker* (Norman, 1994)

Education and the American Indian: The Road to Self-Determination since 1928, 3rd. ed. (Albuquerque, 1999)

Library of Congress Cataloging-in-Publication Data

Szasz, Margaret.
Scottish highlanders and native Americans : indigenous education in the eighteenth-century Atlantic world / Margaret Connell Szasz.
p. cm.
Includes bibliographical references and index.
ISBN 978-0-8061-3861-9 (hardcover : alk. paper)
1. Indians of North America—Education—History—18th century. 2. Algonquian Indians—Education—History—18th century. 3. Iroquois Indians—Education—History—18th century. 4. Indians of North America—Cultural assimilation. 5. Scottish-Americans—History—18th century. I. Title.
E97.S944 2007
371.82997′2—dc22

                                            2007005596

The paper in this book meets the guidelines for permanence and durability of the Committee on Production Guidelines for Book Longevity of the Council on Library Resources. ∞

Copyright © 2007 by the University of Oklahoma Press, Norman, Publishing Division of the University. All rights reserved. Manufactured in the U.S.A.

1 2 3 4 5 6 7 8 9 10

To my colleagues and students
at the University of Aberdeen, Scotland

Contents

List of Illustrations ix

Acknowledgments xi

Introduction 3

1. Land and Cultures of Gaels, Algonquians, and Iroquois 15
2. Highlands versus Lowlands: The Creation of the Highland Line 43
3. Scotland and the Birth of the SSPCK 68
4. Highland Gaels and the "Shocktroops of Presbyterianism" 82
5. The Scottish Society and Native America 115
6. The Algonquians and Iroquois Meet the Scottish Society 134
7. Dugald Buchanan and Samson Occom 162
8. The Edinburgh Connection: Mohegan and Highland Gael in Scotland 197

Conclusion 217

Notes 227

Bibliography 261

Index 273

Illustrations

Figures

Isle of Skye viewed from Isle of Raasay   28
Linlithgow in 1823   59
Neil Gow   61
St. Giles Cathedral   64
Macleod Stone, Isle of Harris   79
Traditional homes in Blackhouse Village, Isle of Lewis   88
Isle of Harris   91
Tay Bridge at Aberfeldy   99
Page from Patrick Butter's journal   103
Raining's School stairs, Inverness   108
Former location of Raining's School   109
Sabhal Mòr Ostaig   114
David Brainerd   127
Joseph Brant (Thayendanegea)   148
The Reverend George Whitefield   172
Kinloch Rannoch   173
Monument to Dugald Buchanan in Kinloch Rannoch   175
Family cottage of Dugald Buchanan   176
Greyfriars Kirk, Edinburgh   184
Graveyard of Little Leny   186
Monument to Dugald Buchanan in Graveyard of Little Leny   187
The Mohegan/Thames River, Connecticut   188
Marker for the Mohegan tribe   189
The Reverend Samson Occom   194
The Reverend Samson Occom   200
Hadrian's Wall   202
Title page, Gaelic New Testament   210

Maps

Scotland   17
North America   26
The Scottish Highlands   45
SSPCK schools, 1774   113
Indians of the northeastern river valleys   130
Southern New England Algonquians   139
Iroquois and southern New England Algonquians   156
Perthshire, ca. 1780   177

Acknowledgments

Research is a humbling experience. Searching archives and manuscript collections, receiving advice from learned scholars, and conversing with people at museums, in libraries, in bed and breakfast lodgings, in shops, on trains, even on the Caledonian MacBrayne (Cal Mac) ferries among the Hebrides all remind us that we would be lost without the community that assists us as we stumble along the path of a storytelling creation. In these pages, therefore, I am issuing a general thanks to all who have added to the writing of this work, whether in the form of ideas, criticism, queries, direction, or, most importantly, humor.

The roots for this book began in the mid-1980s at the University of Exeter. In the temperate climate of Devon, my husband Ferenc M. Szasz, scholar extraordinaire, our younger daughter, Maria, another fine scholar, and I spent a year in various academic pursuits, all based on Ferenc's teaching Fulbright fellowship. During that year we became acquainted with a number of extraordinary colleagues, including, among others, Mick Gidley, David Horn, and Richard Maltby. During the spring of 1986, Mick made the arrangements for the "Colloquium on Cultural Brokers," held in March at the Institute of United States Studies in London, and he kindly invited me to give the keynote address. This opportunity changed the course of my career, thrusting me into the field of comparative ethnohistory, with its stimulating challenges. The year also led to initial research at the National Archives of Scotland (NAS), then known as the Scottish Record Office (SRO), and my first acquaintance with its knowledgeable archivists. Since that introductory foray, I have returned on many occasions, where I invariably found the highest professional expertise from archivists and other staff, including John Fairgrieve, Mandon Mazs, Andy Orr, George Paterson, Robert Gibb, and Jane Jamieson. During that first visit to Scotland we met Mrs. E. M. Donaldson, whose bed and breakfast has become our prized lodging in Edinburgh and whose friendship we have cherished for two decades.

Five years later, in 1991–92, we crossed the Atlantic again, when I accepted a year's teaching exchange with Ted Ranson in the Department of History at the University of Aberdeen, Scotland. During that year we amassed an enormous heating bill, courtesy of the North Sea and environs, while Ted, living in our home near the University of New Mexico, lived so frugally he managed to gain a refund on his heating bill. One year at Aberdeen convinced us that we must return, and in ensuing summers, we participated in the University of New Mexico's Summer Programs Abroad, with the capable assistance of UNM's International Programs staff, especially Rebecca Digman and Ken Carpenter. Rebecca always offered sound advice for the students, reminding them to pack their suitcases, walk around the block with them, and then remove half of the contents.

At the University of Aberdeen we gained colleagues and enduring friendships that we renew virtually every summer. The ideas and advice from these friends have molded this manuscript to such an extent that I hold them partially responsible for giving me the courage to continue despite many adversities. These colleagues include Marjory Harper, whose reading of several drafts of the manuscript provided invaluable comment and detailed assessment. Marjory's guidance can be seen throughout the manuscript. I am also grateful to Tom Devine, who read an earlier draft. Former director of the Research Institute for Irish and Scottish Studies at the University of Aberdeen, he is now Sir William Fraser Professor of Scottish History and Paleography at the University of Edinburgh. Donald E. Meek, former chair of Celtic studies at the University of Aberdeen, and, more recently, Professor of Scottish and Gaelic studies at the University of Edinburgh, has served as my mentor and primary source of understanding for Dugald Buchanan, the Gaelic bard and cultural intermediary. Grant Simpson and David Ditchburn, scholars of Scottish medieval history at the University of Aberdeen, have enlivened many an evening's conversation with their wit and encyclopedic knowledge of their field. Anne Simpson, scholar of Scottish history, has also aided me in many ways. Chris Fraser, a former student at the University of Aberdeen, has searched for materials when I was unable to get to Scotland, and he also read portions of the manuscript. His unfailing humor, alongside that of his wife, Beth, has made him a splendid host and guest, both in New Mexico and northern Scotland.

Other scholars who have read the manuscript include Colin Calloway, Professor of history and Samson Occom Professor of Native American studies at Dartmouth College. Colin and I share a connection in the relatively new comparative ethnohistory field—Scottish Gaels and Native North Americans—and I am grateful for his assessments. Michael C. Coleman, an Irish scholar who teaches in Finland, has contributed his energies to the manuscript, offering perhaps the most detailed comments of any of my readers. His commentary, like his friendship, has been invaluable. Ferenc Morton Szasz read an earlier draft of the manuscript, offering his finely honed skills to improve both style and clarity.

Portions of this manuscript have been delivered at conferences and elsewhere. I would like to thank Robert A. Trennert for inviting me to present a paper before the history department at Arizona State University. His queries about the possible meeting between Buchanan and Samson Occom are reflected in chapter 9. Also at ASU, Peter Iverson has listened to many questions on the manuscript, offering his sympathetic ear. I also appreciate the invitation of the history department at the University of Aberdeen to present a paper at a department colloquium. The late Donald J. Withrington, scholar of the history of Scottish education, asked provocative questions during that colloquium, which I have incorporated into my assessment of the SSPCK schools in the Highlands. Markku Henriksson of North American studies in the Renvall Institute, University of Helsinki, Finland, invited me to give a keynote address at the Maple Leaf and Eagle Conference in 2004, where I delivered another paper that has become part of the manuscript. Both Markku and his wife, Ritva Levo-Henrikkson, of the Department of Communication have welcomed us to Finland with their amazing warmth and energy. Pirkko Koski of the Renvall Institute handled with considerable finesse the complex arrangements for the many scholars who participated in this event. I have also presented papers on this subject at conferences in Vancouver, British Columbia, Cambridge University, England, and the American Society for Ethnohistory gathering in Santa Fe.

Archivists and librarians at a number of institutions have provided essential services. At the University of New Mexico, I would especially like to thank Kate Luger, who has a thorough knowledge of the Scottish sources, as well as the staff in the Inter-Library Loan Office, who have managed to persist despite the disastrous fire of May 2006 that destroyed many of the periodicals in UNM's Zimmerman Library, including all of the history periodicals and many in ethnohistory and anthropology. At the University of Aberdeen, I thank the staff in the Queen Mother Library as well as Michelle Gait and June Ellner, who assisted me when I was working in the Special Libraries and Archives of King's College. I am also grateful to the staff at Special Collections, University of Edinburgh; the Mitchell Library in Glasgow; the Baker-

Berry Library at Dartmouth College; the Hamilton College Library, Clinton, New York; the National Library of Scotland in Edinburgh; the Connecticut Historical Society in Hartford; the Inverness Library in Inverness, Scotland; the Ulapool Museum and Visitor Center in Ulapool, Scotland; and the Speer Library, Princeton Theology Seminary. For those who have assisted me in procuring illustrations, I thank the staff of the Museum of Art, Bowdon College; Kathleen O'Malley at the Hood Museum of Art, Dartmouth College; Rachel Travers at the National Galleries of Scotland; Leanne Swallow, principal search rooom archivist, National Archives of Scotland; Lizanne Garrett of the National Portrait Gallery, Washington, D.C; France Beauregard at the National Gallery of Canada; the Presbyterian Historical Society in Philadelphia; and Ferenc M. Szasz, who shot a number of the illustrations on our research travels.

I am grateful to cartographer Charlotte Cobb for creating the maps of Scotland—one of the country and the second of the Scottish Highlands. Her professionalism is clearly in evidence in these works. I would also like to extend my appreciation to Professor Charles W. J. Withers for his willingness to permit Charlotte to create the third map of the SSPCK schools, which is based on a map in his book, *Gaelic in Scotland, 1698–1981: The Geographical History of a Language.*

At the University of Oklahoma Press, I am indebted to Charles Rankin, whose encouragement and willingness to listen to my description of this story at the Western History Association Conference in the fall of 2005 led me to submit the manuscript early in 2006. It has been a pleasure to work with my editor, Alessandra Jacobi Tamulevich; my copyeditor, Renae Morehead; and also with production manager Emmy Ezell, whose work I have admired since her earlier tenure at the University of New Mexico Press.

My colleagues in the history department at the University of New Mexico who have engaged in many conversations about the themes developed here include Jay Rubenstein, Sam Truett, Charlie Steen, Pat Risso, Lynn Schibechi, and Ferenc Szasz. I am especially grateful to Elaine Nelson, a doctoral student who typed the first draft of the bibliography for me. A number of other graduate students have contributed to this work through discussions in seminars and more informally. These include Lisa Brown, Kent Blansett, Jerry Davis, Shawn Wiemann, Bradley Shreve, Sonia Dickey, Eric Tippeconnic, Kim Suina, Patrick Pynes, and the four who made it to Aberdeen for the Summer School Abroad program—Kathleen Chamberlain, Chris Harrison, Amy Scott, and Janine Dorsey. I also am indebted to the endless discussions with undergraduates during two decades of teaching courses in Native American history and comparative Native American and Celtic ethnohistory, at UNM, the University of Exeter, and the University of Aberdeen.

I would also like to thank the staff in the Department of History: Yolanda Martinez, who, essentially, runs the department; Dana Ellison; Helen Ferguson; and Barbara Wafer. They are extraordinary people who make it possible for the faculty to survive in the academic chaos of the late twentieth and early twenty-first century.

My family members have served as the bedrock for the years that have gone into this book. The Bradleys—Chris and Scott, Tyler, Sean, and Matthew—Eric, and Maria have always been there when I needed them. Helen F. Garretson and the late John L. Garretson have listened, sometimes with puzzlement but always with love and affection, to the strange workings of a historian engaged in research. Ferenc and Mary Szasz heard many of these stories before their passing on. Helen Moulton and Carl E. Connell, my parents, nurtured me in the field of history from my earliest years. C. Rich Connell and his wife, Angie Connell, and Bob Connell, my brothers and sister-in-law, have supported me throughout, especially in recent years with our loss of Carl and Helen. This work would never have been completed without the constancy of my companion, friend, colleague, intellectual counterpart, and husband, Ferenc Morton Szasz.

Scottish Highlanders
and Native Americans

Introduction

> Chan eil air an duine
> sona ach a bhreith
> agus àrach
> The contented person has no needs
> but to be born
> and brought up
>
> > Frank Rennie, *Celtic Culture, Cultar Ceilteach, The Western Isles, Nah Eileanan an Iar*

    Education forms the heart of any culture. For every society, the children represent the future: only the children can carry on the traditions; only the youth have the potential to become the repositories of the society's worldviews. By teaching the old ways to the children, the society ensures the persistence of its culture. When a society surrenders control of the education of its youth, the people relinquish much of their capacity to survive as a unique culture. While eighteenth-century colonialism took on many forms, the efforts of European colonial powers to reeducate the children of a colonized people proved a crucial measure of their success. When the colonizers believed they had weakened the wisdom of those colonized by persuading the youth to adopt their own views of the world, they were moving toward their goals.

    Beginning early in the eighteenth century, a group of Scottish Lowlanders centered in Edinburgh sought to impose Lowland understandings of culture on the Scottish Highlands and the Western and Northern Islands by introducing Lowland education to the children living beyond the Highland Line. After their initial schooling thrust into the Highlands, this group of Lowlanders, known collectively as the Society in Scotland for the Propagation of Christian Knowledge (SSPCK), broadened their design for schooling by expanding across the Atlantic Ocean to the Native peoples living in the Southeast and Northeast

Woodlands of North America. Since the vast distance prevented the society members from controlling Native American schooling from their headquarters in Edinburgh, the SSPCK directors negotiated with American colonials of English, Scottish, and Welsh heritage to direct the SSPCK educational efforts among the Indians. In the end, this cultural thrust across the water juxtaposed Cherokees, Muskogees, Algonquians, and Iroquois against colonial—sometimes Native—schoolmasters and missionaries in the British colonies. By the time of the American Revolution, the enterprise represented a vast network of schools—over 170 in Scotland alone—that extended into the remote regions of the Highlands and the numerous Indian communities of New England and surrounding colonies.

In Scotland, as in North America, in the eighteenth century, the independent status of internal nations within larger political entities was sometimes indistinct. In Native North America Britain recognized indigenous groups as nations by negotiating treaties with them as they did with European powers. Simultaneously, the British sought to denigrate the sovereign status of these nations by physical means such as warfare and some control over trade as well as by cultural means such as missionaries, imposition of British colonial legal systems, and certain modest, private efforts at schooling. In Scotland the political union with England achieved in 1707 implied that Scotland itself no longer retained any separate status. Indeed, it has been suggested that "in the eighteenth century, Scotland, or at least part of it, was less a conquered province than an integral part of the English core state." This becomes problematic, however, when one acknowledges a further internal division, for "in Scotland, the crucial divide, a true internal frontier, lay between the Lowlands and the Highlands."[1]

The blurring of these lines reminds us that the narrative that follows does not fit readily into the paradigm of imperialism that simply contrasts metropole with periphery. In early-eighteenth-century Scotland, for example, Lowlanders perceived the metropole as Edinburgh, but as Scots increasingly shifted their residence to London and beyond the British Isles when they moved outward into the far reaches of the British Empire, the status of the metropole altered in a subtle manner. For some Scots, it even moved outside the borders of Scotland.[2] On the other hand, from the perspective of the Highlands and Islands, as the Lowlanders thrust themselves into this foreign part of Scotland through intensive cultural colonialism and disastrous military defeat, the ordinary clansmen and women began to perceive the metropole as outside the Highlands and in places like Glasgow and, especially, Edinburgh. Yet Linda Colley suggests that the word *Sasannach*, the Scottish epithet for someone who was English born and bred in the eighteenth century, "was used overwhelmingly by Scottish Highlanders as a blanket term to cover English-speaking Scottish Lowlanders as well as the English themselves."[3]

This study, then, will juxtapose one view against another. It will contrast the perspectives of various Native Americans with those of the English colonials in Connecticut, Massachusetts, and beyond and of Highland clansmen and women with those of the schoolmasters sent to teach their children and of the SSPCK directors living in Edinburgh. Given this fluidity of perspectives, the narrative may be seen, in part, as a selected response to earlier scholars who called for a more complex interpretation of imperial history. In the 1980s T. H. Breen suggested that "the new imperial history will focus on the movement of peoples and the clash of cultures, on common folk rather than colonial administrators."[4] In the early 1990s Bernard Bailyn and Philip D. Morgan argued that the general concept of "expansion of the European world outward into a number of alien peripheries or marchlands" was becoming far more complex, "with the colonies [periphery] playing as dynamic a role as the metropolis."[5] Expanding on this theme, Martin Daunton and Rick Halpern pointed out that "there was always some room for a degree of manoeuvre within structures imposed by the imperial state. There were always limits to the extent of imperial power."[6] Some sense of the ambiguity of those limits will appear in the following chapters.

Relations between indigenous people and outsiders were often ambiguous. This description aptly fits the society's endeavors. The nature of the SSPCK's educational encounters with the Highlanders and the Native Americans was scarcely clear-cut. As a rather amorphous entity, this experiment in cultural colonialism proved multifaceted; and on many an occasion, it deflected any effort to achieve clarity. Any assessment of the society's efforts depends on one's perspective; any attempt to generalize about these multiple exchanges provokes a genuine challenge.[7] Although decidedly difficult to pin down, these multilayered cultural encounters in the field of education forged a crucial thread of the eighteenth-century colonial frontiers that lay within Scotland itself as well as in the British colonies. These encounters have long awaited a storyteller.

§

The earlier research and writing that I completed on American Indian and Alaska Native education across Indian Country, compounded by my interest in the role of the "cultural intermediary" or "cultural broker," drew me into this story of internal and external colonialism within Scotland itself and between the Scottish Lowlands and Native America. The cultural broker resides at the focal point of any cultural frontier of humankind. Moving among different worlds, the intermediary seeks to translate—literally and culturally—among the various sides of the cross-cultural equation. Since the mid-1980s, my deep interest in Native American peoples has expanded to include the peoples of Scotland, Ireland, and Wales, especially within the broader framework of comparative indigenous ethnohistory, or a blending of ethnology and history. In the late twentieth century, I found that the significance of cultural intermediaries on North American frontiers was duplicated on the opposite shores of the North Atlantic and, indeed, that the intermediary as a cultural go-between has remained a universal phenomenon of human history.[8]

Living in Scotland during a year's teaching exchange at the University of Aberdeen in 1991–92 and, later, teaching students from the University of New Mexico during several summers on Aberdeen's beautiful campus, I uncovered the rudiments of this story. I made numerous research forays to archives with my husband, Ferenc Morton Szasz, an historian of American intellectual history. Together we traveled across the Lowlands and Highlands and through the Hebrides and Orkneys, and in the process the story began to unfold.

§

The narrative opens long before the eighteenth century. It begins with a brief overview of the early worlds of indigenous peoples who dwelt in the Eastern Woodlands of North America and in the numerous islands—large and small—that lie off the western coast of the European continent. Although these indigenous peoples lived on opposite shores of the North Atlantic, they shared a commonality evinced through their oral cultures, based on myth; their societies, based on kinship; and their mutual dependence on the natural resources available for their survival. On both sides of the Atlantic, the people relied on a reciprocal relationship with the land and its inhabitants, which they voiced via song, origin stories, and a multitude of folk tales. As Native Americans saturated the North American continent with their stories, so too did the clan legends of the Gaelic Highlanders "provide every part of the Highlands and Islands with a local identity and tradition."[9] Of course, there were differences. Christianity reached Ireland and Scotland in the fifth century, whereas it did not reach North America for another millennium. The Irish and the Scots relied on domesticated animals, the Native Americans hunted for deer and other animals. But in terms of their experience of cultural colonialism, their commonalities far outweighed these differences. Hence, the narrative will be rooted in an introductory assessment of these comparative indigenous peoples. It will emphasize how they had already altered their culture and economic base through interactions with outsiders in the many generations before the opening of the eighteenth century.

The saga of the Scottish Society forms the second major theme of this study. Like all reform organizations, the society reflected its times. The SSPCK founders created the organization in direct response to the turbulence that Scotland faced early in the 1700s. Long before the eighteenth century, Scotland had split into two cultures—the Highlands and the Lowlands—and the differences between these two regions, which were divided by a shifting, imaginary marker known as the Highland Line, were legion. With the exception of the far northeast and the Northern Isles, the Highlanders of the mainland and Western Isles spoke Gaelic. Lowlanders spoke the language known as Scots. Almost all Lowlanders had adopted Presbyterianism; Highlanders had accepted a mixture of Episcopalianism, some Presbyterianism, and a remnant of Catholicism. The soil of the Lowlands was arable, while the soil of the rugged Highlands was often unyielding. The Highlanders relied on an ancient but disintegrating clan structure, while the Lowlanders had long accepted a less structured system of societal relationships. Highlanders dressed in tartans; Lowlanders, in a mix of urban and rural attire. Almost all Lowlanders had received some schooling, while most Highlanders had received little or none. By the end of the sixteenth century, when the Stewart king James VI still ruled an independent Scotland, the people who lived on the opposite sides of the Highland Line looked at one another with suspicion, distrust, and downright enmity.

One hundred years later, at the onset of the eighteenth century, Scotland was forced to tackle severe economic and political crises. In recent years, the country had lost a significant portion of its national wealth through an ill-advised venture to establish a colony on the Isthmus of Panama. The nation had already forged a link with England through the Union of the Crowns, completed in 1603, when James VI and I (1567–1625) had succeeded Elizabeth I, becoming monarch for both nations. Although the name was still "Stewart" in Scotland, the English changed the spelling to "Stuart," and it became known as the House of Stuart.[10] A century later, the Parliament of Scotland sealed the royal union with the Union of 1707, when it abolished itself and merged with the Parliament of England at Westminster. Simultaneously, a bitter struggle took place in Scotland in the early eighteenth century as the people attempted to resolve the sharp division between the Whig supporters of the Hanoverian succession to the throne of Britain and the Jacobite supporters of the Stewart line, who longed to restore the monarchy to the deposed Stewarts.[11]

In this tumultuous era, when Scotland had already relinquished much of its political independence, the Scottish Society sprang into being. The society's raison d'être was rooted deeply in the founders' conviction that Scots must strive to become a unified people, a citizenry who shared the same values. Society members relied on the institutions that had been spared through the Union of the Parliaments in 1707 to retain the nation's cultural identity. Despite the political union, Scotland still retained its singular institutions. These included the Kirk, established during the Scottish Reformation of the 1560s; the unique Scottish legal system; and the strong educational system that emerged out of the Scottish Reformation. But in the early 1700s, Presbyterianism and universal schooling largely characterized the Lowlands. The society's founders believed that Scotland's survival as a unique entity depended on its adoption of a unified culture. In this idealized culture, as perceived by the founders, all Scots would become speakers of "English" (Scots); all Scots would become members of the Church of Scotland; all Scots would support the succession of the Hanoverian monarchy; all Scots would be schooled; and most Scots would engage in the type of farming practiced in the rural regions of the Lowlands. Only when the society had attained this goal of homogeneity—through the schooling of the children in the Highlands and Islands—could Scotland, in its entirety, achieve a homogeneous identity. It was to this end that the Scottish Society addressed itself in the early eighteenth century.[12]

The third theme of this narrative will focus on the cross-cultural schooling itself. These sections will contrast the Celtic and Native American cultural encounters between the indigenous pupils and their schoolmasters. The first will assess the experiences of the society's schoolmasters as they crossed the Highland Line to teach their nonliterate pupils through an English-only curriculum in the Gaelic Highlands and the Western and Northern Isles. This educational drama in Scotland began to unfold early in the eighteenth century, and although the SSPCK continued its work until the late nineteenth century, the discussion will focus primarily on the time period that parallels the society's eighteenth-century efforts among Native Americans, roughly to the 1780s. Following this era of society-dominated schooling in the Highlands, the SSPCK began to face competitors, including the Gaelic societies that formed in the Lowland towns in order to encourage the use of Gaelic in Highland schools and, by the late nineteenth century, the public schools that came into being through the passage of the Education Act of 1872. This legislation obviated the society's purpose, although, ironically, it strengthened the society's overall goal—to eliminate Gaelic from the Highlands. Hence, the focus of this book rests largely with the era from 1700 to the American War for Independence (1775–83).

Moving outside Scotland, the second half of the educational encounter will cross the North Atlantic to assess the SSPCK's engagement with Native North Americans. After a cursory look at the short-lived Anglican and Presbyterian missionary experiences among the Muskogees and Cherokees, the story will turn north to evaluate the encounters between the society representatives and the variegated worlds of the Algonquians and Iroquois in New England, New York, and adjacent colonies. The story of the society's involvement with these more northern peoples forms a complex tale of Native communities and their interaction with Native and English schoolmasters; it also includes the cultural colonialism of missionaries, traders, and administrators who represented Congregational, Presbyterian, and Anglican faith backgrounds. In this muddled environment, the unifying event that drew together these markedly different people was the Great Awakening, the religious revival that began during the 1730s in New England and spread its fervor throughout the colonies until the War for Independence. During the mid-eighteenth century, the Great Awakening proved the catalyst for the quickening of the religious spirit in Native American communities, the English colonial communities, and the Scottish Lowlands.

Once the narrative has probed these themes—the diverse indigenous people, the Scottish Society, and the cultural frontier embedded in the schooling itself—the story will shift, coming full circle to the town of Edinburgh, where it began in 1709 with the founding of the SSPCK. The final section will focus on Scotland's capital in 1767, a city that claimed some sixty thousand residents during the mid-eighteenth century, a dramatic era that led contemporaries to describe Edinburgh as one of the key centers of the Scottish Enlightenment. In this singular site, the home turf of the Scottish Society, two Native educational and spiritual intermediaries—one from each side of the Atlantic—walked through the streets of the capital during the summer of 1767. Each of these men had been drawn to Edinburgh because of a unique relationship with the SSPCK.

The first of these intermediaries was Samson Occom, a Mohegan Presbyterian minister and schoolmaster. Although Occom was a strong force within the southern New England Algonquian communities, he had also served as a liaison between the Iroquois and Moor's Indian Charity School, a boarding school founded by Congregational minister Eleazar Wheelock in 1754, and located in Lebanon, Connecticut. Occom had relied on funding from both the Congregational, Boston-based New England Company and the Scottish Society to support himself and his family. The second intermediary was Dugald Buchanan, a Gaelic Highlander who had served as schoolmaster and catechist for the society in the District of Rannoch, located in the uplands of Perthshire. Buchanan had also shared his bardic poetry with the people of Rannoch and in other parts of the Highlands, and he had demonstrated his polished skills as a Gaelic-English translator.

During the mid-1760s, the society attracted these two Native figures to Scotland's capital, and for approximately two months they resided there simultaneously. Occom remained in Scotland during the late spring and summer of 1767, where he and an English colonial minister carried out the Scottish component of a grandiose fund raising tour through the British Isles designed to provide financial security to Moor's Indian Charity School. When Occom arrived, Buchanan was already living in the capital, where he had been supervising the printing of the first New Testament in Scottish Gaelic, a venture initiated and financed by the Scottish Society. When Occom reached Edinburgh with his party, Buchanan had been living there for just over a year and certainly knew the Old Town quite well. As the sole Native American Presbyterian minister in the eighteenth century, Occom remained in demand during his visit, preaching in famous kirks in Edinburgh, Glasgow, Aberdeen, and elsewhere. As supervisor for the printing of the Scottish Gaelic New Testament, Buchanan also remained in demand. Although both men were preoccupied with their responsibilities, they may well have crossed paths, and if they did meet, their exchange would have held dramatic overtones.

The presence of these two cultural intermediaries in the hometown of the SSPCK symbolized the enigmas of the eighteenth-century cultural encounter between indigenous people and outsiders. The lives of these two quintessential Native leaders had been dramatically altered by the Scottish Society. Their strong convictions had bound them to urge their people toward Reformed Protestantism. Yet the deep roots that held them within their indigenous communities had also spurred their fight to retain the cultural sovereignty of Algonquians and Highland Gaels. At the same time, paradoxically, they encouraged their communities to adapt the outsiders' beliefs into their own cultural perspectives. Whether Occom and Buchanan ever shook hands remains an open question, but their residence in Edinburgh during the summer of 1767 served as the cultural epitome of the relationship between the Scottish Society and the people it hoped to change—the Highland Gaels and the Native Americans.

§

One of the most challenging aspects of researching and writing this volume has been retaining a balance between indigenous and outsider perspectives. The archival and printed source material—both primary and secondary accounts—that was recorded by Scottish Lowlanders and English colonials must be interpreted through the cultural lenses of these writers. But the voices of the eighteenth century moved well beyond the figures of colonial power. Eighteenth-century Highlanders remembered their own history through song and story, some of which has been recorded, and through poetry, which was largely vernacular by this time and often written down. Eighteenth-century Algonquians and Iroquois remembered their history with equal concern. They recalled their past via origin stories and folk tales and through individual journals and correspondence.

Although I am neither a Scot—although my ancestry is Scottish and Irish/Scots-Irish—nor a Native American, I have benefited from years of ethnohistorical study, and, as a consequence, I have sought to balance the voices expressed in the many cross-cultural exchanges that follow. Accordingly, I have relied heavily on indigenous sources, such as the diary and correspondence of Samson Occom and letters of other Native Americans from New England and New York, as well as the origin stories and folktales of the Northeast Woodlands as recorded by Native Americans and anthropologists. On the other side of the Atlantic, I have drawn heavily on the rich sources of the National Archives of Scotland, where I read letters written by Dugald Buchanan; and, wherever possible, I have included the translated verse of Highland Gaels. Although the victors often record more battles than the losers, Scottish scholar Donald Smith reminds us that the latter remember well their defeats. After the Jacobite defeat at the hands of the Hanoverians in the Battle of Culloden in 1746, "oral tradition . . . continued under severe social and economic pressure to be a lifeline to the Gaelic past and a resource for the future."[13]

To illustrate these efforts toward balanced perspectives, I offer descriptions of the Gaels drawn from a variety of Scottish perspectives. Derick Thomson, a twentieth-century specialist in Gaelic poetry, described Highland society as "close, kin-based, rural, independent, and self-sufficient in the main."[14] By contrast, in the mid-eighteenth century, the SSPCK chose the following words to describe the same people, who

> spent their time in sauntering from place
> to place in sloth and idleness, and in a total
> neglect of those happy methods by which
> a country is improved, and its inhabitants
> civilized and enriched.[15]

Yet other voices belie this criticism. The Highlanders themselves shared a deep pride in their way of life and their connections with their land. As a Gael wrote of his own part of that land, the Isle of Tiree, in the Hebrides,

> Before a Duke came, or any of his people!
> Or a Kingly George from Hanover's realm
> The low-lying isle with its many shielings
> Belonged as a dwelling to the children of the Gael.[16]

These contrasting sentiments reveal the distinct chasm separating Lowlanders from Highlanders during the eighteenth century and earlier. A similar lack of mutual understanding characterizes the perceptions of English colonials and those of the Algonquians and Iroquois. Eleazar Wheelock, who at one time had dreamed of sending Indian missionaries and schoolmasters throughout Indian Country, and especially among the Iroquois, eventually became disillusioned with his Indian students, observing bitterly, "while I am wearing my life out to do good to the poor Indians, they themselves have no more Desire to help forward the great Design of their Happiness ... but [there] are so many of them pulling the other way & as fast as they can are undoing all I have done."[17] The southern New England Algonquians who left their villages after the American Revolution and settled on lands in upstate New York given them by the Oneidas saw it differently. In a petition appealing for financial aid to enable them to support Samson Occom as their minister, the Indians of Brothertown and New Stockbridge wrote in 1787, "The late unhappy wars have Stript us almost Naked of every thing, our Temporal enjoyments are greatly lesstened, our Numbers vastly diminished, by being warmly engaged in favour of the United States." They added, "The Fountains abroad, that use to water and refresh our Wilderness are all Dryed up, and the Springs that use to rise near are ceased. And we are truly like the man that fell among Thieves, that was Stript, wounded and left half dead in the high way."[18]

One Scottish scholar has noted, "There are two histories of every land and every people, the written history that tells what is considered politic to tell and the unwritten history that tells everything."[19] My goal is to relate a story that falls somewhere between these two poles, one that includes the oral history of the indigenous people who during the eighteenth century still relied on this spoken means of remembering their past. But I also have tried to craft a narrative that balances the Native voices with the accounts that outsiders recorded in written form.

The theme of cultural colonialism remains close to the hearts of many people whose ancestors experienced it firsthand. Hence, the scars from this encounter remain a vivid part of their heritage. But the cultural exchange seldom moved in a single direction. Just as indigenous pupils were changed by their schooling, so too were the schoolmasters changed by their experiences of teaching in the Highlands and among Native Americans. Similarly, the favorable response by Native people to the outsiders' influences cannot be described exclusively in pejorative terms. Throughout this era significant figures representing the indigenous cultures, especially Occom and Buchanan, absorbed the education of the outsiders because they believed it contained far more positive than negative features. The many shades of gray that they encountered in their own experiences of cultural adaptation reveal the ambiguity of these colonialist ventures. I conclude that in these encounters the indigenous people of North America and the Highlands of Scotland chose selectively, accepting what they believed was best for themselves and their communities.

§

In the early twenty-first century, only the readers of Robert Lewis Stevenson's novels will likely have an awareness of the SSPCK. A familiarity with the eighteenth-century adventures of David Balfour—the hero of *Kidnapped*—almost guarantees a nodding acquaintance with the Scottish Society. After his escape from a shipwreck off the Isle of Mull, Balfour travels toward a rendezvous with his Jacobite friend from the ship when he "overtakes "a little stout, solemn man . . . sometimes reading in a book and sometimes marking the place with his finger, and dressed decently and plainly in something of a clerical garb." Balfour's traveling companion, Mr. Henderland, is a catechist "sent out by the Edinburgh Society for the Propagation of Christian Knowledge to evangelize the more savage places of the Highlands." Except for his frequent habit of taking snuff, Mr. Henderland proves a compatible host. Once they reach his dwelling, he serves "porridge and whey" to the Lowland lad. He inquires into Balfour's "state of mind toward God," and, as Balfour recalls, "he soon had me on my knees."[20]

In this intriguing novel, Stevenson creates a symbol for the Scottish Society in the person of Mr. Henderland, who, through the universal appeal of story, achieves for the SSPCK a kind of immortality that no historian has yet imparted. Although the following chapters might not reach the storytelling genre of Stevenson, they have to echo his honest recognition of the efforts of the SSPCK and the complex legacy of the Edinburgh Society.

CHAPTER ONE

Land and Cultures of Gaels, Algonquians, and Iroquois

> Argument from Silence is a hazardous business in the Western Isles, since there is a dearth not only of Facts but of documents of all kinds before 1600.
>
> Francis T. Shaw, *The Northern and Western Islands of Scotland*

In the earliest days of human memory ice lay across the land. It covered everything in the north, carving its path through the valleys and ridges. It was omnipresent. The weight of the ice bore heavily on the earth. On both sides of the Atlantic it pressed south, lowering the sea level, extending the continental shoreline, and linking island with mainland and continent with continent. Then, approximately 10,000 B.C.E., the climate warmed and the great ice mass began to recede. As it melted, the water level in the seas rose until the earth lay under water.

Origin Stories

The origin story of the Iroquois begins here: "all the earth was covered by deep water, and the only living things were water animals. . . . People lived above the great sky dome," and from her home there Sky Woman descended to the earth. As she descended, the waterfowl rose to cushion her fall, and when she landed it was Turtle who held her on the great shell. From there, Muskrat dove to the bottom of the sea to bring up a few grains of earth clutched in his tiny paw. On Turtle's shell the soil began to expand until it stretched far and wide, eventually becoming Turtle Island: "Turtle, the Earth Bearer, is still restless from time to time, and when he stirs there are earthquakes and high seas."[1] Sky Woman gave birth to a daughter, who then bore twins—Sapling and Flint, who was evil.[2] Together the twins set about to create the good and evil conditions that prevail on Turtle Island.

The Northeast Algonquians related a similar story:

> Nanabush, the Strong White One, grandfather of beings,
> Grandfather of men, was on the Turtle Island.
> There he was walking and creating, as he passed by
>   And created the turtle.
> Beings and men all go forth, they walk in the floods
> and shallow waters, down stream thither to the
> Turtle Island.[3]

The Algonquians looked to Cautantowwit, or Kiehtan, the southwest deity and creator. Creating man and woman from a stone, Cautantowwit disliked his first creation and "made a second couple of wood, who became the ancestors of all humankind." Within the corpus of Northeast Algonquian folklore, however, Cautantowwit has remained the sole god, or manitou, "who created and ruled humankind and who sent them their first seeds to grow." Manitous abounded in the fifteenth-century Algonquian world, but only one creator manitou has survived the postcontact pressures. Accounting for the loss of other origin stories among the Algonquians, anthropologist William S. Simmons contends that "Christianity swept this genre away, or rather, replaced it with Christianity's own biblical equivalents."[4] By 1700, when our account opens, the Iroquois, living south and east of Lake Ontario, had retained vibrant origin stories, but the stories of the Algonquians, living in southern New England, were already much diminished.

The once exclusively Celtic islands on the eastern edge of the Atlantic —today's Ireland, Scotland, Wales, Cornwall, Isle of Mann, and England—knew well the impact of the great ice sheet, but the geographical region that bore the brunt of its weight was the Highlands of Scotland. The ice also covered the region known as the Borders, and, to a lesser degree, it bore down on Yorkshire, which lies just south of the Borders. But in the Highlands the ice was over six hundred meters thick. When the glaciers retreated from this region, they left their mark. In some areas they had scoured the soil down to bedrock; in others they had buried the land in sand and gravel; even regions that retained good soil were littered with boulders and stones. Today, a visit to the eastern coast of the Hebridean Isle of South Harris provides ample reminders of the glaciers' legacy.

When the glaciers finally retreated, the land began to rise, "as if it were stretching itself now that it had been released from the dead weight it had borne for thousands of years." Thus, "like a great creature shedding a chrysalis of ice; the land we know as Scotland struggled into

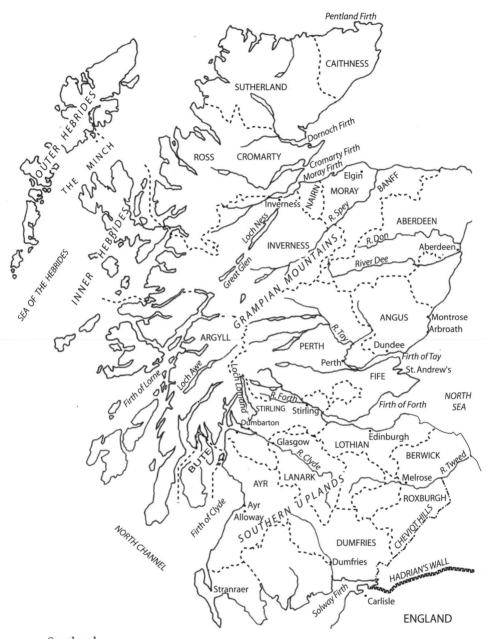

Scotland.
Map by Charlotte Hill Cobb.

the sunlight."[5] As the land rose, so too did the water level, and it began to inundate the land bridge stretching northeast from Britain to Denmark and southeast to France, submerging all of these early corridors beneath the English Channel and the icy waters of the North Sea.

The submerged land that had once linked the Island of Britain with the continent had also bonded Scotland and Ireland, enabling wild horses and giant deer to gambol across the rolling "grasslands of Ireland's heartland." Gradually the moderation of the climate enabled trees to cover the land and to spread up to the mountaintops and across the soggy interior. Later, the first inhabitants of the region, who had walked across the land bridge between Scandinavia and North Britain, probably paddled their dugout canoes across the few miles of water separating Scotland's Mull of Kintyre and present-day County Antrim in Ireland.[6]

The origins of Ireland and Scotland thus enter the grand scene in tandem, and their mythology follows suit. But the core of their mythology—the cosmogony or the origin stories—remains elusive. The mythological cycles of ancient Ireland, later adapted by the Irish or Scotti who moved to Alba (Scotland) early in the sixth century, permeate the landscape of both Ireland and Scottish Gaeldom. There is "scarcely a place that is not connected in some way with the traditionary exploits of the 'Red Branch Champions' or of Finn and his mighty men."[7] The richness of this lore, which was first recorded by medieval Irish monks thereby becoming the earliest written Celtic literature, is also distinctive for its lacunae: it offers no record of Celtic origin stories. Archaeologist Barry Raftery's description of this literature—"an immense body of material combining fact and fantasy, myth and legend, ancient lore, classical interpretation, pan-Christian fables and medieval folk-tradition"—is notable for its lack of any reference to cosmogony.[8]

The reason for this absence may be twofold. It is possible that the Druidic custom of reliance on secrecy and oral tradition may have militated against any perseverance of Celtic origin stories. When the Druids' power was usurped by Christianity, their belief system faded. Secondly, while the Irish and Scottish monks were the crucial catalysts for preserving the oral stories of the Irish mythological cycles, at the same time the monks served as cultural brokers. In this capacity, they stamped the intermediaries' imprint on the message. Thus, they chose to include scriptural narratives of the creation of the universe and of humans, and they failed to allow for parallel Celtic creation narratives. "In the early Irish accounts, therefore, of the beginning of things, we find that it is not with the World that the narrators make their start—it is simply with their own country, with Ireland."⁹ The creation was scripted: Ireland was Irish with a multitude of overtones.

By 1700 the Gaelic Christian Church, formed in Ireland, had merged with Alba's pre-Christian spiritual traditions. The amalgamation began in the early 500s among the Britons of southern Scotland, such as Strathclyde; it concluded 250 years later with the conversion of the Picts, "the last of the Dark Age people of Scotland to accept Christianity."¹⁰ In order for this new faith to enter the lives of the Britons, Anglicans, and Picts, it employed compromise as a successful tactic. Rather than confront certain indigenous traditions, it adapted the Christian calendar to the cycle of the ancient festivals, incorporated the vernacular, and agreed to the people's practice of veneration of ancient shrines, such as holy wells or sacred stones.¹¹

Simultaneously, Christianity brought a nouveau tradition of learning, epitomized by the monasteries, begun in Alba with the arrival of Colm Cille, or St. Columba (521–97), on the Isle of Iona. Many of the monasteries served as church, school, and art center; all of them relied on the written word. Christian myths and stories transcribed by medieval monks served first as an overlay but eventually merged with, and sometimes replaced, the Celtic myths.

By contrast, those bearers of the Christian faith who crossed the water to North America would not arrive among the southern New England Algonquians and the Iroquois for another millennium. The strength of the Iroquois indigenous stories and myths, and to a lesser degree those of the Algonquian, as well as the belated timing of the European Christian missionaries, enabled these Native North American origin stories to persist, despite the eventual inroads of French Jesuits and Dutch, English, and American Protestants. The comparatively late arrival of Christianity in North America empowered the Algonquians and Iroquois, enabling them to strengthen their unique understanding of how the earth and its inhabitants came into being. For these reasons, they were able to preserve their dynamic heritage.

Southern New England Algonquians have been unable to retain the corpus of their origin myths, but this does not preclude their retention of other folklore. In this manner the "ancestral voices continue to speak to the living through oral narratives, and the living in turn attribute new and borrowed customs to ancestral sources."¹²

Like the Algonquian myths, the origin stories of the Gaelic Highlanders have been superceded by scriptural creation mythology. But if their origin stories have been subsumed, the Highlanders still cling to the legends and stories of their ancestors who migrated from Ireland and across other waters as well.

An Amalgam of People

Like their Native North American counterparts, the Highland Gaels have long traced their ancestry through the convoluted peregrinations of intermarriage among different peoples. In the Highlands, "almost everyone is a genealogist," early-eighteenth-century Englishman Edmund Burt carefully noted. Half a century later the indomitable Dr. Samuel Johnson referred to the Highlanders' "recital of genealogies, [a custom which] was anciently made."[13] Both observers recognized the Highland practice of tracing one's ancestry to the distant progenitor of a given clan, such as the well-known Fergus Mór.[14] Fergus Mór was a Scottus of royal blood who moved his family (*cinneadh*) in the late fifth century from Antrim in Northern Ireland to settle in the regions that have become Galloway and Argyll. There he founded in Argyll the Scottish Dalriada, a colony of the Irish kingdom of Dál Riata, marking the earliest Irish intrusion into the land known as Alba or Caledonia.

University of Edinburgh historian Tom M. Devine has argued that "most of these [clan] pedigrees were created and recreated with scant regard for historical accuracy."[15] By 1200 the Scots had emerged as a collective people of many roots. University of Edinburgh historian Michael Lynch characterizes the Scots as "groups of immigrants who have made up the Scottish people over its history."[16] The Picts, who were among the earliest of these immigrants, met their match in the Scots of Dalriada. Residing in Alba from ancient times through the early medieval era, the Picts remain the least known of the Scottish progenitors. Even their name for themselves, recently viewed as a crucial mark of self-identity, has been lost. All that remains is the term "Pritani," a nomenclature applied by the Romans between approximately A.D. 81 and A.D. 155–200 to those people living in northern Scotland.[17]

The Picts may have been a Celtic people, or at least a people led by a Celtic aristocracy, but they eventually intermarried with the Scots of Dalriada and were subsumed by their leadership. By the mid-800s the Picts and the Scots formed the Gaelic stock of the Highlanders and Islanders. During the medieval era, however, the presence of the Norsemen complicated this initial equation. Four centuries of Norse raids and settlement on the Western and Northern Isles and the western and northeastern Highlands ensured a merging of Norse and Celtic cultures that left a linguistic legacy in these regions. On the Isle of Lewis ("Leodhus" for the Norsemen), where the common language was Norwegian, one can still hear the Nordic lilt in the speech of the residents. By 1266, however, following the Scottish-Norwegian Treaty of Perth, Magnus the Law-mender, the Norwegian king, returned to Scotland all Norwegian holdings in the Western Isles, in exchange for an annual fee that Scotland paid into the 1300s.

The Norsemen's presence overlapped with waves of Anglo-Norman as well as Flemish and French immigrants from the continent. Encroaching on the eastern Highlands in the 1100s and 1200s, these continental immigrants introduced into the Gaelic-speaking regions the institution of feudalism as well as the bloodlines of the Stewart, Bruce, Balliol, and other families who would contend for power during the Wars for Independence. Yet these incomers "integrated into existing society rather than conquering it."[18] Although it is likely that the Scottish Lowlands absorbed a heavier influx of non-Celtic peoples, namely, Anglo-Normans and Danes, the Highlands—especially the western and northeastern Highlands—bore the strongest Norwegian influence. By the mid-1200s, with its cultural and ethnic mix largely complete, the Highlands were ripe for the golden age that emerged under the Lords of the Isles (1267–1493). Led by ClanDonald, this semi-independent kingdom, governed by the Council of the Isles and based at Finlagan on Islay, marked the final flourish of Scottish Gaeldom.

The stereotype of the Scottish Highlanders as a people whose ancestry was exclusively Celtic belies their diverse roots; yet the merging of these cultural strands led to a certain common heritage. The Lords of the Isles themselves illustrate this conundrum. While they bore a mixed Gaelic and Norwegian ancestry, the richness of the era that they dominated contributed to the refurbishing of a deep-rooted Gaelic culture through much of the Western Isles and western Highlands. At the same time, in Sutherland and Caithness the Norwegian presence continued to dominate. Hence, an assessment of the Highlands and Islands refutes generalization. The region remained an amalgam of people who varied by subregion and who continued to be affected by historical and geographical conditions. Given this diversity, the single consistent factor of these multiple subcultures proved to be the isolation of the Highlands from the Lowlands, a reality that enabled the people to retain their separateness.

Within indigenous North America, the Algonquian and Iroquoian people also forged separate identities with equally divergent roots. During the early postcontact generations both cultures suffered devastating loss of life due to the new diseases transmitted by Europeans. Ironically, through scourges like smallpox, disease served as an unlikely catalyst for ethnic diversity among these peoples.

The earliest epidemic to strike the Algonquians arrived during the late 1610s. Overwhelming the central coast of New England, it devastated villages, destroying upward of 90 percent of powerful sachemdoms such as the Massachusetts, Pawtuckets, and Pokanokets. The destruction forced once-respected groups like the Massachusetts to contend with the less powerful Micmacs or the Narragansetts, an already strong sachemdom who were to become crucial power brokers between the Native Americans and the English. Through the seventeenth century, small sachemdoms struck down by disease merged with others in ever-shifting reconfigurations of identity. As historian Michael Leroy Oberg notes, "Beyond its dreadful demographic consequences, the smallpox epidemic [of 1633–34] shattered a world in balance."[19]

Members of the Iroquois League—the Hodenosaunee—did not escape the foreign diseases, although their attrition rate did not equal that of other Iroquoian speakers, such as members of the Huron Nation, who suffered horrific mortality due to measles and smallpox. Among the Five Nations that composed the Iroquois League—Senecas, Cayugas, Onondagas, Oneidas, and Mohawks—the Mohawks suffered probably the greatest losses; about two-thirds of their population died during the smallpox epidemic of 1633.[20] At the same time the Oneidas, Onondagas, and Cayugas saw the death of half of their members, and this was only the beginning of the trauma. Disease continued to take its toll among these people well into the eighteenth century.

The devastation wrought by the European pathogens is virtually impossible to comprehend today. The waves of new diseases rent "the social fabric" of the people.[21] The sheer numerical loss, accompanied by the demise of the most able members of the society, along with the Elders, who provided leadership and were the repositories of history and wisdom, led formerly populous groups like the Hodenosaunee to take serious measures to redress the balance. Historian Matthew Dennis has suggested that the Iroquois responded "in a traditional fashion —through adoption." . . . "By transforming enemies into friends, foreigners into Iroquois, they fulfilled Deganawidah's injunction to 'strengthen their house.'"[22]

The league's efforts to replace losses due to disease and war as well as to prevent other tribes from retaining access to European traders with their highly desirable imported goods culminated in the middle decades of the seventeenth century, which "sucked the entire region into a maelstrom of violence and death."[23] Historian Daniel K. Richter has argued that during the "Beaver Wars" replenishment of tribal members through the taking of captives "blended with and often overwhelmed economic motives." He adds, "Although the quest for furs was vital, only an overriding, even desperate, demand for prisoners can explain much of Iroquois behavior."[24] The net result led to an imbalance of population: by the mid-1660s more than two-thirds of the residents in some Iroquois villages were former captives who had been initiated through the complex process of adoption. This alteration of the Iroquois population would lead to numerous domestic difficulties, including the religious division encouraged by the Jesuits, whose presence was requested by former Huron and other Roman Catholic captives, as well as diplomatic pressures encouraged by the pro-French, Christian faction within the league. Despite these internecine quarrels, Richter maintains that much of the fabric for "what scholars know as Iroquois culture was a creation of the melting pot that bubbled during the Beaver Wars."[25]

The Iroquois' drastic measures to replace their losses were never duplicated by the Algonquians during the seventeenth-century warfare within their native lands. The two major conflicts of this region—the Pequot War of 1637 and King Philip's War of 1675–78—split the Natives, pitting sachemdom against sachemdom as well as Algonquians against Pilgrims or Puritans. After the massacre of the Pequots at their Mystic River village in 1637, the Pequot Nation appeared to be dissolved. In reality, as anyone who has recently visited the Mashantucket Pequot "Foxwoods" Casino knows, the Pequots were not dissolved. Some of the survivors merged with the Mohegans and other Algonquian groups. Thus they continued an old Algonquian custom of intermarriage and brought with them some diversity to their new associations.[26] In like fashion, the defeat of the Wampanoags in King Philip's War led to the merging of some prisoners with other tribes, once again encouraging an Algonquian "melting pot" that would come to fruition a century later at the time of the American War for Independence.

By 1700 each of these cultures—the Scottish Highlanders and Islanders and the North American Algonquians and Iroquois—had emerged as a blend of peoples from many different backgrounds, mixtures that would lead to varying degrees of discord in the respective cultures, especially during the major military engagements of the eighteenth century. In Scotland the warfare culminated in the Jacobite Rebellion of 1745, which collapsed with the Battle of Culloden Moor in 1746. In North America the imperial wars culminated in the Seven

Years' War, also known as the French and Indian War, 1754–63, and the subsequent American Revolution.

The Land

The following section will compare the land and climate of these regions. It will also look at the societies that served as the matrix for these cultures, tracing their mythological origins and assessing how they refined the relationship with the land and other beings and crafted the ties of kinship that cemented the peoples' common fate. None of these indigenous societies remained static. Like the snake shedding its old skin with the season, they discarded the old and added new layers while retaining a core of uniqueness. Since the Scottish Lowlanders initially targeted the Highlands and Islands with their cultural emissaries—the schoolmasters—we will begin there.

The Highlands of Scotland are still one of the most beautiful places on earth. Yet, like other regions carved out of stone and mountain, loch and seacoast, they retain a hard and unyielding quality that remains persistently frustrating to those accustomed to a gentle climate and fertile soil. Born from the uplift that once carved the Appalachian Mountains, yet sundered from the Iroquoian "Turtle Island" by a widening crack in the Atlantic, the Highlands were shoved to the northeast until their northernmost regions would lie less than ten degrees below the Arctic Circle. Storms that close in on the Grampian Mountains, which dominate the eastern Highlands, arrive with lightning speed. Only the foolish or the ignorant go walking in these mountains without storm gear and a healthy dose of respect for the unpredictable weather. Maintaining the imprint of that ancient link with Turtle Island, the Highlands themselves are divided by an extension of the same fissure that opened in a series of cracks zigzagging from New England to Newfoundland (the Lake Char Fault) and continuing across the Atlantic to the north and east through the Great Glen Fault straddled by Loch Linnhe and Loch Ness.

Settlement in the Highlands and Islands, including the Inner and Outer Hebrides and the Orkneys and Shetlands, has always been molded by the land and the water. Marked by intense diversity, the Highlands can nevertheless be divided into three subregions—the West Highlands, including the Hebrides or Western Isles; the East Highlands, including the area stretching north from Nairn on the Moray Firth to Caithness at the northeastern tip of Scotland; and the Central Highlands, which include Inverness-shire and Perthshire. Some parts of the Highlands have virtually no mountains. Caithness, for example, is almost exclusively flat, and much of eastern Sutherland, the interior region in the far north, is peat bog.[27] In the West and Central Highlands, however, the high mountains, torrential rivers and burns, and the sea lochs that cut deeply into the coastline dominate the environment, carving almost impossible barriers for travel. In the far north the vast peat bogs of Sutherland further impede easy travel and communication. In the early eighteenth century, much of the Highlands remained barren of trees, wearing only a cover of heather or bracken, or *machair*, over the soil or rocky surface. Traveling through the region in the early eighteenth century, writer Daniel Defoe reacted forcefully to the Highlands, describing the region as "this frightful country."[28]

The lands of the Iroquois and southern New England Algonquians, once contiguous with the Scottish Highlands before the sundering of Turtle Island, lie at the northern edge of eastern North America's arable soil. The Iroquois, who moved north from the Appalachian highlands perhaps a millennium ago, followed the upper tributaries of the Susquehanna River and settled among the fertile flatlands south of Lake Toronto and along the eastward-flowing Mohawk River. They stopped there, avoiding the north side of the lake and the poor soil of the Canadian Shield. For these migrating people, "the rivers that remained in the beds initially carved by the melting ice made Iroquoia the geographical heart of northeastern Indian North America.... Given enough time and good enough canoes, therefore, one could travel literally almost anywhere from Iroquoia."[29]

Located almost due east and a little south of the Iroquois, the southern New England Algonquian homeland lay just south of the marginally arable land of present-day Maine, New Hampshire, and Vermont. Although this Algonquian territory was also scraped clear by the retreating glacier, small patches of land near the streambeds remained arable. The coast also offered fish and shellfish, as attested by the numerous shell middens and the thriving seventeenth-century wampum trade. Largely flat, with the exception of the interior hills of Massachusetts, the Algonquian lands were protected by an oak-hemlock forest, established long after the glacier had retreated, and crisscrossed with streams and rivers that offered good fishing.

Since the Algonquian and Iroquois homelands lay at the eastern edge of a vast continent, their climate was more stable than that of the Highlands. True, Iroquois lands characteristically received a heavier snowfall, blowing east from the Great Lakes, than, say, the lower elevations of the Highlands, but the disrupted terrain of the Highlands

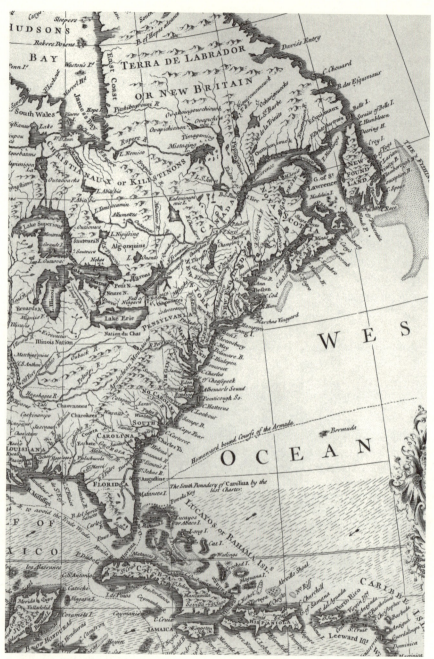

A map of North America.
DRAWN AND ENGRAVED BY RICHARD W. SEALE. ORIGINALLY PUBLISHED IN RAPIN'S
HISTORY OF ENGLAND (1745). FACSIMILE BY CARSON CLARK GALLERY, SCOTLAND MAP
HERITAGE CENTRE, EDINBURGH.

generated a greater diversity of microenvironments than one finds in Iroquoia.

The western Highlands and Islands are invariably foggy. The Norwegians named the Isle of Skye, the largest of the Hebrides, Ealand Skianach (from *ski*, a mist), or "Cloudy Island," and it is a rare day when the Cuillins that rise above Skye are not hidden in showers or capped with mist. But there are exceptions. The Isle of Tiree, south of Skye, is noted for its sunshine—it is said that because it is so low the rain sweeps over it—and Inverness and the Black Isle, to the east, reputedly enjoy some of the best weather between Cornwall and Caithness. Even individual mountains contain separate miniclimates. Fierce winds in the Highlands, and especially in the Hebrides, remain constant. In the 1720s Edmund Burt observed that "Every high Wind, in many Places of the Highlands, is a Whirlwind."[30] Recorded gusts in excess of one hundred miles per hour are not unusual at the Butt of Lewis. On a midsummer's day average winds range between forty and fifty miles per hour. Commenting on the Highlands' climate, former *Glasgow Herald* columnist John MacLeod notes drily, "Highland weather, in truth, boasts infinite variety, and is generally capricious."[31]

In all of these regions the climate and topography would have a profound impact on the peoples who chose to make them their homelands. The land would help to shape the cultures into unique patterns, long before they encountered any outsiders.

Society: Kinship of the Family, Band, Village, and Clan

Describing his early eighteenth-century travels in Scotland, the English engineer Edmund Burt took some pains to distinguish for his London correspondent the differences between the Lowlands and the Highlands. "In England," he wrote, "the Name of Scotsman is used indiscriminately to signify any one of the Male Part of the Natives of North Britain." This, he noted, was erroneous. He cautioned: "the Highlanders differ from the People of the Low Country in almost every Circumstance of Life. Their Language, Customs, Manners, Dress, &c. are unlike." He also noted their dislike for each other: "neither of them would be contented to be taken for the other, insomuch that in speaking of an unknown person of . . . [Scotland] as a Scotsman only it is as indefinite as barely to call a Frenchman an European, so little would his native character be known by it."[32]

Burt focused on the most obvious differences between the Highlanders and the Lowlanders—language, attire, customs, and manners.

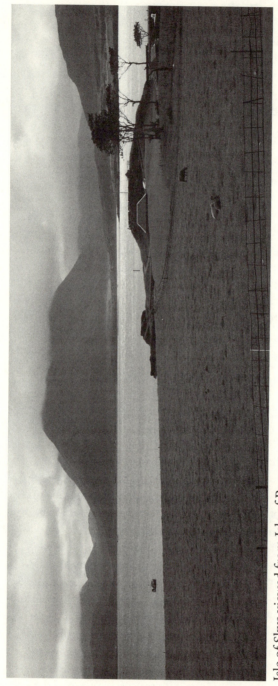

Isle of Skye viewed from Isle of Raasay.
Photograph by Ferenc M. Szasz.

By lifting his words from their eighteenth-century phraseology, we can draw on them as introductory guidelines for a cursory view of the three societies—Highlanders, Iroquois, and Algonquians—that would later be strongly affected by the SSPCK. In each of these societies, the culture embraced its children. In each, all of the members of the community bore some responsibility for educating the children in the ways of the people. Each society consciously molded its youth toward mature adulthood. I will return to the theme of indigenous education later.

Kinship provided the glue that held these societies together. Kinship made it possible for the children to become the cumulative responsibility of a network of people who were all, in one way or another, related to one another. The networks were composed of overlapping bonds of kinship. At the core lay the family. Within this core level, the roles of women and men became the distinguishing feature that strongly influenced child rearing.

Among the Iroquois, men's and women's societal roles remained distinct. The women's domain was the "clearing"—home and children, village and fields. The men's domain was the forest—hunting and war and diplomacy. In Iroquois society lineage was traced through the female line, and the female lineage, or "longhouse families," formed the basic social unit within the Iroquois villages.

Algonquian lineages remained less distinct. For the southern New England Algonquians, gendered division of labor was clear-cut. Men engaged in hunting, warfare, diplomacy, and trade; women prepared game, fished, gathered, planted and harvested, and cared for home and children. But lineage descent, which was probably "in the female line" prior to contact, was modified by those Algonquian generations influenced by colonial English patrilineal structures.[33] Hence, firm evidence on Algonquian lineage structures remains uncertain.

By contrast, Gaelic Highlanders traced their lineage through the father. A Highlander acquired one dimension of self-identity through his or her family name, or *sloinneadh*—for example, Calum mac (son of) Iean vic (grandson of) Coile.[34] Still, although they also worked side by side for some tasks, such as the cutting and hauling of the peat, like their Native American counterparts, the Highlanders also divided much of their labor by gender. The men threshed the grain, while the women ground it. The men dug the ground, but the women did the actual planting. The men built the homes and rethatched the roofs, built and mended the furniture, and made and mended the shoes. Burt, however, insisted that the Highlanders he met in the 1720s and 1730s seldom wore shoes. He told this story:

> There is a Laird's Lady, about a mile from one of the Highland Garrisons, who is often seen from the Ramparts, on Sunday mornings, coming barefoot to the Kirk, with her Maid carrying the Stockings and Shoes after her. She Stops at the Foot of a certain Rock, that serves her for a Seat, not far from ... a Church, and there she puts them on, and, in her Return to the same Place, she prepares to go home barefoot, as she came....
>
> I have twice surprised the Laird and his Lady without Shoes or Stockings, a good Way from Home, in cold Weather.[35]

The women handled all of the dairying chores for the Highland cattle, sheep, or goats; processed the flax and wool for making linen and woolen textiles; and cared for home and family.[36] The men were warriors and hunters. On both sides of the water children learned these gendered assignments.

The key component of the societal glue, the family, remained at the core of the kinship network. Among the Iroquois, this core group was the *lineagehome*, or the longhouse. Each of these indigenous societies expanded the family group outward to include expanding networks. Among the Algonquians, the network encircling the family was the village. The Iroquois and the Gaels, however, created additional intermediary institutions, known as clans and moieties among the Iroquois, and simply as clans among the Gaels. Although major distinctions separated the Iroquois clans from the Highland clans—such as the tracing of lineage—enough similarities remain to pique the imagination. The southern New England Algonquians never developed clans. Thus, the following assessment will contrast only the Gaelic and Iroquois clan systems.

For both the Iroquois and the Gaels, the clans formed the connective tissue for the nurturing bonds of kinship. Beyond this foundation, however, the systems veered apart, moving in directions that reflected the unique circumstances and concomitant worldviews of each society.

Origins of the clans lie deep in the mythic past. In both cases, however, the mythic roots of these peoples shaped their self-perception. In North America, to generalize for a moment, mythology or origin stories recreated a time when humans and animals lived on the earth in forms that enabled them to communicate with each other. In this era, people did not view shapeshifting as unusual. People changed into animals, birds, and fish, and they changed back into their human forms with ease.[37] Later, among hunting and gathering groups, those young men, and sometimes young women, who sought to gain power by means of a vision quest were gifted with that power through the intercession of an animal or reptile, a bird or a fish. For the remainder of the vision questor's life he or she could rely on that source of strength in time of need. This power manifested that mythic era when all living beings on earth communicated with one other.

For North American Natives the mythic era included all of these beings. Native people of this continent, especially those who have retained their origin stories, view their origins through a mythological framework, one "which has roots deep in the prehistoric past."[38] Within this context, Iroquois clans were created during the "formation period" by "Sapling [the Good Twin], who brought cultural benefits to the people after the formation of the earth."[39] Sapling "taught humans how to grow corn to support themselves and how to keep harm at bay through ceremonies of thanksgiving and propitiation to the spirit world." In order for the Iroquois "to keep those ceremonies, Sky-Grasper [Sapling] assigned roles to various camps of people he arbitrarily designated as clans named after such animals as the Wolf, the Bear, and the Turtle."[40] Although each clan displayed its name crest on the longhouse, the clan could also become the name of the community. Colonial Europeans "reported that on the entrance of each dwelling was an image of its lineage's clan animal, announcing that food, shelter and hospitality were available to clan kin from other villages."[41] Although the Iroquois' clan origins lay embedded in mythology, they also served pragmatic purposes—the avoidance of incest, the retention of ceremonies, and the creation of a far-reaching clan network that provided Iroquois men, who were often absent from home, a kinship contact in distant villages.

Only a step removed from their Ulster progenitors, the Gaelic clans of the Scottish Highlands came into being when the fifth-century Irish emigrants, the Scotti, crossed the water linking Antrim with the Kintyre Peninsula to establish a toehold in Alba. The Scotti carried with them the mythology that defined their former homeland.

From the time of the earliest human inhabitants, who arrived after the ice receded some nine thousand years ago, Ireland has been shaped by its mythology. All immigrants who crossed to the island in successive waves from the continent carried their own mythologies, merging these understandings with those of previous arrivals. In this way, Ireland became a home to layers of overlapping myth, told and retold by successive generations of storytellers trained in the art.

All of Ireland's landscape bears the imprint of those mythical figures, whose lives form the substance of Ireland's ancient world. The greatest of all of these myths is "Táin Bó Chuailagné," which relates the story of a war between Ulster, the province of the north, and Connaught, the province of the west, that was fought over the possession of two bulls. Even today the mythical figures of this world—including Cú Chulainn, Ulster war hero; Meadhbh, queen of Connaught; Lugh, god of light; and Brigit, goddess of fire and of poetry—remain embedded in the land, especially in the remnants of Gaelic-speaking Ireland.[42] Michael Dames writes that "mythic Ireland is centered on the story of a divine space-time cycle in which provinces of time continually interact with provinces of space, thanks to a mythic narrative which draws these together as the visible life of the gods."[43] Like Natives of North America, the Irish and Gaelic Highlanders share a symbiotic relationship with the land, a relationship nourished by their respective mythologies.

The Scotti transplanted Irish mythology to Alba, but, like any people shifting away from the myth-laden landscape of their original homeland, they adapted the old stories to the new environment of the Western Isles and western Highlands.[44] But the patterns of a mythopoetic culture remained as integral to their being as the breath of life. Despite their removal, they would scarcely have discarded their literary and spiritual worldview. Given the time period of their migration, it is unlikely that the Christian monks, the native Irish scribes who recorded in the vernacular the overlapping mythologies of the storytellers, would have embarked on this journey. What the Scotti likely transplanted on their initial voyage to Alba were the storytellers themselves. Once they were settled in Alba, later generations could reinforce the oral stories through the transcriptions recorded by the Scottish monks. In Alba these scribes continued the tradition established by the Irish monks following the founding of the mission on the Isle of Iona in A.D. 563 by Colm Cille (St. Columba).

Throughout the medieval era, the Scots, especially those living in the Highlands and Western Isles, maintained close contact with their Irish cousins. The Gaels living on the Inner and Outer Hebrides, Argyll, and the Irish province of Ulster saw the Irish Sea and the Sea of the Hebrides as a connecting rather than a dividing influence. When the "Gaelic cultural province" known as the Lords of the Isles was created in the 1200s, "the Gaelic bardic schools, which trained men for the prestigious office of poet, became responsible for the development of a classical form of Gaelic, used by the 'men of letters' common to both Ireland and Gaelic Scotland, and nowadays called classical common Gaelic."[45] As late as 1513, directly before the Battle of Flodden, a Gaelic poet of Scotland linked the two Gaelic peoples in common cause against the English:

> Meet it is to rise against Saxons ... ere they have taken our country from us ... Fight roughly. Like the Irish Gael, we will have no English Pale.[46]

If the western waterways linked the Irish and Gaelic Scots, the terrain of both Scotland and Ireland discouraged ease of travel and communication by land. In pre-Christian Ireland, lack of communication molded a political structure consisting of "tens of minor tribes, each with its own king and also, to some extent, its own distinctive customs and laws."[47] In the Highlands geography also dictated societal structure and settlement patterns. The nature of the terrain, a jumble of high mountains, broad woodlands, deep lochs—both freshwater and sea—and the sea itself, led each small community to organize itself under a chief, create laws, and conduct its own affairs.[48] Like the Irish, therefore, the MacDonalds, the MacLeods, the MacBeans and other Highland clans emerged from the distinctive features of the land.

For both Scottish and Irish Gaels, however, the clan origins also are rooted in the bardic tradition. The storytellers recounted a mythic era that had uncanny similarities to the mythic era of Native North America. The three Gaelic myth cycles, and especially the third, Finn and the Fenians, which centers on the heroic figure of Finn mac Cumhal (one of whose sons was Oisin, or Ossian, the famous poet and warrior), reveal a strong relationship between humans and all other forms of life. This parallel is best illustrated with a story. As leader of the Fenians, a Native militia composed of exemplary men, each of whom excelled as warrior, poet, and man of culture, Finn was reared to respect the virtues of truth, kindness, gentleness, and trustworthiness. He gained his wisdom, however, by partaking of the "salmon of knowledge," a legendary fish who lived in a deep pool of the River Boyne and was tended by an ancient sage. Finn encountered the "salmon of knowledge" as a youth. After one of the salmon had been caught, Finn was asked to cook it, taking care not to eat any. The expression on Finn's face when he brought the cooked salmon to the sage led him to inquire if Finn had eaten any. "Nay," said Finn, "but when I turned it on the spit my thumb was burnt and I put it to my mouth." Aware that Finn was about to fulfill an ancient prophecy, the sage directed him to eat the salmon, whereupon Finn gained "the wisdom of the ages." Afterward, "he had only to put his thumb under his tooth ... to receive foreknowledge and magic counsel."[49] Finn relied on the salmon for power as the Native North American relied on the figure revealed in the vision quest.

The mythic Gaelic heroes often moved between the interacting worlds of humans and animals, birds, reptiles, or fish. Some possessed the power to shapeshift, which enabled them to assume other guises, as exemplified in this story: "One day that Finn was hunting in Donegal with Ossian [and others] . . . their hounds roused a beautiful fawn [who] . . . suddenly disappeared into a cleft in the hillside." A heavy snow forced them to follow, but when they entered the place (*sídh*) a "beautiful goddess-maiden," the transformed deer, asked for their help "against the army that was coming to attack the sídh." The battle that was joined lasted all night but ended in a victory for Finn and the Fenians.[50] Echoing experiences similar to those of the Algonquians and Iroquois, these mythical figures also depended on other species—raven, eagle, the salmon of wisdom, otter, dog, buzzard, or falcon—for assistance in times of danger.[51]

The mythic clan origins of Celtic and Iroquois people also share commonalities. Both recall this era's reciprocal relationship between humans and other inhabitants of the earth. Within both groups some members had the power of shapeshifting. In both cultures clans are of ancient origin; they spring from mythological into historical time. Like the Iroquois origin stories, the Gaelic clan tales ascribe clans' dominance to ancient roots. The cycle of Finn and the Fenians suggests that clans were integral to the Irish mythological world. As a leader, Finn retained his power only when he maintained an accommodation between the two hostile clans whose rivalry had led to the death of his own father. Yet the totemic roots for Gaelic clans remain unclear. If one accepts the clans' claim for emergence from mythological times, then totemic origin patterns should logically follow. But the only totemic story I have located comes from the Outer Hebrides. Here, Clan MacCodrum of the Uists traces its origins to "a union between the clan's progenitor and a seal woman." Members of this clan "were humans by day and seals by night." It is said that "they were called Clan MacCodrum of the Seals, . . . [and they] became known throughout North Uist and the Outer Hebrides as a sept of the Clan Donald."[52]

Despite these similarities, a number of differences mark the origins of the clans in the two cultures. The Iroquois, like other Native North American groups that maintained clans, derived their totemic designations and clan crests from the animal, fish, bird, or reptile kingdoms. It seems as if the Gaelic peoples followed a different path. Gaelic clan names derive from the patronymic surname, which, as mentioned earlier, derived from several different societal roots well beyond the Gaelic world, including Pictish, Viking, Norman, and Flemish cultures.

The Iroquois clan members perceived themselves as descendants of a common ancestor. Hence, they forbade marriage within the clan. Among the Highland clans choice of marriage partner reflected status: chiefs and members of the *fine* (elite) could marry out (within the Highlands) to achieve strong alliances; if they married within the clan, they chose within the fine. "Ordinary clansmen" generally married within the clan. As Devine argues, "the blood ties between the ruling families and the ordinary clansmen were largely mythical but the *assumption of consanguinity*, suggested in the very word *clan* (i.e., children), gave an emotional bond which helped to cement social cohesion within clanship" (emphasis mine).[53] In the context of the early eighteenth century, Devine employs "mythical" as a synonym for "fictitious." But the Iroquois in this era accorded "mythical" the status reserved for a core tribal value. The core value—no marriage within the clan—relied on the Iroquois belief in a common ancestry for each clan. The Gaelic Scots understood clan as a reflection of consanguinity because clans provided the glue of kinship that held the society together.

All of these societies—Iroquois, Gaels, and Algonquians—tailored their societal groups to suit their unique conditions. Hence, the most fluid of the three, the Algonquians, formed what historian Neal Salisbury calls "village bands" or "collections of extended lineal families" that demonstrated, once again, the bonding thread of consanguinity. They remained flexible because exogamous marriages meant that one had relatives within other bands who could provide a kinship haven outside of the immediate band if one chose to leave. Thus, loyalty to kin superseded loyalty to band. The leadership of the village or band sachems rested on a precarious balance of respect and reciprocity. Sachems lived well, but their sometimes difficult tenure depended on maintaining harmonious relations with the spiritual forces. In this context, they relied on the wisdom of those "capable of communicating with such forces," the shamans or paw-waws; on the judicious selection of "an elite corps of counselors;" and on the providing of gifts to the families who supported the sachem through tribute.[54]

The Iroquois, by contrast, moved toward greater societal complexity. Iroquois families became clans or lineages. Remnants of clans lived in towns, and the towns formed the key groupings of the Iroquois nations. Each nation, such as the Mohawks, consisted of several towns, hamlets, and camps. In the early 1600s, for example, the Mohawks lived in three or four towns and several hamlets.[55]

From the 1100s to the 1600s, the Iroquois towns sustained large populations, ranging from one to two thousand people. Within the towns, matrilineal kinship determined one's residence. Everyone lived in one of the segments of clans (Mohawk, *oh wachira was*) scattered among the ten towns of the Iroquois League. These palisaded compounds, which Europeans dubbed "castles," were defensive bastions that guarded against the omnipresent enemy. Until the mid- to late 1400s, internecine feuding proved intense, and it was this state of perpetual warfare that led Deganawidah (the Peacemaker) and Ayonhwathah to found the Great League of Peace and Power. Five Iroquois Nations, divided into younger and older brothers, formed the confederation: Mohawks, Oneidas, Onondagas, Cayugas, and Senecas.

Women played a crucial role in the governance of the league. Although the fifty-member Grand Council was male, "senior women from dominant clan or lineage segments in each nation each chose a man to serve as a League Chief or sachem." As chiefs died, women chose replacements; if a chief "did not serve his *oh wachira* well, the women could remove his antlers and replace him." Custom required that the Grand Council make all decisions by unanimous vote, reflecting its original raison d'être: "the League was more a mutual non-aggression pact than a political union." From the mid-fifteenth and early sixteenth centuries forward, this allowed each nation or part of a nation considerable latitude in determining policy, but it also made quick decisions in moments of national crisis more difficult.[56]

As anthropologist Dean R. Snow writes, "The metaphysical longhouse of the League stretches across Iroquois. The Mohawks guard the Eastern door and the Senecas guard the Western door. The Onondagas keep the fire at the center. Above them all soars the Tree of Peace, atop which sits an eagle that watches over the peace. Each League Chief . . . is like a tree or support pole of the great longhouse. Together the chiefs link arms and act as one." Following the founding of the Great League, the Iroquois people described themselves—and still do—as the Hodenosaunee, the People of the Longhouse.[57]

The Gaelic Highlanders' societal structure bore more resemblance to the Iroquois' than the Algonquians', for the environmental, cultural, and historical circumstances of these Celts made them a distinctive people. Demographically they differed from both Native American groups because their settlement patterns were scattered. They lived neither in bands nor in villages like the Algonquian nor in sizeable towns like the Iroquois. Before the mid-eighteenth century the largest Highland town, Inverness, was perched on the eastern edge of the region and, according to Burt, boasted only "four Streets, of which three centre at the [Mercat] Cross, and the other is something irregular."[58]

Most Highlanders lived "in little groups of eight or ten houses in the glens or straths or along the edges of inland or sea lochs . . . . There were no concentrations of population, very few villages, few sizeable regions even where large numbers of people lived within easy reach of one another."[59]

Structurally, Highland society was stratified. The chiefs and the leading gentry, known as the fine, provided the magnetic center of each clan. By the sixteenth century, the fine, whose lands were granted by charter from the Stewart monarchs, included the bards and vernacular poets, the hereditary mediciners, factors or bailies, and the traditional specialists, who included standard bearers, quartermasters, or pursemasters.[60] The chief and his fine provided protection and patronage for the clan members. As Scottish historian Allan Macinnes notes, "The personal protection afforded by the chief and the fine was also their clans' assurance of justice."[61]

The chief and the fine were not directly responsible for managing the land; that task fell to certain members of the lesser clan gentry, the *daoine-uaisle*. The *fir-taca*, or tacksman, was "charged to align the estates of the fine with the territories settled by their clansmen."[62] Still, it is likely there was "a general understanding that the chief should provide land for his clansmen rather than that they had rights to specific lands in perpetuity." In addition to the tacksman, on the western coast and in the Hebrides the lesser gentry also included the *buannachan*, or household men, who made up the warrior class of the clan. Charged with the defense of their clan's territory, in the sixteenth century many of them opted to cross over to Ireland, where they served as mercenaries to aid the Irish in their struggle against the English.[63]

Ordinary clansmen, when taking oaths, accorded priority to those sworn by their chief's hand. "In like manner, clansmen when making testaments commended their souls to God and commended their families to the care and protection of their chief."[64] The reciprocal relationship between the chief and his "children" was reinforced by several customs. "The clan virtues were loyalty, courage, obedience, and a sense of common identity between the ruling family and those below with whom they had few blood ties." On a more practical level, as tenants, ordinary clansmen paid to the chief "rentals in kind of cattle, sheep, meal, cheese, hens and geese." On occasion, however, when harvests were meager and clansmen could not provide payment, the fine converted these goods into "subsistence support" for the suffering clansmen and women, thereby providing a form of "social insurance." At the same time ordinary clansmen could share in the glories of the clan through the poetic energies of the bards, who reinforced the clans' historical identity, in part by recounting the epic actions of their ancestors. Among the Iroquois, the orators who customarily related the national mythology performed a similar function. Feasting hosted by the Highland clan chief also solidified the relationship: it demonstrated "the chief's capacities for generosity and hospitality," and it conveyed an important "sense of communal harmony which involved all clansmen," regardless of rank.[65]

Education of Children among Gales, Algonquians, and Iroquois

After the continents drifted apart in ancient geological time, Scotland's proximity to the Arctic Circle meant that the people, especially those living in the Highlands and Islands, had to struggle mightily to survive. Poor soil, numerous rives and lochs, and ever-present mountains made farming difficult. By the early eighteenth century, the Gaelic-speaking Scots were long accustomed to their *run rig* fields of barley and oats, their small herds of cattle, a few sheep, and occasional hunting and fishing. Across the Atlantic the climate remained more moderate, but the natural environment bounded by the Great Lakes, plentiful river systems and the Atlantic Ocean proved equally challenging. Like the Highland Gaels, the Iroquois and Algonquians were long accustomed to tending fields, although they had carved these fields from cleared forests and planted them with maize, beans, and squash, as well as sunflowers and tobacco. Still, they depended more heavily on hunting and fishing and wild plant and berry harvesting because of the absence of domesticated animals, except the dog. In both environments life was difficult and survival contingent on an intimate relationship with the land; acknowledgement of supernatural forces; proper observance of ceremony and ritual; reciprocal ties with the kin group, whether band, tribe, or clan; and persistent teaching of children and youth in the ways of survival and the heritage of the people.

From infancy, children learned the survival skills demanded by their environment, their culture, and their gender. In the Scottish Highlands, the seasons followed a cycle that remained tied to the raising of crops, cutting of peat, and caring for cattle. In late spring women and children drove the cattle to the sheilings—grazing regions in the glens or out on the moor—where they remained until late summer. At the sheilings the boys herded the animals, while the women and girls made the cheese and butter. For the children the season of summer, as recalled by an Isle of Lewis man, was the "best holiday."[66] The boys were expected to prove their manhood through various exploits, such as "lifting" the cattle from neighboring clans or from farms in the Lowlands.[67] When their clan chief alerted them, they were expected to respond by taking up arms against another clan or, in the 1715 and 1745 Jacobite Rebellions, depending on their chief's stance, either for or against the forces of the Hanoverian monarchy. Young men were also expected to learn the numerous skills they would later employ as husbands and fathers. In their largely self-sufficient households, Highland families depended on the men to build and repair homes, thatch roofs, cobble shoes, craft furniture, and thresh grain.

Girls learned quickly that women's contributions to the household were crucial. Although summer dairying chores at the sheilings were perhaps more carefree than during other seasons, women and their daughters were seldom idle. They were responsible for the making of textiles, primarily of wool or linen; they obtained the wool or flax, carded and spun, fulled—often singing as they worked—dyed, knitted, and wove. They created all the family linens and clothing, turning to these tasks "when all of the other work was done."[68]

In the winter they prepared fertilizer for the fields by mixing dung and seaweed, which they turned into the soil in the spring. Before planting, entire families engaged in the annual cutting of the peat(s), a festive, albeit tedious, process that was not completed until they had "lifted" the dried slabs and carried them to their homes, where they provided the primary source of heat through the winter. After helping with the peats, the girls planted *buntata* (potatoes), oats, and barley; when they returned from the sheilings, they harvested the barley and oats and "lifted" the buntata. Then they winnowed, dried, and ground the grain, which they made into bread and other foods. Finally, girls learned all the additional household chores, from childcare to cooking, along with the continuous care for the dairy cattle.

Similarly, among the Algonquian and Iroquois youth, gender shaped the tasks at an early age. Young girls learned that their mothers, aunts, and grandmothers provided stability in the community. Since domesticated livestock were not available before the Europeans arrived, and even then were far less important than in the Scottish Highlands, hunting remained a crucial task that took men away for lengthy trips. In addition, during the seventeenth-century Beaver Wars, Iroquois men were often absent for extended periods to engage in warfare. Only the women and children, the disabled, and the Elders remained in the Iroquois villages during these extended absences.

The eighteenth-century Algonquians, whose proximity to extensive English settlement restricted hunting and curtailed harvests, found older patterns losing their viability. Despite the widening gap between Iroquois and Algonquian economies, gender continued to determine roles for Algonquian youth. Some bands or families continued to move within a short radius as the seasons changed, maintaining a semblance of the old pattern: journeying in the spring from their winter villages to corn field sites by the sea, moving to fishing camps in the summer, hunting in the fall, and returning to the village sites in the winter. Increasingly, the Algonquians of this region engaged in economic exchanges with the English by doing odd jobs, selling goods such as herbs for medicinal remedies, cranberries, brooms, baskets, or other crafts, or working in the whaling industry off the shores of Nantucket or Long Island. Girls learned to perform household chores and helped to cultivate small gardens of maize, beans, and squash, but their skills in crafting clothing and moccasins from animal skins shifted to the making of garments from linen and wool.[69] Boys found it more difficult to adjust because their roles as hunters and fishermen had been largely eliminated. The two pursuits open to men after the English arrived—whaling and military service for the English—promised danger and required considerable absence from home.[70]

Although Iroquois youth followed traditional patterns of learning until the mid-eighteenth century, encroachments on their world brought traumatic changes through the impact of alcohol, loss of land, and French and English religious colonialism. In the early eighteenth century, however, Iroquois boys still trained to be warriors and hunters, orators and spiritual leaders. Girls gained experience in childcare and food preparation, cultivation of crops, weaving baskets, and working with animal hides, especially deerskins. But the divided loyalties of the Iroquois during the era of the American Revolution split the Hodenosaunee, sending many who had allied with the British to a reserve in Ontario, while those who remained found themselves living on islands of Native land within the new republic, where old patterns became increasingly difficult to maintain under the onslaught of Euroamericans.[71]

During the eighteenth century all of these indigenous communities struggled to deal with the increasing pressures from outsiders. What held them together as a people through the uncertainty of change was the persistence of their worldviews, expressed through spirituality, language, and kinship bonds. This cultural legacy formed the linchpin in the education of their children.

Each of these societies transmitted its cultural heritage through storytelling, ceremony, and other ancient forms of teaching. Among Gaelic Highlanders, the bards and storytellers related the mythic past through verse and song. The hereditary posts the bards had once held during the hegemony of the Lordship of the Isles between the mid-1200s and the late 1400s had long since eroded, but their successors of the 1500s and 1600s, who reflected a wider spectrum of Gaelic society, carried on the vernacular tradition across the Highlands and Islands.[72]

> In the ancient books of men of learning and
> and in the gleanings of our ever-fresh poems
> there will remain [on record] each good deed that shall
> be done to me.[73]

In a similar fashion, storytellers and ceremonial leaders among Natives of the Northeast Woodlands taught the mythic and spiritual past. In his exploration of Algonquian folklore, Simmons describes this process as continuum: "Each generation inherited a body of legends, symbols, and meaning from their predecessors and revised this heritage in recognition of their own experiences."[74]

Arguing persuasively for persistence amidst change among southern New England Algonquians, Simmons maintains that "by the mid-eighteenth century Christianity had replaced most core beliefs and almost all myth and ritual." Simultaneously, "some Indian concepts persisted with new English names and focus, and a few indigenous symbols survived intact in the historic period." The means of survival was oral tradition, which emerged as storytelling. As Fidelia Fielding, the remarkable Mohegan storyteller, began to relate a story, she always repeated the old pattern, "It was long before my time, but grandmother knew . . . from her grandmother."[75]

From these myths and legends that retold the stories of creation, culture heroes, and tricksters, the children of Highland, Iroquois, and Algonquian families learned how they were supposed to think and behave. Immersed in the magic of the story, they absorbed ethical lessons reinforced in their daily lives by members of their extended families and kin groups, in the form of band, clan, or tribe. Whether they were educated by the shores of Lake Erie or on the Isle of Lewis, the children learned the concept of self-control at an early age. The ubiquitous cradleboard of North America found an echo in the "rocking cradle" of Scotland, where the infant was "swathed in blankets like a cocoon, with a criss-cross pattern of cord which was passed through rings on the side of the cradle and held the infant firmly in place while it was being rocked."[76] The cradle or cradleboard provided security and safety while it taught patience and self-control. As children matured, each stage of their life reiterated the pattern established during infancy. Their sense of security emanated from the reciprocal relationship with the land, the reassuring presence of kin relationships, the cultural heritage told and retold through stories and ceremonies, and the learning skills deemed necessary for survival. When they achieved maturity, they did so as proud members of the Onondaga or Oneida nations, as Mohegans or Narragansetts, or as MacDonalds or MacLeods.

Into these distinct worlds of tribal and clan societies came numerous outsiders, all of whom sought to gain from their encounters. Some sought material wealth in the form of natural resources; others coveted the land itself; still others attempted to capture the hearts and minds of the young. Their method proved to be the sharpened sword of education.

CHAPTER TWO

Highlands versus Lowlands
The Creation of the Highland Line

In medieval Scotland, Gaelic served the people as the universal tongue. It was "the principal language of civilization, culture and government . . . . [and] in the national life of Scotland . . . Gaelic stood at the centre."[1] Before the fourteenth century, the major boundary that divided the country was the natural geographical barrier created by the Firth of Forth.

By the early seventeenth century, Scotland's linguistic diversity reflected the changes that the country had experienced during the intervening years. Gaelic speakers lived primarily in the Highlands and Western Isles, and they were separated from the Lowland Scots speakers by the famous Highland Line. The Highland Line delineated a geographical and cultural division between Highlands and Lowlands, much as the region dubbed the "frontier line" of North America separated Europeans and other outsiders from Native Americans. Similarly, in nearby Ireland, the River Shannon had divided Anglo Ireland, centered in the Irish Pale, from Gaeltacht (Gaelic Entity).[2]

As a physical barrier, the Highland Line followed a point on the River Clyde north and east through Perthshire and thence north along the Grampian Mountains, remaining inland from the North Sea. Before reaching the Moray Firth, it turned west to Loch Ness, where it veered north again to Caithness and ended in Sutherland at a location near the center of the north coast. The line is strengthened by the mountain range known as the Druim Alban, or the Ridge of Alba (Scotland), which has long served as the backbone of Scotland. Just east of the Druim Alban lie the Grampian Mountains. These erupt as a central massif, known in Gaelic as the Monadliath, or the Gray Mountain, a designation slightly altered by Lowlanders, who dubbed it the Mounth.[3]

As a cultural divider, the Highland Line gained credence between the late fourteenth and sixteenth centuries. In the 1380s the earliest Scot to comment on these cultural distinctions, John of Fordun, chronicler of Aberdeenshire, sharply contrasted the two regions. The "people of the coast," he wrote, "are of domestic and civilized habits," while the "Highlanders and people of the islands ... are a savage and untamed nation, rude and independent ... exceedingly cruel."[4]

With Fordun and other Scottish medieval chroniclers setting the pace, the polarization of Highlanders and Lowlanders became accepted wisdom. Synthesizing his predecessor's commentary, Major John Mair, an eminent sixteenth-century Scottish historian, wrote in 1520, "One half of Scotland speaks Irish [Gaelic] and all these as well as the Islanders we reckon to belong to the wild Scots. In dress, in the manner of their outward life ... these come behind the householding Scots."[5]

The late medieval chroniclers—from Fordun to Mair—merely confirmed the contemporary events of their day. Hence, as Fordun observed, the entity known as the Lordship of the Isles emerged in the fourteenth century. The lordship "was made up of a group of semi-independent clans, some related by blood to the family of Clan Donald, and others taking their land from it, accepting its authority, and contributing to its power."[6] Rising after the Scottish-Norwegian Treaty of 1266 as a "powerful and complex territorial lordship, [the lordship embraced] ... the southern Hebrides and parts of the mainland, mainly in Argyll," providing the region "with a renewed independence of mind and a sense of political identity that amounted to a kingdom within a kingdom."[7] The Lordship of the Isles also enabled the West to enjoy a period of stability that held for over 150 years, ending only as the fifteenth century closed.

The violence that caught Fordun's attention lay closer to Aberdeenshire. On the eastern edge of the Highlands and northwest of Aberdeenshire, the collapse of royal authority among the Stewart descendants of Robert the Bruce (1306–29) led to a violent power struggle exemplified by the "war of attrition" led by Alexander Stewart. Third son of Robert II, and better known as the Wolf of Badenoch, Stewart was responsible for the destruction of the royal burgh of Elgin and its magnificent cathedral, "the lantern of the north," in 1390. It is likely that Stewart's actions were the driving force behind Fordun's emphasis on Highland violence. Similarly, in 1493 the collapse of the Lordship of the Isles led to an era of instability in the Western Isles, which encouraged John Mair's indictment of the Highlands about two decades later.[8] News of these events filtered down to the Lowlanders, persuading them that those Scots who lived beyond the Highland Line were different, and not only in language and dress. They also viewed the Highlanders as the personification of violence.[9]

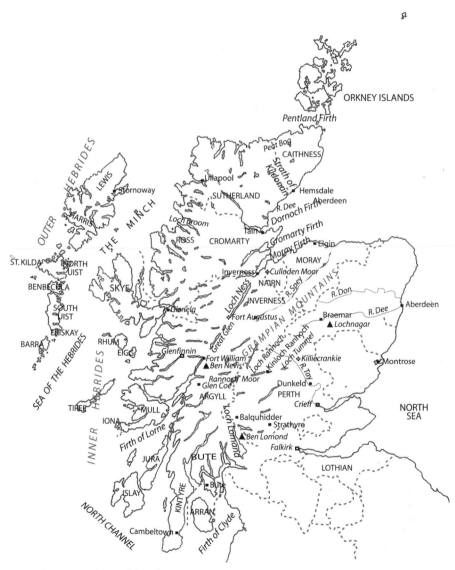

The Scottish Highlands.
MAP BY CHARLOTTE HILL COBB.

By the late sixteenth and seventeenth centuries, the wedge was driven deeper with each generation. After the 1560s, the Scottish Reformation, which engulfed the Lowlands and led to the establishment of the Church of Scotland, or Presbyterian Church, intensified the alienation of Highlanders. At the same time royal power pulled the Highlanders into its net. Touching the Highlands as early as the 1100s under the pressure of feudalism and military action, royal power intensified under James VI and I (1567–1625), whose "contempt for the Highlands" was well known.[10]

When the eighteenth century opened, the Highland Line separated two very different cultures. Divided by religion, language, and dress; by the economic potential of the land on either side of the line; by the existence of the Highland clans, long diminished below the line; and, finally, by a perceived culture of violence versus a more orderly society, it seemed that the two halves of Scotland—the Highlands and the Lowlands—shared little in common. And, indeed, when the founders of the SSPCK brought the society into existence, this is what they believed.

The Highlands, 1590s–1690s: Romanticism versus Reality

Any effort to understand the Scottish Highlanders on the eve of the eighteenth century must cast aside the mist created by early-nineteenth-century Romanticism, plus the nouveau Romanticism of the late twentieth century. The Highlands recast by Sir Walter Scott's pen, which caught the eye of Queen Victoria, strayed a considerable distance from reality. As a ploy for tourist and royalty alike, the novelist's Highlands proved highly successful. As a source for scholars, however, they have evoked extensive ridicule. Allan I. Macinnes, Tom M. Devine, and Donald E. Meek, to name a few, have lambasted Scott's persistent romanticizing of the Highlands, targeting, variously, his misinterpretation of the clans and misunderstanding of the bardic tradition.[11] More recently, films like Mel Gibson's *Braveheart* (1995), pegged by one reviewer as "a star-driven epic that [favors] arrant romanticism," and its contemporary, Michael Caton-Jones' *Rob Roy* (1995), have further befuddled contemporary attempts to understand Highlanders and Lowlanders at the opening of the eighteenth century.[12]

Reality was far more prosaic for most Highland and Hebridean Gaels during the final decades of the Stewart dynasty, long after the Union of the Crowns. Like their Algonquian and Iroquois counterparts, these Gaels lived in a world that demanded a balance between pragmatism and spirituality. Ordinary clan members during this era faced daily challenges that belied romanticism. Parents and kin reared the children, provided food for their families, raised the crops, tended the livestock, and paid the rent.

Religion was integral to their ability to meet these challenges. Although priests and ministers remained scarce, the Gaels took seriously their religious duties, whether they were members of the majority faith of the Highlands, Episcopalianism, or the minority Presbyterian and Catholic faiths. After the Scottish Reformation, Catholicism in Gaeldom became "all but moribund" until the second decade of the seventeenth century, and even then "efforts of Jesuits and other priests to maintain a minimal presence in the Highlands" led only "to marginal but unsanctioned inroads among communities bordering the lowland peripheries."[13] The Catholics remained isolated in remote places like the Hebridean Isles of South Uist and Benbecula, where residents clung to the pre-Reformation Church. Even where Gaels professed the "Reformed faith," however, some aspects of Catholicism persisted in their ritual. Many Gaels, especially those living in the Hebrides and western seaboard, drew heavily from their folk traditions, yet another dimension of their multilayered world. These Gaels still believed in the healing powers of the ancient, holy wells, as well as the multiple powers of specific, venerated stones; they accepted the uncanny accuracy of second sight; and a few practiced the ritual movement following a "sunways" circle.[14] Religion in the Highlands and Islands during this era was complex. Drawing on pre-Christian, Catholic, Episcopal, and Presbyterian traditions, the Scottish Gaels fashioned syncretic faiths that served their needs.

By 1700 the societal structure of Gaeldom was already shifting. Although "the customary relationships between the *fine* and their clansmen" had begun to change in the early seventeenth century, for the ordinary clansman the early eighteenth century was probably not that different from the late seventeenth.[15] Still, if religion, manners, and morals among Western Highlanders and Hebrideans had been little altered by 1700, all of Gaelic society sensed the ongoing shifts in relationships. These shifts had touched every group—the elite; the chief and the fine; the tacksmen, or *fir-taca*; the warriors, or *buannachan*; the bards and *seanachaidh*, or historians; and the ordinary clansmen. Macinnes maintains that the seventeenth-century tribulations of the House of Stewart monarchs—namely, the civil war and Restoration, the revolution, and the reign of William of Orange—profoundly affected Highland society.[16]

However, the lofty medieval position once enjoyed by the chiefs and the fine during the Lordship of the Isles had been in a state of flux since the reign of James VI and I (1567–1625). James's treatment of the Highlanders reflected his conviction that the Gaelic world—as a distinct way of life—should be eradicated from Scottish society. His rigorous policy—initiated when he ruled Scotland exclusively and reinforced after the Union of the Crowns in 1603—incorporated three repressive measures designed to destroy Gaelic uniqueness. Foremost of these measures were the royal legal restrictions, epitomized by the famous Statutes of Iona, signed by selected Gaelic chiefs in 1609. The statutes attacked the clanship of the Gaels by tightening relations between the chiefs and the Crown and forcing the chiefs to account for their actions during regular visits to Edinburgh. Second, James attempted direct colonization by sending the "Fife Adventurers," who, at the turn of the seventeenth century, invaded the Isle of Lewis, northernmost of the Outer Hebrides. Clan MacLeod of Lewis defeated these Lowlanders. Third, James sent half a dozen military and naval expeditions along the western seaboard between 1596 and 1625, "demonstrating to the Highland chiefs that they could no longer count on being left alone."[17]

Through these measures James maintained a pattern of royal interference among the Highlanders. This pattern would gain momentum with his descendants, climaxing with the Jacobite rebellions and their aftermath. By prodding the Gaelic chiefs, James delivered a clear message: the Crown would no longer tolerate the Gaels as a different people. Even though James's domestic repression among Scottish Gaels was less severe than the draconian measures taken in Ireland, these steps would, nonetheless, reverberate among the Scottish clan chiefs. The Statutes of Iona alone would cast a long shadow over Gaeldom. Although historians have long debated the statutes' effectiveness, Rosalind Mitchison and Peter Roebuck have suggested that their aim was "cultural invasion and was not without effect." More broadly, Devine observes, "it is plain that they did have a powerful influence on the clan elites."[18]

The Gaelic chiefs began to sense that influence in 1610. That spring, shortly after the statutes were enacted, the Privy Council summoned the clan chiefs to a late-June conference in Edinburgh. In the early seventeenth century, the royal burgh of Edinburgh was a great distance —both physically and culturally—from the Hebridean and western seaboard homelands of these Gaelic chiefs. Gathering on June 18, ostensibly to discuss the future of the Isles, the chiefs who attended were wary. The underlying purpose of the meetings lay in the Crown's interest in forging links with these powerful, yet remote leaders. The rather frank gesture was well received. Most of the leading chiefs participated in the conference, and it proceeded, perhaps to everyone's surprise, without being interrupted by frequent argument. The Crown was encouraged. Hence, the Privy Council began to summon the chiefs, either individually or a few at a time, for further discussion. The Crown's ploy of monitoring the chiefs' actions seemed to be working. On the other hand, the shrewd Gaels likely had their own reasons for responding to the summons, drawing on generations of political experience. Their favorable reaction and the Crown's willing hand moved the gatherings onto an annual summer trajectory; they persisted for over a decade after James's death in 1625.[19]

Another dimension of the statutes targeted the education of Gaelic youth. Clause 6 ordered that the chiefs "being in goods worth thriescore ky' should educate their eldest son in the Lowlands so that they could speak, read and write English." This clause was directed toward those chiefs whose wealth was the equivalent of sixty cattle, a considerable herd. By 1616, however, the Privy Council had extended the order to include all children of Hebridean chiefs. Lowland schooling for children of the Gaelic elite had become a serious goal.[20]

The intent of the education measures, a virtually universal tactic for colonial regimes, was obvious, but the impact may have been less revolutionary than might appear. Initially, the measure implied that the children of the elite—the chiefs and the fine—had received little or no education, that they were illiterate, and especially that they had no knowledge of Scots, the language of the Lowlands. On the contrary, the Gaelic elite commonly drew on three written languages. These were Gaelic, Latin, and Scots. As John Bannerman reminds us, "Written Gaelic was a literary dialect removed from the everyday speech of the people, while Latin and Scots were the languages of government."[21]

In the sixteenth and seventeenth centuries, the professional orders of Gaelic society had maintained their interest in Latin and Scots alongside written Gaelic, although the ability to write Gaelic was already declining toward the end of the seventeenth century. The bards, whose pivotal role in Gaelic society was seen by the Crown as a threat and hence attracted the attention of the statutes, composed their verse in Gaelic. Consequently, "there had to be an [literate] audience for this poetry." Bannerman reasons, "If the poet required training [seven to twelve years] to become proficient in his art, so did his audience to fully appreciate the results thereof. Because literacy was an integral part of that training... the ability to write Gaelic was likely to be relatively common, at least in the upper levels of lay society to whom the bard addressed the bulk of his output." Bannerman adds an ironic twist, noting that bardic praise for the "traditional attributes of a chief" included the ability to write.[22]

Since the education clause was directed toward the youth of the elite, the fact that they were already literate, at least in their native language, suggests that the Crown failed to acknowledge the educational sophistication of the chiefs and professionals. In some cases, even prior to the signing of the statutes in 1609, certain chiefs had already sent their children to Edinburgh and across to the continent to be educated.[23]

Given these considerations, it appears that the primary impact of the statutes' education clause might have been simply cultural immersion. If the sons and daughters of Gaelic chiefs were already literate and at least bilingual, then they had no need to learn English (Scots). Their familiarity with Lowland customs was a different matter. In the long run, however, even the impact of cultural immersion remains uncertain, since no one has determined the intensity of the response to this royal dictate, and it is possible that very few youth crossed over the Minch to the mainland to make their way to Edinburgh, the city where their fathers had often traveled to attend the summer conferences called by the Privy Council.[24]

It is difficult to speculate on the effect of the education clause because of the lack of statistics, but if even a small number of these youth attended the Edinburgh schools in the early 1600s, they could have had a profound impact. By immersing themselves in Lowland ways, then reentering the kinship-dominated Gaelic world, they could have influenced their own clan elite, thereby compounding the drastic changes introduced by their fathers' trips to the Lowlands. In sum, in the early eighteenth century, when the SSPCK began its Highland and Island schooling program, it encountered a people whose leading figures were already bilingual and literate in one or two languages. Only the ordinary clansmen had remained exclusive Gaelic speakers who were literate neither in Gaelic nor in English (Scots). The children of these ordinary clansmen would become the principal targets of the society's schoolmasters.

Through the seventeenth century, the ordinary members of the clan maintained their sworn loyalty to their chiefs. Simultaneously, a number of the chiefs and perhaps their Lowland-educated children as well, edged closer to economic disaster. The paths they had chosen would wrench the fabric of Gaeldom. The gatherings in Edinburgh that began in 1610 thrust the clan chiefs into the heart of Lowland urban society. Within a short time they cultivated an affinity for this style of life. They enjoyed the fine clothing and the luxurious food, and they may also have derived a certain satisfaction from moving with ease among the cosmopolitan urbanites. Eventually, they began to absent themselves from home for months on end, spending more than their means on clothing, furnishings, and travel expenses. In this way they began to incur enormous debts.

By 1660, when the monarchy was restored under Charles II, the disruptions of the civil war, Oliver Cromwell's leadership, and the interregnum had "transformed the financial picture on many estates from acute financial embarrassment into chronic insolvency."[25] Lack of financial stability impelled the chiefs to search for additional income. Their acute financial need also altered their relationship with Lowland creditors, who forced the chiefs to pledge their lands as security for their debts, a practice known as *wadsetting*, and to incur bonded loans from merchants in Glasgow and Edinburgh.[26]

More important, the chiefs' financial embarrassment began to alter the tradition-bound relationship between them and the ordinary clansmen, who had already begun to be perceived as tenants. The chiefs called upon their clansmen and tenants to furnish more commodities and cash to satisfy their increasing demand for higher rent payments.

In Gaeldom the seventeenth-century rent increases proved startling. They served as a visible reminder of the major shifts in the horizontal structure of the clans that had emerged in the sixteenth and early seventeenth centuries. The ordinary clansmen already shared with their chiefs the responsibility for the support of the fine, especially the *seanachaidh* (historian-storytellers) and pipers, but also the subordinate gentry, the *fir-taca* (tacksmen), and especially the *buannachan* (warriors). Although the buannachan had often served as mercenaries in Ireland, as the need for these skills declined, they resided more frequently within their clan townships, where they became a burden to the ordinary clansmen. In certain regions tenants were required to "maintain the chief's fighting men as members of their own household."[27] The pressures on ordinary clansmen intensified.

As the importance of the buannachan decreased, the importance of the fir-taca increased. During the transition period the warriors became redundant, while the tacksmen gained a more definitive position as financial creditors. In essence, they became estate managers for their chiefs.[28]

Restructuring of the clan society, and hence its reciprocal value system, was integral to the royal desire for government control, but the interference in the Highlands by James VI and I remained benign when compared with his domination of the Ulster Plantation in northern Ireland. The royal mandate for the Highlands foresaw the clan chiefs as nascent proprietors exploiting their estates rather than as traditional chiefs or warlords exploiting the buannachan.[29] Perhaps it was ironic that the Crown's goals dovetailed with the pragmatic reality of the stranglehold of debt upon the chiefs. As leaders who had once been bound by their responsibilities for the clan and who had shared the connection provided by the physical setting that cemented the clanship bond, the Highland chiefs engaged in a subtle yet momentous change of heart. The inexorable power of their indebtedness forced them to reconsider the traditional merits of their land. They began to look at its commercial value. Their change of heart was by no means universal, nor was it immediate, but eventually their altered view of the land would be countered by the claims of their clansmen and women, who "saw themselves as having a customary right to the hereditary possession of their holding, a right known as *duthchas*."[30]

Land was not the only new source of income for the chiefs. They also looked at the prospects for selling the Highland cattle. The clan members had long relied on their few cattle for rent payment and cash and as a source of dairy products, meat, and hides. Edmund Burt observed that during the Highland spring, when "their Provisions of Oatmeal began to fail . . . they bleed their Cattle, and boil the Blood into Cakes, which, together with a little milk and a short Allowance of Oatmeal, is their Food."[31] Scottish journalist John MacLeod describes the impact of the cattle on the environment: "It is hard to grasp how much the passing of these great herds has impoverished the land. . . . Cattle roamed everywhere, their dung enriching the soil, their grazing habits allowing the earth to breathe, and keeping down the coarser plants and sedges."[32] At that time the cattle were generally small. Folklorist I. F. Grant once depicted them as "'Short in the legs, round in the body, straight in the back,' but small in size." Burt described them as looking like Lincolnshire calves. Not all of them were black. Grant notes, "reddish brown was also common . . . [for] these little cattle-beasts, with their long coats, sweeping horns, and gay carriage."[33]

Winter proved the most difficult season in the Highlands. Food was scarce for ordinary clan members and their animals. By spring the cattle were quite weak, "many of them not being able to rise from the ground without help." Although the small animals recovered during the summer, when they were out on the shielings, each fall they returned to face possible starvation in the winter.[34] They did not mature until their fourth year, when they were driven to market.

The tradition of cattle raising had ancient roots among the Gaels. The Irish myths brought to Dalriada by the Scotti were epitomized in the epic saga of Cú Chulainn, the Ulster hero challenged by Meadhbh, queen of Connaught, who was determined to possess the fabulous Brown Bull of Quelgny, in Ulster (see chapter 1). The Gaels called cattle *eudail*, which also translates as "treasure." Among the Scottish Gaels cattle were integral to life. Clan members saw them as a source of wealth, as a means for youth to prove their valor, and as the thread for the seasonal calendar. Beltane (the first of May) was the day when livestock went out to pasturage; Samhain (the first of November) was when they were brought home for the winter. Cattle also played a prominent role in the antics of the Little Folk.[35]

During the mid- to late seventeenth century, the clan chiefs took a long look at these small animals. Eyeing the thriving Lowland trade in black cattle, then dominated by Galloway and the Borders, the chiefs determined to enter the market. Beginning in the 1670s and continuing until the late 1800s, Gaelic cattle drovers, aided by the indispensable skills of their border collies, guided large droves of the small black animals into Lowland markets, first at the Crieff Tryst in Perthshire and later at the Falkirk Tryst outside Stirling.

When the herds made their way out of the hills, they had already traveled a good distance. Those who originated in the Outer Hebrides traveled from North and South Uist in sturdy sailing boats across the Minch, one of the world's most formidable bodies of water. Others—often eight thousand per season—swam the short stretch of water from the Isle of Skye to Kyle Rhea on the mainland. Once on the mainland, they followed the drove tracks, still visible in some stretches, forded the streams, and trudged over the hills and down the glens, always traveling toward the fall tryst or rendezvous.[36]

By the 1720s, the drovers gathered at the fall trysts probably sold between twenty and forty thousand cattle each year. A witness to the gatherings described the drovers as "Highland Gentlemen" and wrote that they were "dress'd in their slashed short Waistcoats, a Trousing . . . with a Plaid for a cloak and a blue Bonnet. They had a Ponyard, Knife and Fork in one Sheath, hanging at one side of their Belt, their Pistol at the other, and their Snuff mull before, with a great broad Sword by their side." The drovers' attendants, "all in belted Plaids . . . spoke the Irish."[37]

During the eighteenth century, these cattle sales influenced the economy of the Lowlands, especially in the Borders, but in the Highlands and Islands cattle sales dominated the financial scene. Grant argues that the chiefs and tacksmen were "dependent on the trade."[38] Income from the cattle sales enabled the chiefs to pay off some of their debts, while *wadsetting* continued to supply their need for credit. But the sales especially benefited the tacksmen because they assumed responsibility for the trade. Initiating the cattle droves by purchasing the animals from the tenants, the tacksmen also arranged for the drovers to drive the cattle to the trysts. The tacksmen thereby commandeered a crucial role in the chiefs' struggle for financial solvency, but their own financial management skills made them the ultimate beneficiaries.[39]

The restructuring of clan relationships due to economic pressure suggests that the Highland Gaels were gradually discarding the garb of kinship obligations for a cloak woven of commercial connections. Chiefs had mortgaged much of their lands and become estate owners; tacksmen had become estate managers; and ordinary clan members had become tenants.

Although this conclusion may have the benefit of logic, it fails to allow for the cultural persistence inherent in a society glued together through the ancient bond of kinship. For over four hundred years, the clans—reformed after the Viking era—had survived through the concept of mutual obligation. Historian Robert A. Dodgshon dubs this relationship "redistributive exchange" or "movements in and out of chiefly centres." He argues that as early as 1500, the "Highland chiefdoms were organized around a landlord-tenant relationship," which relied on tenants paying rent.[40]

In Scottish Gaeldom, tenants paid annual rents largely through in-kind payments of food (i.e., crops), livestock, and dairy products. With no written leases, most tenants probably held their lands on a year-to-year agreement. Seventeenth-century Hebridean traveler Martin Martin explained the arrangement practiced in the Western Isles: "When the proprietor gives a farm to his tenant, whether for one or more years, it is customary to give the tenant a stick of wood and some straw in his hand: this is immediately returned by the tenant again to his master, and then both parties are as much obliged to perform their respective conditions as if they had signed a lease or any other deed."[41]

Without the glue of kinship, the tenant would have been in a precarious position. Each year he hastened to provide his chief with some meal, perhaps part interest in a sheep, some butter, and possibly a load of peats. But the tenant's security did not rest exclusively on these in-kind payments. It also relied on mutual care and concern. In Martin's words, "The islanders have a great respect for their chiefs ... and they conclude grace after every meal with a petition to God for their welfare and prosperity."[42]

Rents paid by clansmen or tenants served other purposes within the socioeconomic order. Cumulatively, they contributed to a "complex amalgam of different dues and obligations" resting on "a core of long-standing obligations kinsmen owed to their chief."[43] For the tenants, this also included a responsibility to provide hospitality to the chief and the fine, which was repaid in kind by the chief.

Kinship relied on the "sense that each class had a distinctive and traditional function as a part of an organic whole [the clan], and that each had something to contribute to the well being of the whole community."[44] For the clan members, the rent was both real and symbolic: "Personal status and connection were valued items not lightly surrendered nor easily eroded."[45] But the chiefs held the power to alter or maintain the old ties. Francis Shaw concludes that "the chiefs themselves, by continuing to uphold many of the old traditions and practices, probably did most of all to maintain the unity of clan society when political and economic forces which spelled its doom were coming into play."[46]

Commercialization, driven by the chiefs' (and the fine's) indebtedness, was steadily eroding Scottish Gaeldom. As long as the bonds of kinship held, the clans could survive. But the erosion continued. It would be accelerated in the eighteenth century by the Lowland schooling that the SSPCK eagerly offered to the children of the ordinary clansmen and women, who were being reduced to the status of tenants.

The Lowlands: Comparisons with the Highlands

By the late seventeenth century, Highlanders had forged specific economic and political links with the Lowlanders. Conversely, few Lowlanders had ventured into the Highlands except the political or military envoys serving on behalf of the Crown. The Crown's engagement stretched from the military expeditions and strong-armed political tactics of James VI and I early in the century to the aggressive actions of William III at the end of the century. After William defeated his father-in-law, James VII and II, at the Battle of the Boyne, Britain's new monarch pursued a relentless policy in Scottish Gaeldom, which included the defeat of James's Scottish supporters in the Rising of 1689, the construction of Fort William in the heart of the Highlands, and the symbolic massacre of ClanMacDonald at Glencoe in 1692. Under William, the Crown's intrusions into the Gaelic Highlands had steadily intensified.

The Gaels themselves had crossed the Highland Line in far greater numbers than their Lowland counterparts. Clan chiefs and their children and members of the fine had resided in the Lowland cities for business, schooling or education, and pleasure. The Highland drovers continued to mingle with those Lowlanders who engaged in the cattle markets at the massive trysts in Crieff, Falkirk, and other venues. Still, these connections remained selective, suggesting that by 1700 "the heart of Gaeldom," the Hebrides and the western seaboard, remained as isolated as ever.[47] While few Lowlanders traveled in the Gaelic world, even among the Gaels, only select members of society visited the Lowlands. The lesser gentry, such as the tacksmen, and the ordinary clan members or tenants remained isolated in Gàidhealtachd, where they were physically and culturally separated from the Lowlands.

At the turn of the eighteenth century, then, most Highlanders and Lowlanders traveled along different paths. In the Highlands, despite their increasing fragility, the clans still enfolded Gaelic society within the embrace of kinship. In the Lowlands, kinship continued to play a role in relationships, but its strength was tempered by other forces that were strongly influenced by commercialism.

The Highland Line also marked a division of Scotland's faith traditions. In the Highlands, many clans were Episcopalian—Macinnes estimates the proportion of Episcopalians may have been as high as 75 percent. A minority of clans, located largely in the southern Highlands, and especially in Argyll and along the northwestern seaboard, had become Presbyterian.[48] Another distinct minority of clans, widely dispersed in both Inner and Outer Hebrides and on the mainland, remained Roman Catholic. In the Lowlands, the northeast, largely Aberdeenshire, flourished as an island of Episcopalians in a sea of Lowland Presbyterians. In the Highlands, the major three faiths often cast a benign eye on carryover beliefs such as second sight or powerful phenomena such as kelpies, shapeshifting figures who emerge from lochs and rivers. By contrast, the Reformed Christianity of the Lowlands—the Church of Scotland—concentrated its energies on feuds within the Established Kirk, having consigned most pagan beliefs and customs to an "unenlightened past."

Access to schooling also distinguished most Highlanders from most Lowlanders. Only the clan chiefs sent their children to Glasgow, Edinburgh, or London for grammar school and university; only the chiefs could afford to hire tutors to prepare their children for these Lowland institutions. In 1700 every university in Scotland was in a Lowland town—Glasgow, St. Andrews, Aberdeen, and Edinburgh.[49] The same geographical restriction applied to most grammar schools. Education for the children of the Gaelic lesser gentry—the tacksmen—and those of the ordinary clanspeople occurred almost exclusively within the family and home, through practical training, the church, storytelling, and song.

Of course, there were some exceptions. Scottish education historian Donald J. Withrington reminds us of the diversity of formal educational opportunity in the Highlands and Islands. He points out that parish schools proliferated in the eastern Highlands—in Banffshire and the uplands of Perthshire—and in the Inner Hebrides—on the Isles of Bute, Mull, and Skye, as well as in two of the few towns in the Outer Hebrides, the port town of Stornoway on the Isle of Lewis and the coastal town of Rodel on South Harris. Elsewhere in the mainland Highlands, only the Badenoch (the northeast and the Moray Firth) and Lochaber (by Loch Linnhe, near Fort William) districts had sufficient parish schools for their residents. Hence, all of the Highland regions north of the Great Glen, and almost all of the Outer Hebrides and even parts of the Inner Hebrides, had very few parish schools and, hence, very little schooling.[50]

The availability of schooling in the Lowlands contrasted sharply with the paucity of schools in the Highlands. Scotland's overarching belief in the uniqueness of its national system of education, long touted by Scots as superior to the English in terms of its deep roots and its democratic ethos, garnered its reputation primarily in the Lowlands. In the eighteenth century, Lowlanders had long benefited from the Scottish tradition of formal learning. As early as the 1490s, children of the elite already had access to schooling, but in 1560, John Knox and his fellow reformers initiated a national system of education with the issuing of *The First Book of Discipline*, which called for elementary schools to be located in every parish, grammar schools for preparation in Latin to be located in towns of "any repute," and high schools for the study of Latin, Greek, rhetoric, and logic, to be located in the larger towns.[51]

By 1700 about 90 percent of the Lowland parishes had established at least one parish school. In the more populous counties, these institutions were grammar schools that prepared students for university, and in some well-populated counties the Kirk had opened more than one parish school. Most Lowland children had access to some form of schooling. If they did not attend their local parish school, they could enroll in a private "adventure school," which proved to be a more than satisfactory venue for the young Robert Burns of Ayrshire. Burns's tutor, John Murdoch, opened an adventure school in 1765, where he taught a small group of local children, including Robert and Gilbert Burns, in the Ayrshire town of Alloway.[52]

For ordinary Lowland children schooling was of a brief duration, usually lasting between two and four years.[53] During this stint the young pupils generally acquired basic literacy. Afterward, they returned to their families, who needed their labor. Lads often served as apprentices, especially for work in the fields; lassies were tutored for their roles as wives and mothers. There was no question of their eligibility for further schooling. Occasionally, an especially able lad from a humble background, known as a "lad o'pairts," would be selected as a bursary scholar for grammar school, followed by university. But these lads were unusual. As for the girls, neither grammar school nor university permitted them to enroll.

Given the time period, however, schooling in the Lowlands had a startling impact. Historian T. C. Smout concludes that by 1700, this admixture of parish and private school led to "a literate peasant society in the Scottish Lowlands that was not merely able to read but apparently loved reading."[54]

The Highland Line also marked a sharp difference in subsistence patterns. In the early eighteenth century, ordinary clansmen supported their families primarily as herdsmen. Since farming plots were small and the soil generally poor, farming, especially in the Hebrides and even in parts of the mainland, engaged only a portion of their time. Likewise, most of them fished only part of the time, if at all.[55] Other seasonal tasks, such as the bringing in of the peats, also demanded their energies. Hence, versatility was a byword for the economic survival of ordinary clansmen and women.[56] And poverty was a given.

At the same time, the largely rural Lowlands wore the mantle of agriculture like a protective cloak. Even the cottars, situated at the lower rung of the economic ladder, just above the servant class, had their own smallholdings, where they raised food for their families in return for the labor they provided to the tenants. Those cottars who were also tradesmen—spinners, weavers, carpenters, blacksmiths—could not survive without their few acres of land. The tenants shouldered responsibility for working the land. They raised the oats, barley, and wheat crucial to the Lowland diet; they grazed the livestock, tended the field through the run rig system of cultivation, and supervised the

Linlithgow in 1823. Harvest in the Central Belt of the Lowlands.
DRAWING BY A. W. CALCOTT, ENGRAVED BY W. R. SMITH.

bringing in of the peats. Between them, these "poor peasant husbandmen"—the tenants and cottars—fed the Lowlands. Still, whether they worked holdings or smallholdings, most of them owned none of the land themselves. Thus, both groups remained beholden to others. While the cottars labored for the tenants, the tenants rented their holdings from the heritors or landowners, and they also owed the heritors additional rent in the form of labor on the "home or mains farm."[57]

Herein lies a crucial difference between Highland and Lowland society. As Devine argues, "the relationship between tenant and landowner in the Lowlands by 1700 was emphatically economic in nature: access to land was given exclusively for rental in money and kind and a range of labour services due to the proprietor." The Lowland tenant-landlord relationship lacked the leaven provided by the reciprocal clan ethos that persisted in the Gaelic world. While the Lowland structure might bear paternalistic overtones, these would never be mistaken for the symbiotic relationship between chief and his *clann*. And without the crucial fabric of kinship, the rural Lowlanders had few defenses against the commercialization of agriculture that spread northward from England during the eighteenth century.[58]

On the cusp of the eighteenth century, Highlanders and Lowlanders seemingly held little in common. Yet their differences—their distinctive religious faiths, the clan system or its absence, the availability of formal schooling, and the varying conditions of farming—were compounded by one further contrast. Perhaps the strongest characteristic of the Highlands and Islands, one that virtually guaranteed their distinctiveness, remained their isolation.

Despite the royal mandate for construction of Highland forts during the seventeenth century plus the building of roads and additional forts during the eighteenth, most of the Highlands, especially along the western seaboard north of the Great Glen, as well as the Hebrides, remained inaccessible. Lochs, mountains, and the harsh winters discouraged Lowlanders from crossing the line and also prevented the Gaels themselves from extensive travel during the winter and early spring. In the west, travel by water, while often perilous, was usually more expedient.

Isolation and extreme poverty, the everyday fare for ordinary Highlanders, reflected the deep imprint of the natural environment on their lives. These features also served as their first line of cultural defense. Their remote locations enabled the Gaels to maintain their language, oral tradition, and religious faiths. The inclement weather, combined with the poor soil, guaranteed a difficult life, but, cumulatively, all of these conditions also molded their unique views of the world.

From late fall through early spring, when the storms swept across the Hebrides, over the Minch, and onto the western seaboard, the Gaels gathered in their cottages or in the Black Houses common to the Isle of Lewis, where they could join in a *céilidh*, a social gathering that enlivened the seemingly endless winter nights. It is not difficult to imagine the scene; it continues, in modified form, into the present—playing old tunes on the fiddle or whistle accompanied by the *bodrain* (drum) and telling the old stories of Cú Chulainn or of Deirdre or recent ones of kelpies or second sight—all shared around a peat fire with its smoke rising through the smoke hole in the roof and reaching toward the dark sky.[59] These evenings helped the Gaels gathered within to put aside their hunger and winter moodiness, to linger on the past and its heroes, or to ponder the mysteries surrounding their own lives.

Rural Lowlanders did not experience the extreme nature of this environmentally imposed isolation, although their winter evenings were also likely to include music as well as the remarkable array of Scottish folk songs, revealed in their richness by the master folklorist Robert Burns. Still, in the early eighteenth century, accessibility and modest economic growth were beginning to draw rural Lowlanders

Niel Gow. Gow was a renowned Perthshire fiddler and Jacobite sympathizer who composed many tunes that remain central to Scottish folk music.
PAINTING BY HENRY RAEBURN. COURTESY NATIONAL GALLERIES OF SCOTLAND.

into the transportation and communication networks that were creeping into their lives. Although some regions lay at the heart of these networks, including the Glasgow-Edinburgh corridor, roads also swung southwest to Galloway and Ayrshire, where Burns would grow up, as well as north to Fife and southern Perthshire and northeast to Angus and the Moray Firth. Improved communication, which linked the large urban centers of Glasgow, Edinburgh, and Aberdeen, plus the expanding ports at Dumfries, Leith, and Clydeside and at the mouths of the River Dee and the River Tay, pushed the Lowland economy toward commercialization.

Estate landowners—the heritors—and their tenants and cottars, the "backbone of the agricultural community," began shifting gears in the early part of the century. Although they were moving more gradually than their rural counterparts south of the Borders, they were slowly turning from subsistence to commercial farming. In the Lowlands, the market economy was making inroads on the old system, although most farms outside Lothian had not yet felt its impact. It was now possible, however, to raise flax, which could be converted into linen in lint plants and then exported, or to focus on subsistence crops alongside a subsidiary cash crop for market.[60]

In the towns, the rising professional classes, dominated by lawyers, merchants, and lairds, lay at the heart of the commercialization affecting certain Lowland regions.[61] But even among the rural lower classes, the economy had already altered to the degree that most cottars were paying their rent in cash rather than in-kind payments. In short, at the turn of the eighteenth century, the gap between Highlanders and Lowlanders was widening dramatically. The intensified pace of Lowlanders' lives as they tasted the market economy drew them even further away from the Highlands, and the persistent isolation of the Gaelic world marked the Highlanders increasingly as a people who were "different."

The Town of Edinburgh in 1700

Of all the major Lowland towns at the turn of the eighteenth century, Edinburgh proved to be the most likely choice for a colonial educational thrust into the Highlands. Glasgow, its chief rival, was soon to embark on its lusty role as Scotland's eighteenth-century center of international trade. But neither Glasgow nor the other population centers of Aberdeen and Dundee could match Edinburgh's claim as the heart of Scotland's political life and the core of its financial network. Even though the Union of the Parliaments would soon mark the dramatic departure of Scottish parliamentarians from Scotland to Westminster, the retention of the courts signaled the continued presence of the legal profession in town. As the focal point for the Church of Scotland and the recently founded Bank of Scotland (1695), Edinburgh also was home to ministers and bankers who jostled with the common folk along the narrow "wynds" and "closes" that entered High Street.

Even Dr. Samuel Johnson, who would walk "arm-in-arm up the High Street" with his friend James Boswell in August 1773, saluted the town with his dismissive words, "Edinburgh, a city too well known to admit description."[62]

Shaped in the medieval era, Edinburgh had often been the focal point for Scotland's convoluted political and religious history. Early in the Reformation era of the mid-sixteenth century, the town hosted the eloquent preaching of John Knox, architect of Scotland's Reformation and minister at St. Giles Cathedral, the High Kirk of Edinburgh. Less than a century later, in 1637, St. Giles was also the scene of one Jenny Geddes allegedly hurling her stool at the preacher, a symbolic gesture of the rebellion against the imposition of the English prayer book that would spawn the National Covenant of 1638. For generations Edinburgh had been on the frontline for the violence of power brokerage characteristic of a nation searching for a means to find its soul and forge its ever-shifting identity.

The status and polity of the Church of Scotland lay at the heart of this quest for identity. During the political uncertainty of the late 1680s, when William of Orange won the throne that had been held by James VII and II, Edinburgh hosted the Parliament of 1689–90, which abolished the Episcopalian polity in the Established Church and restored the Presbyterian form of government that relied on a General Assembly rather than bishops. The restoration of Presbyterianism in 1690 did not, however, assume a perpetuation of the old Scottish Covenants that questioned the Kirk's independence as well as its status as Established Church. A minority of Presbyterians continued to uphold the Covenants in the aftermath of the "killing times" of the 1680s. During these final years of the monarchy of Charles II, his determination to retain Episcopalian polity had met head-on the resistance of the Covenanters (or Cameronians), largely based in Ayshire, who met secretly to hold their own unauthorized religious services. Their rebellion led to violent encounters with royal troops. The widespread suffering that ensued, known as the "killing times," was accompanied by executions and formed an enduring aspect of Presbyterian legend.[63]

Parliament's decision of 1689–90—a compromise that rode roughshod over the martyrdom of this religious minority—was forged in the harsh reality of Scotland's weakened political position. The defeat of James VII and II, combined with the shrewd power brokerage of William, left the Scottish leaders with little room to finesse this aggressive monarch, whose claim to the throne through his wife, Mary, daughter of James VII and II (by his first wife), was reinforced by their Protes-

St. Giles Cathedral, the "High Kirk of Edinburgh."
PHOTOGRAPH BY FERENC M. SZASZ.

tant faith. Surely Scotland, the bulwark of the Reformed faith, would not be so stubborn as to prefer a Catholic Stewart over a Dutchman married to a Protestant Stewart. William's fait accompli forced the Parliament of Scotland to draft a measure that saved Presbyterianism, while abandoning the Covenants and, with them, "the old exclusive claims for Presbyterianism as the only godly form of church government and insistence on independence from state influence."[64]

Parliament's measure of 1690 abolished both Episcopal bishops—the antithesis of Presbyterian polity—and patronage, which meant ministers were appointed by the Kirk rather than selected by the parishioners. It also readopted an earlier declaration of faith known as the Westminster Confession. Under the new conditions, church polity relied on the overarching government of its General Assembly (which meets annually in Edinburgh) and, just below it, the Presbytery. This polity structure was finally in place when the SSPCK was born. In theory, the abruptness of the measure called for the immediate expulsion of all Episcopalian ministers from the established Kirk. In reality, the drastic impact of such a step meant that it would only slip into place over the natural course of one or two generations. The abrupt shift was reminiscent of the early years of the Reformation, when all spiritual leaders were Roman Catholic at the time of the demarcation.

Suppression soon followed. The unyielding tone of Parliament's settlement of 1690 spurred most of Lowland Scotland in general, and Edinburgh in particular, to adopt an intensified atmosphere of religious conformity. Gordon Donaldson puts it this way: "The Westminster Confession, now with statutory authority, became a standard from which men never deviated if not to the peril of their immortal souls, at any rate (if they were ministers or teachers) to the peril of their livelihood." By the 1690s, the prevailing theological position tolerated little deviation: "Anyone whose views diverged from the standards could easily be challenged."[65]

The call for conformity that dominated Edinburgh and the Lowlands at the end of the century was rooted in the Scottish Reformation, but it was nourished by the religious crises that followed during the seventeenth century. Paralleling the Scots' declaration of religious independence, which was perhaps the encoded message of the Reformation, the Scots' turbulent quest for political independence also retained its supporters.

One of the most eloquent expressions of Scottish "patriotism" had appeared some three centuries earlier in the famous letter sent to Pope John XXII on April 5, 1320, known to history as the Declaration of Arbroath. This remarkable statement, aptly described by distinguished Scottish historian Grant G. Simpson as "a blast of highly skilled rhetoric," has been vigorously scrutinized in succeeding centuries. In its latest guise, it galvanized fierce political attention when the Scots and the Welsh raised the question of devolution in the late twentieth century.[66]

While the interpretations of the Declaration of Arbroath represent a panoply of opinions, some more receptive to historical context than others, Simpson offers a commentary that is both balanced and provocative. He writes, "I personally hesitate, unlike some writers, to use the term 'nationalism' in the context of the central middle ages. 'Patriotism' could be a more acceptable word. But since the early thirteenth century there had been growing in the kingdom what I would describe as 'a sense of Scottishness.' This phrase is deliberately a rather generalized one."[67]

Whether the Declaration of Arbroath's famous sentence "For it is not glory, it is not riches, neither is it honour, but it is liberty alone that we fight and contend for, which no honest man will lose but with his life" represented nationalism, patriotism, or the voice of the people remains a subject of debate.[68] More likely, it represents, as Simpson suggests, a voice of "Scottishness" that reappeared during the century and a half before the SSPCK came into existence. In that context, it remains relevant for our story.

The twin concepts of nationhood, or Scottishness, and a government responsible to the people were joined in the 1560s at the time of the Scottish Reformation, leading the Lowland Scots to believe in their nation's unique destiny. This strong sense of self—as a people—is graphically described by Gordon Donaldson. He writes of "the Scottish people's concept of a perpetual contract with God giving them an unique place in the Divine Purpose."[69] Acknowledging a sense of destiny is not unique to the Scots. It lay at the heart of ancient Israel, it motivated the English Puritans who settled in Massachusetts Bay in the 1630s, and it drove those Americans who carried the Church of Jesus Christ of Latter-Day Saints to Deseret (Utah) in the 1840s. In a strange sense, the breadth of this belief—in a given people's unique destiny—forges the link between the post-Reformation Lowland Scots and the eighteenth-century English descendants of the New England Puritans who became ministers and schoolmasters to the Algonquians and Iroquois with the aid of funds from the Scots through the SSPCK.

The Edinburgh founders of the Scottish Society, along with their counterparts elsewhere in the Lowlands, fused a shared belief in the twin destinies of Scotland's Kirk and Scotland's sense of self as a nation.

As Donaldson suggests, some of the founders perceived their "religion not in the individual soul but in the corporate consciousness of the nation."[70] In the early 1700s, the founders of the society realized that their dual vision of Kirk and nation had major flaws. The Scottish nation as a unique corporate entity charged with its own destiny was seemingly split into two separate cultures. In a word, it encompassed a divided people. The Edinburgh gentlemen, who were acutely conscious of the historic role of the Lowlands, especially since the Settlement of 1690, committed themselves to furthering the cause. The faith and the cultural unity of their people—as Scots—must be achieved. In their view, the Highlanders were preventing Scotland from accomplishing its cosmic destiny. They believed that "only by control of the Highlands could the Hanoverian Crown and the Protestant succession be made secure."[71] To this end they would dedicate themselves.

However, if the Highlanders were to be persuaded of the need to participate in this great endeavor, they must undergo a complete transformation. Their religion, their language, their economic base, and their reliance on kinship—namely, the clans—all served as a barrier to Scotland's future as a unified people. Hence, their culture and their way of life must conform to the society and culture of the Lowlands. The isolation of the Highlanders had to be mitigated. Lowland educators should penetrate beyond the Highland Line. And in their forays, they should select as their targets not the adults, who were bound by tradition, but the unshaped minds of the Highland youth, especially the children of ordinary clansmen and women.

Armed with this logic, and a strong sense of their past, a conviction of the justice of their cause, and an equally strong-willed commitment inherent in high-minded philanthropic causes, the gentlemen of Edinburgh, Glasgow, and other Lowland towns created an organization that they called the Society in Scotland for the Propagation of Christian Knowledge. The time to act had arrived.

CHAPTER THREE

Scotland and the Birth of the SSPCK

Like all significant colonialist ventures, the Society in Scotland for the Propagation of Christian Knowledge was forged by the multiple events swirling around its birth. As the society's founders came together early in the eighteenth century, they crafted a movement of like-minded people intent on diminishing the cultural divisions engendered by the Highland Line.[1]

Although the cultural and geographical separation of Scotland into two vastly different regions had begun in the late medieval era, by the turn of the eighteenth century, the contrasts between Highlands and Lowlands were stark. Early in the new century, the whiff of forthcoming economic change in the Lowlands cast the Highlanders and their distinct ways into an increasingly isolated position. A common perception of those Scots who lived in the Lowlands, the disparaging view of the Highlanders as an uncivilized people, played directly into the hands of the society's founders. Their duty beckoned.

The Union of the Parliaments and Its Legacy

In his assessment of the Union of the Parliaments of Scotland and England, historian Bruce Lenman argues that "the incorporating union of 1707 casts a long shadow in Scottish history, both backwards and forwards. . . . [for] all Scottish politics after 1688 were shadowed by the prospect of some form of Union."[2] Among other things, the Union reflected the uneasy status of the throne during the era of the last Stewart monarchs—William and Mary (1689–1702) and, finally, Anne (1702–14). Shortly after his arrival in England, William III made quite clear his sentiments toward the Highlanders. In 1689–90, his forces quelled the first Jacobite uprising supporting the Stewart claim to the throne. In Scotland, this victory for the Williamites unfolded quickly after the death of the Viscount Dundee. Widely known for his leadership skills, the "bonnie Dundee" led the Jacobite forces at the Battle of Killiecrankie (1689). After he was mortally wounded during the battle, the Jacobite rising lost its momentum. Within a few years, William had solidified his reputation in Scottish Gaeldom by secretly ordering the infamous Glencoe Massacre (1692), a brutal event that hardened support in the western Highlands for the deposed James VII and II.[3] Like James VI and I, the grandfather of his wife, Queen Mary, the transplanted Dutch monarch further enforced the royal presence in the Highlands by rebuilding with stone the earthworks structure of the fort at Inverlochy. For Highlanders, Fort William marked the reality of the government's intrusion. For William III, the refurbishing of this Cromwellian structure served as a blunt reminder of his power. A solid military post, the fort commanded a strategic location in the western Highlands, the heart of Gaeldom.[4]

During the reign of William and Mary, the Scottish woes deepened when a severe famine arrived in the mid-1690s. Later, Scots would remember this time as "the Seven Ill Years" (1696–1703). During the years of crop failure, death plagued the land, stalking the poor and the weak. Scholars have estimated that, on average, the famine led to the death of one in twenty persons in Scotland. Still, the impact of the famine ranged widely. Beyond the Highland Line, where the ordinary clansmen and women, or tenants, already lived on the margin, families often found themselves pushed over the edge. In some regions deaths and burials were so "many and common that the Living were wearied in the Burying of the Dead."[5]

The famine only served to intensify the economic distress of Scotland, already weakened by William's war with France. In an era of "imperial rivalry and economic nationalism, marked by mercantilist competition among the leading European powers," Scotland was floundering.[6] Desperate to improve their country's foreign trade and national status, certain enterprising Scots sought a solution by forming in 1695 the Company of Scotland. The company's principal venture, founding the ill-fated colony of Darien on the Isthmus of Panama, suffered multiple blows—Scots remained convinced that part of the blame should be "laid squarely at England's door"—and Darien collapsed in 1700, following a devastating loss of life and fortune. The economic blow to the nation was severe. Scots lost about 25 percent of their country's liquid capital. Ironically, the Darien disaster helped to forge the parliamentary union. After learning of the company's failure, a powerful minority of Scots saw political union with England's parliament as the only viable means to guarantee their country's economic future.[7]

The debate over the Articles of Union—both within and outside the Parliament of Scotland—proved intense. Except for support by members of the Parliament of Scotland itself, virtually every Scot opposed the union of the two parliaments, and they made themselves heard through the protesting mobs that swarmed through the streets of Edinburgh and Glasgow. In this turbulent time, the antiunionists saw the stance of the Kirk as crucial to their cause. Initially the Kirk sided with the opposition. Fearful that its cherished independence would be lost, it emerged as a forceful leader of the antiunionist sentiment; its ministers voiced this stance from almost every pulpit. But the Parliament of Scotland was well aware of the Kirk's power and finessed its opposition by passing a measure known as "an Act of the Security of the Church of Scotland." This legislation appealed to the protective concerns of the Church—it guaranteed the rights of the Kirk and ensured that the Kirk's polity or system of government would become a part of the Treaty of Union itself.[8] With the voice of the Kirk subdued, by January 1707, members of the Parliament of Scotland had ratified the Act of Union and voted their legislative body out of existence.[9]

The Kirk's decision reflected its political pragmatism. Once it had been persuaded that its sovereignty would be assured—Scottish patriotism notwithstanding—it threw its support behind the Act of Union; the Kirk believed that parliamentary union would serve as reinforcement for its own Whig ideology. Although it still retained some doubts about the political merger, the Kirk would have been decidedly uncomfortable with the prospect of a Catholic Stewart on the throne—namely, James VIII and III, son of James VII and II. When the Act of Union committed Scotland to the Protestant Hanoverian succession—which meant a German-speaking monarch on the throne following the death of Queen Anne—the fate of the Kirk and the prospects of the future Hanoverian dynasty became inextricably entwined.

By contrast, the Episcopal faith of many Highland clans—combined with their Jacobitism that led them to abjure the House of Stewart—set them on a collision course with the Kirk. The Church of Scotland denigrated the Jacobites; it accused them of being anti-Whig, anti-Union, and anti-Presbyterian.[10] It was not far off the mark. Hence, with the Act of Union in 1707, the die was cast. The volatile relationship between the Jacobites and the Whigs would be entwined with the equally volatile relationship between the Gaelic Highlanders and the Kirk—the two conflicts form the parameters of this story as it unfolds in Scotland. At the same time, the Kirk's supporters would include a newly forming independent group of philanthropists who called themselves the SSPCK. Given its close relationship with the Kirk and its forceful agenda, the society stood squarely in the center of the eighteenth-century battle of cultures, religions, and political loyalties. Charging into the thick of the battle that pitted Whig against Jacobite, Presbyterian against Episcopalian *and* Catholic, and the Lowlanders' Scots language against the Highlanders' Gaelic, the society sent its "warrior schoolmasters" to the battleground that lay beyond the Highland Line. Within the first decade of the young century, the sides had already hardened, and the political and cultural divisions that were in place would remain firm until the final Jacobite Rebellion of 1745.

After 1707 the Kirk's compromise on patriotism cost it in terms of support. For some, especially Lowland Episcopalians, its once prestigious stature among Lowlanders had become tarnished. By arbitrarily supporting the Act of Union, it had abdicated its traditional role as the nationalist faith. "Confessional nationalism within Scottish Gaeldom . . . [had come] to be rooted in non-juring Episcopaleanism." As the Kirk's role shifted, the way was opened for an independent group like the SSPCK and its members to emerge as "the shocktroops of Presbyterianism" in the Highlands and Islands.[11]

The Founding of the Society

In the decade before the Act of Union, a group of gentlemen living in Edinburgh had formed a praying society that they called the Society for Reformation of Manners (1698), soon shortened to "Manners." An early forerunner to the popular eighteenth-century societies that flourished in Scotland—Edinburgh, Glasgow, and elsewhere in the Scottish Lowlands—in England, on the continent, and beyond Europe, this group avowed a keen interest in "politeness," an attachment that would also characterize a number of the later societies.

At the turn of the eighteenth century, politeness did not simply mean proper social behavior. It also implied the emerging "culture of discussion and argument" that "represented an unparalleled opportunity to spread moral insight and mutual understanding."[12] In 1698 the Manners Society of Edinburgh epitomized this cultural tone. Through correspondence with its counterparts in the English reform societies, the Edinburgh gentlemen learned of an intriguing cause that could potentially change the direction of their reforming instincts. The English reformers described their growing conviction that the education of children from poor families might alleviate their society's religious and political ailments. For the Scots, the analogy proved apt. Members of Edinburgh's Manners Society merely had to substitute "Highlanders" for "English poor," and their reform target leaped into focus.[13]

Yet the founders of the SSPCK, which evolved out of the Manners Society, defined "education" with a broad brush. Their ultimate goal was to change the worldview of the Highlanders. Still, religion lay at the heart of their motivation. The rigor of their Presbyterian faith perspective lent an imperative dimension to their missionary quest, and they eagerly anticipated changing the faith perspective of the Gaels. But their antagonism toward the Irish language, once ubiquitous in Scotland, spurred an equal revulsion toward the Highlanders' Gaelic. Celtic scholar Donald E. Meek asserts that the society "was established in Edinburgh with the express aim of destroying the Gaelic language . . . [and] its missionary programme has a good claim to be seen as a campaign against Roman Catholicism." Allan Macinnes adds that throughout the Jacobite era, the Highlanders themselves viewed Presbyterianism solely as a "missionary denomination."[14]

The SSPCK introduced its missionary and educational work during the Jacobite rebellions—beginning with the "eighty-nine" and ending with the "forty-five" (1689–1745)—each leading to devastating repercussions. The pervasiveness of this cause, which spilled across two centuries, meant that the rebellions would have a wrenching impact on Scottish Gaeldom for the better part of a hundred years. Hence, the society initiated the movement for cultural change amidst the unsettled milieu of divided loyalties and sporadic warfare. The often polarized views of the Jacobite supporters and the members of the society thrust them into an ideological fencing match that continued through the heart of the eighteenth century. Supporters of each position thrust and parried, each striving to sway the hearts and souls of the Gaelic people. The society's schoolmasters, physically ensconced in the Highlands, were caught in the crossfire, and they found themselves torn between the antagonistic stance of the Jacobites, who supported the Stewarts and the prospect of a Scottish Catholic on the throne, and the Whigs, who supported the Protestant and German Hanoverians on the throne. Some SSPCK schoolmasters who were Gaels themselves favored the Jacobite position; others sided with the Whig position, sometimes against their own clans.

During this contentious time, the varying fortunes of the Jacobite cause affected several generations of Scots, casting a long shadow over the society's earnest attempts toward educational reform. The hovering presence of Jacobitism through the first half of the eighteenth century led the society directors to couch the instructions they sent to the schoolmasters in overly zealous language, which can be understood only in the context of the struggle. The stakes were high. For society members, the persistence of the Jacobite cause during the early to mid-eighteenth century broadened their goal. They were not merely attempting to change the Highlanders' culture and way of life. Their view of the Jacobite supporters as opponents meant they also envisioned themselves as "warriors" for Scotland—they faced a perceived enemy who threatened to destroy the unified Scotland they intended to create.

1701: A Pivotal Year

In 1701 the Westminster Parliament passed an act known variously as the Act of Settlement or the Act of Succession. This measure marked the official death knell for the House of Stewart. It provided for the Hanoverian succession to the throne, which had been ruled by the Stewarts since the Union of the Crowns, marked by the ascendancy of James VI and I in 1603. After hearing the news of the death of Queen Elizabeth that year, James VI of Scotland had hastened south, journeying from Edinburgh to London, where he was crowned as James I. In a single moment this event fulfilled his ambition of joining the crowns of Scotland and England. Now, a century later, the Westminster Parliament declared the demise of that historic reign. When Anne, the last of the Stewart monarchs, died in 1714 without a surviving heir, no other member of the family could legally assume the throne. The repercussions of this measure soon filtered north to Scotland, where they reverberated strongly within the membership of the Manners Society of Edinburgh.

In the same year as the Act of Succession, in a royal chateau near Paris, James VII and II, the Stewart monarch in exile, died. He was succeeded by his son, James Francis Edward Stewart, the lad whose birth had occasioned his father's flight from England. Although his enemies dubbed him the "Pretender," this Stewart achieved recognition by Louis XIV, who acknowledged him as James VIII and III. In the year of his recognition, 1701, the heir to the Stewart throne was thirteen years old. Across the water, in the Scottish Highlands, when the Jacobite supporters of the Stewarts heard the news, they interpreted the French recognition of James VIII and III as a sign of hope. Perhaps, they speculated, the rightful inheritor of the crown would someday be returned to the throne.

In this same year, certain residents of the Lowlands found different reasons for hope. In Edinburgh in 1701, at a meeting of the Manners Society, "a few private gentlemen ... formed the design of establishing charity-schools in the Highlands and Islands, and agreed to use their endeavors for procuring, by voluntary subscription, a fund for this purpose."[15] The raison d'être for the SSPCK had been crafted.

Hence, well before the debate over the Act of Union, the antecedent of the SSPCK—an independent organization that would reform education in the Highlands—had already attracted a group of gentlemen in Edinburgh. By the time the Union of the Parliaments had compromised the Kirk's symbolic role as the nationalist faith, the Edinburgh reformers had already laid the groundwork for their Highland mission. Indeed, they had already carried out their first venture. In 1700 they had opened a school in the Highlands, which, by its prompt failure, had confirmed their worst fears. The site they had chosen, in the parish of Abertarff near the head of Loch Ness, lay in "the centre of a country where ignorance and Popery did abound." The schoolmaster had "met with such discouragements from the inhabitants," he had survived only eighteen months before the Edinburgh sponsors had found it "necessary to suppress the school."[16]

Perhaps the Edinburgh gentlemen saw the Abertarff school as a rude awakening, one that might disabuse them of their facile expectations for immediate change. Or they may have interpreted Abertarff as a pragmatic lesson. In one sense, as a group intent on cultural change, they too were "going to school" in order to learn how to revise worldviews and long-held customs of another people. If the Abertarff experiment taught them anything, it was the need to broaden their network of support. Within a year, they had published a memorial justifying their intent of "promoting religion and virtue" in "those countries" beset with "disorders" and outlined the potential means for raising the necessary funds. The members of the Parliament of Scotland in Edinburgh had even drafted a bill "for rendering effectual the scheme therein suggested," but the parliament had failed to act on the measure before it dissolved itself.[17]

The Kirk's General Assembly, the leading body within the Church's polity structure, retained a vested interest in the matter. As one late-nineteenth-century scholar depicted the relationship between the SSPCK and the Kirk, "The Society was not what we would call a scheme of the Church. But the Society was, from its origin most intimately associated with the Church." He added, "Its members and directors were leading Churchmen; it began its work with the Church's free contributions, which were renewed from year to year for half-a-century, and at frequent intervals thereafter."[18]

As the Kirk began negotiating the difficult issues raised by the prospective Act of Union, it welcomed these enterprising gentlemen's proposals. The timing was fortuitous. The Kirk's General Assembly appropriated a select committee; the committee met with the gentlemen to discuss the plan; and the upshot of these meetings was a further publication of the proposals. The General Assembly then offered crucial assistance: its leaders established the necessary connections with people of power and wealth by sending "copies of these proposals, with subscription-papers thereto . . . to all the persons of influence in the kingdom."[19]

Through the tentacles of this far-reaching network, word of the proposals reached the queen, "who was graciously pleased to encourage this design by her royal proclamation." By 1709, "subscriptions having been obtained to the amount of a £1000 Sterling and upwards," Queen Anne granted "letters patent under the great seal of Scotland, for erecting certain of the subscribers into a corporation; the first nominations of whom was lodged with the Lords of Council and Session."[20]

The first patent, issued in 1709, described the "charitable design" of the SSPCK as "the further promoting of Christian Knowledge, and the increase of piety and virtue, within Scotland, especially in the Highlands and Islands and the remote corners thereof, where error, idolatry, superstition, and ignorance, do mostly abound, by reason of the largeness of parishes, and scarcity of schools; and for propagating the same in Popish and Infidel parts of the world."[21]

The Founders and Their Organization

The Edinburgh gentlemen who spurred the formation of the SSPCK reflected the unique environment of Scotland's capital at the time of the Union of the Parliaments. Within their own membership and the contemporary milieu of their cultural and economic environment lay the roots of the famed Scottish Enlightenment that had been gradually emerging, layer on layer, through a mixture of social and cultural changes from the sixteenth century forward. The rise of the professional classes—the lawyers and the ministers—composed a dramatic dimension of this change. In the urban Lowlands, the lawyers, especially in Edinburgh, which served as the heart of an increasingly centralized legal system, wielded a powerful influence on virtually every aspect of Scottish society. Ministers were a close second. And in both professions families "tended to intermarry and each developed the hallmarks of a hereditary caste."[22]

The universities added further yeast to the rich cultural mix of Edinburgh, Glasgow, and Aberdeen. In the congested urban centers, the literati—lawyers, ministers, university staff and students, lairds, and noblemen—congregated in the various societies, where they engaged in stimulating conversation, often enlivened by a glass of claret and a hearty supper. These cosmopolitan gatherings reflected Scotland's "taste for analytical discussion and that spirit of liberal enquiry, to which the world is indebted for some of the most valuable productions of the eighteenth century."[23] Everywhere one could hear echoes of the Scottish Reformation and John Knox's advocacy of schooling for Scottish youth. Simultaneously, the discussions held among these urban Lowlanders retained a persistent thread of morality, one that hinted at the creation of "a new and better kind of society."[24]

The SSPCK emerged as a remolded version of the former Society for the Reformation of Manners, and it proved a mirror image of the search for an improved society. At the first meeting of the society, held on November 3, 1709, the members of the newly formed corporation who gathered that late fall afternoon as the early darkness offered a foretaste of short winter days formed an illustrious group. There "were present several of the Nobility, fourteen of the Lords of Session, many gentlemen of rank and influence, together with most of the ministers of the city of Edinburgh, and in the neighborhood thereof." They attended to business with alacrity. Choosing a president, secretary, and treasurer, they also formed a committee of fifteen directors, who were appointed to meet "as often as they should see needful, for the dispatch of business."[25]

At the next meeting, the directors laid out their goals. They intended to establish schools, "particularly in the Highlands and Islands," where they would teach "Papists as well as Protestants of every denomination." They would select schoolmasters of the "Christian Reformed religion." Scholars who "were unable to pay, should be taught gratis." The directors would "name some prudent persons, ministers and others, to be overseers of those schools." The directors would also encourage "such ministers or catechists" who might give "further instruction of the Scholars, remote from church, by not only catechizing but preaching to them." Finally, they agreed to "extend their endeavors . . . to Heathen nations."[26]

Cognizant of their dependence on voluntary contributions, the directors created a far-flung network of supporters. They "granted commissions to certain persons, as their correspondents in the several counties and principal towns in Scotland." And then, shrewdly, they also arranged for the formation of a board of correspondents in London.[27]

Although the directors and officers were to bear most of the work, they also drew on their local networks of support. Hence, the society's charter mandated that a general quarterly meeting of the members of the society be scheduled "at Edinburgh, in the Town's Hall, the first Thursdays of January, March, June, and November, yearly, in all time coming, at three of the clock in the afternoon."[28]

Reading between the lines of these instructions, it is clear that one goal of the founders involved leaving nothing to chance. Much was at stake. If the Darien disaster had taught the Scottish leaders any single lesson, it was to prepare for all possible exigencies. The founders had planned and organized their effort and shrewdly garnered support. Still, except for the precorporation failure of the school at Abertarff, the members of the society had yet to encounter the reality of life in the Highlands.

The Beginnings: St. Kilda

The first item on the directors' agenda, which, of necessity, preceded any concerns about the reality of life in the Highlands, was to address the society's most pressing need—financial contributions. No schoolmasters could be selected, no schools could be opened until the corporation had garnered a minimum base of £3,700 Sterling, an amount that would draw sufficient interest for operating expenses. As mandated by the patent issued by the queen, the society could not encroach upon the capital. Since all expenditures must, perforce, be drawn from the interest, "it was some time before they could get a sufficient revenue, to enable them to carry their plan into execution."[29]

Given the founders' primary goal of cultural colonialism within the Highlands of Scotland, the initial society directors aimed their appeal toward donors who believed that their personal gifts would aid in improving the lives of the Scottish Highlanders. Many prospective supporters found this idea quite appealing since they were enamored with the idea of the spread of "civilization." Whether the targeted people were the Catholic Irish or the Highland Gaels, Scottish Lowlanders and English alike saw the need for their "improvement" as imperative.[30] The widespread locations of the donors suggested the strength of the network formed by the society directors and the General Assembly. Living, variously, in Scotland, England, and even Ireland, the contributors were largely representative of the SSPCK membership. They were in the professions; they were either from the middle class or the nobility; frequently they were widows of men who came from this background. Those individuals who responded to the society's call for assistance ranged from ministers and merchants to physicians and professors, from a countess and a king to at least one military officer. Their gifts proved equally diverse. Some respondents donated less than £50; others contributed a £1,000 or more; still others endowed the society with the income from their heritable estates.[31]

By 1711, within two years after the queen had bestowed the charter, the society had accumulated sufficient funds to reach the magical figure of £3,700. This sum generated sufficient interest to enable them to open their first school. Appropriately, the society selected as a site for this pioneer institution perhaps the most remote location in all of the Highlands and Islands. Indeed, it was probably the most remote site in the entire British Isles, including Ireland, which was then a part of Britain. In that year the society sent a catechist to St. Kilda, a small group of isles that lie out in the Atlantic, about forty miles west of the Isle of Harris in the Outer Hebrides.

Home to about two hundred Gaels, the islands were described in considerable detail by Martin Martin, a Hebridean who had visited them shortly before the turn of the century, as "being good for pasturage, and [abounding] with a prodigious number of sea-fowl from March till September," which, along with bird eggs, formed the primary diet. Of the people themselves, he noted that they spoke "the Irish language only," that they were of the "reformed faith" (Presbyterian), and that they lived "contentedly together in a little village on the side of St Kilda," which, at two miles in length, remained the largest island.[32] The school at St. Kilda marked the earliest experiment of the society's shocktroops, the schoolmasters and catechists themselves.

In 1711, when St. Kilda was placed under the rigorous scrutiny of the members of the society, its residents seemed ripe for change. The appeal of the islands to these Lowland gentlemen rested in part with their remoteness. From an Edinburgh perspective the central Highlands might be seen as distant, the western Highlands and Hebrides as remote, but St. Kilda was almost literally off the map. In a word, these isolated islands in the Atlantic remained distinctly outside the boundaries of what an urban Lowlander deemed as "civilized" Scotland. Even from South Harris, one can see St. Kilda only from a high point, and, even then, the islands can be viewed only on one of those rare, fully clear days. But St. Kilda held promise. The residents, as Martin Martin pointed out, were of the "reformed religion," a decided advantage for a schoolmaster. Having tasted defeat at the hands of "ignorance and Popery," which the Manners Society schoolmaster had encountered at

Macleod Stone/Clach Mhic Leonid, Isle of Harris. St. Kilda lies forty miles west of this location. At the equinoxes the sun sets exactly due west over St. Kilda as seen from this standing stone. The stone is ten feet, or three meters, high.
PHOTOGRAPH BY FERENC M. SZASZ.

Abertarff, the directors may have been altering their strategy when they chose St. Kilda. Given the two most serious hurdles they perceived in the Highlands and Islands—remoteness and Roman Catholicism—they opted for the less daunting of the two. Their optimism, however, proved ill-founded.

The Crucial Component: The Society's Schoolmasters

The society realized that, second only to the need for funding, its success would depend on the men who would serve as SSPCK schoolmasters and sometimes as catechists. In the early decades, those selected to teach in the Highland schools proved the society's quintessential representatives. Their mission was clear: they were to serve as cultural intermediaries between the Highlands and the Lowlands. They were to bridge the chasm that divided the Lowlanders, who saw themselves as part of the civilized world, from the people of the Gaelic

Highlands and Western Isles and the Orkneys and the Shetlands, who, in a similar fashion, saw the world on their side of the Highland Line as civilized. The schoolmasters were mandated to serve as intermediaries, those who moved on cultural frontiers, interpreting the ways of one culture to another. Yet, from the society's perspective, the message they delivered was intended to move only in a single direction—from Lowland Scotland into the Highlands.

Beginning their work at St. Kilda in 1711, and continuing in numerous, scattered locations through the eighteenth and much of the nineteenth centuries, the schoolmasters served as the cultural shock-troops for the society. They alone lived beyond the cultural dividing line. There is little evidence to suggest that the society directors themselves spent any of their time visiting the people who lived beyond the Highland Line. Rather, they relied on the Kirk inspectors, representing the General Assembly, to evaluate the society's handiwork. On these tours the inspectors traveled from school to school on foot, by horse, or across the water by boat. Later, they wrote detailed reports for the General Assembly offices in Edinburgh. But even the inspectors' visits were intermittent, and, in the long run, only the schoolmasters themselves held the ground for the Lowland architects of reform who had crafted the grandiose design for a cultural colonialism that would incorporate the Highland world into the eighteenth-century society of Lowland Scotland and, eventually, the British Empire.

During the early years, these young scholars found themselves caught between the ideological expectations of the society's directors and the pragmatic reality of Highland and Island life. From the opening salvos in 1711 and 1712, which extended west to St. Kilda and north to Kildonan, a site in Sutherland on the far side of the Great Glen, these intrepid educators came to understand all too well the challenges inherent in the society's plan. They knew far better than the overseers for the schools or the directors for the society the difficulties confronted in attempting deliberate cultural change. The schoolmasters were on location; each day they taught the young Gaels and Northern Islanders; every class session they measured the merit of pedagogical styles; and seven days a week they faced their daunting tasks. When a schoolmaster believed the society was moving in an erroneous direction, he sometimes registered a protest (see chapter 4). This criticism usually reached an unsympathetic ear at the society's office in the heart of Edinburgh.

The directors' unresponsiveness to schoolmasters' innovations reflected the insularity of their world. They retained their distance from the Highlands, both physically and culturally. In their defense, they had other issues to address. Their first priority was to keep the donations flowing into the society's coffers. And even with their closest attention, the society remained on a stringent budget throughout the eighteenth century. Further, the society directors viewed the entire venture from the top down. The society's rejection of the schoolmasters' grievances reminds us of the remoteness of their location, at least from a Highlander's perspective, and the seriousness of their intent. They bore the responsibility that emanated from the society's charter. Further, the directors were in a position to view the entire program; the schoolmasters could see only their tiny corner of the operation. The initial directors had all helped to frame the society's goals. Hence, their conviction on the need for drastic cultural change—the raison d'être for the schools—led them to discount any local criticism from the field.

Furthermore, the society had a vested interest in the schoolmasters because it bore the responsibility for their selection. The hiring of the new masters was not an easy task in the early years, but it became increasingly difficult as the efforts toward fund raising never quite met the reformers' ambitious plans for opening additional schools. Scholars have not agreed on the intellectual merits of the society's schoolmasters, but they do concur that the excessive demands placed on them, exacerbated by their meager remuneration, meant that "the SSPCK had to spread its net widely to find such men."[33]

In short, the society came to expect the impossible from the cultural intermediaries it sent beyond the Highland Line. It demanded that the schoolmasters "be well-educated, sober, serious individuals with a thorough grasp of Calvinist theology. Content to live on a pittance, they had to be suffused with a missionary spirit. On top of all this they had to be Gaelic speakers."[34] The search for individuals who could satisfy these many qualifications was not easy. Yet a good number answered the call, and some of them spent their entire lives wrestling with the challenge.

CHAPTER FOUR

Highland Gaels and the "Shocktroops of Presbyterianism"

Once their capital funding was firmly in place, the society directors turned to the pressing task at hand: finding their schoolmasters. Well aware of the need for relying again on their proven network of connections, they crafted a description of the ideal applicant. "The rules for the conduct of the Society's schoolmasters . . . [were] drawn up with great care and attention."[1] After the society's description met with their satisfaction, they distributed it to various friends and acquaintances who might offer names or suggestions. The portrayal of the ideal schoolmaster provides an astute comment on the society's mindset. The directors requested the services of "men of piety, prudence and gravity, who understood and can speak and write both in the English and Irish languages, and who can write a fair hand and do understand the Rules of Arithmetic, and Cipher exactly and readily."[2]

Perhaps initially the society directors anticipated that their schoolmasters would meet these criteria. The reality would prove otherwise. Through the time span of the society's educational endeavor—1709–1872—the schoolmasters whom they selected ranged widely in their level of success. They varied in age, from seventeen to those in their seventies and eighties; in their commitment to the profession; in their talent; in their ability to adjust to those who lived near the schoolhouse; and in their skills as cultural intermediaries—balancing the interests of the society directors and the people of the Highlands. The "people" included the tenants or clansmen and women, the tacksmen, and the landlords or heritors, who were the former clan chiefs. Successful schoolmasters reached an accord with the people. Among the hundreds of men who served in the SSPCK schools (plus the many women who taught spinning and sewing), a significant number of them failed to meet this standard. Confrontations with local inhabitants frequently elicited pejorative comments that could lead to the dismissal of the schoolmaster or, at the least, his removal to another location. When the inspectors penned terse depictions of schoolmasters that included phrases such as "unfriendly reception," "not accepted," "disagreement with the people," "people indifferent to education," "not esteemed by people," "had not confidence of people," "not welcomed by the people," or "pious but not in harmony with the people," these men seldom survived in their position. One inspector noted simply, "school closed as teacher was not accepted by the people."[3]

The society dismissed other schoolmasters for a variety of reasons. Some men lost their positions for simple "misconduct," or "gross enormities," while John Grant, a schoolmaster at age seventeen, failed to meet his obligations because he "spent his time [in] 'hunting and other diversions.'" Still others failed in their religious mission, such as John Forbes, whose Perthshire "pupils were ignorant of principals [sic] of Christian religion; [the] master lacked discipline and authority." And a few schoolmasters who engaged in Scotland's illegal whiskey trade of the early eighteenth century through the early nineteenth century lost their teaching positions as well, especially when convicted for whiskey smuggling by the Excise Court.[4]

Most of the positive comments on the schoolmaster-Highlanders relationship tended to reflect the position of the society rather than the Highlanders themselves. An exception, schoolmaster Alexander Stewart, who served for three decades, received a "gold watch with inscription from the people of the district" (Bridge of Turk) after he had been teaching for eighteen years.[5] Like Stewart, a small number of men served their entire lives as schoolmasters. Donald Clark taught on the Kintyre Peninsula for almost fifty years. Alexander Grant, who "taught pupils to translate from English to Gaelic," served for fifty-three years (1758–1818); in his final years, "he asked for allowance for a boy to help in winter." William Grassick (1766–1816), who served in some ten different Highland schools, "taught till within a few days of death." When the society inspectors praised the schoolmasters, they employed phraseology such as "an exemplary teacher," "a pious and laborious teacher," "a meritorious teacher," "one of the most successful teachers in the West Highlands," or "one of the best teachers in Shetland." The society also respected teaching by example. Inspector Patrick Butter described John Fraser (1792–1874), who died after thirty-two years of service, as "greatly respected not only for his utility as a teacher of youth but for his exemplary character as a Christian."[6]

Like the mythical Gaelic hero, the Scot who sought to apply for the position of schoolmaster soon learned that he must engage in a series of challenges that would test his mettle. First, he must travel to Edinburgh—finances and distance permitting—"bearing with him an attestation as to his moral and religious character." Second, when he reached the bustling town, he must make his way through the crowded streets to his rendezvous with two of the ecclesiastical directors of the society. These formidable figures then proceeded to carefully examine him in "reading, spelling, writing, arithmatic [sic], church music, and particularly in his 'acquaintance with the Evangelical system' and his ability to communicate that knowledge to others."[7] During his interview, the candidate was put to the test long before his skills could be judged by any future scholars in the Highlands.

For the prospective schoolmaster, the journey to the capital, in itself, could prove a trial of endurance. In 1725, when James Stewart presented himself as a candidate, he "came before [the] Society in Edinburgh having 'travelled upwards of seven score miles.'" For Stewart, however, the rigorous journey proved a sound investment. Later that year he began teaching in the Inner Hebrides on the Isle of Tiree, and he was still serving the society in 1756, when he died. For prospective candidate George Jamieson, the trip was a disaster. En route to his examination by the society in 1806, "he died on 'the passage'"; thereafter, the society gave £3 to his widow. In 1781 John Ross anticipated a similar journey beginning near the Dornoch Firth, north of Inverness. Eventually, Ross found that his effort to reach the capital would earn him a position, but the journey itself would have defeated a lesser man. When Ross "came from Tain to Edinburgh on foot to be examined for the teaching post" at Rosskeen, he would have walked perhaps 150 miles; as the crow flies, the journey was about 130 miles. Although Ross passed the examination hurdle, he was "not well received at Rosskeen" and eventually moved on to other teaching locations until he was "superannuated" (retired) in 1801.[8]

Although the society members seldom traveled to the Highlands themselves, the qualifications they sought for their schoolmasters duplicated the qualifications they had met upon admission to the SSPCK. Society membership was tightly restricted: "no person can be assumed to be such unless he is a donor; one of a sober and religious life, zealously concerned for the success of the design, a sincere Protestant, and one firmly attached to his Majesty King George, and the Protestant succession in his family."[9]

In accord with this membership prescription, once the society directors had approved a candidate and assigned him to a school, yet another, final test awaited him. Before his departure the society held his feet to the fire again, requiring that he sign the "formulae against Popery" and that he take the oath of allegiance to the (Hanoverian succession) government. In this fashion, the society made the candidate acutely aware of the perspective that he represented as an eighteenth-century ambassador to the Highlands. Still, he might have been well advised to take one further vow, that of poverty. SSPCK schoolmasters' wages proved to be well below those of tradesmen or artisans, and their level did not improve during the life span of the society schools. During the 1780s, schoolmaster James Rose, who was teaching northeast of Inverness, caught the attention of the directors when an inspector described his condition: "[he] lived with his family in a barn; starving."[10]

The directors themselves anticipated that their schoolmasters' wages should not be their sole source of income. They asked the ordinary clansmen and women (both tenants and subtenants) to help support their children's teachers. But the realistic potential for community assistance for the schoolmasters relied heavily on the generosity of the clan elite—the heritors, tacksmen, and other influential figures within the parish that surrounded the school. The directors also expected the local chief to provide the schoolmaster with a house to live in and a kailyard for growing vegetables. In Highland communities, the produce from the kailyard provided a crucial addition to the food supply because the crops raised there offered the only source of vegetables for the family of the ordinary clansmen and women. Although the kailyard served as the Highland equivalent of a vegetable garden, its produce was not known for its versatility. Kailyard crops came exclusively from the brassica family, and generally, this meant cabbage (or kale). This hearty green—which grew well in virtually every climate—had been introduced into the Highlands by the sixteenth century, at the latest.[11]

Despite the society's heavy reliance on support from the tacksmen and landlords, it also expected direct in-kind remuneration from the parents of the pupils—the ordinary clanspeople. The directors assumed that the tenants would provide the schoolmaster with "turfs and grass," which meant the peats that served as the winter fuel and sufficient food to maintain a cow through summer and winter.[12]

But Highland reality wore a different cloak. When the society's assumptions proved accurate and lodging, peats, and grass miraculously appeared, the schoolmaster deemed himself fortunate. More often, however, the schoolmaster learned upon his arrival that neither a dwelling nor a schoolhouse, let alone a kailyard, awaited him. Nor had the clanspeople voluntarily provided him with either peats for fuel or forage for a cow. Fuel was crucial, yet it was difficult to procure. Consistent summer rains could prevent the freshly cut peats from drying after it had been cut from the peat bog. When schoolmaster Donald Ramsey, who taught near Inverness, complained that "rainy weather prevented people supplying his winter peats," the society gave him £2. Some tenants simply refused to deliver the peats. In the 1720s schoolmaster Francis Wright reported that he "had to get Lord Strathnaver to compel people to bring fuel to him." While other tenants might be willing to cut the peats, they left it for the schoolmaster to haul. Schoolmaster Thomas Rich found that "people cut but did not carry his peats for which he needed 7 or 8 boat loads." Although the difficulties of procuring a cow and finding forage frequently plagued the schoolmasters, the "Society noted that in all schools the fuel was more troublesome than anything else."[13]

This state of affairs probably reflected the poverty of the people themselves rather than any latent hostility to the opening of a school. These ordinary Gaels remembered well the "Seven Ill Years" of the last great famine, and their lives had remained in the talons of poverty since those days of horror. Two decades after the famine, schoolmaster Andrew Rule found himself teaching in Tullich, in the Aberdeenshire Highlands, where the parents were "so poor that they could not give children more than a little water gruel once a day. They came to school fasting in the morning and got nothing till they returned home at night." During the summer, attendance remained small because the "children were sent to look after cattle."[14] During the 1750s schoolmaster Donald McGregor taught near Stirling, at the southern edge of the Highlands. The families, who worked in the nearby colliery, "were too poor to help with payment" for McGregor, "so salary was raised to £10" by the society. Two decades later, schoolmaster Hew Cuming reported that the crops had failed and "the people could not pay." The society responded to his "distress" by giving him £2.[15] In the fall of 1770, when Lewis Drummond carried out his inspection of the society's schools, his notebooks consistently recorded the omnipresent state of poverty. Relying on terse descriptive phrases, he painted an all-too-clear portrait of the ordinary clanspeople with the often repeated comments "a number of poor cottars," "generally poor," "Some tolerable Great many poor," and "mostly poor."[16]

When the fortunate schoolmaster arrived to find a home and schoolhouse awaiting him, the dwelling was likely to be a single, modest cottage. If he were granted the privilege of a separate structure for a classroom, it probably looked like this Gaelic scholar's description: "Its walls were of turf . . . ; its windows were irregular holes which despised the luxury of glass; its floor was the cold damp earth . . . [and] on the floor blazed a pile of peats and wood, brought by the children from their homes."[17] "The roof also leaked," a Rannoch Highlander recalled of his schoolhouse, "and there being no ceiling, the drops fell straight from the sooty rafters." Some of the raindrops, he added, "must at one time have fallen on the map of Ireland, created there a new river, which rose at Malin Head, and fell into St. George's Channel about Waterford."[18]

Rarely did an inspector of the schools praise the schoolhouse or the lodging. In 1824 inspector Patrick Butter described Norman McLean's lodging on the Isle of Islay as "excellent accommodation," but a more common description was "shamefully bad." In this vein, inspector John Tawse reported that the lodging for Shetland schoolmaster William Pole "had a kitchen and one small garret for a family of 10 persons." And in 1717 schoolmaster Robert Stewart's lodging earned this description: "accommodation not fit 'to lodge swine'; given a 'sheep house' in which he could not stand upright." As a symbol of this frustration, the saga of schoolmaster James Murray eventually wore him down. He began teaching on Orkney in 1713, where he lost his clothes and books when the "ship that brought him from Perth to Orkney sank." From Orkney, he moved back to Perthshire in 1716 to assume a position at Blair Atholl. In 1721 he reported, "rain spoiled clothes, books, furniture, and gave teacher a bad cold." In 1723 he reported, "no seats, no tables; a bridge was needed over the Erochtie Water." In 1726 he "left to study Divinity."[19]

If a single cottage had to suffice for both accommodation and schoolroom, the schoolmaster sought some creative means of dividing the classroom from the living quarters; often this meant carving out a space for the master's family as well, since many of the schoolmasters were family men. While their quarters were cramped, they were not unlike those of the children whom they taught. William Low, schoolmaster on North Uist in the Outer Hebrides, lived in a "dwelling house [that] was a small room boarded off the schoolroom where sewing was taught."[20] Since schools remained scarce among the widely scattered homes of the Highlanders, the society sometimes saw fit to move the buildings themselves. The master "had thus to take up, not only his bed but also the timber of his house and schoolhouse, and to remove to whatever corner of his educational vineyard most needed his services."[21]

A Highland Gael, especially a tenant or cottar (subtenant), would have found such a cottage to be a common sight, even though any outside visitor would have been considerably dismayed at its appearance. Edmund Burt's observations written during the mid-eighteenth

Gearrannan, Baile-Tughaidh. Traditional homes in Blackhouse Village, Isle of Lewis.
PHOTOGRAPH BY THE AUTHOR.

century, suggest his own conditioning to the Highlands. Reflecting from his base at Inverness, initially he observed that "the lodgings of the ordinary people are most miserable." Later, during his wide-ranging travels in the Highlands beyond Inverness, he paused to admire the size of a cottage's roof beam, noting with admiration that it was "fit to resist the violent fluries [sic] of wind that frequently rush into the plains from the opening in the mountain." Dr. Johnson, on the other hand, always remained the self-assured Englishman. During the course of his travels with the Edinburgh native James Boswell, he scarcely altered his initial impressions. When Johnson and Boswell entered the Highlands that Burt had once visited, on their journey west from Inverness, they observed a "Highland hut" along the shores of Loch Ness. In Dr. Johnson's view, its only redeeming quality was the Gael's invitation "to sit down and drink whiskey."[22]

In the early years, when the society was expanding its educational initiative in the Highlands and Islands, the schoolmasters were largely Lowlanders. The candidate who passed the rigorous test administered in Edinburgh might have been living comfortably in a Lowland village or town before making his way beyond the Highland Line. When he reached his assigned location, whether Blair Atholl or Ullapool or the Isle of Mull, he probably faced a shock similar to that experienced by Edmund Burt. But the Lowland schoolmaster poised to take up his new post scarcely found time to whinge about the state of his lodging or the schoolhouse. Once he had managed to find some sort of accommodation, however poor, he turned to the extraordinary challenges of the teaching mandate ordered by the society directors.

Although the master's assignments had been distinctly clarified for him during his rigorous interview and examination by the society, unless he hailed from the Highlands himself, a highly unlikely occurrence during the earliest years of the schools, he had probably composed a mental image of his future pupils, which drew from the pejorative portrayal painted by the members of the society. The schoolmaster had learned well during his Edinburgh encounter that his primary mission would be to impart the educational goals that had inspired these professional Lowlanders. Encoded in his instruction lay the message that any views of the Highlanders and Islanders should attract little concern on his part, especially since they were to about to be replaced.

As the schoolmaster became immersed in the local realities of his *strath*, or glen, of the Highlands or Islands, he soon discovered that he was not instructing the families of the elite. In his everyday teaching he faced pupils who were invariably the children of ordinary clansmen and women. As Cambeltown schoolmaster John Stewart described them, "pupils are exclusively the poor."[23] By the early eighteenth century, Lowlanders and Highland elite had come to describe these people in pragmatic economic terms—as tenants and cottars or subtenants—a shallow depiction that ignored clan connections and the persistence of oral culture.

Like Edmund Burt on his first acquaintance with the Highlanders, the casual visitor would have been blinded to all but the poverty of the ordinary clansmen and women. The astute schoolmaster, however, would soon have become aware that his pupils had already learned the skills requisite for survival in an extremely demanding environment, one that required even greater effort in the eighteenth century to meet the increasing rent demands imposed by the tacksmen. The culturally sensitive schoolmaster who was nurtured in the more amenable environment of the Lowlands would have been struck by the skills that Highland youth had developed to meet this challenge, whether it was caring for the cattle or rethatching the family cottage. It was also likely that the schoolmaster's pupils had earned a close acquaintance with their culture's oral heritage, probably through storytelling; and it was absolutely certain, as Martin Martin pointed out in his *Description of the Western Isles*, that they were steeped in the Gaelic folk worldview that Lowlanders associated with paganism or "Popery." Contrary to the society's fears that "Popery" had been retained as the singular Highland faith tradition, the schoolmasters soon learned that most Highlanders were Episcopalian, a small percentage were Presbyterian, and the Catholics were a distinct minority. In some remote regions the Catholics remained a clear majority, but these areas were the exception. Further, within each of these faith perspectives, the carryover from the pre-Christian world continued to play a prominent role.

As the schoolmaster began his instruction, he discovered all too quickly that his girls and boys were neither literate nor bilingual like the children of the elite, whose ancestors had responded to the educational stipulations of the seventeenth-century Statutes of Iona. Virtually all of the SSPCK school pupils, unless they lived in the far northeast or the Northern Isles, proved monolingual Gaelic speakers who had never had an opportunity to learn to read in either Gaelic or English/Scots. Although an understanding of the Gaelic language remained a prerequisite for the schoolmaster's position—an acknowledgement of the once-universal vernacular tongue of the land that the Scots-speaking Lowlanders had dubbed "Irish,"—the master had absorbed the instructions drilled into him during his interview: he must teach exclusively in English. Within the confines of these linguistic limitations, he began to tackle his many assignments.

The first task was to teach the young Gaelic pupils (or youth of the northeast and Northern Isles) to read, to write, and to do their sums (arithmetic). These were the straightforward basics, and the schoolmaster must have turned to them with some relief. But the society had made it quite clear that his primary task, the most essential reason for his presence in the Highlands, was to teach the principles of the Christian Reformed religion. In other words, he was to impart the theological message of the Church of Scotland. In order to reach this goal, he bore with him specific, detailed instructions. Each schoolmaster was directed to pray with his young scholars twice each day and to catechize them twice each week. As soon as they were able to read, the young scholars quickly became aware of the importance of the Reformed faith. Even in their earliest lessons—mastery of the English alphabet—the master drummed into their heads that the primary goal of English literacy was religious understanding. Hence, all of the pupils

Isle of Harris, west coast. This was a strong Gaelic-speaking region in the eighteenth century; it is one of the few remaining regions with Gaelic speakers in the twenty-first century.
PHOTOGRAPH BY THE AUTHOR.

were expected to improve their level of literacy until they achieved the sine qua non—reading the Bible and other sacred texts in English and without assistance.

Despite the rigor of the instruction, the master's responsibilities did not end with the classroom. Since the SSPCK's long-range goal involved changing the worldviews of those Scots who lived beyond the Highland Line, the society was not content to limit the master's teaching to the pupils in school. With this in mind, the society directed each schoolmaster to expand his instruction into the nearby region that surrounded his school. By serving as catechist for his location, the master could begin to spread the faith among the local families; and when no minister was available, he was also expected to preach the sermon on the Sabbath. The schoolmaster might see his primary task as tutor for his pupils, but he had to be aware of his ultimate responsibility: to relay the tenets of the Presbyterian faith. The society was so confident in the power of its mission that it seemed to expect the people of the Highlands to instantly discard their old faith—once described by a minister at the central Highland community of Kingussie as "gross indolence, ignorance, and superstition"—and replace it with the Calvinist position.[24] For this task, the Society pinned all its hopes on the persuasiveness of the schoolmasters.

Instruction and the Faith Parameters

By 1725 the society had already established twenty-five schools, and the society directors envisioned a rigorous schedule at each of these rapidly multiplying institutions.[25] The school year was endless. It consumed forty-nine weeks, allowing for only a three-week holiday during the long northern days of summer. Although the length of the school week varied slightly, depending on location, generally the master was expected to meet with his pupils in their cottage classroom every weekday, including Saturday morning. On Saturday afternoon the pupils, at least, had a respite, but the master was expected to don his pastoral garb to visit the Elders and the sick who were not able to attend church services.

On Sundays, unless he had been asked to deliver the sermon, the master accompanied his scholars to the church services, where he was responsible for their good behavior. If he served as catechist for the region as well, on Sundays he also catechized the families living in the vicinity of the school.[26] The experiences of William Blair, schoolmaster and minister at Kingussie during the 1770s, epitomized this schedule. As the local catechist, Blair worked a seven-day week: "besides his public exercises on the Lord's Day [delivered] in English and Irish, he travelled about from house to house, from glen to glen, teaching and catechizing and instructing their minds in knowledge of the true God and of the principles of ye Christian religion."[27]

The weekly schedule did not deviate from the Reformed Christianity of the Lowlands. Lest the scholars assume their Sunday to be a day of partial rest, on Monday morning their master reminded them it was not. Demonstrating the society's unrelenting demand for knowledge and memorization of the faith, he tested their recollection of the sermon delivered the previous day by questioning them on its main themes. Each week the master also repeated the instruction on the shorter catechism, in English, of course, until each of his pupils had committed it to memory. No scholar could achieve the ultimate goal of literacy, however, without mastering the reading of the Bible in English.

Textbooks largely fell under the same rubric. As the primary teaching tool of the schoolmaster, the texts bore a decided Presbyterian cast. For example, the society's school at Kildonan in Sutherland proved one of the earliest, coming directly on the heels of the initial effort at St. Kilda. The school was located upriver from the village of Helmsdale, along the Strath of Kildonan, a region largely destroyed by the nineteenth-century "Clearances," when mandated removal dictated by landlords and tacksmen forced the ordinary clansmen and women off the land to make room for vast herds of sheep.[28] When the master at Kildonan ordered books for his classes, they had to fit the textbook template. The young Kildonan scholars struggled with an eclectic assortment of readings, which included Bibles, the Proverbs, the Catechism, the Confession of Faith, Guthrie's *Trial of an Interest in Christ*, and Vincent's catechism. All, of course, were published in English, ostensibly the sole language of instruction in the early decades.[29]

Although the schoolmasters also had specific orders to provide lessons in arithmetic, their instruction on Calvinism held precedence. As mandated, the master was to teach the scholars "to read, write, and do accounts . . . [but] religious instruction was a major part of the curriculum."[30] The society sought to keep track of the scholars' progress, but it also judged the correctness of the master's selection of subjects for the curriculum. One hopes the directors were satisfied with the report from the master at the school in Fort Augustus, located in the parish of Abertarff near the head of Loch Ness. Earlier, this parish had been described as the home of "ignorance and Popery"; it had achieved the singular notoriety of serving as the site of the first short-lived schooling experiment of the Manners Society. By mid-century, however, the schoolmaster must have found it to his liking because he remained there for a dozen years (1749–61). Taking careful note of his scholars' "proficiency in Learning," he also listed the subjects that he taught, which included

> Bibles
> New Testament
> Proverbs
> Catechism
> Writing
> Arithmetic
> Church Musick.

With the exception of writing and arithmetic, Calvinism dominated the curriculum at Abertarff.[31]

In the Highlands, where music had long been interwoven with the clans, church music especially appealed to those schoolmasters who knew the ways of the Gaels. The society expected each of its schoolmasters to incorporate Kirk music into the curriculum. In 1734 schoolmaster Archibald McWatie, located near Dumbarton, learned this lesson abruptly: "unable to teach arithmetic or church music so dismissed." Near the end of the century, schoolmaster Ebenezer Davidson, who taught on the Isle of Coll, "asked leave to go to Glasgow to learn church music. Society refused winter leave when school should be 'throng' and advised him to learn at a nearby Society school at 'next harvest vacation.'"[32]

In this context, even music emerged as a contentious issue in the ongoing debate over teaching Gaelic literacy to the pupils. By 1713, William Mackay, Gaelic-speaking master at the society's newly opened school in Durness, Sutherland, had somehow managed to persuade the directors to permit him to catechize his scholars in Gaelic (even though the directors reminded him that he should never teach them to read in Gaelic). When Mackay pushed the directors further, his powers of persuasion came into play again. He asked permission to pray and sing with his scholars in Gaelic. The directors' favorable response came with yet another proviso: he was to exercise this option *only* with those pupils who had already "mastered English."[33] Mackay's was only one voice, and an unusually persuasive one, but it is unlikely that he was the sole Gaelic-speaking schoolmaster who turned to Gaelic song and prayer in order to find a connection with his pupils. Kirk music might serve well as an overlay, but it could be enhanced when a schoolmaster also relied on the Gaels' traditional music.

In the nineteenth-century society schools, Gaelic music continued to give the schoolmaster a means of bonding with the scholars. However, "in teaching the old 'Gaelic' tunes [the schoolmaster] avoided what was considered a too free and irreverent use of the Psalms of David, and sang the tunes to rhymes of his own making." William Mackay reports that in Glen Urquhart (west of Loch Ness), the following verses ranked among the favorites during Gaelic evening singing classes:

> Buntata prann is bainne leo
> An comhanaidh dha mo bhrainn;
> Nam faighinnsa na dh' ithinn diu
> Gum bithinn sona chaoidh!
> With mashed potatoes and good milk
>   May I be filled for aye
> With them one feed; then shall I joy
>   Until my dying day![34]

In like fashion, the schoolmasters described later (chapters 6 and 7)—Gaelic Highlander Dugald Buchanan, who taught in the Uplands of Perthshire, and Mohegan Samson Occom and Montauk David Fowler, who taught among the Algonquians and Iroquois—found great satisfaction in the leavening quality of song as a powerful means of cross-cultural religious instruction for their Gaelic and Native American pupils. In these instances, music proved a universal language.

The aforementioned "Proficiency in Learning" results, submitted by schoolmasters such as the master at Abertarff, seldom satisfied the society directors in Edinburgh.[35] Reiterating the reality of failure at some of the schools, the society's catechist on St. Kilda, Alexander Buchan (1710–29), admitted after he had been there for fourteen years that his school remained unsuccessful. Although he offered several reasons for this distressing result, citing the poverty of the Gaels, the "stormy weather hindering them to send their children to school," and the sheer difficulty of eking out an existence on the island, the ultimate barrier remained the issue of language. Historian Victor Durkacz argues that the St. Kilda experiment failed because "in a community in which fewer than four or five adults had as much as a smattering of English, he was forbidden to instruct the people in their mother tongue." He adds, "typically, the committee of the SSPCK forbade him to teach any Gaelic reading whatsoever."[36] Summarizing the struggle of the schoolmasters to meet the stringent demands imposed by the society, Scottish historian John Mason writes, "It was a slow and tedious method of imparting knowledge of a foreign tongue, and it is to be wondered how the masters ever succeeded."[37]

Gaelic, "That Nervous, Expressive Tongue"

At the turn of the eighteenth century, almost all of the ordinary clanspeople living in the Highlands and Western Isles spoke Gaelic exclusively—they communicated only in the vernacular. Scotland's Ghaìdhealtachd included the following regions: much of Sutherland; Ross and Cromarty; Inverness-shire; Argyll; the Inner and Outer Hebrides, including St. Kilda; the upper reaches of the River Dee and the River Don in Aberdeenshire; and the Grampian Highlands of Perthshire, reaching almost as far south as Dunblane. This area, as mentioned earlier, was home to about three hundred thousand people, who made up about one-third of Scotland's population at mid-century.[38]

Looking at Scotland's Gàidhealtachd in an eighteenth-century comparative context, Scotland's vernacular still held its own as the dominant tongue north of the Highland Line, even though the exclusively Gaelic-speaking regions had long been confined to the Highlands and Islands. In Ireland, the Irish language may have been more widespread during this century. Although Irish was limited to the regions well beyond "the Pale" (Dublin and its surroundings) and the region west of the River Shannon, including Connemara and parts of the southwest, Donegal, and the southwestern parts of Ulster, Irish remained a virtually universal language in rural western Ireland until the disastrous potato famine of the mid-nineteenth century. In Wales, the Welsh tongue also persisted in the less Anglicized regions—central, coastal, and northwest Wales. In Cornwall, indigenous Cornish was approaching extinction, although some have claimed that a few people still spoke Cornish at the turn of the twentieth century.

Even in the comparatively large area of Scotland's Gàidhealtachd, earlier encroachments had already forced the indigenous language to recede. Consequently, in the border regions, such as the foothills of the Grampian Mountains in Aberdeenshire, the presence of bilingualism—Gaelic and Scots—suggested a cultural frontier where language served as the most telling barometer of cultural change.[39] As the language receded into the hills, the culture receded as well. Still, pride in Gaelic culture in these borderlands persists. Even in the early twenty-first century, the road to Braemar has been highlighted by a large boulder that bears the words "Entering the Highlands."

Since Scottish Gaelic remained in a state of flux in the early eighteenth century, it is virtually impossible to estimate the percentage of Gaelic speakers. An early-nineteenth-century census estimated the number of speakers in the Highlands and Western Isles at "three-fourths of the people."[40] Extensive correspondence located in the National Archives of Scotland suggests that in the regions where the SSPCK sent its schoolmasters, Gaelic served as the only tongue. And this was not limited to the remote Isles of St. Kilda. In 1760, in the parish of Lochanan on the Isle of Harris in the Outer Hebrides, the Hyndman-Dick inspection reported, "The parish is eight miles long and one broad . . . there are no papists in it. It contains 1794 souls, hath only one place of worship. There is a church manse and glebe here—but no parish school. Scarce anyone understands a sermon in English."[41] Inspectors also reported their frequent discoveries of communities where Gaelic remained the sole language. These locations ranged from the Isle of Skye and elsewhere in the Inner Hebrides to Loch Broom on the northwest coast. Most of the western Highlands and Islands were exclusively Gaelic speaking, with the sole exception of the port town of Stornoway, which fronts a natural harbor on the east coast of the Isle of Lewis. Here English had made considerable inroads.

Hence, the schoolmaster who did not speak Gaelic would have been as lost as the eight-year-old English-speaking girl Jean Bain, who in 1898 moved to Braemar, about fifty or sixty miles west of Aberdeen, to live with her uncle Ronald MacDonald and his sister, Charlotte, "who spoke nothing but Gaelic to one another." "For two years," Jean recalled in the 1970s, "I didna ken a word they said, bit efter two years I began to ken." After her understanding improved, Ronald and Charlotte had to send Jean out to the hen house to gather eggs when they chose "to speak privately."[42] Like the seasoned Jean Bain, the society schoolmaster found it necessary to "ken" the Gaelic tongue. He simply could not have related to his scholars without this crucial understanding of his pupils' vernacular. Yet the society persisted in its demands for the "extirpateing of the Irish language".[43]

The schoolmaster was also likely to have some knowledge of Latin, but during the eighteenth century, the society specifically forbade him to teach this classical language. All scholars in the Lowlands who were privileged to attend grammar school were required to learn Latin. When they enrolled at university, they had no further opportunity to study the language through course work because Latin was the exclusive language of instruction and discourse. No scholar applied to university without proven adeptness in the language. In the SSPCK schools in the Gaelic Highlands, however, Latin assumed a different identity. The society enjoined their masters to forbear any Latin instruction because they equated the teaching of Latin with instruction in the Catholic faith. Hence, for society members, the original language of the Christian Church symbolized the threat of Catholicism. In 1720 the Rev. James Robertson of Balquhidder, located in the western Highlands near Ft. William, wrote on behalf of his parishioners, who requested that their children be taught to read Gaelic psalms after mastering the English Bible. The directors replied, "The Society have resolved that none of their Schoolmasters shall teach reading either Latine or Irish but English, and he will take care to see that this be observed in his Schools."[44]

If the teaching of Latin in the Highlands symbolized Catholicism, the teaching of Gaelic symbolized a catering to "barbarism." In the eighteenth century, the society's Gaelic language paranoia was not unusual, given the cultural antagonisms of the previous centuries. It reflected a deep-rooted and widespread Lowland stance toward the language. The Lowlanders' abandonment of Gaelic had begun well before the sixteenth century. As late as the reign of James IV (1488–1573), Gaelic had remained the official language of Scotland's court. In 1320 the authors of the Declaration of Arbroath, while penning their letter in Latin, likely discussed the meaning of its contents in Gaelic. Still, even as early as the thirteenth century, some Scots had demonstrated a "growing amnesia" regarding their own Irish origins, forgetting about the Scotti who had migrated from Catholic Ireland to carry their faith to the pre-Christian Picts of Caledonia.[45]

Antagonism toward the Gaelic language intensified during the Scottish Reformation, when Lowland Presbyterians began to equate the old language with Scotland's pre-Reformation faith. Exploiting this convenient link, the Presbyterians deliberately assigned to Gaelic, once the vernacular, the derogatory label of "Erse." In this manner, Lowlanders were able to link the Gaelic language with Catholic Ireland. When members of the SSPCK called for the destruction of Gaelic, they were flouting their own nation's cultural and linguistic heritage. Their attitude triumphed because the language reminded them of the faith they had come to refute since the days of John Knox. The early society directors "dreaded Gaelic as they dreaded the Pope, with whom they associated it . . . the same regulation that bound their schoolmasters to subscribe the 'formulae against Popery' bound them also to 'discharge' [that is, prohibit] their scholars to speake Earse."[46]

Simultaneously, the SSPCK directors' campaign against the Gaelic language was also triggered by another, equally virulent animosity. Seven years after Queen Anne's charter granted their legitimacy as a corporation, the society members declared, "Nothing can be more effective for reducing these Countries [Highland parishes] to order and making them useful to the Commonwealth, than teaching them their duty to God, their King and Countrey, and routing out their Irish Language, and this has been the care of the Society so far as it could, for all the Schollars are taught in English."[47] The society directors believed that all Scots' "duty to their King and Country" included support of the Hanoverian succession. Hence, they drew an unequivocal association between Gaelic language and culture and rebel support for Jacobitism.

The schoolmasters' stance on Jacobitism varied. Those who maintained their loyalty to the Hanoverian government retained the society's support. During the 1715 and 1745 risings, the society remained leery of their schoolmasters' positions. In 1715 schoolmaster James Johnston "behaved well" during the rising; to avoid the rebels he 'was obliged, notwithstanding the rigour of the season, to lodge many nights in the open fields and travel for the whole night over mountains.' A turncoat to the rebel cause, he also informed the 'friends of the government of the designs of the Rebels.'" By contrast, in 1745, the society questioned the leanings of schoolmaster Ronald MacDonald

Tay Bridge at Aberfeldy. One of forty bridges, plus 250 miles of military roads, built under Field-Marshall George Wade (1673–1748), Commander-in-Chief, North Britain, 1724–40. Edmund Burt served as part of this effort to "civilize" the Highlands after the 1715 Jacobite rising.
PHOTOGRAPH BY FERENC M. SZASZ.

and "decided not to employ him till assured of his loyalty to the Government." Only after MacDonald obtained "certificates of loyalty" from the sheriff clerk at Inverness did the society offer him a position. But in the earlier rising schoolmaster John Clow disregarded these strictures. During the '15, Clow, who was allegedly "intimate with Papists," "'read out to [the] congregation after Divine service the Pretender's proclamation' as minister had refused to do so." The society was quite clear on this stance, and it dismissed John Clow.[48]

As long as Jacobitism hovered as a threat to Scots supporting the Hanoverian monarchy, the society clung to its single-minded opposition to teaching in Gaelic. It did, however, reluctantly agree that a Gaelic-English vocabulary might aid the pupils' learning of English. Therefore, the society itself commissioned the *Galick and English Vocabulary* (c. 1741), a volume destined to become the first secular book published in Scottish Gaelic. But the editor of the *Vocabulary*, Alasdair mac Mhaighstir Alasdair (Alexander MacDonald), was no fan of the society's English-only policy. Nor was he a fan of the Hanoverian government. In 1745, after he was "accused of being 'an offence to sober, well inclined persons' as he went about the country 'composing Galick songs stuffed with obscene language,'" the society dismissed him. In the eyes of the society, his opposition to the government was clear grounds for removal (see chapter 7).[49] A renowned Gaelic poet who had also been schoolmaster and catechist for the society's school at Ardnamurchan, on the western seaboard, Alasdair wrote disparagingly of his employer's monolingual pedagogy: "It is well known that the method of teaching any language by books not written in the people's own language, has been very uneasy to youth and discouraging to their endeavors in the prosecution of their studies."[50]

Not until 1746, after the final defeat of the Jacobite warriors at Culloden, whose cause Alasdair had enthusiastically adopted, did the society begin to weigh the advantages of publishing a Bible translated into Scottish Gaelic. The society's attitude shift did not indicate any growing fondness for the vernacular tongue. Rather, the directors saw only the strategic potential of a Gaelic-English Bible. They had finally perceived that it might well serve as a more efficient means of destroying the language of the Highlands.[51]

Viewed from a larger perspective, it seems that the SSPCK had adopted a singularly shortsighted policy toward Scots Gaelic, especially when its language policy is compared with that of the other two major Celtic countries—Wales and Ireland. The irrational stubbornness of this Lowland organization, which prided itself on its "rational approach" to education, led to the "tragic alienation of language from literacy" within the Scottish Gàidhealtachd. "The Church's refusal to produce and distribute a vernacular Gaelic Bible" was reinforced by the society's conviction that its refusal to allow Gaelic literacy in its schools would help to destroy the language of one-third of Scotland.[52]

By contrast, the Welsh literary tradition remained closely allied with the native Welsh language. An act of Parliament in 1563 authorized the translation of the Bible and the Book of Common Prayer into Welsh, and the first New Testament in Welsh appeared in 1567. Welsh scholar Geraint H. Jenkins suggests that religious publications in the vernacular gave the native language "the priceless advantage of becoming the medium of religion."[53] Similarly, Welsh historian John Davies argues that the Welsh Bible, republished in scores of editions, "was as central to the experience of the Welsh as was Luther's Bible to that of the Germans or the Authorized Version to that of the English."[54] The New Testament in Irish, "printed in a font based on Gaelic script," appeared as early as 1602. The SSPCK, on the other hand, did not begin to consider seriously publishing the Scottish Gaelic translation until a decade after Culloden, and it took another decade for the project to come to fruition. When it finally appeared in 1767, the Scottish Gaelic New Testament lagged far behind its Celtic neighbors—it was published one hundred and fifty years after the Irish translation and two hundred years after the Welsh translation.[55]

Well aware of its forthcoming translation, in 1766 the society appeared to have had a change of heart when it ordered that Gaelic and English could be taught together. In effect, however, the directors were granting to their schoolmasters the authority to teach what they had expressly forbidden during the first six decades or so of the Highland schooling experiment. The initial English-only mandate remained in place long enough to influence at least two generations of Highlanders, enabling the society to take long strides toward "alienating the mother tongue of the Highlanders from both education and religion."[56] By shifting their linguistic methodology in the 1760s, the directors did not alter their stance. Rather, they were simply reminding Highlanders once again that they had supreme confidence in the power of their mission. They chose bilingualism to supersede the English-only policy because bilingual teaching had a stronger potential to hasten the adoption of English by Gaelic speakers. One way or the other, the destruction of Gaelic remained their ultimate goal.

In the Highlands: Voices from Gàidhealtachd

In numerous ways the eighteenth-century Gàidhealtachd in Scotland resembled Indian Country in North America: it was a rich and varied land. This is still true in the twenty-first century. As a result, the concept of a generic "Gaelic voice" has never withstood the test of reality. Hence, the Gaelic voices in this section cannot claim to be totally representative; nor, when they were reported by others, often outsiders, would they necessarily be accurate since they were sifted through outsiders' distinctive cultural views. Finally, these voices remain yet another step removed from the original because they reach us through the often murky voice of a translator. Bearing these caveats in mind, they are all we have at the moment, and they need to be heard. The voices come from schoolmasters, who, after the first generation, were often Highlanders themselves; from catechists, who were sometimes Highlanders; from ministers living in the Highlands; from scholars; from tenants (ordinary clansmen and women) and tacksmen or landlords; and, finally, from the inspectors who toured among the society's schools while they wrote their reports.

The Gaelic pupils and their families suffered from many frustrations in their dealings with the SSPCK schools, but one of the harshest barriers to learning revolved around the English-only policy. This mandate led to such intensive aggravation that it affected virtually everyone connected to the schools, including the pupils themselves, the master, the ministers of the parish, and even the parishioners of the community.

During their perambulations throughout the Highlands and Islands, the school inspectors witnessed the general unhappiness caused by the monolingual pedagogy. Patrick Butter, a particularly well qualified inspector who was not only a "preacher of the Gospel" but also a speaker of Gaelic, proved quite frank in his commentary on the over 225 schools that he had visited during a nine-month tour undertaken in 1824. Although his tour occurred almost sixty years after the society had ostensibly switched to bilingualism, clearly the official permission to read in Gaelic had not reached into every strath and glen. Butter found a significantly higher number of pupils who could not read in English in the areas where residents spoke only Gaelic, which suggests that the masters in these regions were having great difficulty in their attempts to teach literacy. He assumed that the English-only mandate had been motivated by the society's "desire to annihilate the Gaelic." But even the society's official switch to bilingual teaching had continued to alienate those Gaels who wanted to learn exclusively in Gaelic. He wrote, "No Highlander sees the point in part of each year studying and attempting to pronounce a language they will never understand and probably never use."

If the masters had begun by teaching the Gaelic-speaking child to read first in Gaelic and then in English, they might well have been successful. But the schoolmasters Butter observed apparently believed that a Gaelic-speaking child should never learn to read Gaelic, a misconstrued logic that led him to comment, "The fallacy of this prejudice is sufficiently obvious." If the master could not encourage Gaelic literacy, the net result for the child was tragic—this type of teaching led to literacy in neither English nor Gaelic.

The astute Inspector Butter also witnessed the wider community impact of teaching exclusively in English in a region where no one spoke English. In the Gaelic-speaking areas, he observed, "The parent is excluded from all share in judging of his child's programs, and left entirely in the dark respecting the practical application of his studies."[57]

Even as late as the mid-nineteenth century, schoolmasters in the Highlands retained the hard-line antagonism expressed by the society

> Benbecula 10 Sepr. 1824.
>
> There were only 3 scholars in attendance. There were 70 in winter. The house and school house are in bad repair, not well thatched by the people. It is the intention of the factor to have it removed to a more centrical part of the island, where there is a very good house of two storeys, and he has given in writing a promise to the schoolmaster of this house and of the requisite lands. — In the present station garden and cows grass are attached. — Gaelic is the universal language, and in some districts the only language of all these islands. The old people can almost in no instance read, and only a small proportion of the children attend school. — There is a parish school in South Uist not well attended. —
>
> There has been lately organised a Sabbath school taught by the Society schoolmaster under the superintendance of the missionary of the island. It is taught in the chapel during the time of divine service on those sabbaths when the missionary is officiating in more distant parts of his charge, and in the evening when he officiates in the chapel.
>
> upwards

A page from Patrick Butter's journal, Benbecula School Report, September 10, 1824. Butter, Inspector of Highland Schools in 1824 and a "preacher of the Gospel," was fluent in Gaelic.
COURTESY THE NATIONAL ARCHIVES OF SCOTLAND, GD95/9/3.

toward the Gaelic language. Old prejudices die hard. The Highlander from Rannoch who related the story about the roof leaking on the map of Ireland remembered that he was told to "converse in English" during "school hours." His elderly neighbor recalled that "any boy or girl caught speaking Gaelic during school hours was punished by having a human skull suspended round the neck for the rest of the day."[58] The neighbor had been a schoolboy during the 1860s.

Inspector Butter's assessment of the schoolmasters' unwillingness to teach Gaelic literacy was likely true, at least during his school tour of the 1820s. In the early 1700s, however, some society schoolmasters, as well as others who were more sympathetic toward the language, challenged the anti-Gaelic policy of their Edinburgh employers. Their correspondence generally began with a protest, initiated by the master, muddled along for awhile, and concluded with an officious, unrelenting declaration by the society. As early as 1715, only four years after the opening of the school at St. Kilda, the society heard from a Mr. Jamison, who argued that since the children in the schools were expected to learn English, the society ought to consider providing them with "an English vocabulary . . . [and] some words which might be explained to them in their own Language."[59]

Perhaps the most outspoken schoolmaster whose correspondence has survived was James Murray, who taught at the Strowan (Struan) school at Blair Atholl, in the Perthshire Highlands in the early 1700s. Murray would have agreed with Patrick Butter's later assessment of the impact of English-only instruction on the local community. When Murray wrote to the society in 1719, he reported that he had been teaching pupils to read the Gaelic psalms once they could read in English. Like Butter, he sympathized with the parents. Murray explained that he had chosen Gaelic instruction for his scholars "for the good of their Ignorant parents, who understood not the English tongue, that the children, when they go home at night, may be in ease to read to them." Murray maintained his stance for three years, until 1721, when the society forced him to back down. Five years later he had resigned the post. The three-year impasse between schoolmaster Murray and the directors epitomized the clash between the master, who understood the society's goals clearly and who responded creatively to his assignment, and the directors located in far-off Edinburgh, who refused to budge from their ideological stance.[60]

The bilingual experiences of Murray and other Gaelic-speaking schoolmasters thrust them well outside the limited understanding of the Edinburgh directors. The schoolmasters who spoke Gaelic had an entrée into the world of the ordinary clansmen and women. By sharing a common language, these masters were able to move beyond that initial encounter with people accustomed to different worlds expressed through different languages. The Gaelic language expressed the worldview of these clanspeople, and even though this view reflected their "ordinary" position in Highland society, as well as their specific location within the Highlands, it still served as a wellspring of cultural memory. It functioned as a reminder of a common past. The language bond shared by Gaelic speakers set them apart from outsiders. It reinforced cultural exclusivity for a people whose culture had all too frequently come under attack. And it enabled them to embrace a sense of Gaelic identity. By tapping into this language bond, the Gaelic-speaking schoolmasters moved from the crossroads of the cultural frontier to the other side.

By contrast, the members of the society, who were ensconced in Edinburgh and other Lowland towns, may never have understood this sense of identity that the Gaelic-speaking schoolmasters saw with clarity. Even when the uniqueness of Gaelic worldviews came to the society directors' attention, through their correspondence with those schoolmasters who defended Gaelic literacy, they were blinded by their immersion in the changing Lowland urban culture. Still, ironically, the society bequeathed this linguistic bond to schoolmaster and pupil by requiring Gaelic fluency on the part of the masters. In a later, unanticipated measure, the society directors provided further reinforcement for the shared Gaelic culture when it received a generous gift from an expatriate Lowland Scottish merchant by the name of John Raining.

After leaving his native Dumfriesshire, some decades before Robert Burns moved there with his family, Raining had settled in the town of Norwich, in East Anglia. During the eighteenth century, Norwich had attracted sufficient numbers of Scottish expatriates to enable them to form a "society of good will." Raining's financial success did not dampen his fondness for his homeland, and upon his death in 1724, he bequeathed to the Church of Scotland the sum of £1,000 "to plant a school in any part of North Britain where they think it most wanted, and to maintain that institution for the instruction of so many fatherless and other poor children in English, Latin and Arithmetick as the said yearly income will allow." The Kirk's General Assembly promptly named the society directors as managers of the Raining's School bequest.[61]

Spurred by economic and religious aspirations, two communities along the Moray Firth—Tain and Inverness—vied for the coveted prize of a school to be located in their midst. The Rev. Robert Bailie clinched the society's selection of Inverness when he shrewdly appealed to the society's intention of training Gaelic scholars in English. Bailie boasted that "no town in Scotland can afford such a number of Children having Irish, whose povertie renders their Education at Schools impracticable."[62] Reporting from Inverness during the same decade, Edmund Burt would have corroborated both the widespread use of Gaelic and the poverty of the region's children.

In 1727 when Raining's School opened "in four rooms above the Grammar School of Inverness"—the school and the master's house filled the entire third floor—it introduced "the first recorded attempt at teacher training in Scotland." As Scottish education historian Marjorie Cruikshank points out, neither parish nor society schoolmasters in the charity schools had received any instruction in the skills of pedagogy. Basically, "they devised their own methods of teaching," which were invariably hindered by the English-only strictures.

Since the society had discovered rather quickly the difficulty of locating masters who met their stringent qualifications, the directors had already resorted to the use of a type of apprenticeship in the ordinary SSPCK schools. Relying on the masters to choose those pupils—aged twelve to fifteen—who showed some promise as potential apprentice pupil schoolmasters, the society offered each of these scholars a generous incentive. Each apprentice selected to receive a bursary would be awarded a payment of "twelve pennies Scots everyday including Lord's days" for a period of two years. Those apprentices who completed this preliminary training period had the promise of a suit of clothing and a pair of shoes.[63] And those who continued their training for another year received a further reward: the society increased their increment to "eighteen pennies Scots," paid daily, plus a second suit of clothes and pair of shoes.[64]

Given the level of poverty in the Highlands, those pupils who were eager to learn might have been well pleased to receive a bursary or scholarship. For their families, the opportunity was rare. In the 1720s and 1730s two pupils, both with the surname of Tause, Arthur and Charles, who were English-Gaelic-speaking pupils of Glenmuick schoolmaster Andrew Rule, received bursaries. Each of them proved the soundness of the investment: Arthur taught from 1727 to 1742; Charles taught from 1738 until his death in 1798, much of the time in various locations in the Hebrides.[65] Over a century and a half later, in the 1880s, a Gaelic lad by the name of Norman Maclean, who grew up in Skye and later went on to become a renowned Presbyterian minister, recalled the occasion when he was asked to write an impromptu essay that earned him a bursary of £18 a year to attend Raining's School. Maclean reminisced: "If you had never written a line of your own in your life, and were told by a stranger to begin to do so at the age of thirteen, how would you begin? As I looked hopelessly at the paper there came the feeling that this was what my mother waited and prepared for so long—the way of escape! And I began to write."[66]

Maclean's motivation clearly echoed that of his predecessors enrolled in the society's eighteenth-century schools. Offered a bursary, like Maclean, they accepted the increment with considerable satisfaction. By the late 1720s, when Raining's School opened, the bursary could also have meant an opportunity to enroll in this unique institution. Once it was established, Raining's School contacted the society's schoolmasters, especially those teaching in Inverness-shire, requesting that they send their "bursars"—scholarship apprentices—to Raining's. When the young Gaelic scholars arrived in Inverness, they probably found themselves in awe of the town. Since most of them lived in the rural Highlands, for them, Inverness would have seemed an impressive city. Today, it is self-described as the "capital of the Highlands." In the eighteenth century, it was the capital, or largest town, of Inverness-shire.

When the apprentices were settled in at Raining's, they received firm instructions. They were advised to observe the teaching carried on at the renowned institution and also to attempt to improve their English "and get it well rooted" while they were there. Although the society maintained the apprentices for only a brief time at Raining's, they must have returned to their own rural school cottages with a stronger sense of their own worth as bilingual scholars, plus a new awareness of the importance of their role in assisting the master in teaching yet another group of "new beginners."[67]

The Inverness school, which in 1757 finally moved into a splendid building of its own that was located on land donated by the Inverness City Council, served as the "model school" for the SSPCK through much of the eighteenth and nineteenth centuries. By the late nineteenth century, however, Raining's School was caught up in the adverse political decision that discouraged the use of Gaelic within the state schools of Scotland. The controversial Education Act of 1872 chose to ignore the recommendation by the Napier Commission that instruction in Gaelic in the Scottish schools "ought not merely to be permitted but enjoined." Although this legislation proved to be the death knell for Scottish Gaelic, it provided temporary limelight for Raining's School. Raining's soon became the only institution in Scotland that

Raining's School stairs, Inverness. The Raining's School building, once located at the head of these stairs, was completed in 1757 and closed in the mid-1890s. The steep stairs lead from Ardconnel Street down to Castle Street.
PHOTOGRAPH BY THE AUTHOR.

Former location of Raining's School. During the last decades of the twentieth century this unique educational institution of the Highlands was torn down and replaced by a parking lot.
PHOTOGRAPH BY FERENC M. SZASZ.

generated bilingual teachers.[68] Its fundamental contribution to the perpetuation of the Gaelic language was enhanced in 1880, when the school was restructured as a magnate preparatory training college for Gaelic-speaking scholars from across the Highlands and Islands. After graduating from Raining's, these scholars attended normal school to complete their training as bilingual teachers. The success was short-lived. By the mid-1890s, Raining's School had closed its doors, and the society's and Raining's investments had come to an end. The society's campaign against Gaelic, compounded by the Education Act's short-sighted nod to English, had compromised the school's long-range goal —to perpetuate the teaching of Gaelic in Scottish schools.[69]

Ironically, Mr. Raining's linguistic legacy countered that of the SSPCK. By contributing to the spread of bilingualism among the society's schoolmasters, Mr. Raining's gift to the Highlands reinforced the Gaelic worldview that the society had sought so eagerly to vanquish. Some of the most ambitious Raining's School scholars, like Norman Maclean, may have perceived the institution as their ticket out of the Highlands. Maclean and many other pupils who had entered the school speaking Gaelic then made a remarkable leap to St. Andrews,

Edinburgh, or Aberdeen universities in Scotland, or their equivalent institutions in England. From there, the British Empire awaited them, and many never returned to their Highland roots. Others, like Maclean, came back upon their retirement, welcoming the opportunity to reminisce, and, in his case, to write a remarkable memoir. Whether they returned physically, like Maclean, or through the form of bequests, like Raining, their loyalties to their homelands held. And there likely was more than one Highlander who would have agreed with the words that Robert Burns reworked from eighteenth-century Scottish poetry: "My heart's in the Highlands, My heart is not here; / My heart's in the Highlands a-chasing the deer / A-chasing the wild deer, and following the roe— / My heart's in the Highlands wherever I go."[70]

Even today, long after the SSPCK experiment, many Highlanders who have remained in their homeland retain a degree of wariness about outsiders, regardless of their origins. Several years ago a north coast Sutherland woman explained this: "Highlanders are suspicious, if not outright hostile to outsiders. They are even critical towards Inverness."[71] Yet Inverness was the booming town that hosted Raining's School and currently boasts of being the capital of the Highlands.

The persistence of this attitude, which began long before the society's involvement and continues to the present day, is reflected in a story that comes from one of the society's spinning schools. These industrially oriented schools of the mid- to late eighteenth century were established under the auspices of the SSPCK's second letters patent of 1738. Similar to the U.S. Bureau of Indian Affairs boarding schools with their manual labor programs that were introduced in the late nineteenth century, the spinning schools offered pragmatic apprenticeships for Gaelic youth, or, as the patent stated, "To cause such of the children . . . to be instructed and Bred up to husbandry and housewifery, or in trades and Manufactures, or in such like manual occupation as the Society shall think proper."[72]

The charity schools opened under the second patent had a single purpose—to introduce into Gàidhealtachd the economic skills that already were in place in the progressive-minded Lowlands and, of course, in England. To this degree, they augured yet another dimension of Lowland cultural colonialism, this one brimming with expectations for economic improvement. Hence, the society, in conjunction with the trustees for the Board of Manufacturers and the commissioners for the Forfeited Estates, crafted a wide variety of apprenticeship schools, including, for boys, training to be carpenters, various specialties of wrights (cartwrights, wheelwrights, makers of spinning wheels, etc.), coopers, farmers, smiths, tailors, and others; and, for girls, instruction in spinning, weaving, knitting, and sewing, alongside religious instruction, introduced through the reading of Scripture.[73] Some of the boys were "bound out" for various terms of indentures. One group of thirty-five boys included "five as Farmers, seven as Weavers (three of whom also taught Flax-dressing), four as Wheel-wrights, six as Wrights or House-carpenters, (two of whom also taught to make carts and ploughs), three Blacksmiths, three Coopers, two Ship and Boat Carpenters, two Dyers, one Mill-wright, one Flax dresser, and one Shoemaker." Both boys and girls were also taught reading at the society's schools.[74] The women who served as "spinning mistresses" or those who taught "girls to sew seams and weave stockings" often were related to the schoolmaster. Some were wives, others were daughters, and one schoolmaster, Donald Manson, married Sophie Laing, the spinning mistress.[75]

Some of the spinning mistresses found it difficult to pronounce the lengthy names of the Biblical figures. At one of these schools, an older female teacher tried to assist a girl who was struggling to pronounce the multisyllabic names. Finally, in exasperation, she said to the girl, "who stuck fast at a long name about which the teacher herself had doubts, 'just gang ye stracht on Jeanie. Dinna mind hoo ye misca' them. They're a' deid.'"[76]

Reaction of the landed elite in the Highlands and Islands ranged widely. Lady MacKenzie of Cromarty "gave £8 yearly" to the school there; at Ruthven, "the Duke of Gordon gave 2 acres rent free." Still others objected vigorously to the entire principle of education brought in by the outsiders, especially the SSPCK. In more than one instance the landlords refused accommodation for schoolmasters or were unwilling to repair the accommodation that existed. In 1757, when schoolmaster Kenneth Sage arrived at Ardchattan, he found no house available and soon learned he would be ousted—Campbell of Barcaldine "refused to help and closed [the] school." When Sir James Riddell took over the schoolhouse at Strontian (outside Inverness), he "charged for cow grass, and ordered [the] teacher to remove." In 1809 Strathfillan schoolmaster William Rose encountered a new tacksman who "drove [the] teacher's cow off the pendicle."[77] As late as 1824, Patrick Butter, the astute Kirk inspector, summarized these reactions, recording in his journal that "the proprietors, factors and tacksmen... regard the change with considerable uneasiness... education is, in their opinion, prejudiced to the interests of their tenantry."[78] If there were objection to the schools by the elite, their resistance seems to have been based on a different level of reasoning from that of the ordinary clansmen and women. Like the tacksmen and landlords, the tenants, or "people," shared an ambivalent response to the schools. While some were concerned that there simply were too few of the schools to reach all of the Gaelic children who needed to learn to read, others found various personal reasons for their refusal to accept the society men who came to instruct their children. In both instances, when the schoolmasters encountered resistance as outsiders, they usually lost the struggle to maintain their presence.

Still, in retrospect, the issue of language in the schools lay at the core of all of these concerns. Language remained paramount. As Patrick Butter noted, the only motivation that these Highlanders—girls and boys and their parents as well—found for the "education of the young" resided in the reading of the Bible, "especially after its contents are disclosed to them . . . in their own language."[79] An intensely religious people, they understood that the Gaelic language forged the connective spiritual bond for them because it expressed the views of Gàidhealtachd, a culture that retained its separate identity, despite, or perhaps because of, the charity schools established by the society in the eighteenth century. In the nineteenth century, the Highlanders' persistent attachment to the faith introduced by the society schoolmasters in the eighteenth century would emerge with the traumatic Schism of 1843, which divided the Church of Scotland. In this crucial moment, the Highlanders reiterated their cultural independence by splitting from the Church of Scotland and forming culturally tailored denominations reflective of their own syncretic spiritual heritage.

By 1783, the SSPCK had opened over 170 schools in the Highlands and Islands, including 20 spinning schools. During the seven decades between the opening of the first schools in 1711 and the conclusion of our story in the 1780s, tens of thousands of Highland boys and girls had entered the doors of the schoolhouses that were scattered across the region, ranging from North Uist in the Outer Hebrides to the Central Highlands and north to the Orkneys and Shetlands. Scholars have estimated that by the end of the eighteenth century, "nearly 300,000 persons had received religious and moral instruction at the Society's schools."[80]

The instruction offered by the society schoolmasters ultimately sought to change the culture and society of the Highlands, but it left a complex heritage. The cultural legacy was mixed. It ranged from the decline of spoken Gaelic—its poetry, music, and song—to an assertion of Highland cultural nationalism through the declaration of the Gaels' unique faith preferences during the nineteenth century. For a small

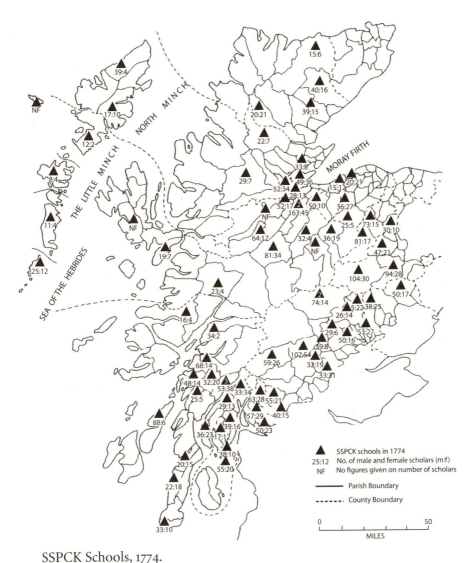

SSPCK Schools, 1774.
MAP BY CHARLOTTE HILL COBB. BASED ON A MAP FROM CHARLES W. J. WITHERS, *Gaelic in Scotland, 1698–1981: The Geographical History of a Language* (Edinburgh: John Donald, 1984), with the kind permission of Charles W. J. Withers.

number of pupils, the mastery of English would spur them to attain further education and, eventually, would lead to emigration to America, England, or the scattered regions of the British Empire. For most pupils, however, the struggles with learning English and the tenets of the Presbyterian faith would scarcely change their livelihood. Whether

Sabhal Mòr Ostaig. At this Gaelic College on the Isle of Skye all teaching is in Gaelic. It is one of fifteen academic partners of the University of the Highlands and Islands.
PHOTOGRAPH BY FERENC M. SZASZ.

they remained in the Highlands or became part of the worldwide Scottish diaspora of the late eighteenth and early nineteenth century, the Highlanders were likely to gain literacy in English while they lost use of their vernacular tongue and, with it, much of the oral dimension of their culture.

The results of the late-twentieth-century renaissance in the Gaelic language and culture—expressed through poetry, dance, music, and Gaelic immersion schools as well as the teaching of the language in Lowland universities and the University of the Highlands and Islands (especially at Sabhal Mòr Ostaig)—appear promising. In January 2006, a proposal to create the first all-Gaelic school in the Highlands at Sleat Primary in the south of Skye raised considerable concern in the community. To date there is just one Gaelic-only school in Scotland—the Gaelic Primary in Glasgow—but there are plans for one in Inverness.[81] But the future of this recent cultural renaissance and the question of whether it will have any lasting effect in the Highlands and Islands remains unknown. Few scholars would disagree, however, that the threads of this decidedly mixed legacy of the society's schools in the Highlands and Islands persist well into the present day.

CHAPTER FIVE

The Scottish Society and Native America

The society's letters patent of 1709 attested to the members' gravest concerns—the perseverance of the Gaelic language and the Catholic religion of the Highlanders. Generation after generation of society directors believed in the power of their schools to effect change. Although their educational outposts may have seemed like islands of civilization within a sea of "Erse-speaking papists," in the minds of these Lowlanders the schools epitomized the promise of the future: a time when all of the Highlanders would become a literate and English-speaking people who had chosen the "true faith" of the Presbyterian Church of Scotland.

After two decades of expansion beyond the Highland Line, by the 1730s, with almost eighty schools in place, the directors had gained sufficient experience to consider other ventures. At this moment, the directors persuaded the society to move in innovative directions. The first change involved the Highlanders themselves, through the second patent, as discussed in chapter 4, which sent the society members scurrying to their financial network to solicit the additional funding necessary for the highly regarded economic training. The Seymour Wood gift of £2,000 Sterling exemplifies the success of the network.[1] The society believed that this type of instruction would guarantee employment for the young Highland men and women who had no apparent manual skills.

Yet another venture had been nagging at their consciences as well. An idea latent with possibilities, it had been embedded in their initial charter, but there it had lain, ignored for over two decades. In the interim years, the society had focused exclusively on targeting schools for the Highlanders. By the 1730s the directors felt sufficiently comfortable with the society's financial status and the continued expansion of schools in the Highlands and Islands. Hence, the directors turned their attention to the phrase in the 1709 charter that promised dramatic action outside Scotland. The phrase read, "And for propagating the same in Popish and Infidel parts of the world."[2] This single phrase universalized the mission of the SSPCK. It seemed to suggest that the society's mandate was to promote Christian knowledge and increase "piety and virtue" to *all* people who suffered from "error, idolatry, superstition, and ignorance."

The reality proved more prosaic. The phrase simply meant that the new mission of the Scottish Lowlanders would be to cross the Atlantic Ocean in order to embrace the Native peoples of North America. It was an ambitious dream. But these members of the society were not merely dreamers. They were skilled administrators; they were shrewd financial managers; they were well-connected professionals who had already proven their ability to garner support from figures of wealth, status, and influence. And, of no little importance, they had surely demonstrated that they enjoyed more than their share of self-confidence. They knew that the task in which they were engaged was not only right; it was justified.

In Native North America they would find new challenges that were invariably compounded by the vast body of water that lay between America and the Outer Hebrides. If the society perceived St. Kilda as "off the map," then America lay virtually beyond their imagining. The sailing vessels that would carry the missives between the society and its missionaries and colonial boards of correspondence moved at an agonizingly slow speed. They always found themselves at the mercy of the storms of the North Atlantic, and, in time of war, they dealt with the threat of human predators under enemy sail. When the Mohegan Presbyterian minister Samson Occom sailed from Boston in late December 1765 as a passenger on the packet *Boston*, he could not have anticipated the fortunes of the crossing. The voyage took six weeks; it spanned two thousand miles. Still, it was a better crossing than his return voyage in 1768, from late March to May 20, when the ship sailed for eight weeks through the spring storms.[3] The difficulties of the Atlantic crossing remained a consideration in the society's calculations through much of the eighteenth century.

The focus now shifts from Gàidhealtachd to Native America, from Scottish Gaels to the Algonquian and Iroquois peoples. Moving across the cultural border between Native North American and outsider, the educational intermediaries on the far side of the Atlantic came from Native and English/Scottish backgrounds. Natives, who became both pupils and schoolmasters, entered the scene as individuals, but each of them identified with an Indian people, whether an Algonquian tribe, especially the Mohegans, Pequots, or Montauks, or one of the Iroquois nations, especially the Mohawks or Oneidas. On the English side of the colonial North American cultural divide, the equivalent figures engaged in Native schooling were members not of tribal nations but of Protestant denominations, whether Presbyterian or Congregational; by birth they were largely of English or Scottish ancestry.

Unlike the society's schooling in the Highlands and Islands of Scotland, the issue of language—Gaelic versus English-only—did not dominate the encounters in Native North America. Rather, the threat of enforced monolingualism was eclipsed by the issues of Native cultural and political autonomy. Although Natives generally remained very sensitive on these issues, outsiders largely ignored them because they were often intent on fulfilling their own private motivations, whether they concerned power, ambition, colonialism, or simply striving for wealth.[4]

Initial Forays and Failures in the Southeast

Between the 1730s and 1750s, when the SSPCK began to cast its cultural net across the Atlantic, its floundering efforts yielded little in the way of results. Initially, the society engaged different nations of Native people who lived in widely scattered regions of the Eastern Woodlands. The Edinburgh directors had already proven that they knew little about the Scottish Gaels; they knew even less about Native North Americans. In the Highlands, the society relied on schoolmasters and catechists to serve as their eyes and ears among the Gaels. In North America, they relied on Celtic and English colonials for advice on how to proceed. They also depended on the judgment of the colonials themselves when they sought men to serve as missionaries and schoolmasters. No candidate for schoolmaster in the colonies ever dreamed of sailing to Scotland for an examination and interview in Edinburgh with the ecclesiastical directors of the society. The dictates of distance demanded more pragmatic methods. In the early years of reaching across the water, the society experimented, and its experiments were widespread.

The short-term, largely unsuccessful early engagements began on the edges of New England. From there, the directors tried other experiments, employing missionaries whom they supported among the Iroquois, as well as smaller Native groups whose villages lay on Long Island.[5] Twice the society tested the educational promise of the southeastern Natives of Georgia, Virginia, and Tennessee.

In Georgia, the society financed a joint venture that was spurred by "a considerable number" of Highlanders who had sailed to the newly founded colony. Well aware of the financial reserves of the SSPCK, in the mid-1730s these emigrant Gaels requested society funds to send a minister to Georgia. They anticipated that he would preach to them in Gaelic and teach and catechize their children in English—a request guaranteed to please the directors—and "instruct the natives as well."[6] The society was interested. Responding favorably to these expatriates, the directors granted a commission to the Rev. John MacLeod, a native of Skye, who soon sailed to Georgia.

MacLeod's stint in Georgia coincided with the brief sojourn of (then) Anglicans John and Charles Wesley and Benjamin Ingham, plus a small group of Moravians, all of whom had sailed on the *Simmonds* to Savannah in 1736. Within this hodgepodge mixture of Presbyterian, proto–Methodist Anglican, and Moravian faiths, the Georgia experience initiated the Scottish Society into the interdenominational milieu of missionary schooling among Native North Americans. Unlike their experiences in the Highlands, where they were the earliest and most aggressive Protestant evangelical group, in North America the society soon learned that they would never enjoy the luxury of being the dominant religious faith intent on crossing the cultural frontier.

As minister to Georgia for the Society for the Propagation of the Gospel in Foreign Parts (the SPG, founded by Anglicans in 1701), John Wesley remained in the colony almost two years, but of the three Englishmen—the Wesley brothers and Ingham—only John's friend Ingham spent much time with the local Creek or Muskogee people. Intent on becoming a cultural intermediary, Ingham began to study Muskogee, the language of the nearby Creek band, a group known as the Yamacraws. In February 1736, after the *Simmonds* had anchored in the Savannah River, Tomochichi, *mico* (leader) of the Yamacraws, and his wife, Sinauky, boarded the ship to welcome the foreigners. Wesley recorded the visit: "Sinauky brought us a jar of milk, and another of honey, and said she hoped when we spoke to them we would feed them with milk, for they were but children, and be as sweet as honey toward them." Tomochichi requested of the strangers, "I would have you teach our children."[7] Among the English passengers, Ingham alone listened to the request and later honored it by opening a school for the Creek children, where he taught, alongside the Moravians, during his brief stay in the colony.

Like MacLeod, his Highland counterpart serving the SSPCK, John Wesley found his intended role as SPG missionary to the Indians usurped by his ministry to the recently arrived immigrants. In the end, the pacifist Moravians and the Gaelic minister MacLeod remained in Georgia longer than Ingham and the Wesley brothers, but even the Moravians and MacLeod fled when war with Spain threatened the fledgling colony.[8] Eventually, the school for the Yamacraw children closed, and the outsiders left. And for many years after their departure, the Creek and Cherokee inhabitants of the southeastern lands claimed by Georgia governor James Oglethorpe dealt with English and Scottish outsiders only through the ubiquitous trade in deer hides. Missionaries to the Native Americans would make little impact in the region until after the United States came into being during the 1780s. In Georgia, the departure of both the SSPCK and the SPG representatives typified the aborted plans of eighteenth-century philanthropic societies among the southeastern Native peoples. Focus on the needs of immigrant groups rather than Native people and frequent disruptions due to warfare meant that these educational and religious endeavors had but a fleeting impact on the southeastern Native peoples before the nineteenth century.

Undaunted, the Scottish Society supported further missionary efforts among the southeastern Native peoples, this time among the Overhill Cherokees who lived in the region that later became Tennessee. This Native group attracted the interest of both Congregational and Presbyterian leadership. In the north, the Boston-based New England Company (Company for Propagating the Gospel in New England, founded in 1649), a missionary organization funded by the Congregationalists, urged the Scottish Society to support an effort to send missionaries to the Cherokees. In the Chesapeake region, the Presbyterians of Virginia also solicited support from Edinburgh for the very same cause.[9]

Since the early 1700s, poverty stricken Scots Irish immigrants, who had fled their northern Ireland Ulster homeland in search of new lands, had been flooding Virginia's Piedmont. Many of them had made their way into the upland region via the ancient Iroquois warrior path/Cherokee trading path that wound its way through the Shenandoah Valley, while others had landed along Virginia's Tidewater rivers and moved west. The Presbyterian Scots Irish had brought with them their own kirk, carried from Scotland to Ireland under the initiative of James VI and I in the early seventeenth century. They also bore a dynamic faith commitment that contrasted sharply with the tepid Anglican faith that dominated the Tidewater. As early as 1740, John Craig, who was ordained as the first Presbyterian minister of Virginia, began to serve his Scots Irish parishioners.[10] By the 1750s, the indefatigable

Samuel Davies, of Welsh ancestry, had emerged as the leading Presbyterian minister of the colony, gaining renown as an ardent spokesperson for the Great Awakening.

At the end of the 1750s, when Davies was tapped to serve as president of the College of New Jersey (Princeton), he had already trained two young ministers. Each had received the support of the Scottish Society and ventured, successively, into the homelands of the Overhill Cherokees, where they sought to establish themselves as missionaries. But by mid-1759, both of them had left the Cherokees and returned to serve among the Scots Irish. Like the ministers in Georgia, they had been defeated by threats of warfare (the French and Indian War, 1754–63), but their departure also reflected the ambivalent reactions to their ministrations by the Cherokee themselves.[11]

While he was training these would-be missionaries, Davies learned of the educational achievements of Samson Occom, a Mohegan who was currently serving among the Montauk Indians on Long Island. Tutored by New Light Congregational minister Eleazar Wheelock, Occom had absorbed a theology bearing a Congregational imprint. Echoing the New England Company commissioners in Boston, Wheelock might well have anticipated that Occom would eventually be ordained into the Congregational ministry. But Davies had other ideas. Recognizing the significance of Occom's Native heritage, Davies perceived the Mohegan as the ideal candidate to serve as a missionary to the Cherokees. And, as a man of action, Davies swiftly urged the Scottish Society's New York Board of Correspondents to press for Occom's ordination, not as a Congregational, but as a Presbyterian minister. The pieces of this interdenominational puzzle locked into place. The Long Island Presbytery promptly ordained Occom as a Presbyterian minister, even as Davies's plans for the Mohegan's mission to the Cherokees collapsed due to the threatened war.[12] In a sense, Davies beat the Congregationalists at their own game: Occom's Presbyterian ordination had scarcely been on their immediate agenda.

Although these events illustrate the missionary networking of colonial America, the brevity of these missionary and educational engagements meant in the long run that they had little impact on the Native people of the Southeast. They also proved a disappointment to a society that had already deemed its Highlands schooling a grand success. Thus, the directors saw an urgent need for a success story in Native North America—one that would persist for more than a decade and would achieve some of the society's goals for religious and educational change among an indigenous people. In short, the directors were searching for a schooling venture that might meet their expectations as a "most agreeable" prospect.[13]

Natives and Missionaries in the Northern Colonies

Only in the northern colonies did the society find the conditions that encouraged such "agreeable" endeavors. Here, a unique mixture of Native peoples and missionary educators, some of whom were Native themselves, worked together with a measure of harmony for more than a single generation. The geographical regions that hosted these relatively stable efforts included the Delaware River valley of Pennsylvania and New Jersey; the Mohawk River valley west of the Hudson River; the Connecticut, Housatonic, Mohegan, and other river valleys of southern New England; and Long Island itself.

Although indigenous people in this broad region represented only two major language families—Algonquian and Iroquois—the people themselves proved more diverse than the language families might suggest. Among the Hodenosaunee (People of the Longhouse) or League of the Iroquois, the schooling and spiritual exchange touched four of the league's six nations—Mohawks, Oneidas, Tuscaroras (who would join the league in the 1720s), and Senecas—although the nations most affected were the Mohawks and Oneidas. Among the Algonquians, a band of Mahicans, or Muhakaneoks, were among the earliest to meet a society missionary, but they were soon followed by the Delawares, or Lenni Lenapes. In the region that Capt. John Smith had once dubbed "New England," the southern Algonquian groups that first engaged Scottish Society schooling and missionaries were the Mohegans, Pequots, Niantics, and Tunxis, the Connecticut Valley bands (Farmington), the Narragansetts, and the Montauks.

These northeastern Native peoples first encountered the missionary educators funded by the society during the 1740s. But some of the figures involved in the exchange between Natives and the Scottish Society, whether Native themselves or of Scottish or English ancestry, remained active in education and the ministry throughout the eighteenth century. Samson Occom, for example, lived until 1792, and the English Presbyterian missionary Samuel Kirkland lived until 1807. The funds that Occom had raised across the water for the Connecticut Indian/English charity boarding school that eventually merged with Dartmouth College dribbled intermittently into the Dartmouth coffers until the early twentieth century. Although it began as a patchy, often competitive effort, the Scottish Society's involvement with the Algonquians and Iroquois left an enduring heritage.

The society's most intensive focus targeted the Algonquians of southern New England. As the focal point for these educational encounters, the region of New England lay at the heart of the Reformed Protestant tradition. Like the Scottish Lowland Presbyterians, New England Congregationalists shared an unwavering faith in literacy. The Puritans and their descendants believed that the Word of God was revealed only in Scripture. Hence, during the seventeenth-century, Puritan missionaries to the Algonquians had taught reading to as many children as they could reach and encouraged Native educators and missionaries to follow suit. During the eighteenth century, the society's missionary educators who engaged Native communities outside New England proper, especially the Presbyterian brothers David and John Brainerd, received their education at Yale, the Connecticut institution, and maintained close ties with fellow New England clergy. During the Revolutionary era, the Iroquois youth living west of the Hudson River also received Reformed Protestant schooling from a New England source. Like spokes of a wagon wheel, the spin-offs from New England extended steadily outward throughout the colonial years.

Thus, by the mid-eighteenth century, when the Scottish Society cast its eye across the Atlantic to New England, it bumped up against powerful forces that were already well established. The SSPCK intruded as the newcomer in a field crowded with many players. First were the Native communities, whose multilevel sparring with the English over several generations had engendered intensive suspicion and mistrust on both sides of the cultural frontier. Second was the New England Company, the Congregationalists' version of the Scottish Society, which had dominated missionary education in the region for almost a century. Its leading Native converts had included the remarkable mid-seventeenth-century figures Cockenoe (Montauk), who had taught the Montauk dialect of Algonquian to the ambitious minister John Eliot; Nesuton (Massachusett), a linguist who had served as Eliot's primary translator for the Massachusett-English Bible; and Wowaus, or James Printer (Nipmuc), whose newly acquired printing skills had thrust him into the midst of the three-year task of printing the bilingual Bible, completed at the Harvard College printing shop in 1663. Interestingly, the Algonquian people of this region had gained a vernacular, bilingual Bible a full century before the Scottish Gaels. Other Native figures such as

Iacoomes (Hiacoomes, Pawkunnaket/Wampanoag), who befriended the English missionary Thomas Mayhew, Jr., and eventually became a minister himself, established close links with the New England Company. These Native converts spread the Word through preaching and teaching among their own families and bands throughout the numerous Algonquian villages of the region.[14]

The lengthy relationship between the New England Company and the Algonquians suggested that in this region the Scottish Society would never achieve the influential position that it had gained in the Highlands. Still the Scots managed to fund several unique educational endeavors that would leave their imprint on this segment of Native American and American culture. Compounding their late arrival to this new field, the Lowland Scots also were handicapped by distance. Responding to this challenge, the directors recalled the society's initial fund raising efforts that had relied on widespread links with prominent individuals and even a board of correspondents in London. Hence, in New England, they sought to alleviate the distance barrier by contacting leading clerics, colonial government officials, and other professionals among the English residents of the region. Once again relying on connections, they engaged a network of leading figures. The arrangement succeeded because both sides perceived it as beneficial. Many of the society's New England contacts proved to be as shrewd as the society directors, anticipating the potential economic windfall as well as the spiritual and educational advantages of allying themselves with the society.

As soon as it became clear that the Lowland Scots had funds, these colonials were willing to help them put those funds to good use. A number of the society's early financial supporters, like John Raining, had earmarked their donations. In another singular instance, Dr. Daniel Williams, a "dissenting clergyman in London," bequeathed to the society his estate at Catworth in Huntingdonshire, but the income from the estate was not to become available until a year after the society had sent "three qualified ministers to abide in foreign and infidel countries." Henceforth, all income from the Catworth estate was to be reserved for these foreign regions of the society's schooling ventures. Other donors were equally exacting in their specifications, and it must have been these targeted contributions that persuaded the directors to embrace schooling for the Native Americans.[15] The donors' endorsement of cultural colonialism among American Indians, plus the internal pressure to spend these restricted funds, likely spurred the society's expansion.

In the northern colonies, the society echoed its organizational network in Britain by agreeing to support several semiautonomous boards of correspondents (the groups alluded to earlier who directed the society's various efforts within their own areas of influence). Located in Massachusetts, New Jersey, New York, and Connecticut, the boards handled the daily decisions, chose suitable persons to serve as missionaries and educators, and determined their salaries as well as the locations where they were to serve. This latitude thrust considerable power into the hands of the board members, but it also encouraged them to compete aggressively for a share of the society's largesse.[16]

Algonquians, Iroquois, and Highland Gaels in the 1730s

Although most historians have overlooked this theme, during the eighteenth century the Highland Gaels and the Natives in the northern colonies shared a number of similarities.[17] Indian Country during the 1730s was not Gàidhealtachd, of course, but the careful observer could find resemblances among the many peoples long settled on the opposite shores of the Atlantic. Although divided by distance and diversity of culture as well as their historical experiences, these indigenous populations also shared a number of commonalities.

By the early eighteenth century each of these cultures—the Gaels, the Algonquians, and the Iroquois—had retained certain core features of their heritage by means of their ubiquitous storytelling and song. Relating the old stories proved a means of recalling mythic time, a merging of the past and the present. Stories proved the best way to pass on cultural values to the young; they reinforced spiritual traditions and provided a form of winter entertainment for multiple generations. Although the Gaelic bards transcribed their songs and poetry, they also engaged in storytelling, and certain clan members—ranging, in eighteenth-century Lowland parlance, from crofter to tacksman—still relied on their oral skills. But the sharing of stories began to lose its power when the common vernacular of the people suffered erosion. Each of these peoples viewed the world through the prism of their own language. Even though the various languages had been modified by the addition of rich words and concepts introduced by outsiders (English, French, Dutch, Viking, Scots), in the eighteenth century the languages themselves still belonged to the people.[18]

Like the Scottish Gaels, the Natives of North America had maintained their ceremonies, customs, and beliefs well into the eighteenth century. All of them were caught, however, by the common dilemma facing minority groups forced to merge the new with the old. True, the Gaels had confronted this merging process many generations earlier, when their ancestors had synthesized indigenous Celtic beliefs with those introduced by Christian missionaries like Colm Cille and, later, Catholic beliefs with Episcopalian and, even later, Episcopalian beliefs with those of the Presbyterians.[19] The Algonquians had encountered Christianity much more recently through the Calvinism of the Congregationalists and, later, the Presbyterians. The First Great Awakening of the 1740s would add yet another layer to their syncretic faiths.[20] South of the Great Lakes, the Iroquois had matched wits with the Jesuits, often by way of the Huron Nation, but some of them, especially the Mohawks, had also encountered the Anglicans.[21] Perhaps as a matter of survival, each group, as well as different members within each group, had cobbled together an endless variety of syncretic and ancient faiths.

Economic poverty had emerged as a common badge of this region of Native North America as it had in Gàidhealtachd. In the Highlands, poverty was rooted in the crumbling of the clans and the economic pressures that the chiefs, via their tacksmen, had laid on the tenants and cottars, once ordinary clansmen and women. Among both Algonquians and Iroquois, the emergence of poverty reflected the vast economic restructuring fostered by European incursions on indigenous farming lands, persistent destruction of hunting and harvesting territories, and, finally, massive population reduction caused by European disease and warfare. Alcohol, for many Native societies, had dealt the final blow; it had destabilized families and communities, destroying old patterns that protected the well-being of the group. The pressure placed on kinship structures—the bedrock of Native American societies and Gaelic society—had been compounded by other incursions.

In short, Native North America and Gàidhealtachd had already been vastly altered before the Scottish Society entered the competition for cultural colonialism among the Native peoples in the northern colonies. We have already had a taste of the alterations in eighteenth-century Gaelic society due, at least in part, to the incursions of the SSPCK. The society's impact among Algonquians and Iroquois would never be as dramatic. In the northern colonies, the society represented only a single group among several competing denominational organizations. Among the Hodenosaunee, they were well matched by the

Jesuits and the Anglicans. Even among the Algonquians, they entered a region long dominated by the New England Company.

In North America, the society's influence would depend on two factors: the commitment and cultural sensitivity of those missionary-educators whom they supported and the responses of those Native peoples whom they approached with the Presbyterian version of Reformed Protestantism. As illustrated in the Scottish Highlands, the results often hinged on the personalities of those individuals who straddled this cultural borderland. In the end, however, the ultimate results rested on the unique cultures of the Native groups themselves and how they responded to the historical circumstances that engulfed them during the mid-eighteenth century.

The Muhakaneoks and Lenni Lenapes:
Life with the Brainerd Brothers

The Muhakaneoks were among the earliest Algonquian people to encounter the Scottish Society. A remnant band of the once powerful Mahican Nation, the Muhakaneoks had come under pressure from both the Mohawks and the Dutch, whose short-lived New Netherlands remained extant from 1624 to 1664. Under these circumstances, most of the River People had been forced to move away from their rich lands along the Mahicanituk River, later renamed after Henry Hudson. This particular band had moved east toward the Housatonic River valley in western Massachusetts, where they had settled in the village of Kaunaumeek, about twenty miles west of the Housatonic.[22]

In the spring of 1743, the people of Kaunaumeek spied a young man on horseback coming toward their village. The traveler was David Brainerd, a twenty-four-year-old Presbyterian missionary who had been a student at Yale during the height of the Great Awakening. Strongly affected by the revival that swept the campus at New Haven, he was eager to begin his life's calling. Moreover, he had been sent to Kaunaumeek by the Scottish Society. Brainerd commented immediately on the pervasiveness of the Scottish influence in the region. Shortly after his arrival he wrote, "Most of the talk I hear is either Highland Scotch [Gaelic] or Indian."[23]

This encounter was to prove a fortuitous experience for both Brainerd and the Muhakaneoks. His short-term residence among the Mahican band would propel David Brainerd into his brief missionary-educator career. Brainerd and the people of Kaunaumeek remained together for only a year. Although Brainerd had already begun to study

David Brainerd (1718–47). Artist unknown.
IMAGE REPRINTED FROM JESSE PAGE, *DAVID BRAINERD, APOSTLE TO THE NORTH AMERICAN INDIAN* (1891).

the Mahican language, at the end of the year he learned that the Scottish Society had selected yet another location and a different Native people for his missionary efforts. He made a perfunctory note in his diary: "Having recvd new orders to go to a number of Indians on Delaware R. in Pennsylvania, & my people here being mostly removed to Mr. [John] Sergeant's, I this day took all clothes books & c. and disposed of them, and set out for Delaware river."[24]

When Brainerd's Mahican hosts learned they could not persuade him to remain, they too decided to leave the site, moving farther east on their exodus to join another band of Muhakaneoks who lived in the Housatonic Valley. Unbeknownst to them, their migrations had only begun. By the 1820s, their descendants—known as the Stockbridge Indians—had already moved north, first to a location in Oneida country in New York and then to Wisconsin, where today their descendants, —the Stockbridge-Munsee Band of Mohicans,—reside on a forty-six-thousand-acre reservation in Shawano County of central Wisconsin.[25]

The small band of Kaunaumeek Mahicans who hosted David Brainerd for this brief interlude in the 1740s retains greater symbolic importance than the band's few numbers might suggest. Their subsequent multiple migrations represent the movement of numerous Indian nations who were displaced from their homelands on repeated occasions. Today, the bands of this Mahican nation are scattered to the four winds, a testament to the migratory history of Native North America. Gaelic history closely paralleled this Native American dispersal as well. The Gaels of the Scottish Highlands and Islands were not far behind the Native Americans when they sailed from their homes during the early years of the epic Scottish diaspora of the late eighteenth and nineteenth centuries.

The saga of the Kaunaumeek Mahicans also formed a crucial aspect of the Scottish Society's mosaic past. In addition to being one of the earliest Algonquian groups to encounter the SSPCK, by hosting David Brainerd they introduced the society's most famous missionary to Native American cultures.[26] The brevity of Brainerd's assignment there may have reflected the proximity of the Kaunaumeeks to the Housatonic Valley, where the New England Company had already staked a claim and where other Mahicans already resided. The society's decision to shift Brainerd could well be perceived as a form of strategic retreat. As Native people migrated—whether through force or voluntarily—the society followed in due course. Hence, the history of the society's link with missionary education in the northern colonies became almost a mirror image of changing Native demographics. As historian Richard

White has pointed out in *The Middle Ground*, trade, disease, warfare, and migration led to a constant shifting and reconfiguration of bands, tribes, and nations. Cognizant of these changes, the society adjusted accordingly.

While his Mahican hosts moved east, David Brainerd mounted his horse again to ride south and west from Kaunaumeek. After crossing the Hudson, the traditional homeland of the Mahicans, he rode south to the Forks of the Delaware in Pennsylvania, where he paused, just a little north of William Penn's old haunts of Philadelphia. Brainerd's new assignment involved the Lenni Lenapes, the Native people who had so intrigued the remarkable Quaker idealist and entrepreneur. The Lenni Lenapes living at the Forks had agreed to the society's offer to introduce a mission.[27]

Brainerd was under no illusions about life among this band of Delawares. Despite the fact that some of them initially appeared interested in his mission, at the end of a year at the Forks, he determined to move again. As he wrote, "My rising hopes, respecting the conversion of the Indians, have been so often dashed, that my spirit is as it were broken, and courage wasted, and I hardly dare hope."[28] Recrossing the Delaware River, he resolved to settle among a few Delaware families who lived in Crosswicks (Crossweeksung), southeast of present-day Trenton, New Jersey. He anticipated gathering a congregation there, one that would respond to his forays into the surrounding countryside and join the small nucleus of a community that was already formed. As he wrote to the society, he was "still hopeful, albeit more cautious."[29]

Repeating the ritual he had initiated among the Mahicans, Brainerd began to study the language, hoping eventually to preach in Delaware. He also opened a school, reaching out to the Lenni Lenape children through teaching. But he discovered that the introduction of group singing and the offer to provide instruction in the evenings attracted the interest of young couples. Once again music offered a universal entrée, as it had proven in the Scottish Highlands. Initially, the Delawares were hostile. One Delaware lamented that other colonials "were want to lie, defraud, steel, and drink worse than the Indians.... [and] brought them [the Lenni Lenapes] to all of these vices which now prevailed among them."[30] Thus, at first they proved very wary.

But it soon became apparent to them that David Brainerd was different. Gradually, he began to attract some followers. Within a short time, others came to live at Crossweeksung, and the few Delaware families he had initially settled among had grown to twenty.

By 1745, however, David Brainerd's fate had turned tragic. He con-

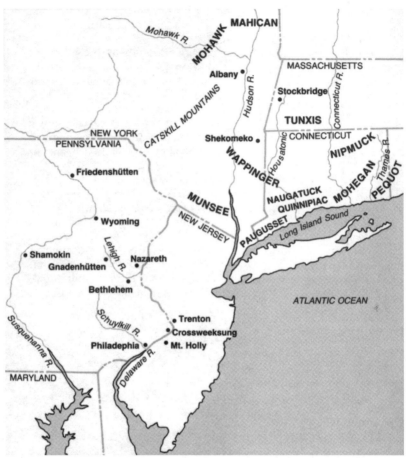

Indians of the northeastern river valleys.
FROM MARGARET CONNELL SZASZ, *INDIAN EDUCATION IN THE AMERICAN COLONIES, 1607–1783* (UNIVERSITY OF NEW MEXICO PRESS, 1998; REPR., UNIVERSITY OF NEBRASKA PRESS, 2007).

tracted consumption (tuberculosis). Despite his illness, he and the community had managed to move about fifteen miles northeast of Crossweeksung, near Cranbury, where they had secured more fertile soil for their crops and better grazing lands for their cattle. With the move, the community continued to grow. It had already doubled in size and included forty families, or well over 130 Delawares.[31]

When David Brainerd had been in his final year of studies at Yale, his younger brother, John, had also enrolled in the college.[32] Having completed his degree in 1746, John Brainerd traveled to Cranbury to join his ailing brother and to minister to the Lenni Lenape community upon David's death in 1747. David Brainerd had served as a missionary and schoolmaster for Mahican and Delaware families for a total of four years. John Brainerd remained as missionary and schoolmaster to this Lenni Lenape community in New Jersey for almost thirty-five years. Yet David, rather than John, emerged as the key figure in the story of eighteenth-century Reformed Protestantism. Immortalized by Jonathan Edwards, the prominent Massachusetts theologian who would have become his father-in-law had David and his fiancée married (they died within a short time of each other), David Brainerd's reputation became secure. His name was on the lips of admiring fellow Protestant clergymen throughout the eighteenth and nineteenth centuries. In retrospect, however, it was his younger brother who was to have a far more lasting influence on the New Jersey and southern New England Algonquian people.[33]

As John Brainerd moved into his brother's position, he saw the need for a larger tract of land to support the thriving community. But this dream would not become a reality for over a decade. Finally, during the French and Indian War, New Jersey's commissioners responsible for the colony's Indian policy purchased for the Delawares a tract of over three thousand acres of trust land located southeast of Willingboro.[34] About two-thirds of the three hundred or so Natives living in New Jersey in the mid-eighteenth century then moved onto the trust lands, forming a community that New Jersey governor Francis Bernard dubbed "Brotherton." While John Brainerd continued to receive some support from the Scottish Society through its New Jersey Board of Correspondents, in 1762 the colony also engaged the missionary to serve the "Brotherton Indians" as their "Superintendent and Guardian." The younger Brainerd brother remained within the community until his death during the American Revolution.[35]

The longevity of John Brainerd's relationship with the Delawares of New Jersey (1746–81) speaks both to the persistence of the Presbyterian missionary schoolmaster himself as well as the Delaware community as a whole. It also speaks to the wisdom of the Scottish Society. Both of the Brainerd brothers and the Lenni Lenapes endorsed the goals of the SSPCK, and their mutual commitment made this settlement one of the most enduring stories of the society's engagement with Native North America. During these years John Brainerd donned the garb of cultural intermediary; he focused on the well-being of the Delaware community and served as a liaison between the community and the outside world. Given the trauma faced by most Native peoples during this era, the Crossweeksung-Cranbury–Brotherton Delaware experience proved unique. Between the mid-1740s and the American War for Independence, this community experienced a relative degree of stability. While the Delawares themselves bore the brunt of responsibility for this record, John Brainerd's commitment to them was essential. The colony of New Jersey's grant of trust land remained vital as well.

John Brainerd's lengthy tenure among the Lenni Lenapes enhanced his role as educational intermediary. As Brainerd grew into his relationship with the Delawares, he became a crucial player in New England's mid-eighteenth-century Native educational network. Relying on interdenominational understanding, the network absorbed Presbyterian, Congregational, and Anglican faiths. Relying on inter-tribal empathy, it mingled youth from many different Algonquian and Iroquois nations. In its full flowering, it proved an ambitious scheme to school Native youth representing a wide range of homelands: southern New England, New York, and New Jersey. The Delawares of New Jersey emerged as the initial catalyst for the schooling network. If the New Jersey Delawares had not placed their confidence in John Brainerd, it is highly likely that the network would have faltered. It is conceivable that it might never have come into being.

Although these indigenous schooling enterprises, like those in the Highlands of Scotland, began with the basic tools of formal education —elementary literacy, writing, and ciphering—as well as vocational skills, they eventually extended well beyond grammar school to include college. Praising his Delaware pupils, John Brainerd once wrote to a friend that "not less than twenty . . . are able to read pretty distinctly in the Bible and repeat most of the Assembly's Short Catechism . . . and some of them can write a decent legible hand."[36] But a small number of Native scholars moved well beyond this level and eventually attended either the College of New Jersey or Dartmouth College in New Hampshire. Throughout this era, which spanned at least two generations, the educational network, including both the girls and boys and the schoolmasters, depended on individual voices of experience, compassion, and wisdom. Some of those voices emerged from within Native communities, whether they were Elders or the cultural intermediaries who had learned to move within the Native American and the outsiders' worlds. John Brainerd, Presbyterian missionary and schoolmaster and little-known second son following a renowned older brother, proved a crucial voice in this regard. The test for the Scottish Society was to listen carefully to these voices in order to determine which of them would prove enduring.

CHAPTER SIX

The Algonquians and Iroquois Meet the Scottish Society

The Great Awakening

David and John Brainerd found a considerable number of kindred spirits when they were swept up by the religious revival during their years at Yale. Beginning in the 1740s and continuing well into the 1770s, converts joined the mood for religious change. They flocked to grassy fields in rural areas, to grand open spaces in colonial towns, and, finally, inside the churches themselves—when they could fit within the walls—where they remained spellbound by the powerful preaching of revival ministers and itinerant preachers. The converts, often called "New Lights," felt extraordinary wonder at their newfound experience of "grace." Collectively, their shared awe became known as the Great Awakening. Later, historians would describe it as the most dramatic religious revival in all of colonial American history.

In North America, the Great Awakening reverberated from one region of the thirteen colonies to another, and it continued to spin its fiery emotion until the outbreak of the American Revolution. In the colonial world, the Awakening cut across all levels of society, including in its expansive grasp a wide range of people. But it was scarcely limited to North America. People felt the power of the mid-eighteenth-century Awakening on both sides of the Atlantic. In North America it affected Native Americans, African Americans, and European Americans; across the water, it attracted Scots, Welsh, English, and continental Europeans. In the colonies the Great Awakening became an influential progenitor for other movements. For the purposes of our story, it formed the primary catalyst for the spread of Christianity and European education among Native Americans. This proved especially true for those living in the northern colonies.

In New England and adjacent regions of the north, the Great Awakening introduced an era of dynamic religious change. It altered the lives of several key individuals in our story, whose new understandings of Christianity convinced them of the need to reshape not only their own lives but also the lives of others. Samson Occom (Mohegan), David Fowler (Montauk), Joseph Johnson (Mohegan), and other Natives during this era were so changed by the great revival that they introduced European ideas into the worldviews of their own people. Those of English or Scottish ancestry, such as Eleazar Wheelock, David and John Brainerd, and Samuel Kirkland, also felt its power; the Great Awakening helped to mold their missionary goals among Native peoples. The careers of all of these people eventually became entwined, but the revival remained their common denominator. The Great Awakening's educational legacy—Native literacy, schooling for Natives, and colleges that attracted a smattering of Native students—would touch each of their lives.

Samson Occom, Native Scholar

Samson Occom emerges as the most articulate Native leader of the eighteenth century.[1] Following his conversion during the Great Awakening, the young Mohegan entered the milieu of English schooling under the guidance of his tutor, Eleazar Wheelock. A New Light Congregational minister, Wheelock completed his studies at Yale in 1733, well before David and John Brainerd enrolled there. Two years later, the members of a church in Lebanon, Connecticut, called him to serve as their pastor.[2] Shortly before Wheelock was installed, the renowned Jonathan Edwards, pastor in Northampton, Massachusetts, led the revival in Northampton that augured the spiritual conflagration soon to sweep across New England.

Like Edwards, Wheelock reverberated with the enthusiasm of the Great Awakening. During the height of the revival, he traveled widely, often preaching twice a day on his speaking trips. As a "popular and pervasive preacher," he caught the attention of his fellow New Light clergymen. Jonathan Edwards even invited him to speak in Northampton.[3] When the revival faded, however, the intensity of Wheelock's involvement led him to search for other means of harnessing his newly unleashed energies.

The key to Wheelock's future career lay in the hands of Samson Occom. During Occom's years of study, Wheelock had been impressed with the young Mohegan's skill at learning. When Occom accepted an offer from the Montauk community on Long Island, where he would serve as schoolmaster and missionary, Wheelock began to ponder the significance of Occom's accomplishments. Always a pragmatist, like the directors of the Scottish Society whose organization later intersected with his career, Wheelock grasped the wider implications of Occom's learning. For Wheelock, Occom's accomplishments seemed to symbolize the untapped learning potential for other Native youth. He reasoned, "after seeing the success of this Attempt, I was much more encouraged to hope that such a Method might be very successful."[4] If Native youth could be gathered into a school, at his invitation, and could collectively absorb the knowledge of the Protestant Reformed tradition of New England (Congregational), they could carry this knowledge back to their own villages as schoolmasters to the children.[5]

As an eminent minister and former tutor of a Native already proven as a Christian scholar, Eleazar Wheelock believed he would be the most qualified individual to head this new institution. Moreover, prospective Native pupils, following Occom's example, might benefit from instruction alongside English charity scholars, who could provide guidance and set an example. Wheelock also reasoned that after his school had opened, the presence of young Indian women—as part-time scholars and part-time domestics living and working in homes in Lebanon—would aid the male graduates. They might eventually serve as wives and Christian helpmates in the mission field. Hence, Wheelock, like his counterparts in the Scottish Society, acknowledged the importance of rudimentary education for women.[6] Through this well-reasoned logic, the idea of a charity boarding school for Indian and English scholars came to dominate Wheelock's thinking. He called it the "Great Design."

Networking for Moor's School

The actual creation of the school required considerably more effort than Wheelock had originally thought. Like the founders of the Scottish Society, Wheelock realized that funding would be the primary stepping-stone to success, and he too emerged as an indefatigable fundraiser. But Wheelock's search for his first Indian pupils posed an equal challenge. In this context, the Scottish Society influenced the formation of his charity school through a rather circuitous route.

In an unexpected turn of events, Wheelock's school eventually became the nexus for Reformed Protestantism in all of southern New England. Through Wheelock and his wide-ranging network—like Samuel Davies's Presbyterian network based in Virginia—the Congregational and Presbyterian leaders began to join forces in the mid-eighteenth century. Although their denominational polity differed, doctrinally, the Presbyterians and Congregationalists shared much in common. Both accepted a neo-Calvinist theology—belief with less emphasis on predestination—and both believed in the power of literacy and education, as well as the necessity of an educated ministry.

Hence, the links fell into place. During the years when the Congregationalist Boston Board of Commissioners for the New England Company were funding Samson Occom's studies in Lebanon, so too were the Presbyterian Scottish Society directors funding David Brainerd and, later, John Brainerd. Eventually, the Congregational network included Wheelock and other clergy, while the Presbyterian network expanded to encompass the Brainerds and, a little later, Occom and Samuel Kirkland.

After Occom settled at Montauk, Long Island, supported by a meager salary provided by the New England Company, Wheelock began to make serious plans for his charity school. In the early 1750s, with funding and the need for Indian pupils foremost in his mind, his thoughts turned quickly to the proven missionary John Brainerd. "I wrote to the Reverend *John Brainerd*, missionary in *New-Jersey*, desiring him to send me two likely Boys for this purpose, of the Delaware Tribe." . . . "He accordingly sent me *John Pumshire*, in the 14th and *Jacob Woolley*, in the 11th Years of their Age; they arrived here December 18th, 1754, and behaved as well as could be reasonably expected." Two years later, when Pumshire became ill, Wheelock sent him home to the Delaware community in Cranbury, where, shortly after his return, he died.[7] Always the pragmatist, Wheelock had anticipated the loss and requested that two more pupils "of that nation" return to the school with Pumshire, "if he survives." Accordingly, "on April 9th, 1757, *Joseph Woolley* and *Hezekiah Calvin* came on the Horse which Pumshire rode."[8]

Since the Delawares had agreed to part temporarily with their own youth, they provided the first pupils at the Connecticut charity school. Their sacrifice meant that, as a people, they bore the primary responsibility for the opening of Wheelock's institution. Although Brainerd's encouragement provided incentive, in the end, the sending of their children remained a Delaware decision. It was made more difficult by the close attachment that Delaware families and kin felt toward their children;—the perseverance of kinship patterns still prevailed among these people. Still, concern for their children's future in a changing world came first, and education promised some tools for grappling with that world. Indirectly, the Scottish Society also helped open Wheelock's school. Their financial support for David and John Brainerd enabled the missionary brothers to bring together the scattered Lenni Lenape families in New Jersey. The SSPCK and the Brainerds contributed to the success of the school experiment, but without the consent of the Delawares themselves, Wheelock would have been forced to look elsewhere for his first pupils.

During its life span of some fifteen years in southern Connecticut, Wheelock's Indian charity school enrolled about sixty-five pupils. Four of the first five pupils were Lenni Lenapes. Later, three additional Delawares—one girl and two boys—also enrolled. Wheelock eventually included approximately sixteen Indian girls. Hence, the seven Delaware pupils, and indirectly the Scottish Society, were responsible for about 10 percent of the total enrollment.[9]

Only one year after Jacob Woolley and John Pumshire rode into the rolling, green countryside surrounding the village of Lebanon, Col. Joshua More, who lived in a nearby village, deeded to the school several buildings, plus two acres of land adjacent to Wheelock's twenty-acre lot in Lebanon. In gratitude, Wheelock named his experiment Moor's Indian Charity School.[10] With the transfer of the land and buildings, plus the safe arrival of the first Delaware youth, Wheelock had emerged as the premier English schoolmaster to the Algonquian youth of southern New England. Later, he would expand his position by obtaining Iroquois pupils as well. This role would dominate the rest of his life; it would also strongly influence all the Native communities who sent their children to Moor's School.

The stability of Wheelock's new venture revolved around several specific conditions. First, he depended on a network of fellow clergy, whether they were Congregational ministers, such as those living in southeastern Connecticut; John Sergeant, missionary to the Mahicans and Housatonics, known collectively as the "Stockbridge Indians"; Presbyterian ministers, such as John Brainerd; or the Anglican priest George Whitefield. During the 1740s, Whitefield was best known for his charismatic preaching in both Britain and colonial America. He ignited the fires of the Great Awakening by attracting massive crowds who thronged to hear him during his various tours throughout the colonies.

But Wheelock's links with religious figures was matched by his network of financial donors. He never ceased in his assiduous efforts to gain financial aid from an eclectic variety of sources—governing bodies and churches, private organizations like the New England Company and, eventually, the Scottish Society, and various influential individuals. Whitefield seemed to know virtually everyone who was of any social, political, or financial importance.[11]

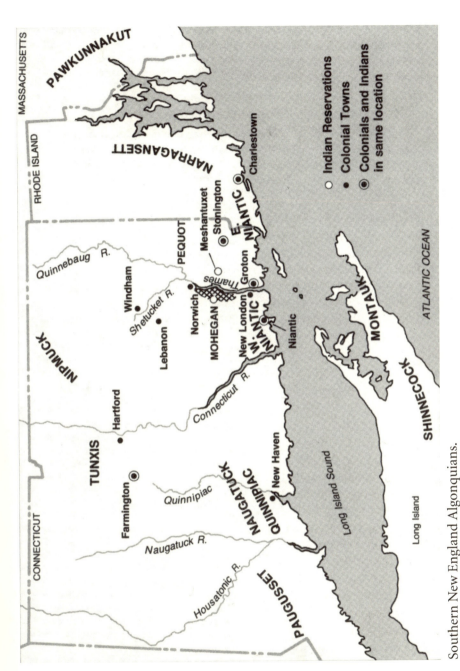

Southern New England Algonquians.
FROM MARGARET CONNELL SZASZ, *INDIAN EDUCATION IN THE AMERICAN COLONIES, 1607–1783* (UNIVERSITY OF NEW MEXICO PRESS, 1998; REPR., UNIVERSITY OF NEBRASKA PRESS, 2007).

Further, as the significant role of the New Jersey Delawares confirmed, Wheelock remained entirely dependent on Native parents and their communities; the existence of Moor's School rested on their support. The Narragansett widow who provided five children to Wheelock's care entrusted their lives to the minister. When she sent one of her sons, Sarah Simons wrote to Wheelock, "I have sent my Lettel Son James up to you, take him to your self and keep him in subjection. Keep him as Long as you ples til you think that he shall be capabel of bisness."[12]

Finally, Wheelock's promotion of his southern Connecticut school rested on the shoulders of his first pupil, Samson Occom. By 1759, after Occom's ordination as a Presbyterian minister, the charity school had been opened and had survived its early years. Without Occom's steady example, Wheelock might have faltered in his idealistic determination to remold the youth from the Algonquian villages into Calvinist farmers and schoolmasters, aided by the presence of their schooled wives by their side.

Native Pupils at Moor's School

Although it was located in southeastern Connecticut, Moor's Indian Charity School drew scholars from a wide area. Many came from nearby communities in southern New England. They made their way west from Narragansett lands in Rhode Island. They traveled north from the communities of New London and Groton. But they came from other regions as well. Some crossed Long Island Sound from the Montauk village where Occom lived. Those who came from the New Jersey Delaware band rode north and east, a distance of about 150 miles to Lebanon. The Iroquois students traveled the greatest distance. Their lengthy journey of perhaps 300 miles began in their homelands along the Mohawk River, continued down the Hudson River, and finally concluded overland to the more benign climate of Lebanon.[13] After Wheelock moved his school to Hanover, New Hampshire, still other Indian scholars traveled south from Ontario. Although some, like the Delawares, may have arrived on horseback, most of the students probably traveled by foot or in boats, making their way in rain, wind, and snow. The best travel accounts of trips like this were recorded by Samson Occom himself, when he entered brief notes in his diary during his many journeys from Connecticut to Oneida country and home again.[14]

Native kinship patterns served as a powerful magnet in attracting potential scholars. Over half of the Indian nations represented at Moor's School were Algonquian. Most of these pupils came from the Delaware, Mohegan, Pequot, Narragansett, and Montauk nations. Many were related. David and Jacob Fowler were the brothers of Mary Fowler Occom, the Montauk wife of Samson Occom. Brother and sister combinations were not unusual, and some families sent all of their children to Moor's School. Still other pupils formed connections during their years in Lebanon. When David Fowler, Occom's brother-in-law, was teaching in an Oneida village, he grew lonely for companionship. He also grew weary of fending for himself. He complained that he was doing his own "housework" and gathering subsistence foods, in addition to his struggles to communicate with young Oneida pupils who could speak neither an Algonquian dialect, such as Fowler's own Montauk, nor English, Fowler's second language. "I find it very hard to live here without the other Rib," he wrote to Wheelock.[15] In desperation, during the fall of his second year among the Oneidas, he made the long trek south to Lebanon, where he courted and married Hannah Garrett, a Pequot student who came from a highly respected family. But the young couple remained at Oneida for only one full winter before settling at Montauk.[16]

In many ways the journeys of the Native scholars to Moor's School and the travels of the Gaelic pupils in the Highlands and Islands to their schools were comparable. Despite the vastly different topography, they shared some similarities. On both sides of the water, the journeys proved challenging. As the young scholars made their way to school or returned home, they struggled across rivers, walked through valleys, gorges, and glens, climbed hills (here the Gaels had the greater challenge), and carried few amenities along the way to ease their journeys.

Upon their arrival at Moor's School, the new scholars often greeted cousins or brothers or sisters whose presence in Lebanon had drawn them there in the first place. The kinship connection at Moor's School followed a common pattern for Indian pupils in colonial America. Once established, this pattern would persist through the long, difficult history of the Indian boarding school experience, whether federal, tribal, or mission school, from the eighteenth century forward.[17]

At Moor's School the role of kinship reflected the strength of Native community life and the interlocking ties that bound members within a single village or beyond the boundaries of villages and bands, where intermarriage and clan connections linked different families and groups. Potential Native pupils, whether Algonquian or Iroquois, who chose to attend Moor's for kinship reasons brought their customary social patterns with them into an institution pledged to replace these patterns. Therefore, the persistence of kinship relations within this colonial English institution suggests that Moor's School could never be totally isolated from the Native cultural influence. It also suggests that this charity school belonged to its Indian students as much as it was shaped by the handful of English charity students like Samuel Kirkland, who would later serve as missionary to the Senecas and Oneidas. Even though the Native scholars, like David Fowler, generally became schoolmasters while the English scholars, like Kirkland, generally became ministers or missionaries, while they attended Moor's School, the Native pupils outnumbered the English. Thus, by their very numbers, they must have set the social tone of the institution.

In order to assess the students' impact on the school's milieu, I would like to explore briefly the general environment at Moor's School. By looking at the daily routine, the curriculum, the relationships among the pupils themselves, plus the connections between students and staff, as well as students and the nearby community, one can catch a glimpse of the dynamics engendered by this unusual eighteenth-century ethnic and cultural mix.

When Indian youth entered Moor's School, they encountered a rigorous level of discipline and punishment. This proved quite foreign to their customary upbringing. Their own communities relied on other proven means to guide the youth to maturity.[18] Native children were always loved, and they seldom received physical punishment. They were taught to endure hardship and suffering without complaint. The school's discipline seemed foreign to their understanding; it was matched by a rigorous course of learning, which focused on religion, European languages, European culture and history, and mathematics. Wheelock designed all of the instruction within the framework of an intensive, highly introspective Reformed Protestant faith. For the Native pupils, this proved the ultimate pressure.[19] Even though many of the Algonquian pupils had been reared in partially Christianized communities, some of them dissolved under the religious pressure of the school's environment.

By necessity, Moor's School was founded as a boarding school. Unlike the Scottish Society's schooling in the Highlands, where the directors expected the schoolmasters to travel some distance to the students' Highland locations, Wheelock expected potential Native American pupils to travel from their villages to his southern Connecticut town. Lebanon boasted no Indian communities in the immediate vicinity, and given eighteenth-century transportation, children simply could not return home at the end of the day. The persistent pressure, day in and day out, allowed for little respite. This contrasts sharply with the Highlands and Islands schooling, where most of the students could return home to their families each evening. There they would find themselves once again in the embrace of their familiar language, and, poverty notwithstanding, they could return to the customary pattern of life followed by families of clansmen and women. In Connecticut, according to the tenets of Wheelock's Great Design, the charity school itself was to serve as a replacement home where Native scholars adapted to English ways. The lingua franca was, of course, English, and the acceptable worldview derived its values from the eighteenth-century New Englanders, largely of English descent. The amenities available for the charity scholars—whether English or Native—included the common beverages of tea and coffee. These were not foreign to the English pupils, but, like the language and the foreign worldview, they helped draw the Native pupils away from their own customs and slowly pulled them further into English colonial ways.

Although the structured daily schedule must have seemed foreign to entering Native pupils, it was commonplace for English schooling of the day. Still, Natives arriving from their villages found it to be an extraordinary change of pace and environment. One of the most overwhelming differences that the young scholars had to adjust to was the necessity of remaining indoors for a good part of each day. In their own communities, they remained outside for most of the day.

The school day began early. For six days of the week the boys—some of whom were young men, like David Fowler, who had entered the school at age twenty-four—remained in class all morning. There they were instructed in the mastery of the languages deemed important in eighteenth-century New England, specifically Latin and Greek, and, occasionally, Hebrew; arithmetic; and the basic tenets of Reformed Protestant theology. After a two-hour break at midday, they returned to the classroom, where they remained until five. In the evening, they were required to engage in their studies until bedtime.

Still, there were exceptions to this pattern. Since the boys were deemed responsible for keeping the school farm in good order, they were expected to attend to specific farm chores, which Wheelock viewed as partial payment for their board and room. In addition, Wheelock promoted the practice of husbandry, viewing it, like blacksmithing, as a skill that might provide jobs for those students who did not become schoolmasters or ministers.[20] But most of the boys viewed farming as simply the repetition of endless chores. In Native societies, farming was "women's work." Whether Algonquian or Iroquois, the women traditionally bore the responsibility for cultivating the family's crops. Of the search for blacksmithing positions for his Indian pupils, Wheelock complained, "I find it difficult to put out the boys, who are designed for blacksmiths, to places suitable for them; and the greatest difficulty is, that their fellow apprentices, viz. English boys, will despise them, and treat them as slaves, which I apprehend will be of hurtful and ruinous consequences to them."[21] The omnipresent instruction of the Reformed Protestant faith, which provided the matrix of learning for both Gaelic and Native scholars in their respective charity schools, created a rather somber tone. As in the Highland schools, Moor's School began each day with the morning prayer and catechism. It closed with the evening prayer and worship. Sundays were set aside for worship.

When Wheelock made the bold decision to include girls in this environment, he assigned them specific roles that reflected his culture, rather than the culture of the Algonquian and Iroquois pupils. In New England, the English colonial perception of women differed from the views on women in other regions, especially in the Carolinas and Georgia. Even in the eighteenth century, these descendants of the English Puritans retained their belief in literacy and extended it, albeit more modestly, to include literacy for women. Hence, the female pupils were deigned the privilege of classroom instruction one day a week, a mere fraction of the boys' six days. On their single day of instruction, the Indian girls learned basic reading and writing skills and how to do sums. Wheelock saw no need to offer them the rigorous academic instruction deemed necessary for the boys; pragmatically, he believed it would prove too expensive for his stringent budget. He defended his position by reasoning that the girls' education was to prepare them "to accompany these Boys, when they shall have Occasion for such Assistance in the Business of their Mission."[22]

Ever concerned about finances, Wheelock scrimped on the girls' accommodations. He lodged them in nearby homes rather than at the school and "hired women in this neighborhood to instruct [them] in all the arts of good House wifery."[23] This domestic instruction for the girls bore a strong resemblance to the boys' training in husbandry or blacksmithing. The local wives and mothers who lodged the girls probably treated them as servants, although one historian has suggested that their treatment may have approximated that of slaves.[24]

The rigorous pace of the week at Moor's School was partially broken by the Sabbath. On Sunday, Wheelock permitted the boys to disregard their complete conjugation of Latin or Greek and the girls to leave behind their household chores. On the Sabbath, attendance at the meetinghouse dominated their schedule. Built in 1743, the year that Occom began his studies with Wheelock, the meetinghouse was situated on the green, at the crossing point of the two main roads. In 1755, after the first two Delaware boys had arrived, the parish voted to "set apart for the boys 'the pew in the gallery over the west stairs'" and, when Wheelock enrolled the first girls, to give the "Indian girls liberty to sit in the hindseat on the women's side below."[25]

During meetings, which were interspersed with catechism classes for both girls and boys, the students took their places in their assigned rows of pews, either separate from or directly behind the English members of the congregation. Despite the seating discrimination, some of the pupils chose to become members of the church.[26]

Given the pervasive prejudice against the Indian youth as well as the unaccustomed punishment meted out to them, plus the Calvinist intensity that pervaded the instruction, one could scarcely describe Moor's School as an idyllic world. The tensions revealing the cracks in the institution's façade were complex. Although it might appear that cultural divisions drove the primary wedge between Indian and English, in reality, race and ethnic issues also tore at the deceptive calm. The students devised their own methods for addressing these issues, as the following story illustrates.

On a September day in 1765, seventeen-year-old English student David M'Clure reported, "When the sun was about two hours high" several students were "standing near the woodpile" when John Wheelock, Eleazar Wheelock's eleven-year-old son by his second marriage, challenged William, a mixed-blood, freckle-faced Mohawk who was probably between eleven and thirteen, to fight Joseph Johnson, a Mohegan, who was fourteen. John Wheelock instigated the fight by calling William a "speckle face white eye," and when Johnson repeated the taunt, the fight was on.

"Both boys strip of their waistcoats, prepare for an incounter, and in the meantime the most of the school boys were greather'd around. When Johnson called William a son of a Bitch, and I think, Indian Devil, at last they came to blows." They continued "domineering over each other until sundown"; then the fight spread among the other students, until, "finally, one nation seemed to be at variance with another." Only when M'Clure intervened by threatening that the students would be sent home or "be whipt when Mr Wheelock comes home" did peace return.[27]

M'Clure signed the letter he wrote to Wheelock—with the flourish common to the literate, mid-eighteenth-century colonials—as "Promoter of Piece Tranquility & Good order. Animus Quietus. D.M.C." He did not find it necessary to explain the underlying causes for the "incounter" because everyone at the school, including Wheelock himself, already knew.

The most obvious source of the fight was the issue of prejudice toward the school's mixed-blood scholars, as expressed by the taunts issued by Wheelock's son and the Mohegan lad Johnson. Everyone within the school environment knew that William, the maligned Mohawk, was a son of William Johnson, the Irish-born superintendent of Indian Affairs for the Northern District. Everyone also knew that his mother was probably Molly Brant, the strong-willed sister of Joseph Brant, who had been an earlier pupil at Moor's School, and if not Molly, then certainly another Mohawk woman.[28] Hence, the accusations of "speckle face white eye" and "son of a bitch." To add fuel to the flame, according to Eleazar Wheelock, William had become troublesome because of "his Pride and the Violence of his Temper [which] rendered him troublesome and obliged me to be severe with him."[29]

Wheelock's attempt to understand Indians was often colored by his chastising of what he perceived as his pupils' "Indian Pride." When the young scholars demonstrated any spirit of independence, he resorted to this single, pejorative term to denigrate their sense of self worth.[30] However revealing Wheelock's response might have been, it remains less important than the fight itself. The fight has survived as one of the few recorded instances when the internal conflict that lay beneath the surface at the school emerged, belying the often wordless tension that could never be recorded. And even this graphic fistfight would have been lost if Wheelock had not been away from Lebanon and M'Clure had not taken it upon himself to tattle.

Reformed Protestantism and Moor's School Scholars

Although M'Clure later carved out a career for himself in the ministry and coauthored the earliest biography of Wheelock, he was scarcely as famous as the first of Moor's School's English charity pupils, Samuel Kirkland. Kirkland shared both bitter conflicts and friendship with the Indian students, whether at the school itself or in the Iroquois villages during Wheelock's 1760s experiment of sending the students to New York to teach Iroquois children.

Kirkland was of Scottish ancestry, although his father had graduated from Yale and become a Congregational minister. By contrast, Kirkland completed his theological training at the College of New Jersey, an institution founded by Presbyterians during the Great Awakening. Afterward, he returned to Lebanon in 1766, where he was ordained as a Presbyterian minister. Like Samson Occom, Kirkland began his studies under Congregational auspices, but he shifted to the Scottish denomination that reflected the faith of his ancestors. By 1770 Kirkland had split with his former mentor over financial matters and personal issues, but his commitment to the Oneidas as a Presbyterian missionary and educator convinced the SSPCK directors that they should fund his work. Clearly eighteenth-century politics were enmeshed with philanthropic funding, a not-uncommon pairing.[31]

By the time of the Battle of Bunker Hill in 1775, Kirkland's following among the Oneidas persuaded this Iroquois nation to ally themselves—following Kirkland's urgent plea—with the American rebels. The Oneida decision would wreak havoc within the Hodenosaunee during the war, pitting Oneidas, allied with the Americans, against the Mohawks and other Iroquois nations, allied with the British, a split that emerged dramatically in the Battle of Oriskany in 1777. The stance of Kirkland and the Oneidas had even further implications. It thrust two former pupils from Moor's School—Kirkland and Joseph Brant—against each other. The Mohawk leader Thayendanegea, better known as Joseph Brant, would eventually become the most powerful Native ally of the British. After the American victory in 1783, he would lead his people north to a grant of land that the British set aside for the Iroquois in Ontario—the Grand River Reserve—beyond the new borders of the United States.[32]

Oddly, while Brant and Kirkland were enemies during the war, in earlier times they had been linked by their mutual connection with the SSPCK. Brant's enrollment at Moor's School depended directly on the largesse of the Scottish Society. In 1761 two of the society's colonial boards of correspondence offered to fund an Iroquois recruiting trip for the school. Under the proposal, Occom and his brother-in-law, David Fowler, traveled to the Six Nations in search of "a Number of Indian Boys, not exceeding three, to be put under Mr. Wheelock's Care and Instruction."[33]

One of the "Indian boys" they recruited within the Mohawk Nation was Joseph Brant. As Molly Brant's brother and brother-in-law of William Johnson, the canny trader to the Mohawks, the young Brant had already gained experience in multicultural diplomacy. His brother-in-law had hosted many a negotiation between Iroquois nations and

Joseph Brant (Thayendanegea), Mohawk leader. The brother-in-law of Sir William Johnson, Brant attended Moor's School. Later he led the Iroquois when they sided with the British during the American War for Independence. After the war he moved to the Grand River Reserve for the Six Nations (Iroquois) in Ontario. Painting by William Berczy.
Courtesy the National Gallery of Canada.

government leaders of New York and other land-hungry colonies. Brant had also absorbed the Anglican religious faith that Johnson, an Anglo-Irishman, reflected.[34] During Brant's two years at the Indian charity school, he could not have avoided absorbing some of the Reformed Protestant faith, but he remained true to the earlier teachings. Regardless of their faith background, all pupils were instructed in the Congregational view of the world. Later, this brokerage would serve Brant in good stead when former school friends became enemies.

At Moor's School, Brant's Anglican background provoked further tension because of the denominational differences. After the American Revolution, when Brant and other Iroquois loyalists settled in Ontario, he strengthened the Anglican position among the Mohawks.[35] The experiences of Brant and, indeed, his nephew William illustrate how the multiple levels of conflict at Moor's School—race, ethnicity, religious faith, and the many kinds of prejudice—led to misunderstandings that the pupils would carry back to their home communities after they left Lebanon.

Since Congregationalism lay at the heart of the charity school's message, the pupils quickly learned that it would dominate their lives as long as they remained there. For Wheelock, the Great Awakening with its strong emphasis on the conversion experience had been a pivotal moment in his life. As an "enthusiastic" preacher, Wheelock had been "indefatigable, dogmatically sure of his beliefs, [and] self-sacrificing in his zeal." As director of the school, he transferred this zealous passion to the religious training of the pupils.[36] Unlike their young counterparts in Scottish Society schools in the Highlands and Islands, the Moor's School pupils experienced no release from the constant pressure to conform to Reformed Protestantism. Neither their evenings nor their weekends offered any relief from the all-pervasive worldview of the eighteenth-century evangelical mindset.

Rebellion among the pupils emerged in different forms. The famous fight between Joseph Johnson and William Johnson was one expression of frustration. Leaving school and returning home was another. Still other students found release in "frolicks" and bouts of heavy drinking. After these excesses, they generally expressed repentance through written apologies to Wheelock. A Mohegan pupil even wrote an apology on the day of her arrival, confessing, "I Hannah Nonesuch do with shamefacedness acknowledge that on the evening of the 8th Inst I was . . . guilty of being at the tavern and tarrying there . . . for a frolick . . . I am heartily sorry & desire to lie low in the dust and do now beg Forgiveness."[37]

Still other students later wrote bitter letters to Wheelock. While he was a scholar at Moor's School, Narragansett Daniel Simon, who later became a missionary to Algonquian groups after his graduation from Dartmouth College, complained to Wheelock about the ever-present farm chores that served as partial payment for room and board: "if the doctor will let me follow my studys I shall be thinkful . . . if we poor Indians shall work as much to pay for our learning . . . I say now wo unto that poor Indian or white man that should ever come to this school, without he is rich."[38]

The underlying tensions that gnawed at the common fabric of Moor's Indian Charity School did not appear to discourage Wheelock, at least during the initial years. In the early 1760s, after his institution had been in place for almost a decade, he was still sufficiently sanguine about the school's progress to embark on further ambitious educational dreams that would involve the Scottish Society even more directly.

The SSPCK and the Connecticut Board of Correspondents

All of the threads that formed the fabric of Wheelock's Great Design came together during his prolonged campaign to transfer Moor's School from Algonquian country in Connecticut to the Iroquois nations that stretched west from the Hudson River to the Genesee River, south of Lake Ontario. Although Wheelock's plan stumbled over barriers that would have confounded a less-determined protagonist, his persistence brought the dream to fruition, albeit in a form somewhat different from what he had envisioned. Throughout the struggle, Wheelock remained a pragmatist; he was constantly aware of the need to revise his plan. In this instance, the necessity for revision compromised both his initial ideal and those of some of his key allies.

Spurred by the two-decade-old relationship between Occom and Wheelock, the proposed move relied on Occom's willingness to serve as liaison between two Iroquois nations—the Mohawks and the Oneidas—and the Indian charity school. During the early 1760s, despite the ongoing Seven Years' War, Wheelock's two ambassadors to the Iroquois—Occom and David Fowler—had persuaded both the Mohawks and the Oneidas to send a number of their youth southeast to Lebanon to be schooled.

The motivation for sending Occom to Iroquoia was not confined to recruitment of new students. The Scottish Society's New York Board of Correspondents also urged Occom—with a greater abundance of words than financial aid—to respond to the Oneida's request for a missionary. During the summers of 1761 to 1763, Occom traveled to the Oneida Nation villages as a potential missionary. But he received a mixed response to his overtures.[39]

During the winter following their first trip north, Occom and Fowler both became fluent in the Oneida tongue, aided by the guidance of an Oneida who had returned with them. Although the mastery of the new language suggests Occom's optimism about a proposed missionary assignment, that same fall (1761) he was also much discouraged by the return of his rheumatism from "lying on the wet ground" during the nine-week sojourn to the north. The visits of the second and third summers were brief, especially in the summer of 1763, when the threat of Pontiac's rebellion sent Occom home and cancelled all missionaries' ventures among the Iroquois.[40]

During this impasse in Occom's career, Wheelock began to take further steps to ensure the success of his own goal. Occom and David Fowler—both supported by the SSPCK—had provided crucial aid in expanding the enrollment of Iroquois pupils, but Wheelock still planned to establish the firm presence of Reformed Protestantism directly in Iroquois country itself, and by the end of 1763, it became clear to him that Occom had pulled back from living in the north. Hence, by 1764 Wheelock resolved to send a number of his students—both Native and English—to serve as schoolmasters and missionaries among the Iroquois. If he could not move the school to the Iroquois, he could at least move some of his pupils there. And they would serve as his educational entrée to the Hodenosaunee.

At the same time, Wheelock achieved a tour de force that linked him directly to the Scottish Society and gave his school the firm stamp of legitimacy that he had been unable to achieve during its first decade. Seeking his own regional board of correspondents for the society, he had applied to the society directors in Edinburgh in 1762 and 1763, but he had to wait until June 1764 for the SSPCK's approval.[41] Almost ten years after the first Delaware students arrived, he finally gained recognition from a powerful overseas funding agency. His new link with the Scottish Society promised a degree of stature and independence and some freedom from the need to rely on irregular regional funding from willful groups such as the New England Company, which tended to find numerous faults with Wheelock's enterprise.

Initially, the society played into Wheelock's hands. Responding favorably to his suggestions, it approved of Wheelock's nominations for the board, which consisted largely of his personal cadre of friends and colleagues in the ministry. On July 4 of that year, the members of the board held their first meeting. Through this means—the Connecticut Board of Correspondents—the newly formed board of trustees for Moor's School had sprung to life. Its life span would parallel that of the school. Wheelock relied on his dual-purpose board as a viable entity as long as the school remained in Lebanon. When he moved the school to New Hampshire in 1769, where it was eventually subsumed by Dartmouth College and began to rely on funds procured in England and Wales and, to a lesser degree, in Scotland, the Connecticut Board of Correspondents lost its raison d'être.[42]

While Wheelock schemed, Occom—still based at Montauk—searched for a stronger base of financial support for his growing family. Since his ordination in 1759, his options had seemed to broaden, but none of the prospects, including the position of serving as a missionary to the Oneidas, had proved feasible. Early in 1764 Occom received a promising offer from the Boston commissioners for the New England Company, the group that had provided a minimal stipend for him at Montauk. The offer, to serve as a missionary to the Niantic Nation of southern Connecticut, appeared to resolve the Occom family's financial woes. It promised a salary of £30 a year, roughly double what he was being paid at Montauk.[43] Accepting the offer, Samson and Mary Occom left Montauk with their six children and moved into the house that Occom had been building on his lands at Mohegan. At last he could come home.

At this fateful juncture in Occom's life, Wheelock intervened. Flexing the muscles of his newly formed Connecticut Board of Correspondents, he persuaded the Boston commissioners to release Occom from his Niantic obligation by promising them that the Connecticut board would send Occom back to the Iroquois. This scheme, while plausible from Wheelock's perspective, had two flaws. First, it discredited Occom's independent decision to accept the Niantic position, and, second, it did not provide any assurance that George Whitefield—the assumed source of funding for Occom's service in missionary work among the Iroquois—would concur with the plan. In this regard, Wheelock had put forth Whitefield as security for his promise, but he had failed to alert Whitefield himself.

The Connecticut board sent a hesitant Occom, accompanied once again by David Fowler, to New York, where they were instructed to secure Whitefield's agreement to fund the new missionary attempt. As Occom had feared, Whitefield not only balked; he was incensed at Wheelock's lack of foresight. After their rejection by the normally generous Whitefield, Occom and Fowler rode back to Connecticut empty-handed.⁴⁴ Fowler returned to his studies at Moor's School, where he remained until the following spring, when he left for his schoolmaster position with the Oneidas. Occom returned to his family and their partially constructed house at Mohegan.

The net result of Wheelock's scheming scarcely benefited Occom. He had left his old position at Montauk, been forced to forego his new position among the Niantic, and been rejected for the position at Oneida. Although he had the good fortune to be back at Mohegan, his house was only half built, and its completion depended upon Wheelock's promise to finance the rest. Occom had no job, and he had no prospects of immediate future employment.

Moor's School Students among the Iroquois

The bleakness facing Occom was magnified among his fellow Algonquians whom Wheelock had sent to teach amidst the Iroquois. Despite his setback, Occom was able to remain among a people who spoke his own language and shared some of his Algonquian worldviews. When Wheelock began to craft the Iroquois plan, he did not even consider the language and cultural barriers that his Algonquian students might face in the villages of the Iroquois nations. He continued to espouse the superiority of Native missionaries and schoolmasters serving among other Indians because he had never actually known Native people in their home environment. Despite his years of directing an Indian charity school, he never seemed to comprehend the variety of the cultures of his Native students.

Pleased with his accomplishments in Lebanon, Wheelock began to dream about expanding his schooling enterprise among the Iroquois. Convinced that he could shift Moor's School from Connecticut to New York, he believed he could establish his own charity boarding school among the Hodenosaunee. Rather quickly, however, this idea stumbled against a formidable barrier in the person of William Johnson. If Wheelock saw himself as a figure of power vis-à-vis his connections with the southern New England Algonquians and the nearby Delawares, the authority of his voice among the Algonquians was decidedly weak when compared with the power that Johnson wielded in his relations with the League of the Iroquois and especially his neighbors, the Mohawks. A shrewd trader and businessman, by the 1760s Johnson had lived among the Mohawk for about three decades. Further enhancing this connection, from the late 1750s until his death in 1774, he had shared his household with Molly Brant, who bore his children and served as "housekeeper and hostess" at Johnson Hall, where she was "a strong influence in Indian affairs."[45] Wheelock's relationship with the Algonquians bore absolutely no resemblance to Johnson's situation. Wheelock had not lived within an Indian community; he had never married an Algonquian woman; nor is there any evidence that he had learned any Iroquois or Algonquian languages.

Above all, however, Wheelock remained a pragmatist. When it became clear to him that the Iroquois boarding school of his dreams had vaporized, he chose another route to the Hodenosaunee, one that would extend his influence by way of day schools staffed by his own students and Reformed Protestant missionary ventures, also led by his own pupils. Almost all of those whom he would send north had already come under his supervision in Lebanon. The SSPCK's Connecticut board immediately gave their approval to the new plan.

In the spring of 1765 the society's Connecticut board examined and approved the first large group of candidates who were to serve as reinforcements to those sent in the previous fall. The event was reminiscent of the Scottish Society's examiners questioning their first applicants in Edinburgh for the position of schoolmaster in the Highlands and Islands. In Lebanon, Connecticut, those chosen for the journey included two English missionaries, who were ordained before their departure; three Algonquian schoolmasters, including David Fowler; and five "ushers," or assistant schoolmasters, who were younger and less experienced. Four of the ushers were Mohawk, and the fifth was Jacob Fowler, David's brother.[46]

Within a few years, the Connecticut board had sent more than twenty missionaries, schoolmasters, and ushers into Iroquois country. All but one of them had trained at Moor's School. Of the nine English missionaries, eight had studied with Wheelock. Of the roughly thirteen schoolmasters and ushers, over half were from Algonquian villages, and four or five came from Iroquois villages.[47]

In 1764 and 1765, at the beginning of this audacious plan, Wheelock and his Connecticut board had high expectations for their educational-missionary extension into Iroquois country. But reality struck all too quickly. The Algonquian schoolmasters and ushers were the first to admit to defeat. Within a short time they learned of the difficulties of adapting to life among these northern people. The English missionaries were next. Only Samuel Kirkland remained more than a few years, and he was unique. He adapted far better than any of the other missionaries and spent the remainder of his life among the Oneidas. He even outlasted all the Algonquians. Unlike the others, the Iroquois students who were assigned as ushers found themselves returning home, and they saw no need to leave their homelands. Only one of them remained in teaching, but others became interpreters.[48]

Like their mentor, Eleazar Wheelock, the Algonquian students who became schoolmasters or ushers could never have imagined how extensively their lives in southern New England differed from those who lived within the villages that formed the League of the Iroquois. Even though the Algonquians were Native Americans, the shock they received upon their arrival in Oneida or Mohawk villages could easily have paralleled that of the early Lowland schoolmasters arriving on the Isle of Harris or the Strath of Kildonan or Fort Augustus. For the Algonquians, the villages of the Iroquois were literally a foreign country; for the Lowlanders, the scattered communities in the Highlands and Islands seemed equally foreign. A kaleidoscope of impressions must have whirled through their senses during those first days at their new schools—the inability to communicate, especially for the Algonquian schoolmasters; the widespread poverty and meager diet; the almost exclusively oral culture; the different forms of religious expression; the overwhelming sense of isolation; and, finally, an awareness of the strong sense of kinship and community among those whom they came to teach. Taken together, this meant that those who lived in one of the Iroquois nations were insiders; those who came to teach—Native or English—were outsiders.

Reared in their home villages in southern New England, Long Island, or New Jersey, the Algonquian pupils had already made a tremendous leap when they journeyed from their communities to Moor's School. But once they were settled in at the school, they remained sequestered within its closed environment, except when they visited their families or sought release in nearby taverns. And once again, they had managed to adapt to the school's conditions. The three-hundred-mile journey to the Iroquois villages, which transported them into another, far more powerful culture made the earlier journey to Moor's School a more modest adventure than it had once appeared.

Here in this new culture they were distinctly out of their element. When they spoke, whether in an Algonquian dialect or in English, no one in the village understood them. When they faced their Mohawk or Oneida pupils, no one comprehended their words. Even though they were already bilingual in Algonquian and English, and some of them were literate in Latin, Greek, and even some Hebrew, no one had given any thought to their need to learn another Native American language such as Iroquois. Delaware schoolmaster Hezekiah Calvin, who was

Iroquois and southern New England Algonquians in the eighteenth century.

From Margaret Connell Szasz, *Indian Education in the American Colonies, 1607–1783* (University of New Mexico Press, 1998; repr., University of Nebraska Press, 2007).

not yet twenty when he stood in front of a group of Mohawk children for the first time, articulated the frustration shared by his peers when he wrote to Wheelock that he felt "as a dumb stump that has no tongue to use."[49]

Provisions were another matter. The Algonquians had completed, often grudgingly, the farm chores at Moor's School, but none of them, with the exception of David and Jacob Fowler, had developed any interest in husbandry. As was customary among the Iroquois, Algonquian women had always tended the sacred trilogy of corn, beans, and squash; Iroquois men had generally contributed to farming by preparing the soil in the spring, but their responsibilities ended there. Their milieu was the forest and the warpath. When English husbandmen observed the Iroquois, especially when the Natives faced starving times during the drought of the late 1760s, the English concluded that their farming techniques were superior. Even Wheelock's English farmers, who supervised the crops grown at Moor's School, had reflected this attitude of superiority when they directed the Algonquian male students doing their chores in the fields. Among the Indian schoolmasters, only David Fowler attempted to teach English-style farming methods to the Iroquois. Planning a journey to Lebanon in the spring of 1766, he wrote to Wheelock that he could not travel until he had planted, "so that I may be able to tell my [Oneida] Children how they must manage the Garden in my Absence."[50] But Fowler's tenure among the Oneidas was cut short before he could have any extended effect on their lives.

Until they began living among the Iroquois, the Algonquians had also remained unaware of how accustomed they had become to the basic necessities—clothing, food, and drink—plus the other conveniences supplied for them at Moor's School. Wheelock had also provided amenities that they had taken for granted after extended stays at the school—coffee and tea, clean linen shirts, plus breeches and stockings. But those amenities that had become so familiar to the Algonquian students had not yet become common in the Iroquois villages. At the end of their three-hundred-mile journey to Iroquois country, the Indian schoolmasters found none of those amenities. In the 1760s deprivation formed the common fare of all.

Earlier, when Samuel Kirkland had been a missionary for eighteen months among the Senecas, he had "lived almost wholly upon Indian fare." While he resided there, his diet was "Sometimes nothing but a roasted Squash or a little bullet Corn for Breakfast and Supper." Later, at the Seneca's "fishing quarters," he had "lived and fared as they did" and "had no Flesh nor Bread for six weeks save once." Following his ordination, Kirkland had shifted his missionary work to the Oneidas, whose homelands were not as remote as the Senecas'. At Oneida, the rigor of his earlier experiences shaped his attitude toward his former fellow students. He had little sympathy for the Algonquian schoolmasters, who "would often murmur at their Hard Quarters." Kirkland chided them as well for not living like Indians. He wrote to a Delaware schoolmaster who had inquired about tea and coffee, "I should advise you to make use of those teas which nature had provided us in the wilderness such as pine buds, sassafras blows & the bark of the root spice wood." Not content with this degree of irony, he even suggested that the young Delaware adopt Indian attire, adding, "It will be no disgrace to your characters and colour."[51]

For the transplanted students from Moor's School, Iroquois country lay far away from what they had come to perceive as "civilization." The schoolmasters' frustration with the language barrier and the absence of what they felt were basic necessities, as well as the luxuries they had adopted at school, were compounded by their religious sensibilities. Their own spiritual training, whether in the Christianized Algonquian communities or at Moor's School, spoke all too clearly when they described their young charges as "pagans." For Hezekiah Calvin, who lived among the Mohawks for two winters, returning to his familiar, Christianized Delaware surroundings under the tutelage of John Brainerd came as a relief. Of his Iroquois hosts, he wrote, "I should be very glad to see my Brethren [the Mohawk] become christians and live like Christians."[52]

Yet the Mohawks had not been ignored by Christian missionaries. In this context, the Algonquian schoolmasters' views of Mohawk religion resembled the Lowland schoolmasters' views of Scottish Highlanders' religion—both people were chastised for believing in the wrong kind of Christianity (Anglican for the Mohawks, Episcopalian or Catholic for the Highlanders). Moreover, they were also criticized for retaining residual strains of Native or pre-Christian belief and ceremony.

Surely the Iroquois' feelings for the schoolmasters must have been as mixed as the schoolmasters' assessments of their hosts. When Calvin demonstrated little remorse at leaving his Mohawk pupils, they may well have shared his sentiment. One missionary wrote of Calvin's leaving that the Mohawk "did not seem to lament his departure."[53] The ignorance of Wheelock, who had only a minimal knowledge of the historic imbalance between the weak southern New England Algonquians and the powerful Iroquois, was partly responsible for the boldness of this scheme to place Algonquian schoolmasters within Iroquois villages. It is highly likely, however, that one of the reasons why the schoolmasters found it impossible to remain was rooted in this historic imbalance. The dominant Iroquois League had played a significant role through much of the seventeenth and eighteenth centuries. Both in its size and its ability to negotiate power, the league carried much more weight than the smaller Algonquian nations, most of whom had been subdued during the previous century. The irony of schoolmasters traveling from these much-weakened Native nations to teach the children of the Hodenosaunee was probably not lost on the Iroquois leaders.[54]

But the schoolmaster experiment retained some exceptions. David Fowler, for example, expressed considerable pride in his "singing evenings" with his Oneida pupils. He also progressed in his efforts to learn their language and persevered in his attempts to teach them English-style husbandry. It is likely that had he not been angered by the arrogant behavior of fellow Moor's School student Samuel Kirkland during the second winter there he might have remained to see further progress in his pupils' learning.[55] But Fowler remained the exception. By 1769 the Connecticut Board of Correspondents was no longer sending any new schoolmasters to the Iroquois villages. By 1772, with the exception of the ushers who were themselves Iroquois, only Samuel Kirkland remained in Oneida. Unfortunately, he had already distanced himself from Wheelock.

The Scottish Society's Role among Algonquians and Iroquois

The Scottish Society's educational investment in Native North America differed, of course, from its sustained educational efforts in the Highlands and Islands. Although a number of conditions highlighted the contrast, the vast expanse of the Atlantic was the most formidable. The body of water that separated Scotland from North America prevented the SSPCK directors from exerting any measure of tight control over the colonial boards of correspondence, let alone over the schooling ventures themselves. They could have no immediate supervision over the forays of Wheelock's students among the Iroquois youth.

In southern New England, the society entered a competitive field already dominated by the Congregationalists. The ensuing interdenominational cooperation between the two strands of Reformed Protestantism—Congregational and Presbyterian—called forth a spirit of unity that persisted well into the nineteenth century. For Lowland Presbyterians, accustomed to a secure position as the dominant faith for much of Scotland's population, the cloak of ecumenicalism that they donned in southern New England and surrounding colonies required some adjustment. It was an unaccustomed garment for the proud members of the Church of Scotland.

Yet pragmatic adjustment remained essential. The society became a competitive player in this region only because its directors were willing to alter the rules that they had so readily applied to the Highlands. If the SSPCK expected to extend its message of English literacy and Reformed Protestant faith among Native Americans, the directors reasoned that they would have to loosen their reins of power. A strong measure of control, they discovered, proved impossible to maintain on the western shores of the Atlantic. Hence, the society directors acknowledged obvious limitations. They could not select the schoolmasters for Algonquian or Iroquois schools; nor could they dictate the schoolmasters' qualifications. They officially retained the power to approve—or disapprove—petitions from the colonial boards of correspondence, as in the case of the Connecticut board. But in reality, they granted the selection of the board members to the colonial figure who provided the primary impetus for that body—Eleazar Wheelock.

The society's cooperation extended to ministers of both Congregational and Presbyterian denominations. Still, it is likely that society members were surely pleased to learn that Samson Occom and, later, Samuel Kirkland had been ordained as Presbyterian ministers, especially since they had been initially tutored by the Congregational minister Wheelock. But the society also worked directly with Wheelock himself and, peripherally, with the Anglican George Whitefield. The Great Awakening in this instance provided commonality rather than dissonance. But the ecumenicalism of the society directors was frequently stretched as they negotiated schooling ventures for Algonquian and Iroquois youth. By contrast, their ready support for David Brainerd and his brother, John, and, later, for Kirkland proved less taxing because the Brainerds and Kirkland, like the society members, were Presbyterians.

Most of the Algonquian and Iroquois youth who had been sent to the Iroquois villages were less directly affected by the Scottish Society. In two Native communities—the Delawares of New Jersey and the Oneida Nation—the entire community came under the tutelage of the Presbyterian ministry. Both David and John Brainerd taught the faith of the Scottish Lowlanders among the Delawares, and Samuel Kirkland taught the theology he had learned at the College of New Jersey— probably mixed with some of the Congregational lessons of Moor's School—when he was among the Senecas for a brief time and, later, in his permanent position among the Oneidas. Samson Occom ministered to the Montauk community as a Presbyterian clergyman, despite his initial training by a Congregational minister.

Beyond these figures, however, the Native students at Moor's School, especially the Iroquois students, were probably unaware of the role of the SSPCK in their lives. The Moor's School students sent to the Iroquois nations knew they had to be approved by the Connecticut board, but they might not have been cognizant of this board's source of funding or of the importance of the society's approval that had initially brought it into existence.

In most of these interactions between the SSPCK and Native Americans, the society retained a degree of anonymity that belied its powerful presence in the Gaelic Highlands. Yet the society proved integral to a number of schooling ventures among Native youth in the northern colonies. It also gave direct financial support to Presbyterian missionaries and educators based among Native groups in both northern and southern colonies. Still, the physical distance from North America, compounded by the religious diversity within the colonies, limited the scope of its power and assured a relatively low profile for a powerful organization long accustomed to the limelight. Perhaps the highest profile that the society attained in the field of Native American education during the colonial era came about because of yet another schooling scheme devised by Eleazar Wheelock. The issues involved in this story will be addressed in the next chapter.

CHAPTER SEVEN

Dugald Buchanan and Samson Occom

During the seventeenth and eighteenth centuries, the vast expanse of water that separated Turtle Island, or North America, from Scotland was, in many respects, an invincible frontier dividing the Native peoples of North America from the Gaels of the Highlands. Like the Highland Line that separated Highlanders from Lowlanders, the Atlantic Ocean seemed to form a permanent barrier. But occasionally Natives could breach that barrier. Those few Natives who made the journey, however—including Pocahontas (Matoaka) of the Powhatans and Tomochichi, the Muskogee leader who greeted the Wesley brothers and Benjamin Ingham—remained in England during their visits. Pocahontas lived through the shock of a single winter in London. Just as her return voyage set sail, she died at a location downriver from the city, near the mouth of the Thames. She was buried at Gravesend. Like the thousands of Indian youth attending boarding schools in later centuries, Pocahontas failed to physically master the overwhelming strangeness of a foreign world that was compounded by the climate of London.

Within the multiple perspectives of the northern colonial schoolmasters and missionaries—whether Algonquian, Iroquois, or English/Scottish by heritage—the notion of traveling to Scotland remained beyond their ken. The missionaries associated the SSPCK with Scotland, but, in reality, they grounded that link in one fundamental need—increased funding for Native schooling. For the Algonquian students and schoolmasters, proximity to homes and villages superseded all other values. They were decidedly uncomfortable in the midst of foreign cultures. This attachment to homeland and community precipitated the return flight of the Algonquian young men who taught or assisted briefly in the schools among the Oneidas and Mohawks. Although overlapping considerations hastened their departure—the Iroquois language, the foreign culture, and the lack of amenities—the three hundred miles or more separating them from their people proved the last straw. By contrast, the Iroquois ushers or assistant schoolmasters who traveled north saw no need to return to the foreign country of the Algonquians when they could remain in their homeland.

The Natives' enduring attachment to land and kinship network eluded the students' mentor, Eleazar Wheelock. Still, Wheelock might have gained some understanding of their needs had he pondered how little he himself had traveled in Indian Country. During all of the negotiations with William Johnson, Wheelock never saw the Mohawk lands; he also failed to visit John Brainerd and the Delaware community in New Jersey, despite the generosity the Lenni Lenapes displayed in sending their youth to Moor's School. Nor did Wheelock plan a trip to Scotland, where he might have spoken face-to-face with the society directors. He remained in New England, always too committed to fund-raising and administration. Still, he was not alone in his colonial provinciality. Like Wheelock, none of the Congregational or Presbyterian missionaries within the Reformed Protestant network during this era crossed the water to visit Scotland, with the exception of Samson Occom. Despite their indebtedness to the SSPCK, the Presbyterian ministers and educators John Brainerd and Samuel Kirkland had too little income to consider the voyage; they communicated with the society either through direct correspondence or, indirectly, through the colonies' regional boards of correspondence.

Like their colonial counterparts, the Scots demonstrated little interest in sailing across the Atlantic. Despite their eagerness to expand the mission of the SSPCK to Native North America, concern over the society's finances persuaded them to rely on writing letters. Given that the society directors failed to visit the SSPCK schools in the nearby Highlands, one could hardly expect them to set aside the many weeks necessary for an Atlantic crossing. They also probably weighed the dangers of the voyage. On both sides of the water, then, the expense, the time, and the risks of transatlantic crossings seemed to militate against their benefits.

Only George Whitefield and Samson Occom would break the mold. They alone engaged the risks of Atlantic travel and moved beyond the customary caution reflected among other religious figures of this era who negotiated the cultural borders. But the famed Anglican evangelist, who seemed at home on both sides of the Atlantic, was in a category by himself. As for Samson Occom, when he agreed to make such a voyage, he could scarcely have anticipated its consequences.

Occom's journey would prove an extraordinary event that altered the lives of the key figures in this story and led to unforeseen results within northeast Native America as well as in Scotland.

The Common Worlds of Mohegans and Gaels

Despite the distance separating Native Americans from Gaelic Highlanders during the mid-eighteenth century, a number of connections linked these seemingly disparate people. Earlier chapters have described the pre-eighteenth-century commonalities between Native North Americans and Gaels; this chapter will look at the eighteenth-century connections that the Scottish Society forged through its role in Reformed Protestant schooling. It will also contrast the distinctive cultural backgrounds of Native American and Gaelic people through the lives of two towering eighteenth-century brokers—Samson Occom and Dugald Buchanan. Further, it will explore how their particular positions within their indigenous cultures helped shape their respective relationships with the Scottish Society.

In its dealings with these two men, the Scottish Society might have viewed Occom and Buchanan as symbols of their cultures, but in reality they did not necessarily represent their indigenous societies. If one were to place Occom and Buchanan on a spectrum ranging from conservative to liberal or progressive, they would clearly fall into the liberal camp. By "liberal," I mean a member of a society who remains open to outside ideas and is willing to add foreign worldviews to those already held by the community. A "conservative" represents the opposite position—a person adamant about retaining the worldviews and customs that have been held for many generations. The conservative remains indifferent or is outright hostile to outside ideas. On this spectrum, a "truly representative figure" would fall somewhere between the two extremes. Neither Occom nor Buchanan could have been perceived as representative because each had welded a strong alliance with Reformed Protestantism and thus had made a commitment to the outsiders' faith.[1]

Even though Occom and Buchanan were not representative members of their societies, they still reflect the conflicts common among cultures that lie in the path of expanding powers. In both the Scottish Highlands and New England, their people confronted an unrelenting colonialism that threatened their existence as unique entities. Outside pressures on these indigenous people exacted a daily toll in their lives. The southern New England Algonquians and the Gaelic Highlanders were, perforce, in a constant state of flux. Forced on the defensive, they tried numerous tactics, from modifying their economic base to carving out a syncretic religious faith, from communicating in their indigenous languages to retaining portions of their oral literature and history. But the greatest challenge for these two brokers lay in forging a consensus that would enable their societies to respond to the unrelenting foreign pressure. In this context, cultural intermediaries helped to determine which aspects of the outside cultures would benefit the people. As spiritual and educational leaders within their communities and liaisons to the foreign worlds that lay outside, Occom and Buchanan negotiated paths that would allow for the preservation of some older beliefs and customs, especially language, song, and story, while supplanting traditional spiritual practices with the teachings of Reformed Protestantism. By taking a firm stand, they often thrust themselves into untenable positions. Their actions were almost guaranteed to please some of their people and elicit fierce opposition from others. Theirs was not an easy choice. But the conviction of their chosen faith suffused them with an unwavering commitment to follow the paths that beckoned.

Occom and Buchanan epitomized the goals of the Scottish Society. As schooled indigenous leaders who accepted the Presbyterian faith and promoted its implicit message of literacy, they represented the inclusive transformation that the society desired. The SSPCK intended to create Christians rather than schooled indigenous people who could read. Simultaneously, Occom and Buchanan reshaped the SSPCK goals to accommodate their own societies' values. Unwilling to discard indigenous customs in their entirety, they retained the need for community and kinship and the accompanying sense of responsibility to the people; they chose to speak in their Native languages; and they truly loved their songs and stories, augmented by those emanating from Christian traditions. Despite the degree of transformation that they experienced, they remained committed members of their indigenous societies. The individualism that often accompanied Reformed Calvinism was not their style. Still, they were undeniably changed, and in order to understand the breadth of that change, we must take a look at their lives writ large.

Dugald Buchanan: The Remolding of a Highlander

Dugald Buchanan was born in 1716, on the ancestral lands of the Buchanan clan in the region known as the braes of Balquhidder.[2] These lands lay along the northeast shore of Loch Lomond, extending farther east for about twenty-five miles under the shadow of Ben Lomond. The Buchanan clan had held its lands in the southern Highlands since at least the thirteenth century, but when compared with the holdings of their neighbors, such as the Campbells or Macleans, the lands claimed by the Buchanans proved quite modest.[3] From the late sixteenth century, as the Highlanders chafed under the tight control exerted by James VI and I, the larger clans, and especially the Campbells, acquired additional title to the lands of less powerful clans. Consequently, they squeezed out the smaller clans like the MacGregors, some of whose lands were directly adjacent to the Buchanans'. In response, the MacGregors began "feuding with Campbells and . . . raiding the girnal houses [granaries] of the Buchanans and Dukes of Lennox."[4]

Dugald Buchanan himself encountered the MacGregors and other disaffected clansmen after the 1745 Jacobite rebellion, known as the '45, or Forty-Five. In this manner, the events reshaping the clans during the early eighteenth century also helped to shape the direction of Buchanan's life. His view of the world as a young man was just coming into focus as the Jacobite clans clashed with the Lowland Scots, the anti-Jacobite clans, and the English troops during the final military rebellion against the Hanoverian monarchy. Well before the Forty-Five the Highland chiefs had altered the relationship between themselves and ordinary clansmen and women, reshaping the kinship bonds almost beyond recognition. Still, following the rebellion a spark of pride remained that would be rekindled in the aftermath of the late-eighteenth- and early-nineteenth-century Clearances. But by then, well over a century later, few Highlanders remained in their homeland to carry the torch. By the mid-nineteenth century, the clans had already been dispersed, and the Scottish diaspora had sent most of them across the water and around the earth. The last Jacobite rebellion, then, set the tone for Buchanan's youth and early manhood. He was only thirty years old when the Jacobite clans met their dénouement at Culloden Moor in 1746.

A child of the Highlands, Buchanan bore the legacy of his heritage throughout his life. His fluency in the Gaelic language, his loyalty to clan, and even his attire spoke to the persistence of his native culture. The pleasure he derived from writing poetry and song attested to his schooling in this Scottish Gaelic heritage. In his youth Buchanan dressed in the tartan, which remained his ordinary attire until the wearing of the plaid was proscribed by the Disarming Act of 1746, passed by parliament directly after the Battle of Culloden.[5] Enforced until 1782, the Disarming Act starkly reminded more than one generation of Highlanders of the harsh feelings expressed toward all clansmen and women by both the Lowlanders and the Hanoverian monarchy. As Highland Gaels remembered, it was all due to "mi-run mor nan Gall" (the great ill will of the Lowlanders).[6]

The Hanoverian hostility to the Highlanders taught Buchanan that his life would also be one of change. Like many of his compatriots, he learned that he could not remain immune from outside pressures. During the Forty-Five Buchanan suddenly found himself in the awkward position of being a distinct minority, even among his clansmen. The landing of Prince Charles Edward Stewart in the Outer Hebrides on August 2, 1745, followed by the raising of the Stewart standard by hundreds of Camerons and MacDonalds in Glenfinnin on August 19, led his friends in Balquhidder to take up the Jacobite cause. Buchanan immediately threw his support to the Whigs, a stand that placed him in direct opposition to his clansmen. It was even said that when some of his acquaintances saw him, they scoffed, "There goes the Whig." When his friends "donned belt and claymore and marched away over the hills to follow Prince Charles," Buchanan stayed at home and "would have nothing to do with the rising."[7]

It is in the context of the Forty-Five that scholars have frequently contrasted Dugald Buchanan with Alasdair mac Mhaighstir Alasdair (Alexander MacDonald, c. 1690/95–1770), once described as "the outstanding Gaelic poet of the 18th century."[8] A bard of great breadth and one of the last of the Scottish Highlanders to write in classic Gaelic—the literary link that had united Ireland and Scotland in the medieval world—mac Mhaighstir Alasdair's innovative work "left a deep mark on eighteenth-century Gaelic poetry as a whole" and on Dugald Buchanan, "marginally at least."[9]

Like Buchanan, mac Mhaighstir Alasdair taught in an SSPCK school, but, unlike Buchanan, his political stance was Jacobite, which led him to resign his teaching position to follow the prince. Mac Mhaighstir Alasdair was a western Highlander who bore a "notable" MacDonald heritage. His cousin was Flora MacDonald, the renowned young woman who was imprisoned by the Hanoverian government for her role in the escape of Prince Charles during his six-month flight from British soldiers seeking his capture after Culloden. Fighting alongside the prince as his comrade in arms yet serving primarily as his bard throughout the ill-fated campaign, mac Mhaighstir Alasdair pledged himself to the cause of the Jacobites. But Derick Thomson, foremost critic of Gaelic poetry and a respected poet himself, qualifies mac

Mhaighstir Alasdair's support for the Jacobite cause. Thomson suggests that "the mainstream of this, however, was not a narrow dynastic loyalty to the House of Stuart, but a dream of Gaelic independence."[10] The ultimate goal for a patriot of that ilk remained simply the regaining of the throne by the Scottish royal descendant whom the Jacobites perceived as the lawful heir.

Derick Thomson's interpretation of mac Mhaighstir Alasdair's motivation establishes the common bond shared by these two eighteenth-century Gaelic bards, a link that lifted them above their obvious political differences. Although their responses to the Forty-Five were polarized, they were united in their abiding ties to Scottish Gaeldom. This is clarified by Buchanan's reaction to the treatment of the Highlanders at Carlisle. After the Jacobite forces retreated from their long march down into England—they came within 120 miles of London—they marched to the border town of Carlisle. At Carlisle a meager group of four hundred Highlanders faced with the impossible task of defending the post against the Hanoverian forces were defeated and hanged as rebels. Included among those who lost their lives were Buchanan's own kinsmen; he wept for his fellow Gaels: "The greater part of my relations were concerned in the rebellion, some of them fell in battle, and others suffered at Carlisle, but though the cause was bad, yet I was heartily grieved, and could not forgive those who, by their power and false witnesses, were instrumental in their death."[11]

Reading between the lines in one of Buchanan's few extant letters, one finds further suggestion of moral outrage at what he perceived as an outsider's deliberate misrepresentation, even vilification, of the annexed district of Rannoch, the region of upland Perthshire where Buchanan would serve as SSPCK schoolmaster and catechist for many years.[12] Even though Buchanan and mac Mhaighstir Alasdair may have disagreed on the methods necessary to defend their people, their shared love for Gàidhealtachd remained a steady flame in their lives. The shattering impact of the Forty-Five on these two Highland bards points to its devastating power to wreak havoc on the fortunes of so many Highland Gaels during the mid-eighteenth century.

Parents, Schooling, and a Search for Understanding

Buchanan's outrage over the Hanoverians' treatment of the Highlanders at Carlisle, including the members of the Buchanan clan, reflected his childhood nurturing. Reared within traditional clan lands, Buchanan grew up on a farm at Ardoch, near Stratheyre, in the Perthshire Highlands. Later, he came to respect the strong guidance of his "religious parents," "who took every care to train me up in the fear of the Lord, and early taught me my duty."[13]

His mother, Janet Ferguson, held sway over his life. "My tender mother," he wrote in his "Confessions," "taught me to pray as soon as I could speak, following all the means used for my improvement."[14] Ferguson died when Buchanan was only six years old, but her strength of character influenced her son throughout his life. The immediate effect of her death traumatized the lad. Later, he recalled, "From the time of her death I was not so well taken care of, either as to correction or instruction. Hence, I discouraged myself to be what I really was. The corrupt root began to bud, and there being none to lop off the branches, I got leave to do what was right in the sight of my own eyes." What Buchanan perceived as freedom, however, exacted its own toll. For about two years after Ferguson's death he found his nights to be haunted "with terrible visions . . . that the day of judgement was come." The dreams seemed to be a reproof for his actions, "for when I began to grow remiss and thoughtless . . . [the Lord] always visited me with another of those terrible dreams, which generally drove me again to my prayers."[15]

Buchanan was fortunate in that his father was a practical man. As the sole parent responsible for his son's welfare, he decided that Dugald should receive as much education as possible. After Ferguson's death, the senior Buchanan sent his son to enroll in the SSPCK school that had opened near Ardoch.[16] Here, the young lad's natural aptitude for learning served him well. Although a native Gaelic speaker, he moved rapidly toward the society's goal of learning to read the Bible in English. By the time he reached the age of twelve his remarkable progress toward English literacy had already qualified him to serve as a tutor. Shortly thereafter, he obtained his first job: "I was called to a family for the purpose of teaching the children to read."[17]

The young tutor remained with the family for only five months, but in that short time he felt his mother's positive influence weaken under the pressure of the family's pervasive behavior. All too soon he succumbed to the family's "wickedness, each one of its members exceeding the other in cursing, swearing, and other vices, except the mistress, who, I believe, feared the Lord." When Buchanan returned home to live with his father, he told himself he must "abandon my cursing and swearing; but no sooner did I get out of [my father's] sight than I was as bad as before."[18]

Once more, the senior Buchanan took charge of his son's life; he was determined that the lad receive a thorough education. When Dugald was fourteen, his father sent him to Stirling, where he continued his formal studies. From Stirling, Buchanan sent his son to Edinburgh for further schooling. Like the seventeenth-century sons of the fine, he was thrust into Lowland society. In Edinburgh Dugald found himself without the steadying rudder of his father's counsel. Far removed from the influence of any direct kin or clan members, he lost his direction. Ostensibly he was living in the Lowland towns to acquire further education, but he confessed that he met "corrupted youths like myself, and we added one sin to another; and . . . I was always the foremost man."[19] It is likely that his seventeenth-century counterparts, perhaps even their fathers, shared experiences similar to Buchanan's during their enforced Lowland schooling years.

At this juncture his father intervened again, ordering Dugald to return home. While the young Buchanan may have been removed by distance from his kin group, he still found the Highland kinship network difficult to evade. Six years had elapsed since he had left his position as tutor. Buchanan was eighteen years old. He chafed against his father's reassertion of authority: "my father would have me to make choice of some business, to which I was very aware, for I loved my loose way of living so well, that I could not think of any other." But his father was adamant: "I therefore made choice of the occupation of house carpenter, and went to Kippon [sic], where I engaged for three years with a friend of my own."[20]

Having served two years of the three-year apprenticeship in Kippen, a community near Ardoch, Buchanan broke with his master and moved south to Dumbarton, a town located on the River Clyde, just outside Glasgow, where he "engaged for six months with another [carpenter]."[21] These newly gained carpentry skills may have qualified him for gainful employment, but Buchanan still had not found any peace within himself. His personal contest with "sin," a very real internal battle that had troubled him since his mother's death, continued to stalk his daylight hours. The resolution of this persistent aggravation still eluded him, and it would continue to plague his thoughts for well over another decade. Buchanan was in his mid-twenties, but his life seemed to be moving in an uneventful pattern, punctuated only by his struggle to find an accommodation with the religious faith that he had been taught as a youth.

The Cambuslang Wark and the Forty-Five

In 1742, when Buchanan was twenty-six years old, he heard news of a religious revival just outside the bustling port city of Glasgow. Since it took place at the town of Cambuslang, it would be dubbed the Cambuslang Wark.[22] His curiosity piqued, Buchanan traveled to Cambuslang to witness the event. Once he had arrived at the revival itself, he walked among the crowd, and admitted to being "greatly comforted to hearing the people speaking of their experiences to one another." The focal point of the revival was George Whitefield, who had traveled north on one of his many peregrinations during the Great Awakening that took him across to the British colonies in North America and throughout England, Wales, and Scotland. Immersed in the crowd of salvation seekers, Buchanan listened to the compelling words of the preacher. Later, he wrote, "Mr [George] Whitefield lectured from Matt. XIV, and there was an uncommon concern among the people."[23]

Buchanan's response to the revival has been disputed by his biographers. The issue revolves around his own statement declaring that the revival had not changed his life. He wrote, "although I heard great threatenings denounced against sinners of all descriptions, yet I was not in the least affected thereby, and saw that unless the Spirit of God wrought upon me, it was beyond the reach of any mortal to do it."[24] This statement may have been written as a youthful expression of bravado. At this stage in his life, Buchanan had been battling the concept of sin for two decades, and he may have convinced himself that attending a single wark, even the famous Cambuslang Wark, could not have a significant impact on his much-troubled soul. It is more likely that at Cambuslang he felt the first murmurings of a renewed spirit, murmurings that would increase in volume and intensity during the 1740s. But in the months directly after Cambuslang, he could have been unaware of their presence.

The decade of the 1740s proved a difficult time for Buchanan. The Cambuslang Wark occurred in 1742. The Forty-Five rebellion ended with the Battle of Culloden Moor on April 16, 1746. Like the wark, the Forty-Five had an almost mesmerizing effect on Buchanan, tearing him loose from his moorings. Although he had once considered himself a solid Whig, after Carlisle and Culloden he could not rid his mind of the resentment that he felt against the Hanoverians and their treatment of his kinsmen. Revenge overwhelmed him. He found himself once again beset by turmoil within, bitterly juxtaposing the merits of revenge against those of Christian forgiveness.[25]

Not until 1750, eight years after Cambuslang and four after Culloden, did Buchanan resolve these issues. During the summer of that year, when he was thirty-four years old, he found the "religious contentment" (peace) that he had sought since the death of his mother.[26] No

The Reverend George Whitefield (1714–70). Whitefield was an Anglican leader of the Great Awakening in the American colonies and a renowned preacher on both sides of the Atlantic. He influenced both Samson Occom and Dugald Buchanan. Mezzotint by John Greenwood after Nathaniel Hone.
COURTESY THE NATIONAL PORTRAIT GALLERY, SMITHSONIAN INSTITUTION.

Kinloch Rannoch. This was the residence of Dugald Buchanan and his family during the 1750s and 1760s. The village lies at the east end of Lock Rannoch, Perthshire.
PHOTOGRAPH BY FERENC M. SZASZ.

single event or person had enabled Buchanan to achieve this serenity—neither the preaching of George Whitefield at Cambuslang nor the influence of Margaret Brisbane, daughter of the land steward of the Earl of Louden, whom he married in 1749, and who returned with him to the family farm at Ardoch. Still, Buchanan could not have found contentment in his faith without the assistance of these individuals; cumulatively, they helped him find peace through an internal resolution of the faith issues that had distressed him.[27]

Given the significance of that spiritual contentment, it could be argued that Dugald Buchanan's life finally "began" in 1750, when he was in his mid-thirties. Although Buchanan and his wife, Margaret, had recently moved to Ardoch, he had not found it easy to take up his father's trade of husbandry, a skill "to which apparently he was ill adapted by disposition and training."[28] Consequently, he abandoned both husbandry and his earlier training in carpentry, and in that year he turned to itinerant teaching. For two or three years he taught without a permanent post, but by 1753, it was likely that he was teaching school at Drumchastel when the Scottish Society offered him a permanent teaching position as schoolmaster in the township of Kinloch Rannoch within the District of Rannoch.[29] His skills as a teacher had finally been recognized.

Rannoch Schoolmaster and Catechist for the Kirk

The villages of Kinloch Rannoch, Drumchastel, and Bunrannoch lay snugly at the eastern edge of Loch Rannoch, southwest of Glen Garry and Blair Athol and perhaps thirty miles west of Pitlochry. To the west was Rannoch Moor, and beyond that, Glencoe and Loch Linnhe and Fort William. To the east lay the River Tummel and Loch Tummel. From Ardoch and the Buchanan family farm, Loch Rannoch was a trip of perhaps fifty miles as the crow flies, but it was considerably farther via eighteenth-century transportation, which was likely to be on foot or on horseback. (See map on page 45.)

After he began teaching school in the District of Rannoch, Dugald Buchanan's stature began to grow in the eyes of his fellow Highlanders. Here, in the southern Highlands, he spoke to the hearts of those Gaels who had been won over to the Lowland Presbyterian faith. Although the society had granted him recognition as a schoolmaster, his legacy among the Highland Gaels emerged through the other roles that he assumed in these years. In addition to his teaching, he responded to a call from the Church of Scotland to serve as catechist for the region. Largely through his frequent preaching, as well as his singing of poetic hymns, he influenced many of those Highlanders who heard his evangelical message. In spite of the fact that the Kirk never licensed him as "preacher and pastor in the parish," he gained greater fame than some of those who had been awarded an official license to preach.[30]

Above all, Buchanan proved a spiritual poet whose songs and lyrics found their way into the lives of many Highland Gaels. These years were the culmination of his life, a final stage that had become a reality only through his agonizing search for spiritual understanding. Once he reached this level of understanding, he spoke from the heart, through his preaching, poetry, teaching, and singing. The message that he delivered struck a deep chord within the Highlands, especially in the gloomy years after the defeat at Culloden.

In the mid-eighteenth century, northwest upland Perthshire, which included the District of Rannoch, was "strongly Gaelic" in language. To the southeast, in the Lowland town of Perth, the dominant language had already shifted to Scots. Upstream from Perth and straddling the border between the Lowlands and Highlands, the town of Dunkeld,

Monument to Dugald Buchanan in Kinloch Rannoch.
Photograph by Ferenc M. Szasz.

Family cottage of Dugald Buchanan. Buchanan and his family lived here during his years of teaching and serving as a catechist in the vicinity of Kinloch Rannock. Artist unknown.
SKETCH REPRINTED FROM A. SINCLAIR, REMINISCENCES OF THE LIFE AND LABOURS OF DUGALD BUCHANAN, FORMERLY TEACHER AND EVANGELIST AT RANNOCK, PERTHSHIRE (1885).

situated along the banks of the River Tay, was "'divided equally' between Gaelic speakers and English speakers."[31] As the old administrative center of the pre-Reformation Scottish Catholic Church, Dunkeld served as a reminder of the linguistic and cultural divide that split eighteenth-century Scotland into the Highlands and the Lowlands.

Since the District of Rannoch lay squarely in the heart of the Gaelic-speaking region of Perthshire, it proved an appropriate home for a Gaelic religious poet and schoolmaster. But in 1746 Rannoch also bore the reputation of being a lawless region. It was "a notoriously unstable area . . . [struggling] with its problems of social control." Like several other Highland districts, Rannoch was targeted as a refuge by followers of clan chiefs who had lost their lands through various means and thus remained unable to support their clansmen and women. Dubbed the "broken men," these landless clansmen brought an element of instability into the townships of the Rannoch District. Their restless pattern of movement led to a "constant turnover" among township

Perthshire (the County of Perth), ca. 1780. One of a series of regional maps of Scotland by British map maker Thomas Kitchin. Originally published for inclusion in the *London Magazine*, a monthly journal for gentlemen covering all things political, geographical, and scientific.
FACSIMILE BY CARSON CLARK GALLERY, SCOTLAND MAP HERITAGE CENTRE, EDINBURGH.

residents, and their disregard for the "common moral code" disrupted an otherwise peaceful environment.[32]

A contemporary account described Rannoch as a district where "the prevailing names are Camerons and MacGregors (who have assumed other names), a few MacDonalds, all of them originally refugees, come to Rannoch not for building of Kirks."[33] When Buchanan moved his family to Rannoch, he encountered these MacGregors and "broken men" from other clans. Soon after he arrived, he received a message from the Forfeited Estates Commissioners, who requested that their catechists for the district, including Buchanan and others, " 'put the fear of God before the eyes' of the broken men. This they did fearlessly."[34] Shortly thereafter a contemporary report from the region suggested that "many formerly noted for dishonesty and licentiousness are now becoming sober, honest, and industrious."[35]

Buchanan responded rigorously to the challenge issued by the Forfeited Estates Commissioners. Within half a dozen years his fame had spread so widely that he had "every Sunday an audience of 500 people." By the 1760s Rannoch's reputation had turned around: "With respect to theft so universally well-known . . . but for two years past not a single beast has been stolen."[36]

Buchanan's mettle may have been tested by this challenge, but it is unlikely that his dealings with the "broken men" were that different from his everyday dealings with others. When he perceived injustice of any sort, he was quick to respond, relying on his wits, along with his knowledge of the situation, to defend the wronged and confront the guilty. In a November 1753 letter to Mr. Ramsay, the factor on the newly confiscated estate of Strowan (Struan), he defended both Ramsay and "the country" (i.e., the District of Rannoch) from the charges leveled by a Mr. Small, who was a farmer. Buchanan was particularly offended at Small's accusation that "the country [Rannoch] is in confusion." Buchanan labeled this charge "an untruth." He wrote, "I believe that on all the Forfeited Estates there is no such care taken in the instruction of youth as in Rannoch." Moreover, "those villages that are now restrained by the Law, now have their children in all those amiable virtues which has a godly prospect to prosperity." And, on the schools themselves, he added, "we have this winter upwards of three hundred and fifty boys and girls instructed not only to Read, but some of them to spin and knit stockings."[37] Clearly an orderly state of affairs had ensued since the schoolmaster's arrival, not only in the schools, but also in the townships throughout the district.

Highland Schoolmaster as Spiritual Bard

It was in this new, orderly context that Buchanan began to rely heavily on song (*oran/orain*; and *duan*, poem). But his composition of poetry and song had woven its way into his life well before he settled in the District of Rannoch. Donald MacLean, one of his early biographers, suggests that Buchanan wrote "An Gaisgeach" (The Hero) as a poetic response to the execution of the Gaels who surrendered at Carlisle in 1746. Instead of the traditional Gaelic hero who physically conquered his enemies, the poem extols the qualities of the Christian Gaelic hero:

> A hero he who has subdued
> The dread of death, the fears of life
> And who with manly fortitude
> Encounters fate in fearless strife.[38]

Buchanan composed lengthy poems on religion and ethics during his years in Rannoch, but it is highly likely he destroyed the secular poems he had written earlier. Hence, his reputation as a Gaelic sacred bard rests on the sacred poetry. In 1767, when Buchanan oversaw the publication of this collection in Edinburgh, his reputation as poet was ensured. Since that date, at least twenty-four editions of the slim volume of eight poems—the longest, "Là a'Bhreitheanais" (The Day of Judgment), contains five hundred lines—have appeared under the title *Laoidhe Spioradail, le Dùghall Bochannan*. In the late-eighteenth and nineteenth centuries, Buchanan's poetry profoundly influenced the religious faith of the Highland Gaels as they absorbed the Lowlanders' Presbyterianism and reshaped it to suit their own societal values. After the Bible and the catechism, *Laoidhe Spioradail* proved the most widely printed Gaelic publication. But, as Scottish Gaels gathered on the Sabbath to listen to the reading of his poetry, Buchanan's words also entered into the oral heritage of these people.[39]

For most Highland Gaels during the eighteenth century, the printing of Buchanan's poetry meant they would listen to these poems rather than read them. With the exception of the clan chiefs and their families, including the small number of children of the fine who been sent to the Lowlands for school, most Highlanders could not read Gaelic, even though it was the first language of Gàidhealtachd. Neither could the majority of Highlanders comprehend written or spoken English. And even the minority who could read Gaelic had no access to a Scots Gaelic New Testament until 1767, the same year that Buchanan published his poems.

The first Gaelic-English vocabulary, completed in 1741 by Alaisdair mac Mhaighstir Alaisdair, preceded the New Testament by about twenty-five years. Still, even though the New Testament had yet to be translated into Scottish Gaelic, Highlanders seeking knowledge of Presbyterian doctrine could listen to one key source—the Presbyterian Shorter Catechism. The Church of Scotland catechists like Dugald Buchanan used the Shorter Catechism as their primary printed teaching tool, and it served them well during their lengthy itinerant circuits. As they traveled from glen to loch to river, and over brae and ben, they had confidence in at least one statement of faith printed in the vernacular, but it was still no substitute for a Bible in Scottish Gaelic.

If the Highland Gaels were ever to understand the faith that had so challenged Buchanan for over half of his life, they had to come to it orally. For the mid-eighteenth-century Highlander, oral expression of the culture meant less the spoken word than the word expressed through song and music. John MacInnes described this process of learning: "A people to whom music and poetry was as the breath of life needed something more than sound doctrine, more or less ably expounded. They needed to sing their faith. The spiritual bards amply supplied that need."[40] By mid-century, SSPCK schoolmaster Dugald Buchanan was emerging as the foremost figure among these spiritual bards.

The Gaels who responded to Buchanan's *dain spioradail* were "passionately fond of verse and were endowed with accurate and tenacious memories." Through many generations they had absorbed "ballad literature and the poetry of the secular bards." During the long summer days spent at the shielings and on the long winter nights when they attended the *ceilidhs*—the evening gatherings of song and storytelling—they listened and they sang. In the eighteenth century, with the arrival of Presbyterianism in much of the Highlands, they merely broadened their repertoire of poetry by learning *dain spioradail* through the same communal gatherings.[41]

In the northern and northeastern regions of Caithness and Sutherland, the people shared an unusual relationship with Dugald Buchanan. Even though he never physically traveled to these remote lands, he reached out to those who lived there through his music. The connection came about in the following manner: In the immediate aftermath of the Forty-Five, when the Hanoverian government was zealously extinguishing any sparks of further rebellion, the Perthshire border town of Dunkeld served as a central location for the stationing of militia assigned to keep watch over the Highlands. One group of Sutherland militia, numbering twelve men, found themselves assigned to watch the District of Rannoch, where they had to deal with the lawless element, or the "broken men." Shortly after their arrival, upon inquiring about Sabbath services, they learned of Buchanan, the schoolmaster, who, it was said, "was in the habit of addressing all who chose to hear him." Over time, two of these Sutherland men became "quite attached" to Buchanan; they sang for him [the] *dain spioradail* of Sutherland that John Mackay, a Sutherland spiritual bard, had composed. In Caithness and Sutherland the "Gaelic hymns were very popular, and were repeated around the peat fires of the far north-land." By weaving these songs into the southern Highlands musical tradition,

Buchanan enriched the verse of his own people, but the admiration of the Sutherland Gaels for Buchanan's songs enlarged his audience as well. Many of those Gaels "who could not read a primer could sing these songs by the hour as well as secular and Ossianic poems of many hundred lines."[42]

As Buchanan absorbed influences from John Mackay and other Sutherland bards, his poetry gained followers across both the southern and northern Highlands. Yet Buchanan's writing also reflected the works of several well-known English writers. His first exposure to English authors may have come when he was employed as a tutor at the age of twelve, where he encountered the writings of Milton and Shakespeare.[43] Derick Thomson suggests that Buchanan "was probably more widely read in English than any of his contemporary Gaelic poets."[44] Biographer Donald E. Meek observes that Buchanan was also influenced by the well-known hymn writer Isaac Watts, along with James Thomson and Edward Young ("Graveyard School of Poetry"). "Curiously," Meek notes, "substantial sections of his poems are unacknowledged translations or paraphrases of hymns by the 'father of English hymnody.'" In this context, however, Meek adds that "spiritual power from the Lowlands and England contributed very substantially to the making of Highland religion."[45] One might suspect that this borrowing did not move in a single direction.

By the 1750s Buchanan had achieved a position of considerable stature. He proved a familiar figure to the school children and Gaelic Presbyterians who lived in the uplands of Perthshire. Described by A. Sinclair MacLean as "above the average height, of dark complexion, dark hair, and large expressive eyes," he was recognized by many of his neighbors as a figure of considerable influence within the community. A few years later Benjamin Rush, the famous medical doctor from Philadelphia who studied at the University of Edinburgh in the 1760s, portrayed Buchanan as "an old Highlander of plain manners . . . [one] who 'possessed an original mind.'" When Rush became acquainted with Buchanan in the capital, the Gael was likely wearing an urban attire and would have been clad in "knee breeches, a blue great-coat, and a broad blue bonnet." In his youth, however, he had worn "the kilt, the common dress of the country."[46]

Although he had become the best known of the Highland spiritual poets, Buchanan also garnered respect for his felicity in English, which he combined with a command of his native Gaelic. During a conversation with Rush, he confessed that "he always prayed and dreamed in his native language."[47] Since Buchanan's linguistic abilities were matched by his gift for speech and song, it may well have been this combination of talents that led to his leadership role in the Scottish Gaelic New Testament project.

In the early 1760s, after considerable delay, the SSPCK finally commissioned the translation of the New Testament into Scottish Gaelic. Contrary to appearances, however, this did not mean the society had undergone a change of heart; rather, it had only changed tactics. Despite its commitment to the translation project, the SSPCK did not swerve from its original goal—the eventual replacement of Gaelic with English. Still, the society had modified its attitude toward Gaelic, a pragmatic change that could be attributed to the outcome of the Forty-Five. The Lowlanders whose blood had chilled when Prince Charles Edward Stewart had occupied Edinburgh were vastly relieved when they learned of the Jacobite defeat at Culloden. And, in a scenario later to be very familiar to Native Americans, when the Jacobites lost their final battle, the Hanoverians and their Lowland supporters found other means of imposing their will in the Highlands. These included further schooling; changed styles of farming, known as "improvement"; and, eventually, the introduction of vast numbers of Lowland sheep. But the SSPCK's belated interest in a New Testament translation may also have been spurred by Dr. Samuel Johnson, who submitted a highly publicized opinion favoring the Scottish Gaelic translation.[48] In 1766 Johnson wrote to William Drummond, one of the society's directors, "I did not expect to hear that it could be in an assembly convened for the propagation of Christian knowledge, a question whether any nation uninstructed in religion should receive instruction; or whether that instruction should be imparted to them by a translation of the holy books into their own language. To omit . . . the most efficacious method of advancing Christianity . . . is a crime."[49]

When the society selected an official translator for the project, it chose the Rev. James Stuart. Stuart was the Church of Scotland minister at Killin, an upland Perthshire village that lay south of Loch Rannoch, near Loch Tay. When the translation itself was completed, it was probably Stuart who requested that Buchanan be selected to supervise the next stage of the project—the printing—which would be undertaken in Scotland's capital. It would be Buchanan's responsibility to shepherd the translated text from handwritten draft to final printed publication.

At first Buchanan's willingness to take on this mammoth task might seem puzzling, for it meant a move to Edinburgh, in the heart of the Lowlands. Although he had lived in the capital as a youth, the town was far removed from his current position. Moreover, it remained some distance from his residence among his Gaelic kinspeople in the Rannoch District. Further, returning to Edinburgh in the 1760s—as a respected schoolmaster, catechist, and spiritual bard and serving the society and the Kirk as cultural intermediary in the Perthshire Highlands—promised to be a stark contrast to his wayward days there as a youth, when, by his own confession, he had joined with his friends in a life filled with sin. On the other hand, Buchanan's commitment to his faith taught him the significance of the assignment. In the mid-1760s, few Highland Gaels could comprehend the King James Version of the New Testament. Hence, the translation could prove a crucial catalyst for their understanding of the faith that Buchanan was teaching.

Ultimately, Buchanan became the man of the hour—no one had a better command of the shifting meanings that divided the two languages; no one could move as deftly from one language to the other; and no one else had the unique spiritual commitment of a Highland Gael who was also Presbyterian and who had a strong desire to see the work completed. In short, despite the distance of travel, the difficulty of living away from home, family, and kin, and the complexities of the task itself, Buchanan possessed all the prerequisites for the role of printing supervisor. He accepted the position.

Highland Gaels in Edinburgh

In the spring of 1766 Buchanan left the District of Rannoch and moved down to Edinburgh for what proved to be a lengthy stay. During his sojourn in the capital, he divided his energies among his several assignments. His primary attention focused on revising the proofs and supervising the printers, who were laboriously crafting the ten thousand copies of the New Testament that had been ordered by the society.[50] But he also engaged in other projects, one of which involved the supervision of the printing of his own poems, as previously mentioned.

Learning of Buchanan's arrival through the Highlanders' urban network, his countrymen and women living in Edinburgh urged him to serve as their minister during his residence there. An early biographer of Buchanan has suggested that these displaced Highlanders sought approval for Buchanan's ordination by the Kirk's leadership, which was based in the General Assembly offices located in Edinburgh. Although I have not located any pertinent correspondence on this issue, this biographer suggested that Buchanan attended classes in natural philosophy, anatomy, and astronomy at Edinburgh University in preparation

Greyfriars Kirk, Edinburgh. The Kirk of the Grey Friars (Franciscan) was built in 1620; after its destruction, it was rebuilt in the early 1700s. Dugald Buchanan preached here in Gaelic to Highlanders living in the capital. PHOTOGRAPH BY FERENC M. SZASZ.

for the possible ordination. The ordination never occurred. Still, Buchanan responded to his kinsmen's needs by preaching—in Gaelic—at the Greyfriars Kirk to these urbanized Highlanders. In this manner, the earliest Gaelic congregation of Edinburgh was gathered.[51]

The milieu of the Edinburgh that Dugald Buchanan settled in to during the mid-1760s reflected one of the most dramatic eras in the capital's often tumultuous history. A town whose population approached sixty thousand people, Edinburgh thronged with activity. Ideas and plans for change abounded. The New City would soon be constructed. Buchanan's residence there coincided directly with the Scottish Enlightenment, "that extraordinary outburst of intellectual activity" that culminated in the thirty-year period—1760–90—that historian David Daiches has described as the golden age.[52] The intellectual stimulation brought to town figures like David Hume, Adam Smith, and James Watt.[53] In this environment Buchanan found the opportunity to meet and, on occasion, match wits with some of those figures, such as David Hume, who were drawn to the cultural florescence that characterized the Lowland urban settings.[54] It was here too that he met and had several conversations with the colonial medical student Benjamin Rush.

Buchanan's residence in the capital was cut short when he learned that his family had been suffering from an epidemic of fever. He returned home to nurse them but caught the fever himself and died, surrounded by his family, on June 2, 1768. He was only fifty-two. On his death, those family members who survived him—his widow, Margaret, and their two sons and two daughters—left Loch Rannoch and returned to the old family farm at Ardoch. Buchanan's kinsmen from Balquhidder marched north to Rannoch, persuaded the local residents that they should be allowed to retrieve the bard's body, and carried it back to Balquhidder. There, once again in his homeland, they buried him "in the churchyard of Leny on the banks of the Teith . . . . [where] only persons of the name of Buchanan . . . are buried."[55]

Samson Occom, Mohegan

Across the Atlantic Ocean, some seven years after Buchanan's birth, Samson Occom was born. His mother, Sarah (Wauby or Sampson) Ockham, bore Sampson in the wigwam that she shared with her husband, Joshua Ockham, and an older son, also named Joshua. Like the Gaelic bard, Samson Occom was born into a tribal network and an oral culture. Although his mother's family background remains uncer-

Graveyard of Little Leny. The burial site of Dugald Buchanan, this graveyard is located just outside Callander and not far from Buchanan's birth site in Ardoch, Strathyre.
PHOTOGRAPH BY FERENC M. SZASZ.

tain, according to tradition, she was descended from Uncas, the powerful seventeenth-century Mohegan sachem who had guided his people for over fifty years until his death in 1683.[56] The Mohegan (Munhicke) background of Occom's father can be traced only as far as Sampson's grandfather, Tomockham, alias Ashneon. In the late seventeenth century, Tomockham moved south from the region between the Shetucket and Quinebaug Rivers onto the lands that lay west of the Mohegan River (which the English renamed the Thames). Settled in a location near Uncas Hill, he became a follower of Uncas. It is likely that Joshua Ockham was born on these lands, which would eventually become the southeastern corner of Connecticut. It was also said that Samson Occom was born here, near Uncas Hill, overlooking the river that the Mohegans named after their own people.

Occom's lineage was mixed, a reflection of the multiple generations of connections between the Pequot and Mohegan nations whose members resided on the northern shore of Long Island Sound.[57] In a pattern that echoed the divisions among the Gaelic clans, the old antagonisms

Monument to Dugald Buchanan in Graveyard of Little Leny. Dedicated in 1925.
PHOTOGRAPH BY FERENC M. SZASZ.

among these Algonquian peoples ran deep. Although Uncas himself bore Pequot, Mohegan, Narragansett, and other Algonquian ancestry, as a Mohegan sachem, after the English became major figures in the region, he and his Mohegan followers allied with the English in their war against the Pequots. The Mohegans joined in the infamous Mystic Fort Massacre (1637) and the ensuing swamp fight slaughter that ended

The Mohegan/Thames River, Connecticut. Samson Occom was born near this location in southeastern Connecticut. The river is identified by the Mohegans as the Massapequotuck River. English immigrants changed the name to the Thames River.
PHOTOGRAPH BY FERENC M. SZASZ.

the Pequot War that same year. This clash left perhaps as many as half of all the Pequots dead, and those who survived were enslaved or merged among their neighbors, especially the Mohegans. Although political and kinship ties between Pequots and Mohegans persisted through the postwar generations, the old enmity has endured to the present time.[58]

Prior to the 1630s, these two Native peoples—Mohegans and Pequots—had spread across most of southeastern Connecticut. The Pequot had claimed the Mystic River valley; the Mohegans, the Mohegan River valley. But relentless English expansion during the seventeenth century had destroyed most of their aboriginal land base. By the time of Occom's youth, in the 1720s and 1730s, the English had been settled in the region for almost four generations, forcing Native people to become an "almost invisible minority [living] around the edges of the . . . English farming villages, seaports, mill towns, and commercial centers that sprang up in the Indians' original territories."[59]

Despite the overwhelming encroachment of the outsiders, in later

Marker for the Mohegan Tribe. Descendants of the Mohegan tribe who remained in Connecticut when Occom and others moved to Oneida lands gained federal recognition as a sovereign nation in 1994. The New York Mohegan descendants live in Wisconsin and struggle for federal recognition.
PHOTOGRAPH BY THE AUTHOR.

years, Occom still maintained that his parents, Sarah and Joshua, "had Livd a wandering Life as did all the Indians at Mohegan, they Chiefly Depended upon Hunting, Fishing & Fowling for their living and had no Connection with the English, excepting to Trifle [trade] with them in their small Trifles."[60] Although these words document Occom's memory, even during his childhood the English were pressuring the Mohegans to relinquish their remaining holdings, and as soon as the Natives had been physically subdued, the English shifted their tactics to a form of "spiritual colonialism."

Seldom subtle, the English saw material gifts as a persuasive incentive for religious conversion. They were not far off the mark. Occom recalled that "Once a Fortnight, in ye Summer Season, a Minister from New London used to come up, and the Indians to attend." Yet he remembered that the Mohegans found the appeal of their offer in its economic, rather than spiritual, merit. It was, as Occom put it, "not that they regarded the Christian Religion, but they had Blankets given to them every Fall of the Year and for these things they would attend."[61]

Like their Puritan ancestors, such as John Eliot, the earlier missionary to the Algonquians, these eighteenth-century English Congregationalists saw literacy as an inseparable dimension of their faith. But during Occom's youth, as he recalled, schooling was merely an intermittent exercise that he avoided whenever he could. He remembered a "Sort of School," but "there never was one that ever Learnt to read any thing." Nor was the "man who went about among the Indian Wigwams" to make the children read any more successful: "The Children used to take Care to Keep out of his way;—and he used to Catch me Some times and make me Say over my letters, and I believe I Learnt Some of them. But this was Soon over too."[62]

In Occom's recollection, through most of his childhood the English remained peripheral. Then things began to change. Toward the end of the 1730s, "When I was 16 years of age, we heard a Strange Rumor among the English, that there were Extraordinary Ministers Preaching from Place to Place and a Strange Concern among the White People."[63] The Great Awakening had reached New England, and it promised to leave its mark upon English and Algonquian alike.

"Some Time in the Summer . . . some Ministers began to visit us and Preach the Word of God." Within Occom's family the first member to be touched by the revival was his mother. David Jewett, the local Congregational minister, converted Sarah Wauby Ockham sometime in the early 1740s. Well beyond the confines of the Mohegan world, the revival struck the English with a throbbing intensity heightened by the preaching of ministers like Eleazar Wheelock and his brother-in-law, James Davenport. In 1743 Davenport preached in New London, which lay south of the Mohegan villages and, by its proximity to them, was the equivalent of today's Indian "border town," such as the Navajo border town of Gallup, New Mexico, or the Yakama border town of Wapato, Washington.

George Whitefield's entry into New England may also have brought the famous Anglican before some Algonquian listeners, but it is not clear if Occom heard him then, during the height of the revival, or if he met him later. What is clear, however, is that Occom was struck by the revival preaching: "I was one who was imprest with the things we had heard. These Preachers did not only come to us, but we frequently went to their meetings and Churches."[64]

Like the spiritual breakthrough for Dugald Buchanan, Occom's conversion, coming at the age of seventeen, proved pivotal: "From this Time the Distress and Burden of my mind was removed, and I found Serenity and Pleasure of Soul, in Serving God." Occom came to believe that he could best serve God by serving his own people—"my Poor Brethren," as he often phrased it. For months he struggled to teach himself to read, reasoning, "if I could once Learn to Read I would Instruct the poor Children in Reading." He tackled the New Testament, which only whetted his appetite. "By this time I Just began to Read in the New Testament without Spelling,—and I had a Stronger Desire Still to learn to read the Word of God."[65]

As Occom struggled to enter the path he would eventually follow for a lifetime, one of instructing his "poor Brethren" through "an Uncommon Pity and compassion" for them, he and his mother, Sarah, searched for a means to fulfill his dream. Sarah Ockham was an astute, determined woman. In 1743, when she and Occom learned that Mr. Wheelock, the revival minister in Lebanon, "had a Number of English youth under his Tuition," they concurred that it was time to act. They agreed that Sarah would travel to the minister and ask "Mr Wheelock whether he would take me a little while to Instruct me in readings." Wheelock was interested. He instructed Sarah Ockham that he wanted to see her son "as Soon as possible." "So I went up," Occom recalled, "thinking I should be back again in a few Days."[66] The days stretched into months, and the months stretched into years.

When Occom went to Lebanon he was probably about twenty. His mentor, at age thirty-two, was twelve years older. When Occom reached the age of twenty-six, having studied with Wheelock and other ministers in the local area for six years, he found himself suffering from severe eye strain, a condition that prevented him from entering Yale to continue his education. At this juncture, he began to search for a position where he could use his newly acquired skills. During his years of study, he had become acquainted with most of the Algonquian villages in the region. Sailing across Long Island Sound on a fishing trip one day, he visited the village of Montauk, located on the eastern end of Long Island, where he learned the people were in need of a minister and teacher. With Wheelock's blessing and some financial aid from the New England Company commissioners in Boston, he accepted the position. He had stumbled into the first stage of his life's work.

Steeped in intensive studies of English, Latin, Greek, and some Hebrew during his years of learning within the ministerial community of southeastern Connecticut, Occom must have felt isolated at Montauk. Still, even when he was a student, he had maintained his kinship links with the mainland Native villages because he served as a counselor for the Mohegans, which required that he remain in touch with other Algonquian communities. And it was in this capacity that he dealt with the Mohegan land dispute with Connecticut and other matters that plagued his tribe's declining population of perhaps four hundred members.[67] Occom's responsibilities on the mainland also encompassed a strong Native network that stretched well beyond Mohegan. From his student days forward he had continued to strengthen the links among the Native communities in the area. In his travels he dealt with the Pequots of Groton, the Eastern and Western Niantics, the Naragansetts of Rhode Island, his own people at Mohegan, and his new charges across the Long Island Sound, the Montauks.

When Occom arrived among the Montauks to take up his position, he was well prepared. One of his biographers has suggested that his studies were so thorough that he "was probably no more poorly educated than many a preacher of his day, and in eloquence, earnestness and simplicity, superior to not a few."[68] It is perhaps ironic, then, that Occom probably shared less in common with his fellow ministers of New England, all of whom were English, than he did with someone he had never heard of: Dugald Buchanan. Occom and Buchanan both ministered to a people forced to negotiate with increasingly powerful cultures intent on domination. Their shared ability to communicate in the language of their people set them apart from outsiders intent on some form of colonialism, and their similar minority status—Mohegan and Gael—lent a commonality to their lives. Simultaneously, their unique role as Native people set them apart from the general membership of the Reformed Protestant denominations of eighteenth-century New England and, across the water, the Church of Scotland. In this context of cross-cultural faith, Occom's arrival at Montauk resembled Buchanan's arrival at Kinloch Rannoch. During the early 1750s, each stumbled upon what would become his life's work.

Occom's dozen years of residence among the Montauks proved a time of testing. Although he cemented his commitment to the community through his marriage to Mary Fowler, a Montauk woman, he felt keenly the economic disparity that separated him from the English ministers. The commissioners of the New England Company paid him a salary that was significantly less than his English counterparts, just as it had similarly discriminated between Native and English schoolmasters during the previous century. During these years at Montauk, Mary Fowler bore the first six of their children, but Occom's pleading for further remuneration to support their growing family was generally ignored. Hence, he nurtured a growing sense of disappointment that emerged from his singular treatment. Gnawing at his consciousness, this feeling of resentment must have served as a prelude for all future enterprises that involved his doing the bidding of the English. This bitterness so corroded the naiveté of his youth that it eventually led to his unwillingness to cooperate with the English in any further joint plans.[69]

Hard pressed to support his family during these early years of their marriage, Occom reawakened skills he had once absorbed as a youth: "I Planted my own Corn, Potatoes, and Beans. I used to be out hoeing my Corn Some times before Sun Rise and after my School is Dismist, and by this means I was able to raise my own Pork." Fishing and hunting also gained importance: "Some Mornings and Evenings I would be out with my Hook and Line to Catch Fish . . . and I was very expert with my gun, and fed my Family with Fowls. I could more than pay for my Powder & Shot with Feathers." He also added new skills: "At other Times I bound old Books for Easthampton People, made wooden Spoons and Ladles, stocked Guns, & worked on Ceder to make Pails, Piggins, and Churns, etc."[70] One wonders if Buchanan's low salary and large Gaelic family persuaded him to engage in similar survival tactics.

The economic stringency forced upon Mary and Samson Occom during the Montauk years might have forewarned Occom to move more cautiously in his future arrangements with the English. In this early stage of his career, however, he still believed the English to be the lifeline for his "poor brethren." English power and English wealth loomed as an invincible network that he could not avoid, except at the peril of himself and his family.

The unfolding of Occom's story during the decade of the 1760s reveals the Mohegan as a willing player in all the outsiders' plans. At this time, Occom did not raise serious objections to the idea of his being swept up in the momentum of English and Scottish proposals for education and conversion of Native people. Invariably, these proposals seemed to hinge on the role of Occom as a central figure. Both the English and the Scots needed Samson Occom, the famed "Indian Minister."[71] As the only ordained Native Presbyterian in the American colonies, his symbolic role proved of inestimable value to Reformed Protestants on both sides of the water.

As for Occom's side of the equation, he was initially amenable to this position because he still believed in the cause that his sponsors promoted, and it had a deeper meaning for him than they may have realized. Occom felt indebted to Wheelock and his other tutors. He also had faith in Whitefield's willingness to advance funds or offer advice.[72]

Given Occom's frame of mind, the SSPCK board of correspondents

The Reverend Samson Occom (1723–92). Painting by Nathaniel Smibert.
COURTESY BOWDOIN COLLEGE MUSEUM OF ART.

based in New York did not find it difficult to persuade the Mohegan that he should fulfill the Oneida Nation's request for a missionary educator who would live within their villages.[73] Nor did Wheelock find it difficult to persuade Occom that he should shoulder the burden of Iroquois recruitment for Moor's school during his several visits to the Oneida in the early 1760s. Nor did Wheelock meet opposition from the Mohegan minister when he asked Occom to raise funds for the financial stability of Moor's School, which had not yet gained a sufficient operating base. Yet when Occom acted—in good faith—in almost every instance he found himself disappointed. When that disappointment was compounded by suspicion of deceit, he lost faith in many of those outsiders who had always secured his commitment solely on the strength of their word.

Occom's trips to the Oneida Nation in the early 1760s (see chapter 6), illustrate his declining confidence in the schemes plotted by outsiders. By 1764 Occom knew quite well that the proposed missionary post among the Oneidas suited neither his health nor his desire to remain in the land of his birth, among his own people. Yet Wheelock persisted, using the leverage of his newly formed Connecticut Board of Correspondents to persuade all of the parties involved of the wisdom of sending Occom back to the Oneidas. Occom seemed to believe he had little choice in the matter. Well aware of Wheelock's stubbornness, and deferring once again to his authority, the Mohegan agreed to try. But his correspondence hints at the onset of his rebellion.

In late August 1764, Occom wrote to Wheelock, probably while he and David Fowler were aboard the boat sailing from Norwich to New York: "I'm Sorry you couldn't get at Least Some Money for David [Fowler], it looks like Presumption for us to go on long Journey thro' Christians without Money, if it was altogether among Indian Heathen we might do well enough—But I have Determined to go. Tho no White Missionary would go in Such Circumstances."[74] As he concluded the letter, Occom recalled that he was indebted to Wheelock for the survival of his family, whom he had just left at their partially completed home in Mohegan. Begging Wheelock's aid, he wrote, "I leave my Poor Wife and Children at your feet and if they hunger, Starve and die let them Die there." He followed this request with his customary profession of humility: "Sir, I shall endeavor to follow your Directions in all things." Then he signed the letter, "Your Good for Nothing Indian Sarvant, Samson Occom." Although his voice vacillated, the dissatisfaction, or, to borrow Blodgett's term, "truculence" expressed in this missive was clear.[75] These words suggest that Occom saw himself as a mirror image of Wheelock's perception of Indians; yet the potential for change already lay within him.

Occom was finally beginning to see himself as a pawn in the English game. Still, he was not without a few ploys of his own. In the game of chance that he was playing with Wheelock, he was careful to let his mentor know that he too held some cards. He would follow Wheelock's orders by initiating this scheme, but in so doing he engineered the arrangements so that Wheelock was in his debt. Through Occom's acumen, Wheelock acquired the responsibility for funding the house construction: "I leave my House and other Business to be done upon your Credit, and it will be Dear Business [expensive] in the End." Occom had negotiated with a Mr. Peabody in Norwich Landing to "Carry on" his business and "by vertue of the Paper you [Wheelock] put into my Hands, he is to get all the Meterials that my House will require, and to Hire Hands and to pay them at any Marchants who will except and trust to your obligation." Nor did Occom stop with the responsibilities for the house. He drew Wheelock further into his debt by announcing that "my family now wants Cloathing—and provision they must now have, or my Business can't go on."[76]

When Occom and Fowler were forced to return from New York, it was clear that the Mohegan minister had won this round. Wheelock was furious, but Occom's business affairs, foremost of which was the house at Mohegan, remained Wheelock's responsibility. In the next round, however, both players of the game suffered losses; at the same time both gained specific benefits that would alter their future lives. Occom's trip to the British Isles would permanently change the relationship between former mentor and former Indian pupil, but it would also affect the relationship between Natives of the Northeast and the Scottish Society.

CHAPTER EIGHT

The Edinburgh Connection
Mohegan and Highland Gael in Scotland

In many respects the initial idea for a fund-raising tour of the British Isles, like most English or Scottish schemes that involved Samson Occom, came about without his knowledge. Even before the fiasco in New York, Eleazar Wheelock's ministerial network had been considering new methods of raising money to support Moor's Indian Charity School. That spring Charles Jeffrey Smith wrote to Wheelock with a prescient piece of advice: "When the Indian War is a little abated, would it not be best to send Mr. Occom with another Person home a begging? An Indian minister in England might get a Bushel of Money for the School."[1] By early July, Wheelock had persuaded his Connecticut Board of Correspondents to support the proposal to send Occom to Britain. But all through these years George Whitefield had been well ahead of Wheelock. The Anglican's connections on both sides of the water had led him to introduce the idea of raising funds in Britain even earlier. As early as 1760, Whitefield had nudged Wheelock with a subtle suggestion: "Had I a converted Indian scholar that could preach and pray in English, something might be done to purpose."[2] Hence, others had been speculating on travel plans for Occom well before they had troubled to notify the key player.

In the fall of 1765, after Occom had agreed to participate in the venture, the preparations moved into high gear. Wheelock drew on his network of contacts to secure endorsements, calling on both Occom and Nathaniel Whitaker, the Norwich minister who joined him on the tour, to secure testimonials. The most daunting opposition to the proposed tour reflected the political realities of denominational sparring in the missionary field. The criticism came from the New England Company commissioners in Boston, who may have felt slighted because their financial support of Occom at Montauk seemed to be overshadowed by Wheelock's intervention. Oddly, those who had been most reluctant to award Occom a decent salary now claimed the Mohegan as their man. In the midst of this dispute, the intense uproar caused by parliament's passage of the Stamp Act made it difficult for the ship's master to obtain clearance papers to sail. After weeks of waiting, however, all was ready, including the twenty-guinea payment for Occom and Whitaker's passage, which was covered by John Hancock, part owner of the packet *Boston*.[3]

When Samson Occom sailed from Boston on December 23, 1765, en route to London, he plunged, perhaps unwittingly, into the final episode of the game of chance that he and Wheelock had engaged in since they first met in 1743. This round would cast the Mohegan Presbyterian minister and his mentor, the English Congregational minister, as fellow players in Wheelock's grand design to transfer Moor's School from Lebanon, Connecticut, to Hanover, New Hampshire, where it would continue under the auspices of a new college to be named in honor of the Earl of Dartmouth. But at the beginning of this round in 1765, all of the cards were not yet laid on the table. A consummate player of the game of fund-raising and educational politics, Wheelock held some of his cards close to the vest, not revealing them to Occom until he had returned from England, some two and a half years later. Throughout his journey Occom believed the goal of the trip was exclusively to establish a fund that would enable Moor's School to achieve financial stability. The role that he envisioned for himself was to serve as the primary fund-raiser. But Occom's education abroad was not precisely what he had envisioned as he boarded ship on that late December day. Rather, it served as the final embellishment for the learning trajectory that had begun almost twenty-five years earlier under Wheelock's tutelage.

The Indian Minister in England and Wales

The ship's master, John Marshall, sighted land on February 2, 1766, and, as Occom wrote, "the next Day which was ye 3 of February We went a Shore on great Briton, in a Fish Boat, and Land at a Place Call'd Bricksham [Brixham] on Tor Bay."[4] They had landed just offshore from the West Country, not far from Exeter, Devon, and they were still two hundred miles from London. By the evening of the sixth they had arrived in the capital, and, after spending the first night with a friend of Wheelock's, they were taken to George Whitefield's home.

Almost all of those involved in the fund-raising tour hoped for a resounding success. They were not disappointed. The figures initially responsible for that success included Occom's fellow fund-raiser, Nathaniel Whitaker. Selected to accompany Occom after several other ministers had declined the opportunity, Whitaker was a member of Wheelock's ministerial circle of friends and also served on the board of directors for the Connecticut Board of Correspondents, which had agreed to employ Occom when he moved back to Mohegan. Despite his credentials, Whitaker did not impress the English, who created an English board of trustees to supervise the funds collected in England and Wales. Increasingly, the English supporters began to rely on Occom himself.[5] Although Whitaker administered a successful smallpox inoculation to Occom a month or so after they arrived, beyond that initial gesture, the two men were not especially companionable, even though they were thrown together for almost thirty months.

Most of the tour's success must be attributed to Occom, whom the English quickly dubbed the "Indian minister." Aided by the astute shepherding of Whitefield, they moved among the highest circles of British society, including the nobility. They even visited the "royal robing-room," where they watched the youthful George III as he was being "arrayed for Parliament." Whitefield, their genial host, arranged for Occom to deliver his initial sermon in his tabernacle, where he "made a decided and very favorable impression."[6] As the Anglican wrote to Wheelock, "Mr Occum hath preached for me with acceptance, and also Mr Whitaker."[7] Whitefield also introduced them to the most important religious figures in London, including Selina, the Countess of Huntingdon. They met Methodists, Quakers, Independents, and Anglicans. They "waited on the Archbishop of Canterbury" and attracted the interest of the archbishop of York.[8] Later, in Scotland, they moved in the midst of a powerful cadre of Presbyterians. The Countess of Huntingdon, who was a strong patron of Methodism and a close friend of Whitefield, emerged as an important catalyst for their widening group of supporters in England. She had also been one of the early contributors to the SSPCK and had helped eased the financial burden of Moor's School. Occom and Whitaker had a ready entrée into this circle because of Wheelock's many supporters but also because of the persistent interest—by the English, the Welsh, and the Scots—in the "Red Indians." When the British met Occom firsthand, they were overwhelmed.

Occom became an instant celebrity. His initial advantage lay in his uniqueness. Since no Native American minister had previously traveled to the British Isles, Occom bore a hint of the exotic, reminiscent of the aura cast by Pocahontas during that winter of 1616–17. But Occom could not have won the support of the crowds who flocked to hear him merely because he was the "Indian minister." His singular style of preaching—he spoke simply and from the heart—and his distinctively Native appearance, plus his warmth of manner, broadened his appeal

The Reverend Samson Occom. The "Indian minister" in England. Mezzotint by J. Spilsbury from an oil painting (now lost) by Mason Chamberlin.
COURTESY THE HOOD MUSEUM OF ART, DARTMOUTH COLLEGE.

and increased the adulation. Never in his life had he been the subject of such respect. Harold Blodgett quipped that "what Occom preached was no great matter, but what he looked like was material for a Pepys."[9] Had he been a vain person, this celebrity status might well have led to vanity or that "Indian pride" that Wheelock discerned so easily among his Indian students. But Occom's humility stood him in good stead. In June 1766, after he had been in England for almost six months, he learned that "the *Stage Players*, had been *Mimicking* of me in their plays, lately." Puzzled, he added, "I never thought I Shou'd ever come to *that Honor*. O god wou'd give me a greater Courage."[10]

Beyond Hadrian's Wall: Occom in Scotland

After some fifteen heady months of preaching in London, throughout the West Country, in the eastern counties, and across Wales, Occom and Whitaker traveled north, following the western route by way of Liverpool. Whitaker had advised Wheelock two months earlier, "We are now going into Scotland i.e. to beg along the western road thither. . . . . May the presence of the God of Jacob go along with us, & make our way prosperous. The thing Seems to have got dead in London; but I hope to be Successful in the Country."[11] Begging in Liverpool profited them little, and Whitaker was unimpressed with the town. He wrote, "Liverpool is a pool of error and wickedness, the Ministers here are Socianians one Armenian & a Baptist the Same. . . . Ichabod! 50 years ago the Gospel flourished here—O that God may preserve America."[12]

By early May 1767, they had crossed to the Pictish side of Hadrian's Wall at Carlisle, where Dugald Buchanan's relatives had fallen two decades earlier, and entered Scotland. Finally, if only for a brief time, Occom was in Buchanan's homeland, the country the Gaelic bard knew in his native tongue as "Alba."

The Scottish tour had multiple ramifications. It brought Occom to the home of the General Assembly of the Church of Scotland, in Edinburgh, the birthplace of the denomination in which he was ordained. It also connected him with the directors of the Scottish Society, who had influenced his career, and his income, through the Connecticut and New York boards of correspondents. Further, the tour enabled the Scots themselves to meet their first "Red Indian" Presbyterian minister. In terms of revenue, Occom and Whitaker's Scottish visit proved an overwhelming success. In two months their tour in Scotland raised, proportionate to the population of the country, a larger sum of money than they would collect in twenty-eight months in all of England and Wales. And finally, it is highly likely that Samson Occom and Dugald Buchanan may have shared a little time together during their mutual residence in Edinburgh.

Given these considerations, it is puzzling that Occom's tour of Scotland has received virtually no attention from historians. Neither W.

Hadrian's Wall. This structure was built in A.D. 122 under the Roman emperor Hadrian to protect the frontier from the Picts of Caledonia. Traveling by way of Carlisle, Samson Occom entered Alba in the late spring of 1767.

PHOTOGRAPH BY FERENC M. SZASZ.

DeLoss Love nor Harold Blodgett deemed this portion of the fund-raising trip to be worthy of much attention. Love devoted at best a single page to the subject; Blodgett, less than a page. Even Leon Burr Richardson, whose edited work *An Indian Preacher in England* (1933) gathered a singular collection of the writings of those figures on both sides of the Atlantic who engaged in this remarkable fund-raising venture, could spare only a small portion of the collection to letters written during the two months in Scotland.[13] Hence, the following story is, perforce, based largely on primary research in the National Archives of Scotland, the National Library of Scotland, and the newspapers and other primary sources that I was able to track down during my various research trips there, as well as extensive wandering about Old Town Edinburgh, Aberdeen, and Glasgow, the Lowland towns where the "Indian minister" spent most of his time.

Occom and Whitaker remained in Scotland for just over two months. The two ministers' party arrived in early May; they left for Ireland in mid-July. It is extremely difficult to follow the tracks of their stay. They traveled light. By searching the minutes of the committee meetings of the SSPCK and comparing them with occasional newspaper articles, I found some clues but never enough to compile a definitive, day-by-day account. Since the primary goal of the two ministers was to raise funds, Occom and Whitaker negotiated immediately with the society directors to urge that the General Assembly serve as official sponsor for the fund-raising. Within two weeks of the party's arrival, Occom and Whitaker learned that this effort had failed. From that moment forward the entire fate of the mission lay in the hands of the SSPCK directors and Occom and Whitaker. Theirs was a successful joint venture.

Occom, the Society Directors, and the Lowland Churches

Certain circles in Edinburgh had eagerly awaited Occom's arrival. When his party finally rode into town, on the evening of May 12, both the Scottish Society and the local newspaper took note. The report of the society's governing committee was low-key and bureaucratic in tone: "It being represented that Mr Nathaniel Whitaker and Mr Samson Occum from America were arrived here lately in order to sollicite Contributions for an Indian School or Academy . . . they agreed that another meeting be held tomorrow to consider further of this matter."[14] Still, the official report may have squeezed dry any interest expressed by the members, who had long awaited the pair of ministers. The story printed in The *Caledonian Mercury*, one of Edinburgh's two newspapers, proved far more dramatic. Reporting on the sixteenth, the newspaper noted, "Tuesday evening arrived in town, from London, the Rev. Messrs. Nathaniel Whitaker and Samson Occom, ministers of the gospel in New England." While Whitaker received only a single mention, the reporter for the *Mercury* was intrigued with Occom. The reporter had also done his homework: "The Rev. Mr. Occom is of the *Mohegan* tribe, and was the first scholar educated by Mr. Wheelock. After being employed as a schoolmaster in the wilderness, he was ordained as a minister of the gospel by the *Suffolk* presbytery on *Long-island*, where his influence among the Indians is very considerable. He is the *first Indian preacher* that ever *set his foot* in *Britain*." The reporter was also impressed with the expression of strong support for Wheelock's plan: "We are informed that the Design on which these gentlemen have come, has been very strongly recommended by *Sir William Johnson*, and many of the governors and assemblies in North America."[15] Wheelock's plan for Occom and Whitaker to secure testimonials before their departure had proved a shrewd investment.

Of the two institutions—the governing committee of the SSPCK and the *Caledonian Mercury*—the society's committee faced the greater challenge. The newspaper reporter was looking for a good story, and he certainly found one with Occom's arrival. But the committee, which did hold a meeting on May 23, shouldered the burden of coordinating the fund-raising campaign.

According to the minutes, the committee members first considered the role that the General Assembly might play in the campaign. The highest body of the Church of Scotland, the General Assembly maintained its offices at the edge of Old Town, a location overlooking the swampy region north of Old Town, which would be soon drained before it became the fashionable New Town, linked to Old Town through a series of bridges connecting the medieval with the "modern." With its stunning location, the General Assembly buildings would later serve as a temporary home for the members of the new Scottish parliament of 1999, who awaited the completion of the controversial Holyrood parliament building in the fall of 2004. As Occom and Whitaker were traveling to Edinburgh, the General Assembly staff was preparing for their annual meeting, a gathering of Presbyterians from all across Scotland, arriving in such numbers they must have dominated the capital every year during the last two weeks of May. Whitaker knew well that their trip to Scotland must coincide with the anticipated opening of the annual meeting. Two months earlier, he had advised Wheelock that they would travel north "till we come there to the Gen. Assemly which meets about the Midle of May." But he also anticipated the assembly's refusal to support their endeavor, adding, "I fear Success at the Genl Assembly of S. but God reigns."[16] When the two colonials arrived, Kirk leaders were anticipating the opening of the meeting, which lay only nine days away. Considering the immediacy of Occom and Whitfield's request, which they delivered in the form of a memorial on "Mr Wheelocks Indian School," the group agreed to appoint several committee members to meet with several members of the assembly "to converse with them as to the expediency of Presenting a Petition to the Assembly for a Collection."[17]

Four days later, on May 27, the society committee met again. The news was disastrous. Those delegated to "converse" with the assembly members had made no headway. The members pondered the next step. Finally, they resolved that "a Narrative of Mr Wheelock, Proceedings be printed & circulated to Presbytrys in name of the Societys recommending a Collection for said School to be under the management of the Society & their Board of Correspondent Connecticut and appended to that Contribution be Transmitted to Mr John Forrest, Mr Arch Wallace and Mr Rob Scott Moncrieff Merchant in Edinburgh." The committee recommended that Dr. Alexander Webster, minister of Tolbooth Kirk in Edinburgh, Whitaker, and Occom "prepare said narrative for the Press."[18]

By reaching this decision, the committee had taken a firm stand after being rebuffed by the General Assembly. Their immediate action was reminiscent of the founding years, when the earliest members boldly struck out on their own because they believed, correctly, that the parish schools established by the Kirk did not begin to meet the needs of the difficult terrain, let alone the vastness of Highlands and Islands parishes. If one accepted the premise that sufficient schools for Gaelic youth had to be established beyond the Highland Line, then the stand of the society would eventually be proved right. In the interim years, the society and the General Assembly had often cooperated. In this instance, the society found itself without its old ally. But by the 1760s, it had garnered considerable experience in appealing to the financial largesse of Scottish Presbyterians, and it would draw on this during the remaining weeks of the two colonials' visit.

By June 3, when the society governing committee met again, Occom and Whitaker were in attendance, and they, presumably with Dr. Webster, reported that they had completed the "Memorial." Although their voices at this meeting remained unrecorded, it is likely they also approved of the decision to read the "Memorial" to the "General Meeting" of the society, scheduled for the following day. One week later, when the committee met again, they encountered yet another challenge—how to persuade their fellow Scots that "Wheelock's Indian School" should be supported through their contributions. With their usual aplomb, they resolved "that copies of the Narrative & Memorial should be transmitted by Couriers to the Ministers of All the most Considerable Places in Scotland" and, further, that the memorial "be asserted with some alterations in the Edinburgh News Paper."[19]

In this propitious manner, the word passed from household to household. On Monday, June 15, 1767, the *Caledonian Mercury* devoted a full page to the memorial, printing the entire text, which, incidentally, was signed only by "Nath. Whitaker," and following it with a commendation by the SSPCK, signed by the Marquis of Lothian, president of the society. The society's statement reflected its customary pragmatism. It reconfirmed the goals of "Mr Wheelock's plan for the conversion and civilization of the Indians." Then it went directly to the point. " 'Tis desired," the marquis wrote, "that the money collected on this occasion, may be lodged with [the following]." The names that appeared were leading figures, whether merchants, provosts, or mayors of Scotland's key towns. Significantly, they included Edinburgh and Glasgow, in the central Lowland corridor; Perth, Dundee, Montrose, and Aberdeen, the urban centers that hugged the coastline of the North Sea above Edinburgh (except Perth, which was upstream along the River Tay); Inverness, the only town of any size in the eastern Highlands but a border Highland town; and, finally, Dumfries, the single town representing the West Country, where Robert Burns would later make his home.

The virtual advertisement in the *Caledonian Mercury* was a classic example of the society at work, except in this instance, the publicity benefited considerably from the assistance of Occom and Whitaker, who must have written much of the memorial. But the cleverness of the newspaper publication and the shrewd selection of the towns reflected the society's well-honed experience in raising funds for their own primary cause—schools among the Highlanders. The finishing touch was the distribution of the funds to key individuals in each town and the instruction that "the money received by these respective collectors, be transmitted to Mr John Davidson, Treasurer to the Society." The society left nothing to chance. But it also encouraged the notion of self-determination within each institution collecting funds, advising, "as they propose, for the satisfaction of all the contributors, that the money should be under their own direction." Occom and Whitaker could have not selected more able partners in their venture.[20]

The campaign could well have foundered without one additional dimension: the call for help issued by preaching in the churches. Throughout their stay, both Occom and Whitaker took their cause to individual churches throughout the Lowlands. The record is not clear as to exactly how many churches welcomed them. Still, by piecing together the fragmentary primary accounts, I have concluded that, cumulatively, they spoke in at least ten churches or other venues. I suspect that they may have addressed perhaps twice as many congregations during their two-month stay.

In some instances we know who spoke; in others, the account does not mention which one spoke where. Both of them preached in Edinburgh itself. The society invited Whitaker to preach there on several days directly before he and Occom left for Ireland.[21] But Occom must have been the first Native American invited to speak in Scotland, as he had been in London. Less than two weeks after their arrival in the capital, the "Indian minister" preached at the famous Tolboth Kirk, where Alexander Webster—the society committee member who had joined Occom and Whitaker in the writing of the memorial—presided.[22] In early to mid-June, both men were in Glasgow for at least a week, if not longer, where they apparently resided with a Mr. George Brown, a merchant of Tronsgate, Glasgow.[23] The *Glasgow Journal* announced to its readers, "Last week arrived here the Rev. Mr. Occum the Indian preacher, and Mr. Whitaker from North America, they preached in several churches in town."[24] Clearly, the *Journal* gauged which of the two men would be of interest to its readers. Writing to Whitaker during the Glasgow visit, Alexander Webster noted the response of the Glaswegians: "it gives me great pleasure that you have met with so favorable a reception at Glasgow."[25] Outside Glasgow, in mid-July, when Whitaker was preaching in Edinburgh, Occom delivered a sermon at a church in Paisley, a town just outside Glasgow.[26] As elsewhere, the churches or other venues responded to the energy released by these sermons to collect funds for Moor's School. The *Glasgow Journal* reminded its readers, "we hear a collection is to be made next Sunday in the Church of Relief, for the Indian charity-School."[27] Assuming they also preached elsewhere in these two leading towns, Occom and Whitaker carried their message across the entire central belt of Scotland.

Beyond the two main towns, it is quite possible that at least one of them, probably Occom, also spoke to congregations in Perth, and perhaps Dundee and Montrose, en route to Aberdeen. It is doubtful if either of them traveled as far north as Inverness. And there is no indication that they were able to travel to the West Country to visit Dumfries. But among the towns along the North Sea, the tour had a strong impact on Aberdeen, which, thanks to its location well up the coast from Edinburgh, was probably the farthest outpost for their travel. Occom made it as far as the Granite City, which lay between the River Dee and the River Don, by the end of June. On Monday, June 29, the *Aberdeen Journal* informed its readers, "Yesterday, the Rev. Mr. Occum, the Indian Minister, preached in this place to a very crowded Audience." Aberdeen, which was one of the towns listed in the society's piece published on June 15 in Edinburgh's *Caledonian Mercury*, responded with alacrity. On July 6, just a week after Occom's popular appearance, the *Journal* reported, "Yesterday intimation was given from the pulpits of this city, that a public collection is to be made at the Church doors next Lord's day, for Mr. Wheelock's *Indian Academy*, and, when made, to be paid to Baillie *Abercromby* . . . to be transmitted along with whatever private contributions shall be sent him, according to the recommendation of the *Society for propagating Christian Knowledge*."[28] Exactly one week later the *Journal* announced that the collection "for Mr. Wheelock's *Academy, for educating Indian missionaries* had amounted to 78/ [£78]." It also noted, "we hear that some contributions have already been sent privately to Baillie Abercromby, and others will probably be sent . . . there is reason to believe, that there will be a very considerable addition to the contributions from this city, before they be remitted to the Society at Edinburgh."[29] Pride in the generosity of the Aberdeen churches and private donors could be read between the lines of the local newspaper editor's announcement.

The society's governing committee, alongside Occom and Whitaker, could be proud of their combined effort toward fund-raising. The *Scots Magazine* of June 1767 reported the following sums collected: (all figures in pounds) Aberdeen church-doors, 78; South Leith church, 56; Relief church at Edinburgh, 74; Relief church at Glasgow, 94; Glasgow, 299; Paisley, 52; Kilmarnock, 36; East Kilbridie, 33; Cambuslang, 26; Sheetleslon church, 18; Greenock, 14; Carmonoch, 13; Blantyre, 13. This totals approximately £806 (numbers were rounded off to the pound), and it is not a complete figure since the magazine appeared before Occom and Whitaker left Scotland. It also contrasts sharply with the mere £39 raised in their stay in Liverpool. The total amount raised in Scotland during the two months was £2,529. By contrast, the total amount collected in England and Wales in a period of over two years was £9,497.[30] The Scots had outdone themselves.

Occom and Buchanan in Edinburgh

During the Scottish tour Samson Occom and Dugald Buchanan walked the same streets of the capital. Reconstructing the Occom and Whitaker visit suggests that Occom clearly did not spend all of this two months in Edinburgh. He was in Glasgow for perhaps two weeks; the trip to Aberdeen may have taken him out of Edinburgh for perhaps a week or two. But it is likely that he remained in the capital for at least a month, if not longer. Buchanan's lengthy residence in Edinburgh occurred at the same time.

Returning to the major venture that drew Buchanan to Edinburgh, it is a challenge to reconstruct the exact timing of his residence, but the following account may shed some light. The meetings of the governing committee of the SSPCK record that Buchanan's first involvement in the translation of the New Testament occurred when he participated in a proposed revised translation that was to supersede the one that James Stuart had already finished. Although Stuart (whose name is spelled both "Stewart" and "Stuart" in the minutes) had completed a translation by the fall of 1764, the committee found itself in the uncomfortable position of agreeing to this version or acknowledging the criticism of West Highlanders, who argued that Stuart's translation could not be understood by Gaelic speakers in the West.[31]

Throughout the winter and spring of 1764–65, the committee members vacillated over giving approval to Stuart's translation. In the interim, they engaged other Highlanders literate in Gaelic and English to revise Stuart's translation of the New Testament. Buchanan entered the scene for two reasons. The society already knew of his work as schoolmaster and catechist, and earlier they had engaged him to "translate the mother's catechism into Earse [Gaelic]," which he had completed in the summer of 1758.[32] Hence, his reputation was assured. This time, the society asked him to be one of the transcribers for the revised translation, ordering "that Mr. Dougald Buchanan be conjoined with those already employed in transcribing it." The Highlanders engaged in the revision included a minister of Inverness and a minister of Slate. The latter was probably from Sleat, at the southern end of the Isle of Skye.[33] By February 1765 the committee had agreed to pay "the several lads employed in transcribing the Gaelic version of the New Testament ... for their trouble in this work ... at the rate of six pence [per page]." Essentially, Buchanan and his fellow transcribers were engaged in piecework that acknowledged their considerable skills. Few were qualified for such an intricate and complex assignment.

In the end, their combined effort appeared to have favored Stuart. By

Title page, Gaelic New Testament. Dugald Buchanan assisted in the translation and directed the printing of this major work, which appeared in 1767.
COURTESY THE NATIONAL ARCHIVES OF SCOTLAND, GD95/11/15.

the summer of 1765, Stuart had persuaded the society's governing committee that his translation should emerge as the official Gaelic New Testament. However, the minutes, which are recorded in the same bureaucratic tone maintained during Occom and Whitaker's visit, do not reveal all of the machinations involved in this translation dispute. But the net result granted James Stuart the victory, at least temporarily. In early January 1766 the committee requested that Stuart, with the assistance of his son and Dugald Buchanan, "superintend the Printing."[34] During the remaining few weeks of January and February, however, the committee heard further complaints from West Highlanders. Still, by the first week of March, they had finally conceded to the persuasive powers of Stuart, who was shrewd enough to attend the first meeting of that month. Given the arrival of "Mr Stuart [who] had come to town . . . and . . . was waiting in the next room . . . . the committee ordered . . . . that the work be put in the Press with all convenient speed." Stuart's presence had worked miracles, and the committee ordered "that 10,000 Copies of said Testament should be printed for the Society."[35]

By the first meeting of April 1766, which occurred on the third of the month, the minutes recorded that Buchanan, "one of the Societys masters [is] presently in town overseeing the translation of the New Testament."[36] Assuming that Buchanan had begun to supervise the printing in the spring of 1766, this means that he had been living in Edinburgh a little more than a year when Occom and his party reached the capital. The New Testament had not been completed by May 12, 1767, the day Occom and Whitaker arrived in Edinburgh, but by June 26, during the middle of Occom's visit, the committee learned "that Mr Stuarts Gallic version of the New Testament would be finished within a few days."

The committee's response to this dramatic news was pragmatic. They did not pause to cheer, or at least the secretary did not record any applause. Rather, they addressed their immediate responsibility, which was to consider "what further remuneration shall be given to Mr Stuart & Dugald Buchanan for their trouble in their work." They solved this question neatly, by appointing a subcommittee to study the matter. It was likely that Occom was out of town at the time of this meeting, since he was preaching in Aberdeen on the twenty-eighth. On July 2, when the committee met again and agreed that Buchanan should "be allowed the further sum of £30—for his trouble in superintending the Press over and above the weekly allowance of 12 sh agreed to be paid to him of former minute," Occom was probably back in

Edinburgh. He did not preach in Paisley until the tenth, over a week later.[37]

The question of dates and of whether or not Occom and Buchanan's presence in Edinburgh overlapped suggests that they were both in town for a substantial part of Occom's stay, even though he was moving about the Lowlands for his various preaching assignments. This brings us back to the issue of whether Occom and Buchanan had an opportunity to meet. I conclude that it is highly likely that they did meet. Although no one has yet discovered definitive proof of their meeting, given the size of Edinburgh, the publicity granted to the Scottish visit, the extensive involvement of churches across the Lowlands, and, finally, the closely linked society of the Lowland figures involved in Reformed Protestant schooling, whether in the Highlands or among the "Red Indians," it would be astonishing had they not. At the same time, I also conclude that whether or not they met is probably less important than the symbolic value of their simultaneous presence in the heart of Edinburgh and the homeland of the Scottish Society.

The Edinburgh Connection

A speculative assessment of the proposed Occom-Buchanan conversation suggests the significance of their likely meeting. It is worth pondering how these two eighteenth-century men might have reacted to each other in the spring and early summer of 1767. Even on their initial acquaintance, Occom and Buchanan might well have learned how much they shared in common. They would have discovered how they were linked by their indigenous backgrounds, by their encounter with Reformed Protestantism, and by their openness to merging the Reformed faith tradition with their own cultures. In this context, they would also have discovered another immediate connection, one that was rooted in their steady reliance on the medium of an oral tradition. Both of their cultures relied on speech and song, poetry and story. Their commonalities were legion.

During this meeting, they would have communicated in English, a second language for each. Since these sparks of recognition might well have startled the two men, they could have easily moved the conversation in any number of different directions. Each of these spiritual intermediaries would have recognized that the other was unique. Together, they would have seen that each was a crucial figure of his own culture and that each was most comfortable moving within his culture. At the same time, they would have been instantly aware that both of them had traveled in circles outside their cultures and had sought to bring to their own people some of the faith tradition that had appealed to them as individuals. The ultimate recognition would have come when they realized that each of them held the cultural integrity of his people above all other values.

Hence, as Native spiritual intermediaries, they might have forged an instant bond. They would have found far more in common with each other than they shared with the other Reformed Protestant figures who had brought them together in Scotland's capital as mutual inheritors of the Great Awakening. Had this event occurred in the twenty-first century, the conversation between Occom and Buchanan would have been audio- or videotaped. Major television channels would have featured this unusual meeting, and all of the appropriate individuals would have issued pithy sound bites about its significance. The contrast is overwhelming and serves as a stark reminder of the changes brought about by technology and communication. In reality, any awareness of this speculative mid-eighteenth-century conversation had to be constrained by the technology of the era. Hence, it continues to be bounded by that era and must remain, like so many other events of the eighteenth century, largely a fabric woven by our imaginations.

The Repercussions of Occom's Tour Abroad

After they left Scotland, Occom and Whitaker traveled briefly to northern Ireland and then back to London by way of North Britain and the east coast. Occom returned to Connecticut in the spring of 1768 with a far more sophisticated understanding of the British Empire and the structured society that lay behind it. He also carried home an awareness of his own personal fame, which was partly responsible for the growing division between him and his former mentor. Wheelock continued to view Occom as a "child" who was prone to "that Indian distemper, *Pride*."[38] But the full rupture between the two men only came when Occom learned that the months that he had spent across the water, a lengthy time that had absorbed his energies and separated him from his wife and children, would not contribute to the maintenance of Moor's School at Lebanon. Rather, the school was to be shifted away from the villages of his people—ranging from Montauks to Mohegans and from Delawares to Narragansetts—and moved north to the forested lands of western New Hampshire. Dartmouth College, which incorporated Moor's School and was opened by Wheelock in 1769, would primarily address the needs of those English who sought to become missionaries to the Indians, not the Natives themselves.[39] Occom was horrified. Eventually he broke off relations with Wheelock. He never afterward visited the "hypocritical institution" known as Dartmouth College.

Occom found himself in considerable difficulty on his return. His break with Wheelock served to compound his economic woes. The Boston commissioners had relinquished his services at Wheelock's request; the Connecticut Board of Correspondents—which had promised to pay his salary—basically lost its raison d'être when the English board of trustees was created during the fund-raising tour. Wheelock was still convinced that Occom should become a missionary to the Iroquois, but Occom resisted this plan. Occom wanted only to remain in his homeland. But this choice obviated the possibility of any regular income. Although he received occasional donations from his friends on the English board of trustees, this was quickly spent, and, in the end, he was left without resources.

Following a brief time of depression during the early 1770s, Occom found himself caught up again in a local Native religious revival, one that echoed on a small scale the Great Awakening, the movement that had served as a catalyst for his life's career as minister and schoolmaster. Occom's works also came into print during this time, an event that further enhanced his reputation. Acting on a hunch, a New Haven printer ran off a 1772 edition of a sermon on temperance that Occom had been asked to preach at a public hanging of a Mohegan who had committed a murder while intoxicated. The printer's instinct paid off. As the first printed sermon delivered by a Native minister, it sold out and eventually went through a number of printings as a temperance tract.[40]

Two years later Occom's second publication, *A Choice Collection of Hymns and Spiritual Songs*, appeared.[41] Like Buchanan's spiritual songs, Occom's hymns reflected the influence of British hymnists, but, unlike Buchanan, Occom had met most of the prominent hymnists during the fund-raising tour. Although the majority of the 108 hymns in the 1774 edition were written by Isaac Watts and others, Occom himself wrote a "considerable number" of them, which historian W. DeLoss Love notes "have distinctly his earmarks in certain expressions." The most famous of Occom's hymns, "Wak'd by the Gospel's Pow'rful Sound," remained an integral part of nineteenth-century American hymnody. The others served Occom and his Algonquian people.[42]

Shortly before the outbreak of the American Revolution in 1775,

Occom also became a driving force for a dynamic migration of his people—the southern New England Algonquians from Connecticut, Rhode Island, and Long Island—who planned to move onto Oneida lands west of the Hudson River. Convinced that it was time to leave the increasing levels of English pressure, these Natives would eventually leave their Mohegan and Pequot communities, the Tunxis community in Farmington, Connecticut, and the Narragansett, Niantic, and Montauk villages. Although a small number left for Oneida country before the war, the main body of emigrants stalled until after the Peace of Paris in 1783.[43]

In 1784 Occom joined with members of these other communities, which included some of his own family, to make the long-awaited trek to Iroquois country. The war had ended; it was time to move on. A year later the displaced Algonquian people organized themselves formally, naming their new community Eeyamquiltoossuconnuck, or Brothertown. Several years later, in her second wrenching move, Mary Occom left the family home at Mohegan to join her husband at Brothertown. For Occom, the move to the Brothertown community, where he spent the last years of his life, led to some of his most contented days. There he could preach to his people in their own language, sing with them, often using the hymns that he had written, go fishing with his relatives and friends, and watch the transplanted community grow. The last entries in his journal reflect the peace that he had found among his own people, a considerable distance away from his former English neighbors in Connecticut and even farther from those figures he had come to know in England, Wales, and Scotland.[44] In 1792, when Samson Occom died, eight years after the move to Brothertown, Indians traveled from great distances to attend the funeral and to cherish the memories of their remarkable spiritual leader.

When Occom and Buchanan made their agonizing career choices, they found themselves poised on the cusp of the universal experience characterizing the relationship between peoples subjected to cultural colonialism and the colonial powers themselves. Their actions epitomized the decisions of leaders who have faced those choices of how to remold their societies as their people encounter the outsiders. The decisions these two men made enabled them and their followers to find a new path that combined a faith tradition from the outside with some of the older ways and worldviews that had come down to them through word and song within their families and communities.

The path of a cultural intermediary has never been an easy one. Both of these men encountered criticism among their own people, whether Gaels or Mohegans. Even Occom's wife, Mary, was distressed that her husband returned from England with English ways that seemed foreign to the Montauk ways that she preferred.[45] In Scotland during the late-nineteenth and twentieth centuries, Gaelic Highlanders still remained divisive over Buchanan's influence. Gaelic poet Derick Thomson wrote that Buchanan's "obsession with the pains of Hell . . . [has] festered in the Highlands ever since Buchanan's time."[46]

Yet antagonism toward Buchanan also retained a vivid presence in the Highlands. In his autobiography, the Skye-born Presbyterian minister Norman Maclean, who had been a pupil at Raining's school in Inverness during the 1880s, recalled a comment of his childhood friend Sam. As the two lads were fishing one day, Sam told him that he might be refused baptism because of his father's beliefs. "You see," he explained to Norman, "my father was a great whistler. . . . And then he loved to sing the old Gaelic songs. It was no use his asking baptism for his children for he would be told that he must stop whistling and singing worldly songs. And he couldn't do that, and he didn't like the songs of Dugald Buchanan."[47]

Still, these two intermediaries continued to believe that crossing the boundary that separated them from outsiders did not mean that they could never return. Both Occom and Buchanan *did* return. They were able to cross and recross the line, stepping back and forth into new and old. They continued to rely on their Gaelic or Mohegan language; they retained their sense of community and their connections with the land; and they maintained their obligations to their people. At the same time, they were unwilling to relinquish the imported Calvinism that had changed their lives and the lives of the Gaelic Highlanders and the southern New England Algonquians. Hence, while they merged their cultures through a unique form of syncretism, they brought that syncretism home. Their home always remained within their Native communities. And in that context—selecting their place and their kinspeople, those with whom they were most comfortable—they clearly preferred the Mohegans and the Gaelic Highlanders.

Conclusion

When the Scottish Society held its inaugural meeting on November 3, 1709, the members of the SSPCK were poised to amalgamate their country into a single cultural entity. Their idealism was palpable. Their organization was astounding. Within two years, with some assistance from the Church of Scotland's General Assembly, the society had cast a financial web that stretched through Scotland, England, and Wales and across to Ireland. The support made available through this financial network enabled the SSPCK to send the earliest of its Gaelic speaking schoolmasters and catechists to the Highlands and Islands, where they would teach the body of knowledge that the Lowlanders deemed "civilization."

The first of their representatives to carry the Presbyterian banner beyond the Highland Line was a catechist who in 1711 sailed beyond the Outer Hebrides to the remote isles of St. Kilda, where he found all the residents to be Gaelic speakers. The second, sent in the following year, was a schoolmaster who traveled north to Sutherland to open a school inland from the North Sea, along the Strath of Kildonan. Stimulated by the opening of its schools in the Highlands and spurred by contributions from donors who had earmarked them for the Christianization of Native people outside Scotland, within three decades of Queen Anne's letters patent the society had extended its influence across the Atlantic. Reaching into Native communities along North America's eastern seaboard, the society initiated its North American venture rather haphazardly but finally found its footing among the Native Americans of the Northeast. Shortly thereafter, in 1738, the society received its second letters patent, which expanded the schooling in order to provide for industrial training for Highland youth, such as the spinning schools that were introduced for girls and young women.

During the initial decades, when the SSPCK sent its Lowlands representatives beyond the Highland Line, its schoolmasters and catechists came up against a Gaelic society that had yet to suffer the repercussions of the Forty-Five, the final Jacobite rebellion. For the SSPCK schoolmasters and catechists, the resistance rooted in the Jacobitism of the early eighteenth century meant that the first educational encounter sometimes bore a hard edge. The mood for rebellion was engendered, at least in part, by the anti-Hanoverian sentiment shared by a number of the clans. In 1700 the culture of the Highlands and Islands that would be altered beyond recognition by events of the eighteenth and early nineteenth centuries still clung to some of its earlier ways. Ordinary clansmen and women continued to rely on the oral tradition of Gaelic song, storytelling, and bardic verse. Through this means, they carried the past into their lives and crafted an ongoing commentary on the present. In their religious faiths, most of the ordinary clanspeople were Episcopal, not Lowland Presbyterian, and almost all, whether Episcopal, Presbyterian, or Catholic, retained some pre-Christian beliefs and remnants of old ceremonies. At the same time, ordinary clanspeople had found economic survival more difficult due to the increasing financial demands of the clan chiefs as imposed by their tacksmen, but the clan members continued to provide for their families through herding and by raising a little barley and oats, as they had before. Some, however, had become drovers for the expansive cattle trade in the Lowlands.

In the decades before the Forty-Five, the society adopted a singular approach to its self-appointed goal of bringing Presbyterianism and English literacy to the Highlands. This approach would differ from its later stance. Initially, the society heeded its own proscription against the use of Gaelic in the schoolroom by delivering a stern warning to the masters who traveled to Edinburgh for their initial interview. The gist of the warning was that the schoolmasters should use no Gaelic during their instruction. Even though some of the early schoolmasters rebelled against the stricture, the society held fast until mid-century. The society directors stubbornly refused to thaw their frozen linguistic stance until after the Battle of Culloden Moor. Only when the Jacobite clans had been defeated did the society reconsider its prohibition of Gaelic; only then did it offer to provide funding for the publication of a bilingual New Testament in Scottish Gaelic. And even then its apparent change of heart belied the society's conviction that the use of Gaelic instruction in the schools might further its ultimate goal—the destruction of the Gaelic language. Since teachers who served in the Highlands schools in the mid-nineteenth century still punished their pupils for speaking Gaelic in the classroom, the society's original mandate against the vernacular tongue demonstrated an astonishing power of persistence.

By the late eighteenth century, the society's plan for replacing the culture of the Highlands with its own belief system—the culture of the Lowlands—had bequeathed an enduring legacy in the regions beyond the Highland Line. Music had once played an important role in Highland life. Lowland Presbyterianism modified this role. The relationship between Scottish Calvinism and music is an uneasy one. As recently as the early 1990s, when I lived in the Lowlands, the Presbyterian church that I attended briefly did not provide any musical accompaniment for the hymns. The hymnals included only the words for the hymns; there was no score available. If the visitor did not happen to know the tune, he or she could only follow along with the other voices. During the eighteenth century, some of the Highlanders who eagerly accepted the Presbyterian form of Calvinism also endorsed the belief that playing the fiddle was a form of sin. In several instances, fiddlers discarded or destroyed the instruments they had played throughout their lives. From a Calvinist perspective, which frowned on musical accompaniment, these fiddle destroyers were justified because they were rejecting the "instrument of the devil."

During the Scottish diaspora of the late eighteenth and early nineteenth centuries, the Highlanders carried with them the memories of their folk music as well as their instruments in the ships that bore them across the water to Nova Scotia and elsewhere around the world. In this manner, the pre-Calvinist tunes, often lost in the Highlands themselves, retained their life among the emigrants. Today, in the early twenty-first century, the descendants of those emigrant Scots living in Nova Scotia retain their reputation for excellence in performing traditional folk music of the Highlands.

Music was not the sole casualty of this cultural encounter. In the Gaelic-speaking areas, the SSPCK contributed widely to the loss of the indigenous language. By the mid- to late eighteenth century, after the society had modified its approach to the question of teaching in Gaelic, its pejorative attitude toward the vernacular tongue had already rubbed off on the Gaels themselves. By then, parents urged that their children be taught English in school, reasoning that they could speak Gaelic at home. English became synonymous with "progress"; Gaelic with "backwardness." Without English one could not "get ahead" in the modern world. Across the generations, the relevance of Gaelic seemed to diminish, and it gradually became the "language of the past." Although some Gaels continued to speak Gaelic, most deemed knowledge of the native language as archaic, in part because it failed to guarantee any future for young people. In the early twenty-first century, those Gaels who continue to speak their language in the home and who enjoy listening to Gaelic radio live in the Hebrides or Glasgow and its environs. Some Glaswegian Gaelic speakers come from the Highlands and Islands, such as the Patrick Highlanders, largely from the Isle of Lewis; other Glaswegians brought their Gaelic (Irish) with them when they immigrated to Scotland from Ireland.

By intruding into the Highlanders' culture with their own beliefs, the society introduced further dissension into the once-powerful clan system. Already caught in the downward spiral begun in the seventeenth century with the financial indebtedness of the clan chiefs and exacerbated by the era of Jacobitism, military defeat, and the Hanoverian revenge exacted after 1746, the society's introduction of Lowland education further dismembered the culture. Although the clan children of ordinary Highlanders represented a culture already torn, the schoolmasters, catechists, and ministers continued to hammer relentlessly at the Scottish Gaels' understanding of the world. The weakness of the clan chiefs, whose debts had driven them to become landlords rather than chiefs, compounded by the defeat of the Jacobite warriors and the post-Culloden restrictions, crumbled further under the Presbyterian attack against the Gaelic language, the Episcopalian religion, and the unique worldviews once sheltered by the isolation promised by the Highland Line. The cultural encounter engendered by the SSPCK further diminished the folk culture of the Gaelic Highlanders; it did not fully disappear, but it did retreat to the more remote regions of their land.

When the SSPCK entered the crowded field of educational colonialism on the western shores of the North Atlantic, it encountered diverse indigenous attitudes toward outsiders, which proved difficult for Scottish Lowlanders to comprehend. For the society, generalizations about Native peoples served no purpose because each group bore a different story. Each village, tribe, or nation had lived through different kinds of historical experiences, both pre- and post-Columbian, and these experiences, as well as the cultures they brought to these encounters, had molded their lives and their kinship systems. Indigenous Americans had always been changing; adaptation was an integral part of their lives. Generations of Native peoples had rubbed shoulders through trade and warfare long before the new outsiders arrived in their lands. Well before 1492, these Natives had learned to blend some of their ceremonies and faith traditions. The introduction of the society's faith perspective, explained by schoolmasters and missionaries, was scarcely a new experience for Native Americans. Presbyterianism, ensconced in its formal classroom educational instruction, merely merged with their ongoing story as yet another instance of change.

Hence, Algonquian villagers of the Northeast, like the Delawares who chose to send their youth to Wheelock's Indian charity boarding school, had already altered their religious views through the Reformed Protestantism taught by missionaries like the Brainerd brothers. Although they feared to part with their children, these villagers viewed Moor's School as an opportunity for the Delaware youth to gain further knowledge of English ways in order to benefit the people. Since they had already modified their religion by incorporating a syncretic faith, from their perspective Moor's School promised further lessons in that tradition of adaptation.

By contrast, the Iroquois interaction with European cultures proved more eclectic. Well before the arrival of Europeans, the Iroquois had undergone tremendous societal changes, particularly during the era when they formed the League of the Iroquois. The Iroquois encountered a diverse group of Europeans, ranging from the French to the Dutch and the English, each of which was accompanied by representatives of its respective faith. Various Iroquois nations, and especially the Huron Nation, met the Jesuits, who had dominated French-Native relations during the seventeenth century, but other Iroquois encountered the Dutch Reformed Church, which had arrived with the early Dutch settlers along the Hudson, and the Anglicans, who had accompanied the English. When the Reformed Protestants, like Samuel Kirkland, arrived in the mid- to late eighteenth century, they were making a somewhat tardy appearance among these Iroquois nations. But the Hodenosaunee had two distinct advantages over the Algonquians. The first was their more remote location; the second was their population of some thirty to forty thousand people. Due to their sheer size as well as the power of the league, plus their considerable distance from the initial English settlements, by 1700 they still retained a greater body of their Native worldviews and ceremonies than their Algonquian counterparts.

The Scottish Society's role among the Native peoples of North America did not replicate its strong influence in the Highlands and Islands. In southern New England and adjacent regions, it had been preceded by the Congregationalists; within the Iroquois League, despite Kirkland's influence among the Oneidas, it ran squarely into prior claims of the Church of England and the Jesuits; and among the Cherokees and Creeks, its ventures stumbled before they were ever put in place. Still, the society carved out a role for itself in the north. It funded English and Native missionaries, including the Brainerd brothers, Kirkland, and Occom. The society directors were shrewd enough to delegate their authority through the regional boards of correspondence, and the society exerted considerable influence over Moor's School, Samson Occom, and the schoolmasters and ministers sent to the Iroquois villages by the Connecticut Board of Correspondents. Later, it would extend that influence to Moor's School and Dartmouth College in Hanover, New Hampshire.

Still, the largesse of the Scots, reflected by their generous contributions to the Occom-Whitaker fund-raising tour in the Scottish Lowlands, remained almost exclusively in Scottish hands. When Wheelock founded Dartmouth College in 1769, he and his descendants quickly learned that the Scottish Society was unwilling to loosen its control over the funds raised by Occom and Whitaker in 1767 unless Dartmouth could prove that the money would be used to educate Native, not English or European American students who were training to become missionaries to Native peoples. Also, even when it agreed to support Native students, the society restricted the use of those funds, informing Dartmouth that the college could only draw on the accrued interest. By the late eighteenth century, the society's financial prudence had become a revered tradition among its members. Early in the century, when the SSPCK first secured funding upon receipt of its initial letters patent in 1709, its working funds could not dip into the principle. It was only logical that decades later the society would extend this financial precedent to its relationship with Dartmouth College.

By contrast, the English Trust, formed during Occom and Whitaker's lengthy stay in England and Wales, proved quite willing to release to Dartmouth the funds that the two ministers had garnered in England and Wales. The Scots' refusal seemed almost a symbolic gesture, testifying to an intense commitment to a source of financial support that would exist in perpetuity. The Scots had absorbed the crucial lesson about retaining a "nest egg." They also felt more comfortable with the funds under their own control. They shrewdly guessed that the newly independent Americans might spend, with little compunction, all those contributions that the Scots themselves had raised, largely through the Lowland church members who donated some of their earnings, but also as an expression of their idealism. These Lowlanders reaffirmed the worthiness of the Moor's School cause that Occom and Whitaker promoted in Edinburgh, Glasgow, Aberdeen, and surrounding towns because it reminded them of their own civilizing cause among the Scottish Highlanders.

In 1716, only five years after the society had sent its first representative to St. Kilda, Dugald Buchanan, society schoolmaster, catechist, and translator extraordinaire, was born on the ancestral lands of the

Buchanan clan, just northeast of Loch Lomond. Buchanan was seven years old when his Mohegan counterpart, Samson Occom, schoolmaster, Presbyterian minister, and adviser to southern New England Algonquian communities, was born, probably on Uncas Hill, just above the Mohegan River, on the ancestral lands of the Mohegan, in the colony of Connecticut.

In the twin trajectories of their lives, Samson Occom and Dugald Buchanan epitomized the link between the Gaels of the Scottish Highlands and Islands and the Native peoples of North America. The Mohegan Algonquians and the Perthshire Gaels completed this link through their parallel connection with the Scottish Society and the Presbyterian Kirk. So too did the ambiguities that framed their lives reflect the ambiguities of indigenous people as they faced the choices regarding adaptation and change in their daily lives.

While Occom and Buchanan appeared to embrace fully the Reformed Protestantism introduced by both Congregationalists and Presbyterians in New England and the Church of Scotland in the Highlands, in reality, theirs was a selective appropriation. Both of these spiritual intermediaries faced dozens of choices during the course of their lives. Oftentimes they seemed to choose the outsiders' faith, the outsiders' worldview, and the outsiders' approach to life. But they never moved fully out of their Native American and Gaelic worlds. Despite their written publications and their respective journals, they remained committed to an oral culture of word and song. And in every instance, they chose on behalf of their people in their struggle to adjust to the world of the outsiders. After the American Revolution, Occom determined to migrate northwest with his people to Brothertown—the community located on lands the Oneidas had reserved for the southern New England Algonquians—because he could no longer abide living among the English of Connecticut. To Occom, the English seemed to have all of the power, all of the wealth, and all of the influence. When Buchanan chose to move away from his beloved Highlands and down to Edinburgh, he intended to remain only for the length of time required to supervise the printing of the New Testament. He agreed to move not because he wanted to live in the capital but because he was convinced that he was contributing to the future of his people. Buchanan believed that a Gaelic translation of the New Testament would be essential for his people's understanding of God's message because the only way they could comprehend the Word was through their own language. Only a Gaelic rendering of God's word could reach their innermost consciousness.

In their role as intermediaries, Occom and Buchanan sought to retain an entrée into each of the brokered cultures that defined their lives—the colonial English, the Lowland Scots, and their own people. Yet each stumbled in the process. Each met critics on the various sides of the cultural divide. Gaels criticized Buchanan for accepting too eagerly the faith of the Lowlanders and simultaneously discarding the folk traditions and faith of his Gaelic kin. Or, as Derick Thomson wrote:

> Although Calvin came
> he did not steal that love out of your heart:
> you loved
> the tawny moor, . . .[1]

The Algonquians were critical of Occom for stepping too far across the divide. Those who lived in Mohegan and the other communities—even his own wife, Mary—criticized Occom for accepting too eagerly the customs of the English, both in Connecticut and in England. Throughout their marriage, Mary Occom remained more attached to Montauk traditions than her husband did, but, in his defense, he had garnered far more experience with the outsiders through his immersion in English culture during those years of schooling in Lebanon, his relations with Wheelock and the SSPCK boards of correspondence, and his lengthy stay in England and Wales, plus the brief weeks in Scotland.[2] Occom reflected that influence throughout the years in Connecticut and on Long Island.

In their moments of stumbling and their sheer inability to maintain the balance—striving toward adaptation without falling into the abyss of assimilation—Buchanan and Occom served as a mirror reflecting the stance of their own respective people. Gaels and Native Americans accepted some aspects of cultural colonialism, yet in so doing they relinquished certain portions of their societies' worldviews while they gained new understandings. They learned they could not have it both ways completely, but this did not prevent them from trying to achieve some form of compromise. In a similar fashion, the society became aware, when it listened to the schoolmasters, that it could not change a people entirely. Still, this did not prevent the directors from attempting to reach that elusive goal. Cultural colonialism, by its nature, assumes the superiority of one civilization over another. The concept of superiority proved a difficult barrier for the Mohegan minister and the Rannoch bard, and it complicated further their search for cultural balance.

Had these two men engaged in conversation in Edinburgh during the spring and summer of 1767, they might have shared the common anxieties that plagued their efforts. But their mutual sense of achievement—merging the Calvinist faith with the traditions of their own peoples—could have sealed their brief acquaintance. They were, after all, engaged in the same game—both had pledged their lives to protect the integrity of their Native cultures, while offering their people a faith perspective to help them negotiate with the most recent outsiders who had come into their worlds. Drawn together by the compelling nature of the Great Awakening, which had encompassed the Atlantic world and, in turn, by the schooling endeavors of the Scottish Society, they could well have found a common cause during that brief moment in Edinburgh that encapsulated the Scottish connection.

Notes

Introduction

1. Bernard Bailyn and Philip D. Morgan, eds., *Strangers within the Realm: Cultural Margins of the First British Empire* (Chapel Hill: Published for the Institute of Early American History and Culture, Williamsburg, Virginia, by the University of North Carolina Press, 1991), 17, 19.

2. Eric Richards argues, "Precisely because so large a part of the old elite could not afford to attend London (until about 1760), it continued to regard Edinburgh as its natural focus, provincial or not." "Scotland and the Uses of the Atlantic Empire," in Bailyn and Morgan, 67–114, quote on 74.

3. Linda Colley, *Britons: Forging the Nation, 1707–1837* (New Haven: Yale University Press, 1992), 14–15. Professor Donald E. Meek refutes Colley's broad interpretation of Sasannach. Personal communication, November 26, 2006.

4. T. H. Breen, "An Empire of Goods: The Anglicization of Colonial America, 1690–1776," *Journal of British Studies* 25 (October 1986): 473.

5. Bailyn and Morgan, *Strangers within the Realm*, 1, 9.

6. Martin Daunton and Rick Halpern, eds., *Empire and Others: British Encounters with Indigenous Peoples, 1600–1850* (Philadelphia: University of Pennsylvania Press, 1999), 10.

7. In his evaluation of British and American Indian identities, Philip D. Morgan emphasizes the complexity of this aspect of colonial relations. He contrasts the "myriad alternative identities" among the British, with the "amazingly diverse array of peoples" encountered by the British during the expansion of the empire. "Encounters between British and Indigenous Peoples, c. 1500–c. 1800," in Daunton and Halpern, *Empire and Others*, 45.

8. On the cultural intermediary, see ibid., 53; Margaret Connell Szasz, ed., *Between Indian and White Worlds: The Cultural Broker* (Norman: University of Oklahoma Press, 2001); Francis Karttunen, *Between Worlds: Interpreters, Guides, and Survivors* (New Brunswick, N.J.: Rutgers University Press, 1994); Eric Hinderaker, "Translation and Cultural Brokerage," in *A Companion to American Indian History*, ed., Philip J. Deloria and Neal Salisbury, 356–75 (Malden, Mass.: Blackwell, 2004).

9. Donald Smith, *Storytelling Scotland: A Nation in Narrative* (Edinburgh: Polygon, Edinburgh University Press, 2001), 42.

10. For the purposes of this narrative, and to avoid confusion, I shall retain the Stewart spelling.

11. The last ruler of this dynasty was James VII and II (1685–89), grandson of James VI and I.

12. Eric Richards suggests the irony in the search for homogeneity. He argues that "the redefinition of Scotland after the Union entailed a deliberate contraction of its language, identity, and pride. The process was led by the landed classes in Scotland in a self-anglicization and voluntary assimilation toward London." "Scotland," 85.

13. Smith, *Storytelling Scotland*, 47.

14. Derick Thomson, *An Introduction to Gaelic Poetry* (London: Victor Gollancz, 1974), 58.

15. "State of the Society in Scotland for Propagating Christian Knowledge, in the Year 1769" (N.p.: N.p., 1769), 2. Copy of this manuscript was located in Hills Library, Andover-Newton Theological School, Newton Centre, MA.

16. John MacLean of Balemartin qtd. in I. F. Grant and Hugh Cheape, *Periods in Highland History* (1987; repr., London: Shepheard-Walwyn, 1997), 252.

17. Eleazar Wheelock to Mrs. Symons, June 27, 1768, qtd. in James Dow McCallum, ed., *The Letters of Eleazar Wheelock's Indians* (Hanover: Dartmouth College, 1932), 225–26.

18. Indian Papers, Connecticut Historical Society, Hartford, qtd. in W. DeLoss Love, *Samson Occom and the Christian Indians of New England* (1899; repr., Syracuse: Syracuse University Press, 2000), 276.

19. Smith, *Storytelling Scotland*, 46–47.

20. Robert Louis Stevenson, *Kidnapped* (New York: Tom Doherty Associates, 1991), 107–11.

1. Land and Cultures of Gaels, Algonquians, and Iroquois

1. This is a synthesis of several versions of the Iroquois origin story; the quotes appear in Dean R. Snow, *The Iroquois* (Oxford: Blackwell, 1996), 2–3.

2. Sapling was also called Tharonhiawagon, Upholder of the Heavens, or Sky Grasper.

3. Daniel G. Brinton, ed., *The Lenape and Their Legends, with the Complete Text and Symbols of the Walum Olum* (1884; repr., New York: AMS Press, 1969), 179.

4. William S. Simmons, *Spirit of the New England Tribes* (Hanover: University Press of New England, 1986), 7, 38, 41. For a comparison of the symbolism of this couple and that of Adam and Eve, see Neal Salisbury, *Manitou and Providence: Indians, Europeans, and the Making of New England, 1500–1643* (New York: Oxford University Press, 1982), 136–37. These authors also point out that both southern and northern New England Algonquians recognized large numbers of gods, or manitous, but for the Micmacs and Abenakis, Gluskap was the culture hero and transformer.

5. Stewart Ross, *Ancient Scotland* (Moffat: Lochar, 1991), 12. Michael Dames questions the argument that science is not myth: "The recent appreciation by

Popper [K.] and others that 'scientific discovery is akin to explanatory storytelling, to myth-making, and to the poetic imagination' places science in the broad mythic field where, in any case, it was born and nurtured." *Mythic Ireland* (London: Thames and Hudson, 1992), 10.

6. Katharine Scherman, *The Flowering of Ireland: Saints, Scholars, and Kings* (Boston: Little, Brown, 1981), 14; Barry Raftery, *Pagan Celtic Ireland* (London: Thames and Hudson, 1997), 17.

7. Charles Squire, *Mythology of the Celtic People* (1912; repr., London: Bracken Books, 1996), 4.

8. Raftery, *Pagan Celtic Ireland*, 13.

9. T. W. Rolleston, *Celtic Myths and Legends* (New York: Avenal Books, 1986), 95.

10. Ross, *Ancient Scotland*, 158; Michael Lynch, *Scotland: A New History* (London: Pimlico, 1993), 30–38.

11. See Nigel Pennick, *Celtic Sacred Landscapes* (New York: Thames and Hudson, 1996), 39–78.

12. Simmons, *New England Tribes*, vii.

13. Edmund Burt, *Burt's Letters from the North of Scotland* (Edinburgh: Birlinn, 1998), 200; Samuel Johnson and James Boswell, *A Journey to the Western Isles of Scotland and the Journal of a Tour to the Hebrides* (London: Penguin Books, 1984), 114.

14. The Gaelic word for clan is *cenél* or *fine*. See Tom M. Devine, *Clanship to Crofters' War* (Manchester: Manchester University Press, 1996), 3, 6.

15. Ibid., 7. Devine's position is not universally accepted. "Whether the Dal Riata had settled in Scotland before the advent of Fergus Mór Mac Eire c. 500 is open to argument, but there is little doubt that in his person the Dalriada dynasty removed from Ireland to Scotland. . . . There is no indication that Fergus Mór relinquished his authority over his Irish territories when he left for Scotland." John Bannerman, *Studies in the History of Dalriada* (Edinburgh: Scottish Academic Press, 1974), 1.

16. Lynch, *Scotland*, xiv.

17. Stewart Ross notes that "classical sources suggest that *Pritani* was the name which people of the Iron Age used to describe themselves"; the word translates as "the picture people," a reference to the custom of the Celtic Iron Age people who painted or tattooed designs on the skin. Ross, *Ancient Scotland*, 121; on the identity of the Picts, also see 12–17.

18. Lynch, *Scotland*, xiv.

19. Michael Leroy Oberg, *Uncas: First of the Mohegans* (Ithaca: Cornell University Press, 2003), 45.

20. Daniel K. Richter, *The Ordeal of the Longhouse* (Chapel Hill: University of North Carolina Press, 1992), 59.

21. Snow, *Iroquois*, 94.

22. Matthew Dennis, *Cultivating a Landscape of Peace* (Ithaca: Cornell University Press, 1993), 264. Deganawidah founded the League of the Iroquois (c. 1450), which included the Onondagas, Mohawks, Oneidas, Senecas, and Cayugas.

23. Snow, *Iroquois*, 111.

24. Richter, *Ordeal of the Longhouse*, 65.

25. Ibid., 73.

26. Oberg, *Uncas*, 72; Kevin A. McBride, "The Legacy of Robin Cassacinamon: Mashantucket Pequot Leadership in the Historic Period," in *Northeastern Indian Lives, 1632–1816*, ed. Robert S. Grumet (Amherst: University of Massachusetts Press, 1996), 74–75.

27. For a clear description of the land see John MacLeod, *Highlanders: A History of the Gaels* (London: Hodder and Stoughton, 1997), 9–14.

28. Daniel Defoe, *A Tour through the Whole Island of Great Britain*, ed. P. N. Furbank and W. R. Onans (New Haven: Yale University Press, 1991), 365.

29. Richter, *Ordeal of the Longhouse*, 11.

30. Burt, *Letters*, 179.

31. MacLeod, *Highlanders*, 21.

32. Burt, *Letters*, 153–54.

33. Bert Salwen, "Indians of Southern New England and Long Island: Early Period," and William N. Fenton, "Northern Iroquoian Culture Patters," both in *Handbook of North American Indians*, vol. 15, *Northeast*, ed. Bruce G. Trigger (Washington, D.C.: Smithsonian Institution, 1978), 160–67, 309–10; Richter, *Ordeal of the Longhouse*, 22–23; Joy Bilharz, "First among Equals? The Changing Status of Seneca Women," in *Women and Power in Native North America*, ed. Laura F. Klein and Lillian A. Ackerman (Norman: University of Oklahoma Press, 2000), 101–107. Also see Salisbury, *Manitou and Providence*, 39–41; Oberg, *Uncas*, 30.

34. Robert A. Dodgshon, "'Pretense of Blude' and 'Place of Their Duelling': The Nature of Scottish Clans, 1500–1745," in *Scottish Society: 1500–1800*, ed. Robert Allen Houston and Ian D. White (Cambridge: Cambridge University Press, 1989), 177. Also see Burt, *Letters*, 123. Pictish ancestry, however, was traced through the female side. See "Clans" in *Collins Encyclopedia of Scotland*, ed. John Keay and Julia Keay (London: Harper Collins, 1984), 159–63, citation appears on 161.

35. Burt, *Letters*, 235–36. While I was researching in a small community on the north coast of Sutherland in 1998, a woman told me of a relative who had walked barefoot from a location about fifty miles southeast on the east coast to visit a relative who was ill. The relative then returned in the same manner.

36. I. F. Grant, *Highland Folkways* (London: Routledge and Kegan Paul, 1980), 198–218.

37. There are numerous illustrations of shapeshifting in the stories collected in Richard Erdoes and Alfonso Ortiz, eds., *American Indian Myths and Legends* (New York: Pantheon Books, 1984), and in Jarold Ramsey, ed., *Coyote Was Going There* (Seattle: University of Washington Press, 1999).

38. Mary A. Druke, "Linking Arms: The Structure of Iroquois Intertribal Diplomacy," in *Beyond the Covenant Chain: The Iroquois and their Neighbors in Indian North America*, ed. Daniel K. Richter and James H. Merrell (Syracuse: Syracuse University Press, 1987), 30.

39. William N. Fenton, *The Great Law and the Longhouse: A Political History of the Iroquois Confederacy* (Norman: University of Oklahoma Press, 1998), 3–4.

40. Richter, *Ordeal of the Longhouse*, 10–11. For the Iroquois names of the clans of the Six Nations, see Fenton, "Northern Iroquoian Culture Patterns," 313.

41. Richter, *Ordeal of the Longhouse*, 21. Also see Fenton, "Northern Iroquoian Culture Patterns," 306.

42. For a synthesis of "Táin Bó Chuailagné," see T. W. Rolleston, *Celtic Myths and Legends* (New York: Avenal Books, 1986), 202–25. For further reading, see Dames, *Mythic Ireland*; Joseph Campbell, *The Hero with a Thousand Faces* (New York: World Publishing, 1971), 116–18, 220–21, 330–34; and Squire, *Mythology*.

43. Dames, *Mythic Ireland*, 17.

44. The question of migration and transfer of myth has universal implications. In Native North America it has affected the many tribes who shifted their homelands under pressures of war and removal. Native students and colleagues have pondered the complexity of this issue with me in many a conversation.

45. Donald E. Meek, *The Scottish Highlands: The Churches and Gaelic Culture*, Gospel and Culture Pamphlet 11 (Geneva: World Council of Churches Publications, 1996), 12.

46. W. J. Watson, ed., *Scottish Verse from the Book of the Dean of Lismore* (Edinburgh: Scottish Gaelic Texts Society, 1937), as qtd. in Lynch, *Scotland*, 68.

47. Ibid., 8.

48. A. J. Youngson, ed., *Beyond the Highland Line* (London: Collins, St. James Place, 1974), 15–16.

49. The three Gaelic myth cycles are the Tuatha Dé Danann, the Heroes of Ulster, and Finn and the Fenians. The latter became popular in Scotland through medieval ballads, which led to the assignation of specific Scottish locations for incidents from the stories. "Finn mac Cumhal (Fionn mac Cumhall, Finegal, etc.) Celtic Hero," in *Collins Encyclopedia*, 371. In Scotland the poems concerning the Fenians employed Fingal, rather than Finn, and later came under the rubric of Ossianic ballads due to the once-controversial eighteenth-century publications by James MacPherson, including *Fragments of Ancient Poetry, Collected in the Highlands of Scotland* (Edinburgh, 1760); *Fingal, An Ancient Epic Poem, Composed by Ossian, the Son of Fingal* (London, 1765); and *The Poems of Ossian* (London, 1773), which created a literary sensation in Europe and attracted the admiration of Thomas Jefferson. For a brief account of MacPherson, see *Collins Encyclopedia*, 671–72. There are many versions of the story quoted. This one is borrowed from Squire, *Mythology*, 210–11, and Rolleston, *Celtic Myths and Legends*, 255–57. Also see Miranda Green, *Animals in Celtic Life and Myth* (London: Routledge, 1998), 190–96.

50. Squire, *Mythology*, 212–13.

51. In the story "The Bore Stripping Hangman," a tale of Irish brothers Cormac and Alastir, contemporaries of Finn and the Fenians, John Matthews describes these "animal helpers" as "animal totems." *Classic Celtic Fairy Tales* (London: Blandford, 1997), 46–47, 67. In this context, the term "guardian spirit," drawn from a Native North American context, might be seen as a close parallel.

52. Smith, *Storytelling Scotland*, 42–43; Donald Smith, *Scottish Folk-Tales and Legends Retold by Barbara Kerr Wilson* (Oxford: Oxford University Press, 1989), 7.

53. Devine, *Clanship to Crofters' War*, 8. On marriage customs, see Burt, *Letters*, 116–17, 243.

54. Salisbury, *Manitou and Providence*, 41–44.

55. Richter, *Ordeal of the Longhouse*, 17.

56. Snow, *The Iroquois*, 62.

57. Ibid., 64. Also see J. N. B. Hewett, "A Constitutional League of Peace in Stone Age America," in *An Iroquois Source Book*, vol. 1, *Political and Social Organization*, ed. Elisabeth Tooker (New York: Garland, 1985), 531.

58. Burt, *Letters*, 20.

59. Youngson, *Beyond the Highland Line*, 16.

60. "Within Gaeldom as elsewhere in Scotland, the granting of charter giving title to estates was accepted as part of the royal prerogative." Allan Macinnes, *Clanship, Commerce, and the House of Stuart, 1603–1788* (East Linton: Tuckwell Press), 5.

61. Ibid., 15.

62. Ibid.

63. Devine, *Clanship to Crofters' War*, 6–7, 11.

64. Macinnes, *Clanship*, 3.

65. Devine, *Clanship to Crofters' War*, 10.

66. Recollections of Angus MacLeod. Oral History Collections, Siabost School Museum, Isle of Lewis [hereafter cited as OHC, SSM].

67. Cattle could be sold in late summer or early fall, providing cash to Highlanders to buy meal, pay the rent, or purchase products they could not make themselves, such as iron. For further reading, see Grant, *Highland Folkways*.

68. Recollection of a woman at Draeger, age 83. OHC, SSM. For a graphic description of "waulking" or "fulling" see "The Waulking Day," *Transactions of the Gaelic Society of Inverness* 13 (1886–87): 201–17.

69. On women's craft production and adaptation of clothing, see Jean M. O'Brien, "'Divorced' from the Land: Resistance and Survival of Indian Women in Eighteenth-Century New England, in *After King Philip's War: Presence and Persistence in Indian New England*, ed. Colin G. Calloway (Hanover: Dartmouth College and University Press of New England, 1997), 149–50.

70. Ibid., 153–55; Daniel Vickers, "The First Whalemen of Nantucket," in Calloway, *After King Philip's War*, 90–113.

71. Fenton, "Northern Iroquoian Culture Patterns," 197–303, 306–14.

72. During this era "the entire Hebrides and the West Highland coastline formed a single Atlantic principality, and the Lords of the Isles conducted their affairs and governed this dominion as independent rulers in the west." Ronald Williams, *The Lords of the Isles: The Clan Donald and the Early Kingdom of the Scots* (London: Chatoo and Windus, the Hogarth Press, 1984), xiii. Also see Grant, *Highland Folkways*, 26; Kenneth MacKinnon, *Gaelic: A Past and Future Prospect* (Edinburgh: Saltire Society, 1991), 36.

73. These lines were probably written by one of the MacEwen family, c. 1641–45. Thomson, *Introduction to Gaelic Poetry*, 40.

74. Simmons, *New England Tribes*, vii.

75. Ibid., 64; Frank G. Speck, "Mohegan Traditions of 'Muhkeahweesug' The Little Men," *Papoose* I (7): 11–14, qtd. in ibid., 236.

76. Amy Stewart Fraser, *Dae Ye Min Lansyne? A Pot-pourri of Games, Rhymes, and Ploys of Scottish Childhood* (London: Routledge and Kegan Paul, 1975), 4.

2. Highlands and Lowlands

1. MacKinnon, *Gaelic*, 26. This generalization excludes the Orkneys and Shetlands, where Norwegian persisted. Also see Barbara A. Fennell, *A History of English: A Sociolinguistic Approach* (Oxford: Blackwell, 2001), 192.

2. Today the remaining Gaeltacht areas in Ireland are in Donegal and Galway, including the Aran Islands and portions of Mayo, Kerry, and County Cork.

3. Carolyn Bingham, *Beyond the Highland Line: Highland History and Culture* (London: Constable, 1991), 13–14.

4. Lynch, *Scotland* (London: Pimlico, 1993), 67–68. In the quote Lynch replaces "race" with "nation" (68). Also see Devine, *Clanship to Crofters' War*, 1–2; Meek, *Scottish Highlands*, 7. Meek spells the name Fordoun (2).

5. Meek, *Scottish Highlands*, 8.

6. David Daiches, ed., *The New Companion to Scottish Culture* (Edinburgh: Polygon, 1993), 196.

7. Robert A. Dodgshon, *From Chiefs to Landlords* (Edinburgh: Edinburgh University Press, 1998), 3.

8. For this interpretation I am grateful to Devine, *Clanship to Crofters' War*, 4–5; and Lynch, *Scotland*, 67–69.

9. Lynch argues that in the fifteenth and sixteenth centuries the Highlands was neither "more [n]or less" violent than the Lowlands. Lynch, *Scotland*, 69.

10. Daiches, *Companion to Scottish Culture*, 167. On the economic impact of the relationship between James VI and I and the Highlanders see Dodgshon, *From Chiefs to Landlords*, 103–107.

11. Donald E. Meek, *The Quest for Celtic Christianity* (Edinburgh: The Handsel Press, 2000), esp. the introduction and chapters 1–4; Macinnes, *Clanship*, ix, x; Devine, *Clanship to Crofters' War*, 8–9. Also see Lynch, *Scotland*, 354–55; T. C. Smout, *A Century of the Scottish People, 1830–1950* (New Haven: Yale University Press, 1986), 10–12.

12. Derek Malcolm, "Mel Takes the High Wood," *Guardian Weekly*, September 17, 1995. In *The Quest for Celtic Christianity*, Donald Meek reminds us of how easily present views are imposed upon the past.

13. Macinnes, *Clanship*, 78, 93.

14. Ibid., 78. On Roman Catholicism among the Gaels, Macinnes points out that "the Kirk was as much concerned by practices of latent Catholicism—such as visits to wells and chapels—as with the actual presence of priests, friars and other religious orders," ibid., 11. On the persistence of folk tradition see Martin Martin, *A Description of the Western Isles of Scotland c. 1695: A Voyage to St. Kilda* (1703;

repr., Edinburgh: Birlinn, 1999), 71–83. Martin's well-known description of second sight is on 180–99. His references to holy wells are on 93, 141, 148, and 168. He mentions venerated stones on 50, 107, and 139–40. The "sunways" circle references are on 69 and 80–81. Finally, on the persistence of Catholicism among Protestants, see 139 and 142.

15. Devine, *Clanship to Crofters' War*, 17, quote on 80. On the economic dimension of the fine-clansmen relationship, also see Dodgshon, *From Chiefs to Landlords*, 107–14. After the Union of the Crowns in 1603, the Stewart kings of Scotland, whose name originated as "steward," became known as the Stuart kings of Great Britain.

16. Allan I. Macinnes, "The Impact of the Civil Wars and Interregnum: Political Disruption and Social Change within Scottish Gaeldom," in *Economy and Society in Scotland and Ireland, 1500–1939*, ed. Rosalind Mitchison and Peter Roebuck (Edinburgh: John Donald Publications, 1988), 58–69.

17. On the final failure of the attempted colonization of Lewis, see Donald Gregory, *History of the Western Highlands and Isles of Scotland from A.D. 1493 to A.D. 1625* (Edinburgh, 1836; repr., Bowie, Mo.: Heritage Books, 1996), 334–38. The colonization attempt spanned a decade, from 1597–1608.

18. Mitchison and Roebuck, *Economy and Society*, 13; Devine, *Clanship to Crofters' War*, 13. Comparing policy in Scotland's Highlands and Ireland, Mitchison and Roebuck explain, "the English Crown exerted much greater pressure on Irish society than either the king or his Privy Council brought to bear in the Highlands." *Economy and Society*, 2. For an opposing view on the effectiveness of the statutes see Julian Goodare, "The Statutes of Iona in Context," *Scottish Historical Review* 77, no. 203 (1998): 54. Goodare also compares policy in the Highlands and Ireland: 32–33, 54–55. I am indebted to Grant Simpson for supplying me with a copy of this article.

19. Goodare, "Statutes of Iona," 41–43. The Edinburgh gatherings continued until 1637 and thus "formed probably the first occasion on which government and chiefs talked to one another without arguing" (43).

20. Ibid., 52. On the extension of 1616, see Francis T. Shaw, *The Northern and Western Islands of Scotland: Their Economy and Society in the Seventeenth Century* (Edinburgh: John Donald, 1980), 146. Goodare points out that some chiefs had acquired a Lowland education before 1609.

21. John Bannerman, "Literacy in the Highlands," in Ian B. Coward and Duncan Shaw, eds., *The Renaissance and Reformation in Scotland: Essays in Honor of Gordon Donaldson* (Edinburgh: Scottish Academic Press, 1983), 14.

22. Ibid., 214, 225, 229. Bannerman writes that "it is difficult to note how far down the social scale literacy extended" (230).

23. Ibid., 215, 221.

24. Bannerman, "Literacy in the Highlands," 217. Bannerman describes Ruarri Mór MacLeod (of Dunvegan) who sent four sons to Glasgow University. All of them matriculated in the 1620s and 1630s. Goodare questions whether the Statutes of Iona ever were implemented. Also see Shaw, *Northern and Western Islands*, 146.

25. Macinnes, "Civil Wars and Interregnum," 62.

26. Devine, *Clanship to Crofters' War*, 15.

27. Robert A. Dodgshon, "West Highland Chiefdons, 1500–1745: A Study In Redistributive Exchange," in Mitchison and Roebuck, *Economy and Society*, 30.

28. Macinnes, "Civil Wars and Interregnum," 61–62.

29. Ibid.

30. Dodgshon, *From Chiefs to Landlords*, 45. On changing perceptions by the chiefs, see 114–15. On the concept of *duthchas* as "heritable trusteeship," also see Macinnes, *Clanship*, 5. Macinnes adds the complementary concept of *oighreachd*, or the "heritable title [of the fine] to their estates and institutional jurisdictions." He points out that this differentiated the Scottish from the Irish Gaels, "whose equivalent concept of *duthchas* was not complemented by that of *oighreachd*." Ibid., 6. On the concept of *duthchas*, also see James Hunter, *Last of the Free* (Edinburgh: Mainstream Publishing, 2000), esp. 172–73.

31. Burt, *Letters*, 204; Shaw, *Northern and Western Islands*, 114.

32. John MacLeod, *Highlanders: A History of the Gaels* (London: Hodder and Stoughton, 1997), 101–102.

33. Grant, *Highland Folkways*, 77–78; Burt, *Letters*, 207.

34. Grant, *Highland Folkways*, 73–76; Martin, *Western Isles of Scotland*, 100.

35. Grant, *Highland Folkways*, 66–67.

36. A. R. B. Haldane, *The Drove Roads of Scotland* (Edinburgh: Birlinn, 1997), 70–73, 75–79. On the swimming of the cattle from Skye across one of the kyles to the mainland, see Martin, *Western Isles of Scotland*, 127–28.

37. This implies that the drovers themselves may well have spoken English. Grant, *Highland Folkways*, 69–71, quote on 71. For further statistics and details on the trysts, see Haldane, *Drove Roads of Scotland*, 135–49.

38. Grant, *Highland Folkways*, 70. Also see Macinnes, "Civil Wars and Interregnum," 64.

39. Macinnes, "Civil Wars and Interregnum."

40. Dodgshon, "West Highland Chiefdoms," 27–29.

41. Martin, *Western Isles of Scotland*, 85; Shaw, *Northern and Western Islands*, 68.

42. Martin, *Western Isles of Scotland*, 130. Martin cites instances of the chief's care for the Elders and those in need of his aid. See, e.g., "Isle of Barra," 67–68. Shaw describes this reciprocity as the "benevolent regard . . . some of the chiefs held for their tenants, with the respect which many tenants had for their chiefs." Shaw, *Northern and Western Islands*, 69.

43. Dodgshon, "West Highland Chiefdoms," 28.

44. Shaw, *Northern and Western Islands*, 197.

45. Mitchison and Roebuck, *Economy and Society*, 2.

46. Shaw, *Northern and Western Islands*, 197.

47. Lynch, *Scotland*, 299.

48. Macinnes, *Clanship*, 176.

49. The Highlands would not gain a university for another three centuries. The University of the Highlands and Islands (UHI), which relies heavily on long-distance learning, opened at the beginning of the twenty-first century.

50. Donald J. Withrington, *Going to School* (Edinburgh: National Museums of Scotland, 1997), 17–18.

51. Elementary schools taught reading and Scripture for five to eight year olds; grammar schools were for children of eight to twelve years; and high schools, for those who were fourteen to sixteen years. H. Cowper and W. Pickard, "Education," in Daiches, *Companion to Scottish Culture*, 88.

52. T. C. Smout, *A History of the Scottish People, 1560–1830* (London: Collins, 1969), 456; Robert Allen Houston, "Scottish Education and Literacy, 1600–1800: An International Perspective," in *Improvement and Enlightenment*, ed. Tom M. Devine (Edinburgh: John Donald, 1989), 453; Withrington, *Going to School*, 16–17.

53. H. M. Knox, *Two Hundred and Fifty Years of Scottish Education, 1696–1946* (Edinburgh: Oliver and Boyd, 1953), 10; Houston, "Scottish Education and Literacy," 454, 459.

54. Smout, *History of the Scottish People*, 460.

55. Adam Nicholson points out that in Lochs, Isle of Lewis, before the families were evicted in the Clearances, they depended on fishing, especially cod and ling, which "were at their best between February and May." *Sea Room* (London: Harper Collins, 2002), 46.

56. Even today Hebrideans must engage in many kinds of work in order to survive and remain in their homelands. Author's field notes, May 26–30, 2003, Isles of Lewis and South Harris.

57. Rural Aberdeenshire is strewn with sites containing the place name "The Mains," a nomenclature that has survived the eighteenth-century usage. In this section I rely heavily on T. M. Devine, *The Scottish Nation, 1700–2000* (London: Allen Lane, Penguin Press, 1999), 124–34.

58. Ibid., 126.

59. Author's field notes, May 30, 2003, Isle of Lewis. Also see Smith, *Storytelling Scotland*, 49–50.

60. Tom M. Devine, *The Transformation of Rural Scotland* (Edinburgh: University of Edinburgh Press, 1994), 5, 9, 16; A. J. G. Cummings, "The Business Affairs of an Eighteenth-Century Lowland Laird: Sir Archibald Grant of Monymusk, 1696–1778," in *Scottish Elites*, ed. Tom M. Devine (Edinburgh: John Donald, 1994), 57–58.

61. Cummings, "Business Affairs," 43.

62. Johnson and Boswell, *Journey to the Western Isles*, 35, 166.

63. David Stevenson, *The Covenanters: The National Covenant and Scotland* (Edinburgh: The Saltire Society, 1988), 64–67.

64. Ibid., 69.

65. Gordon Donaldson, *The Faith of the Scots* (London: B.T.D. Batsford, 1990), 103. Ironically, Donaldson notes, "At the same time . . . [it] created a breeding ground for discord on matters of doctrine."

66. When the Parliament of Scotland opened in 1999, sentiment lay with a singular notion. Many believed that the thrust of independence had followed a circuitous route moving from the Declaration of Arbroath to Thomas Jefferson's words in the American Declaration of Independence, "Governments . . . derive

their just Powers from the Consent of the Governed," and Robert Burns's famous line "A man's a man for a' that." Although there is little proof for these connections, the sentiment of the day led the new members of the parliament to join in the singing of Burns's words.

67. Grant G. Simpson, "The Declaration of Arbroath: What Significance When," unpublished manuscript in author's collection, 8. On historical interpretations of the Declaration of Arbroath, see Terry Brotherstone and David Ditchburn, "1320 and A' That: The Declaration of Arbroath and the Remaking of Scottish History," in *Freedom and Authority, Scotland, 1050–1650: Historical and Historiographical Essays Presented to Grant G. Simpson*, ed. Terry Brotherstone and David Ditchburn (East Linton: Tuckwell Press, 2000), 10–31.

68. "Letter of Barons of Scotland to Pope John XXII, 1320, otherwise called the Declaration of Arbroath" (trans., pub. in 1689), in Gordon Donaldson, ed., *Scottish Historical Documents* (Glasgow: Neil Wilson, 1999), 55–58, quote on 57.

69. Donaldson, *Faith of the Scots*, 88.

70. Ibid., 89.

71. M. G. Jones, *The Charity School Movement* (Cambridge: Cambridge University Press, 1938), 172.

3. Scotland and the Birth of the SSPCK

1. "It is in that struggle—Highlander versus Lowlander—that Highland history is best defined." MacLeod, *Highlanders*, 7.

2. Bruce P. Lenman, "Union, Jacobitism, and Enlightenment," in *Why Scottish History Matters*, ed. Rosalind Mitchison (Edinburgh: The Saltire Society, 1991), 65.

3. On July 27, 1689, the death of John Graham of Claverhouse, Viscount Dundee, who had led the Highlanders to victory over the government forces until a stray bullet took his life, left the royalist supporters of James VII and II, or Jacobites, without a leader, and by May 1, 1690, they had suffered a final defeat at Cromdale, near what is now Grantown-on-Spey. The Glencoe Massacre symbolized William's determination to gain control over the Highlands, but the viciousness with which it was executed by the Campbell clan's attack on the MacDonalds of Glencoe encouraged the Jacobites; it also attached a stigma of "atrocity" to the Campbells. Lynch, *Scotland*, 305–307; Frank McLynn, *The Jacobites* (London: Routledge and Kegan Paul, 1988), 11–13.

4. In 1702 William's horse stumbled on a molehill and threw the king; the accident eventually led to his death. When the Jacobites heard the news, it is said that "from then on they would drink exultent toast to 'the wee gentleman in velvet'—the mole which had caused the king's fall." Magnus Magnusson, *Scotland: The Story of a Nation* (New York: Atlantic Monthly Press, 2000), 534.

5. Donaldson, *Scottish Historical Documents*, 265. In Aberdeenshire, the mortality rate may have exceeded 20 percent. Lynch, *Scotland*, 307.

6. Macinnes, *Clanship*, 160.

7. Devine points out that England withdrew its investment and "refused to send

provision or succour" to the ailing colony. *Scottish Nation*, 5–6, quote on 5. See also Lynch, *Scotland*, 308–309; Magnusson, *Scotland*, 547–48. The fallout from the Darien Company persisted until the Act of Union in 1707, which "shrewdly included compensation with interest for all investors." "The Darien Venture," in *Collins Encyclopedia*, 220.

8. Devine, *Scottish Nation*, 12; "Act for Security of Church of Scotland," in Donaldson, *Scottish Historical Documents*, 275–77.

9. "In the outcome, . . . the terms of the Union were less total, less obliterating of Scottishness, than expected. The settlement left room for maneuver and for a markedly Scottish response to the redefined world as it emerged in the following half-century." Eric Richards, "Scotland and the Atlantic Empire," 73.

10. Macinnes, *Clanship*, 176. Macinnes argues that "episcopaleanism not only provided a religious complement to the hierarchical nature of clanship, but inculcated a spirit of obedience and submission to royal authority."

11. Ibid., 178.

12. David Allan, *Scotland in the Eighteenth Century* (Edinburgh: Longman, 2002), 129–30. Allan points out that by 1799, Scotland hosted more than 320 clubs, societies, assembly rooms, Masonic lodges, subscription libraries, and other meeting places and voluntary associations.

13. Jones, *Charity School Movement*, 176. Their correspondents included various members of their English organizational counterpart, the SPCK, especially James Kirkwood, an "outed" Episcopalian minister who was the SPCK's corresponding member in Scotland. Aware of conditions in the Scottish Highlands, Kirkwood was a catalyst for the Edinburgh society's first schooling venture, which survived for eighteen months.

14. Meek, *Scottish Highlands*, 17; Macinnes, *Clanship*, 177.

15. *An Account of the Society in Scotland for Propagating Christian Knowledge* (Edinburgh: A. Murray and J. Cochrane, 1774), 5.

16. Ibid.

17. Ibid., 4.

18. "The Church and Education in the Highlands," *Transactions of the Gaelic Society of Inverness* 7 (1877–78): 15.

19. *Account of the Society in Scotland*, 4–5.

20. Ibid., 5.

21. Ibid., 54. In the early eighteenth century, almost one-third of the population of Scotland lived in the Highlands and Islands, but they were served by perhaps one-seventh of the country's parish ministers. For the contrast in size of Highland and Lowland parishes, see Peter G. B. McNeil and Hector L. MacQueen, eds., *Atlas of Scottish History to 1707* (Edinburgh: The Scottish Medievalists and Department of Geography, University of Edinburgh, 1996), 402–403.

22. Lynch, *Scotland*, 254–56, quote on 255. John Clive, "The Social Background of the Scottish Renaissance," in *Scotland in the Age of Improvement*, ed. N. T. Phillipson and Rosalind Mitchison (Edinburgh: Edinburgh University Press, 1996), 228.

23. Clive, "Social Background," 226, also see 235; Allan, *Scotland in the Eighteenth Century*, 132. The persistence of these Scottish institutions—the law, the Church, and the schools—owed a debt to the Union of the Parliaments. Eric Richards points out that the Union enabled Scotland to retain "control of its educational system, its church government, and its legal system. The law, the courts, the burghs, the electoral system, the schools, the universities, and the church remained intact." "Scotland and the Atlantic Empire," 74.

24. Allan, *Scotland in the Eighteenth Century*, 132.

25. *Account of the Society in Scotland*, 5. A later account described the founders as "nine Peers and seventy-three Commoners." "State of the Society." Also see John Kerr, *Scottish Education, School, and University, from Early Times to 1908* (Cambridge: Cambridge University Press, 1910), 184.

26. *Account of the Society in Scotland*, 5–6.

27. Ibid.

28. Ibid., 6, 55.

29. Ibid.

30. On the parallels of these attitudes toward "others," including the Irish, the Welsh, the Gaelic Highlanders, and those indigenous people who came under the rubric of the British Empire, see Bailyn and Morgan, *Strangers within the Realm*, 17–19.

31. For the "Schedule of Donations" and the "State of the Funds Belonging to the Society at Whitsunday 1774," see ibid., 63–68. The first donor on the list, whose title will always be linked with the Highland Clearances of the late eighteenth and early nineteenth centuries was the "Rt Hon Jane, Countess-dowager of Sutherland."

32. Martin, *Western Isles of Scotland*, 170–74. Martin voyaged to St. Kilda in 1697. The last residents of St. Kilda, numbering thirty-six people, all of whom were Gaelic speakers, were evacuated at their own request in 1930. Today the islands have been designated a World Heritage Site, but one can travel to St. Kilda through tours operated by the National Trust of Scotland. The crossing from Oban, undertaken only during a calm sea, is fourteen hours. Rob Humphreys and Donald Reid, *Scottish Highlands and Islands: The Rough Guide* (London: Penguin Group, 2000), 316.

33. Victor Edward Durkacz, *The Decline of the Celtic Languages: A Study of Linguistic and Cultural Conflict in Scotland, Wales, and Ireland from the Reformation to the Twentieth Century* (Edinburgh: John Donald, 1983), 57.

34. Ibid. In the early twentieth century, William Mackay observed that the standard of measurement for the society's schoolmasters was not as high as that applied to applicants for the Kirk's parish schools. Still, he noted, some "were good classical scholars." William Mackay, "Education in the Highlands," *Transactions of the Gaelic Society of Inverness* 27 (1908–11): 265–66.

4. Highland Gaels and the "Shocktroops of Presbyterianism"

1. "State of the Society," 7.

2. June 8, 1711, 196–97. GD95 2. General Register House. National Archives of Scotland, Edinburgh [NAS]. The society asked all of its members as well as the principals of the Scottish universities to suggest names of possible applicants. Aberdeen University responded quickly, offering five names; in the early searches Highland synods and presbyteries offered other suggestions.

3. A. S. Cowper, *SSPCK Schoolmasters 1709–1872* (Edinburgh: Scottish Record Society, New Series, 1997), 35, 37, 63, 84, 87, 90, 100, 105.

4. Ibid., 21–22, 30, 35, 89. On the Whiskey Wars of this era, see Ian R. Mitchell, "The Whiskey Wars in Scotland," *History Scotland* 5 (November–December 2005): 34–39.

5. Ibid., 97.

6. Ibid., 8, 17, 32, 34–35, 69, 96.

7. John Mason, "Scottish Charity Schools of the Eighteenth Century," *The Scottish Historical Review* 33 (April 1954): 4. Some of those candidates who failed to pass received tutoring for several weeks at the society's expense by one of its approved teachers, and then they were reexamined. No candidate knew if he received an appointment, however, until the society notified him (5). Also see Durkacz, *Decline of the Celtic Languages*, 57; Mackay, "Education in the Highlands," 266.

8. Cowper, *SSPCK Schoolmasters*, 41, 92, 98.

9. "State of the Society," 5.

10. Jones, *Charity School Movement*, 190–91; Cowper, *SSPCK Schoolmasters*, 90.

11. This description was found at a kailyard located at the Highland Folk Museum in Kingussie, a town in the central Highlands. It also noted that the "peculiar 'D' shaped wall [by the kailyard] is very commonly found in field excavations of kailyards in old deserted settlements." Author's field notes, June 4, 1998.

12. Jones, *Charity School Movement*, 190–91; Mason, "Scottish Charity Schools," 3.

13. Cowper, *SSPCK Schoolmasters*, 87–88, 105.

14. Ibid, 93.

15. Ibid., 20, 56.

16. "Reports and returns made by Mr. Lewis Drummond during his visits to the Society's schools—in terms of minutes of meeting of October and November 1770," 25, 38, 44. GD 95/9/2. NAS; also see Jones, *Charity School Movement*.

17. Mackay, "Education in the Highlands," 263.

18. James Robertson, "Memories of Rannoch," *Transactions of the Gaelic Society of Inverness* 51 (1978–80): 202.

19. Cowper, *SSPCK Schoolmasters*, 69, 84, 86, 99.

20. Ibid., 45.

21. Mackay, "Education in the Highlands," 264.

22. Burt, *Letters*, 62, 169–70; Johnson and Boswell, *Journey to the Western Islands*, 54–55. For further description, see Mason, "Scottish Charity Schools," 4.

23. Cowper, *SSPCK Schoolmasters*, 98.

24. William Blair, minister and schoolmaster at Kingussie, Memorial, 1775, General Assembly Papers, 345–56. CH1/2/118/1775. NAS.

25. Cowper, *SSPCK Schoolmasters*, n.p.

26. Jones, *Charity School Movement*, 188–89.

27. Blair, Kingussie, Memorial, 1775. NAS.

28. In *SSPCK Schoolmasters* A. S. Cowper includes a number of references to school closures during the nineteenth century due to the arrival of the sheep. Inspectors reported school locations where the region had been "depopulated" because it had been turned into a "sheep walk." See, e.g., 63–66. One schoolmaster was reportedly "burned out at the evictions" in Kildonan. See Evan McPherson, 75.

29. A. S. Cowper and I. Ross, "The SSPCK and Kildonan, 1709–1827." T33/50/53, 3. NAS.

30. For this background, I am grateful to Francis Ross for her knowledgeable advice, which she provided as staff member at the Ulapool Museum and Visitor Centre. Author's field notes, June 8, 1998.

31. Schools in the Presbytery of Abertarff: Fort Augustus. "Proficiency in Learning," 1749–61, 44–45, GD95/9/1, NAS. Fort Augustus is located at the southwest tip of Loch Ness. In 1730 Gen. George Wade, the well-known builder of roads in the Highlands, replaced the barracks built after the Jacobite Rising of 1715 with a fort that he named after William Augustus, the nine-year-old son of George II, also known as the Duke of Cumberland. "Sixteen years later, after a few months in Jacobite hands, the fort became the residence of the Duke, who used it as a hunting lodge to flush out and butcher the fugitives from Culloden." *Collins Encyclopedia*, 391.

32. Cowper, *SSPCK Schoolmasters*, 22, 77.

33. Durkacz, *Decline of Celtic Languages*,

34. Mackay, "Education in the Highlands," 266. Mackay does not date this singing, but the verse does raise implications for the use of Gaelic in teaching. If news of these Gaelic singing classes had reached the society, one can imagine the resulting furor.

35. In "Scottish Charity Schools," John Mason suggests that the society's "policy of attempting to supplant Gaelic by English may have been responsible for the slow progress of certain schools" (8). Durkacz concurs. In *Decline of Celtic Languages*, he observes, "One historian has claimed this ill-conceived policy was the real reason for the slow progress of the society's scholars" (61). Durkacz cites here Mason, "Scottish Charity Schools," 8–9.

36. Durkacz, *Decline of Celtic Languages*, 59–60.

37. Mason, "Scottish Charity Schools," 8.

38. Among scholars, Michael Lynch uses the lowest estimate of the Highlands population in 1755, suggesting the figure of 115,000. *Scotland*, 367. I. F. Grant and Hugh Cheape estimate that in 1755, the Highlands population was 337,000. *Periods in Highland History*, 209. Alexander Webster's estimate for 1755 is 1,265,380. *Collins Encyclopedia*, 780–81. John MacLeod argues that in 1745, the population of the Highlands was one-third of the population of Scotland. MacLeod, *Highlanders*, 4.

If Scotland's population was 1.2 million mid-century, one-third was close to Grant and Cheape's estimate of 337,000.

39. Lynch argues for the Grampian foothills as a bilingual region. My sources from Aberdeen have argued that this region held Gaelic speakers as late as the early twentieth century. Author's field notes, 1991–2000; Adam Watson and R. D. Clement, "Aberdeenshire Gaelic," *Transactions of the Gaelic Society of Inverness* 48 (1980–82): 373–403. Watson and Clement located a Gaelic speaker in Braemar, at the headwaters of the River Dee, in the 1970s, leading them to conclude that "Braemar Gaelic had not died." Ibid., 387.

40. According to John Kerr, "a careful investigation . . . as to the condition of the Gaelic districts . . . and the extent to which Gaelic was the spoken language of a population of 171 parishes, [it was] ascertained by the census of 1821 to contain 416,000." In these parishes, which excluded the non-Gaelic regions of Caithness, Orkney, and Shetland, "Gaelic was the language of three-fourths of the people." *Scottish Education*, 188.

41. 1860 Hyndman-Dick Report, 40. CH8/212. NAS.

42. Watson and Clement, "Aberdeenshire Gaelic," 388.

43. Ibid., 377.

44. January 15, 1720, 342. GD95 2/2. NAS. Cited in Durkacz, *Decline of Celtic Languages*, 62.

45. Quote is in Brotherstone and Ditchburn, "1320 and A' That," 24. On the Lowlanders' general fear of "the Gaelic language and its associated culture," see Durkacz, *Decline of Celtic Languages*, 49–50.

46. Mackay, "Education in the Highlands," 267.

47. March 5, 1716. 95. GD95 2/2. NAS. Cited in Durkacz, *Decline of Celtic Languages*, 50–51.

48. Cowper, *SSPCK Schoolmasters*, 18, 41, 51.

49. Ibid., 48.

50. Derick S. Thomson, ed., *Gaelic Poetry in the Eighteenth Century* (Aberdeen: University of Aberdeen, 1993), 13. Quote taken from the *Vocabulary*'s preface is located in Durkacz, *Decline of the Celtic Languages*, 65. Also see Rev. A. MacDonald, *The Poems of Alexander MacDonald* (Inverness: Northern Counties Newspaper and Printing and Publishing, 1924), xxvi.

51. Durkacz, *Decline of the Celtic Languages*, 52.

52. Ibid., 62.

53. Geraint H. Jenkins, "From Reformation to Methodism, 1536–1750," in *The Tempus History of Wales 25,000 B.C.–A.D. 2000*, ed. Prys Morgan (Stroud, Gloucestershire: Tempus, 2001): 159.

54. John Davies, *A History of Wales* (London: Penguin, 1993), 242–44, quote on 244.

55. Nicholas Williams, "Literature in Irish," in *The Oxford Companion to Irish History*, ed. S. J. Connelly (Oxford: Oxford University Press, 2002), 332. Donald E. Meek, "The Gaelic Bible," in D. F. Wright, ed., *The Bible in Scottish Life and Literature* (Edinburgh: The Saint Andrews Press, 1988), 14. Meek points out that a Roman font was used for printing in Scotland.

56. Quoted in Durkacz, *Decline of the Celtic Languages*, 62. Also see Mason, "Scottish Charity Schools," 9.

57. Patrick Butter's Journal, 1824, 45, 47, 49–52. GD R42/95/93 SPCK Records. NAS. Butter noted that Gaelic had been "almost universally banned from the parish schools." Until the introduction of the "Gaelic Schools" in 1811, the only schools that taught Gaelic were "those in which the minister or Society schoolmaster happened to be successful in exciting the attention of the inhabitants to a serious consideration of the great truths of religion." Had teachers taught in Gaelic from the beginning, however, Butter still believed it would have led "ultimately" to "the suppression of the Gaelic language." Ibid., 53–54.

58. Robertson, "Memories of Rannoch," 204. Punishment stories abound in the various reminiscences. See, e.g., Mackay, "Education in the Highlands," 266.

59. "Some Considerations to be Laid Before the Committee of the Society," April 22, 1715. GD95/10/58 SSPCK Records. NAS.

60. February 4, 1719, 259. GD 95 2/2. NAS. Cited in Durkacz, *Decline of Celtic Languages*, 62–63. Quote is on 62.

61. In this section on Raining's School, I rely on Durkacz, *Decline of Celtic Languages*, 266–68; Thomas M. Murchison, "Raining's School, Inverness: A Seedbed of Talent," *Transactions of the Gaelic Society of Inverness* 52 (1980–81): 405–59; and Marjorie Cruikshank, *A History of the Training of Teachers in Scotland* (London: University of London, 1970). I would also like to thank Chris Fraser, whose research on the school was crucial. Murchison deduces that Raining "may have come from the Dumfries area," 409. Raining's School has largely escaped the attention of scholars and has also proven to be of little interest to contemporary Inverness, which demolished the building in the 1960s or 1970s to enlarge a car park. Today, the only physical reminder of the school is the very steep set of "Raining's Stairs" that ascend from Old Town's Castle Street to Ardconnell Street in Colt or Barn Hill. When the town council granted the site it became the only structure in the entire "plain"; currently it is a middle-class residential area. In the car park there is a small sign acknowledging the school.

62. Mr. Raining's legacy, June 20, 1724, 266–268. GD 95/2. Rev. Baillie's correspondence, September 10, 1724, 281. GD 95/2. Both quotes cited in Durkacz, *Decline of Celtic Languages*, 59.

63. In 1724 a suit of clothing for a "poor scholar" cost £18 sterling and a pair of shoes, £1/8. Cowper, *SSPCK Schoolmasters*, 24.

64. Cruikshank, *Training of Teachers in Scotland*, 21; Durkacz, *Decline of Celtic Languages*, 58–59; "State of the Society," 9.

65. Arthur asked to remain in Glenmuick "till he be of more growth being of low stature." His request was approved, and the society gave him a suit of clothes. The two pupils were probably brothers or cousins. Cowper, *SSPCK Schoolmasters*, 101–102.

66. "Dr. Norman Maclean, Pupil of Rainings, 1882–85," in Murchison, "Raining's School," 437. Murchison quotes here from *Set Free* (1949), the second of Maclean's three wonderful autobiographical volumes.

67. Cruikshank, *Training of Teachers in Scotland*, 21.

68. The Napier Commission (1883–84) was a royal body called to investigate the Crofters' War (1881–83). Its recommendations led to the passage of the Crofters' Holding Act of 1886 that restricted the power of landlords and gave small tenants security of tenure and fair rentals. Quote from Smout, *Century of the Scottish People*, 219. Also see Devine, *Scottish Nation*, 299, 400–401. Kenneth Mackinnon points out that the Education Act of 1872 "actively discouraged" the use of Gaelic in the schools, but it is likely that this measure merely intensified the already common use of punishment against pupils who spoke Gaelic. *Gaelic*, 75.

69. Between 1890 and 1893 two-thirds of the capital assets remaining in the Raining's fund were used to form the Highlands and Islands Education Trust, while the society retained one-third of the funds to further religious work in the Highlands and Islands. There was some debate over the school's future as a possible training center for Gaelic teachers, but the momentum had been lost. By 1900 the building had been sold, and the remarkable source of Highlanders' Gaelic education had ceased. Funds from the sale established "the Raining Bursary" for a Highland's scholar to go to university.

70. *Poems and Songs of Robert Burns*, ed., James Banks (1955; repr., London: Harper Collins, 1991), 510.

71. Interview with anonymous Sutherland source, June 9, 1998, which concurred with an anonymous Wester Ross source, June 7, 1998. Author's field notes.

72. "Proceedings of the Society under the Second Patent," in *Account of the Society*, 20. The society was not permitted to use any of the funds raised under the auspices of the first patent for these schools, which delayed any durable school experiments until the 1750s. According to the "Proceedings of the Society," "many young women have been taught to spin; and many young men have been instructed in various branches of trade and manufacture" (20–22).

73. John Mason, *A History of Scottish Experiments in Rural Education From the Eighteenth Century to the Present Day* (London: University of London Press, 1935), 3–45. Westminster formed in 1727 the Board for Manufacturers and Fisheries, which was assigned the task of improving the Scottish linen, woolen, and fishing industries. Devine, *Scottish Nation*, 57–58. Commissioners for the Forfeited Estates administered the remaining Jacobite estates (those not sold off) confiscated by the Hanoverian government after the 1745 rising and held between 1752 and 1784.

74. Seymour Wood, Esq, of London, "bequethed to the Society the sum of £2000 Sterling, to be wholly expended and applied for the purposes of their second patent, and *not let out at* interest." "State of the Society," 13, 14, quote on 13.

75. Cowper, *SSPCK Schoolmasters*, 13, 16, 39, 78, 85, 95. Cowper mentions girls as students at the SSPCK schools in a single reference under the John McKay listing: "Society asked minister to deal with parents to send their daughters as well as their sons to school," 62. Even this reference, like those mentioned earlier, may be referring to the instruction in spinning or sewing. But girls as well as boys attended the SSPCK schools, sometimes forming half of the total number of stu-

dents. See, e.g., Harray School, presbytery of Kirkwall, March 1712–April 1731, SSPCK Records, GD 95/91, NAS. In 1748 all 134 of the society's schools enrolled boys and girls, but at each school the enrollment of boys was higher: for boys the total enrollment was 5,187; for girls it was 2,617. "List of Schools Maintained by the Society for Propagating Christian Knowledge, 1748." GD 95/91, NAS.

76. Kerr, *Scottish Education*, 185.

77. Cowper, *SSPCK Schoolmasters*, 40, 68, 79, 91–91.

78. Butter's Journal, 1824, 38. GD R42 95/93. NAS.

79. Ibid., 39.

80. Graham Andrew, *A Brief Survey of the Society in Scotland* (Edinburgh: C. J. Cousland and Sons, 1957), 5. Statistics are also drawn from James Scotland, *The History of Scottish Education*, vol. 1, *From the Beginning to 1872* (London: University of London Press, 1969), 101. Scotland notes that by 1795, 94 spinning schools had opened. Cowper states that there were 323 schools in 1795. This figure likely included the spinning schools. Cowper, *SSPCK Schoolmasters*, n.p. Also see Donald Meek, "Scottish SPCK," in *Dictionary of Scottish Church History and Theology* (Edinburgh: T and T Clark, 1993), 761–62. In 1769 the society reported that the total enrollment in the schools between November 1768 and November 1769 was near eight thousand children, both boys and girls. "State of the Society," 10.

81. On the University of the Highlands and Islands, see catalogue published in 2000.

5. The Scottish Society and Native America

1. "State of the Society," 13–14.

2. *Account of the Society*, 54.

3. W. DeLoss Love, *Samson Occom*, 136, 138. On the return voyage in 1768, Occom sailed in Capt. Robert Calef's ship, *London Packet*. Ibid., 150.

4. This assessment of outsiders paraphrases a comment made by Samson Occom, qtd. in ibid., 123.

5. *Account of the Society*, 14–15; "State of the Society," 16.

6. Ibid., 14–15.

7. *The Journal of the Rev. John Wesley, A.M.*, ed. Nehemiah Curnock, 8 vols. (London: Epworth Press, 1938), 1:159–60.

8. On Macleod, see *Account of the Society*, 14–15; "State of the Society in Scotland," 16. On Wesley, see Wesley, *Journal*, 1:31. In his own diary John Wesley admitted that his "chief motive" of "embarking for Georgia" was "the hope of saving my own soul. I hope to learn the true sense of the gospel of Christ, by preaching it to the heathen." Ibid., 8:288–89. For an overview of the Anglicans and Moravians in Georgia, see Margaret Connell Szasz, *Indian Education in the American Colonies, 1607–1783* (Albuquerque: University of New Mexico Press, 1988), 149–71.

9. For Virginia Presbyterian minister Samuel Davies's links with Scotland, see Douglas Sloan, *The Scottish Enlightenment and the American College Ideal* (New

York: Teachers College Press, Columbia University, 1971), 53–54; *Account of the Society*, 15.

10. For further background on Craig and the southern Shenandoah Valley Scots Irish, see Howard McKnight Wilson, *The Tinkling Spring Headwater of Freedom* (Fishersville, Va.: Tinkling Spring and Hermitage Presbyterian Church, 1954), 25, 72, 84. I am grateful to my maternal grandmother, Mabel Carson Moulton, for this citation.

11. After some of the Cherokees allied with the French during the Seven Years' War, the "mission was soon given up." William G. McLoughlin, *Cherokee Renascence in the New Republic* (Princeton: Princeton University Press, 1986), 72. Also see Henry T. Malone, *Cherokees of the Old South* (Athens: University of Georgia Press, 1956), 96. For a more detailed explanation, see Samuel C. Williams, "An Account of the Presbyterian Missions to the Cherokee, 1757–1759," *Tennessee Historical Magazine* ser. 2, I (1931): 125–38. This article includes part of the diary of the second missionary, William Richardson.

12. S. Williams, "Presbyterian Missions," 126–129, 137; Love, *Samson Occom*, 50–51.

13. The society applied these words to the "diligent and successful labours of the Reverend Mr Samuel Kirkland," who served as missionary among the Oneidas during the era of the American Revolution and afterward until his death. Quote is in *Account of the Society*, 17.

14. For an insightful history of the New England Company see William Kellaway, *The New England Company, 1649–1776* (London: Longman, Green, 1961). Also see Connell Szasz, *Indian Education*, 111–23.

15. *Account of the Society*, 7–8, 63. One donation of £1,000 was bequeathed by a Mr. Spreull, a Glasgow merchant. His surviving sisters specified that it was to be reserved as capital stock and only the interest spent, one-half of which was designated for the Highlands, "particularly in such places where is the greatest danger of Popery," and the other half, in North America. Ibid., 66.

16. Ibid., 14–15. Formed in 1764, the Connecticut board was the last to be created.

17. On comparative cultures see Donald E. Meek, "Scottish Highlanders, North American Indians and the SSPCK: Some Cultural Perspectives," in *Records of the Scottish Church History Society* 23, part 3 (1989): 386.

18. On the impact of the Viking tongue on the Hebrideans, Adam Nicholson writes, "The words used here for boats and the sea all come from Old Norse and the same descriptions have been on people's lips for a millennium." *Sea Room*, 31–33, quote on 31.

19. On the fictions of the "Celtic church" see Meek, *Quest for Celtic Christianity*, 103–21. Meek argues that no single institutional Celtic church existed. He suggests that more identifiable names for this faith would be a "'Gaelic church' . . . in the Gaelic speaking regions of Ireland and Scotland," and in Wales, a "Welsh church," and in Cornwall, Brittany, and Northumbria, the "corresponding entities" in each. Ibid., 105.

20. Simmons, *New England Tribes*, 64.

21. On the Jesuits and the Iroquois, see Dennis, *Landscape of Peace*, 180–86, 234–38; Snow, *Iroquois*, 115, 117–18; Richter, *Ordeal of the Longhouse*, 104–29. On the Anglicans and the Iroquois see Richter, *Ordeal of the Longhouse*, 229–34.

22. For clarification of the complex history of this Indian nation, see T. J. Brasser, "Mahican," in *Handbook of Northeastern Indians*, vol. 15, *Northeast*, ed. Bruce Trigger (Washington, D.C., Smithsonian Institution, 1978), 198–212. In the early seventeenth century, when the Dutch arrived, the nation numbered between four thousand and forty-five hundred people.

23. "The Life and Diary of the Rev. David Brainerd: With Notes and Reflections," in *The Works of President Edwards*, by Jonathan Edwards, 8 vols. (Leeds: Printed by E. Baines, 1806–11), 3:140, quote is on 145. The Scottish Society's contemporary description of David Brainerd is in *Account of the Society*, 15, 18.

24. Brainerd, "Life and Diary," 3:179–180.

25. Patrick Frazier, *The Mohicans of Stockbridge* (Lincoln: University of Nebraska Press, 1992), 58–59; Love, *Samson Occom*, 231–46, 316–23; Dorothy W. Davids, "Stockbridge-Munsee (Mohican)," in *Encyclopedia of North American Indians*, ed. Frederick W. Hoxie, (Boston: Houghton Mifflin, 1996), 611. In the 1990s, the Stockbridges and the Munsee Delawares, who joined them in Wisconsin, had about fourteen hundred members, of whom approximately half lived on or near the reservation. Also see Dorothy W. Davids, "Stockbridge-Munsee," in *Native America in the Twentieth Century*, ed. Mary B. Davis (New York: Garland, 1994), 619–20.

26. Two years earlier, in 1741, the society had engaged the Rev. Azariah Horton through its New York Board of Correspondents to serve as missionary to the Shinnecock people of Long Island, where he remained until 1750. Love, *Samson Occom*, 42–43.

27. Clinton Alfred Weslager, *The Delaware Indians: A History* (New Brunswick, N.J.: Rutgers, 1972), 262.

28. Brainerd, "Life and Diary," 3:229.

29. Weslager, *Delaware Indians*, 262. In his diary, Brainerd noted, "Spent some considerable time in writing an account of the Indian affairs to go to Scotland; but enjoyed not much sweetness and satisfaction." "Life and Diary," 3:185.

30. *Memoirs of the Reverend David Brainerd*, ed. Edward Parsons and Edward Williams, in *The Works of President Edwards*, by Jonathan Edwards. 8 vols. (1817; repr., New York: Burt Franklin, 1968), 3:411.

31. Weslager, *Delaware Indians*, 263.

32. Thomas Brainerd, *The Life of John Brainerd* (Philadelphia: Presbyterian Publication Committee, 1865), 51–54.

33. In the early nineteenth century the American Board of Commissioners for Foreign Missions (Presbyterian/Congregational), or the ABCFM, named its first mission school among the Cherokees after David Brainerd. For an assessment of the paradox of the brothers' fame, see Connell Szasz, *Indian Education*, 214–16.

34. The commissioners paid £740 for the lands, and the magnitude of this sum,

in addition to the £1,000 cash settlement that New Jersey agreed to give to the Six Nations—Nanticokes, Tutelos, Unamis, Munsies, Mahicans, and Pomptons—in October 1858, led the commissioners to conduct a lottery to repay the colony's government some £1,600. The thirty-two hundred tickets were offered to residents of New York, New Jersey, and Pennsylvania. Between 1761 and 1763, tickets sold for £4. There were three series, and the prizes were £800 for the top two and others. Weslager, *Delaware Indians*, 267–71.

35. By the outbreak of the Revolution, the number of Delawares living on the trust lands had declined. In 1801, two decades after John Brainerd's death, the remaining remnant accepted the invitation of the Stockbridge Indians, who suggested that the Brotherton people "'pack up their mat' and 'come eat out of their dish,' adding that 'their necks were stretched in looking toward the fireside of their grandfather till they were long as cranes.'" The Delawares joined the Stockbridge community, which had moved after the Revolution to lands set aside for them by the Oneidas. Weslager, *Delaware Indians*, 274–75. The Stockbridge community included the band met by David Brainerd in 1743.

36. Brainerd to a friend in England, October 4, 1752, cited in Brainerd, *Life of John Brainerd*, 255.

6. The Algonquians and Iroquois Meet the Scottish Society

1. Sources on Occom include Love, *Samson Occom*; Harold Blodgett, *Samson Occom* (Hanover: Dartmouth College, 1935); Margaret Connell Szasz, "Samson Occom: Mohegan as Spiritual Intermediary," in Connell Szasz, *Between Indian and White Worlds*, 61–78; Margaret Connell Szasz, "Samson Occom, Mohegan Leader and Cultural Broker," in *The Human Tradition in Colonial America*, ed. Ian K. Steele and Nancy L. Rhoden, (Wilmington, Del.: Scholarly Resources, 1999), 237–55.

2. James Dow McCallum, *Eleazar Wheelock, Founder of Dartmouth College* (Hanover: Dartmouth College, 1939), 3–11; James Axtell, *The Invasion Within: The Contest of Cultures in Colonial North America* (New York: Oxford University Press, 1985), 204–15; David McClure and Elijah Parish, *Memoirs of the Rev. Eleazar Wheelock* (Newburyport, Mass.: Edward Norris, 1811); Connell Szasz, *Indian Education*, 194–96, 218–21.

3. Quote in Edwin Scott Gaustad, *The Great Awakening in New England* (1957; repr., Chicago: Quadrangle Books, 1968), 45.

4. Eleazar Wheelock, *A Narrative of the Original Design, Rise, Progress and Present State of the Indian Charity-School in Lebanon* (Boston: Printed by Richard and Samuel Draper, in Newbury-Street, 1763), 29.

5. Ibid., 24–25.

6. Ibid., 15. On the women at Moor's School, see Margaret Connell Szasz, "'Poor Richard' Meets the Native American: Young Indian Women at School in Eighteenth-Century Connecticut," *Pacific Historical Review* 49 (May 1980): 215–35.

7. Wheelock, *Narrative*, 29. The cause of Pumshire's death is not clear, but its

significance in the history of Indian schooling remains to dominate the story. Of Wheelock's first two pupils, a 50 percent death rate is not surprising. The cemetery at Carlisle Indian School, Pennsylvania (1879–1919) offers a mute testimony to the physically damaging effects of the extreme adjustments that Native children experienced in boarding school. James Dow McCallum points out that Wheelock and others "knew little about the physical (or mental) needs of his charges." Discipline was "severe," school days were long, and the children were "subjected to an overemotionalized, soul-probing religion." McCallum concludes, "the wonder is that any of them . . . survived." *Eleazar Wheelock*, 80–82.

8. Wheelock, *Narrative*, 29–30. Between 1763 and 1775, Wheelock published nine *Narratives* that served as direct promotional literature for the school, thereby becoming another means of securing funding.

9. Enrollment figures for the charity school vary considerably. A conservative estimate is about sixty pupils. Wheelock's own figures were much higher. On the Delaware pupils see Love, *Samson Occom*, 58–59, 64, 69.

10. Love maintains that the charity school was not located in a village. It was "only this group of buildings [including the meeting house, school buildings, and Wheelock's home] where two highways of travel crossed." Love, *Samson Occom*, 31, 61–63; description of the physical structures of Moor's School is on 31.

11. Wheelock, *Narrative*, 29–30.

12. Qtd. in ibid., 71.

13. Given Europeans' critical attitudes toward Indians during this era, the students probably carried all of their own provisions.

14. Occom's trips to and from the Iroquois are the only detailed accounts I have located for travels by Indians in this region during the eighteenth century, and they indicate that, despite his fame as "the Indian preacher," he often slept outside and on the ground. Transcript of Samson Occom's Journal [Diary], three volumes, Dartmouth College Archives [DCA], Hanover, New Hampshire, vol. 3.

15. Fowler to Wheelock, June 15, 1765, file 765365, DCA.

16. Connell Szasz, *Indian Education*, 226–27; Connell Szasz, "Poor Richard," 228–30.

17. Michael C. Coleman, *American Indian Children at School, 1850–1930* (Jackson: University Press of Mississippi, 1993), 69; K. Tsianina Lomawaima, *They Called It Prairie Light: The Story of Chilocco Indian School* (Lincoln: University of Nebraska Press, 1994), 35; Brenda J. Child, *Boarding School Seasons* (Lincoln: University of Nebraska Press, 1998), 23–24.

18. George A. Pettitt, *Primitive Education in North America* (Berkeley: University of California Publications in American Ethnology and Archaeology, 1946); Patricia Riley, ed., *Growing up in Native America, An Anthology* (New York: William Morrow, 1993); Margaret Connell Szasz, "Native American Children," in *American Childhood: A Research Guide and Historical Handbook*, ed. N. Ray Hiner and Joseph M. Hawes (Westport, Conn.: Greenwood Press, 1985): 311–42; Margaret Connell Szasz, "Native American Children," in *The Chicago Companion to the Child* (Chicago: University of Chicago Press, forthcoming).

19. Classic studies on colonial European education include Bernard Bailyn,

Education in the Forming of American Society (New York: Vintage Books, 1963); Lawrence A. Cremin, *American Education: The Colonial Experience, 1607–1783* (New York: Harper and Row, 1970). Wheelock's punishment of the children finally led to repercussions when the Oneida Nation pulled their children out of the school in 1769. Later, they explained their avoidance of Wheelock's school and the need to educate their own children. Tagawaron speaker, Reply to "Speech to the Chiefs of the Oneida Tribe (in the name of Mr. Avery)," February 22, 1772. February 1772 folder, correspondence files, Samuel Kirkland Papers [SKP], Hamilton College Library [HCL], Clinton, New York. Also see Axtell, *Invasion Within*, 212.

20. As James Axtell points out, however, the prejudice against Indians, especially during and after the Seven Years' War, made it highly unlikely that they would find employment in any English community in New England. Axtell, *Invasion Within*, 208–11.

21. Wheelock to Whitefield, April 18, 1764, in McClure and Parish, *Memoirs of Eleazar Wheelock*, 244.

22. Should they need an alternative career if they did not marry a missionary or a schoolmaster, the girls were to be instructed until they were "fit for an Apprenticeship, to be taught Men's and Women's Apparel." Wheelock, *Narrative*, 34. This plan is reminiscent of the SSPCK's Highland spinning schools.

23. Ibid.

24. McCallum, *Eleazar Wheelock*, 89. It is likely this varied from household to household, but, like their male counterparts, the female students encountered strong prejudice from the English community. Even Wheelock, a slave owner himself, referred to one of his female students, a Delaware, as an "amiable little black savage Christian." Wheelock to Dennys de Berdt, November 16, 1761, file 761616, DCA.

25. Love, *Samson Occom*, 61.

26. Ibid.

27. David M'Clure became a master at Moor's School in 1769. McClure and Parish, *Memoirs of Eleazar Wheelock*, 208. David M'Clure (Animus Quietus) to Wheelock, September 25, 1765. Quoted in McCallum, *Eleazar Wheelock*, 92–93. On William's lineage and behavior, also see Axtell, *Invasion Within*, 211.

28. For a biography of Molly Brant, see Lois M. Feister and Bonnie Pulis, "Molly Brant: Her Domestic and Political Roles in Eighteenth-Century New York," in Grumet, *Northeastern Indian Lives*, 295–320.

29. Love, *Samson Occom*, 67–68, quotes on 68. Love also reported that Wheelock sent William home about fourteen months after the fight. The Mohawk's sojourn at the school lasted from November 30, 1764, to December 10, 1766. McCallum, *Eleazar Wheelock*, 136. A decade later, William, like his fellow Mohawks, fought with the British during the American Revolution; he was killed during the war.

30. On Wheelock's perception of "Insufferable [Indian] pride," see Axtell, *Invasion Within*, 211.

31. The best source on Kirkland is Walter Pilkington, ed., *The Journals of Samuel*

Kirkland (Clinton, N.Y.: Hamilton College, 1980). On his split with Wheelock, later "papered over, but the old close relationship was never resumed," see 41. As missionary among the Oneidas, Kirkland also depended on funding from the Corporation of Harvard College and the New England Company. See *Account of the Society*, 17–18; November 1770 folder, SKP-HCL (original document on the Harvard College meeting of November 13, 1770, is located in the Massachusetts Historical Society as 71.k.96). On Kirkland's final agreement with Wheelock, see "Articles of agreement between Kirkland and Wheelock, 1771," October 1771 folder, SKP-HCL.

32. Barbara Tuchman, *The Iroquois in the American Revolution* (Syracuse: Syracuse University Press, 1972), 39–40, 52–53, 55–58, 115–16. Located on either side of the Grand River, the reserve encompassed 2,842,480 acres. Olive Patricia Dickason, *Canada's First Nations* (Norman: University of Oklahoma Press, 1992), 190.

33. Wheelock, *Narrative*, 39. The New York board also intended to send Occom on this journey in order to explore the Oneida request for a missionary. Love, *Samson Occom*, 84–91.

34. Although most Irish were Catholic—except in Ulster, where James VI and I had settled immigrants, largely Presbyterians from Scotland's west country—the Church of Ireland was Anglican, a reflection of the centuries-old power struggle between England and Ireland. In Ireland the Anglicans were descendants of settlers from England, the earliest of whom had arrived in the 1100s after the Norman conquest, beginning the era of English colonialism. Following the English Reformation of the 1530s, they had become Anglican.

35. Molly Brant also remained active in the Anglican Church on the Grand River Reserve, Ontario. Feister and Pulis, "Molly Brant," 317.

36. McCallum, *Eleazar Wheelock* 27, 38.

37. Hannah Nonesuch Confession, March 11, 1768, file 768211.1, DCA.

38. Qtd. in McCallum, *Eleazar Wheelock*, 86. On Simon's career, see Love, *Samson Occom*, 242–43.

39. For details of Occom's relations with the Oneidas, see Love, *Samson Occom*; and Connell Szasz, "Samson Occom: Mohegan Leader," 244, 251–53.

40. Love, *Samson Occom*, 92–98, quote on 96. Occom Diary, 1:44–61, DCA.

41. A letter from the Rev. John Erskine to Wheelock, March 15, 1764, accompanies the SSPCK commission for a board of correspondents in Connecticut. McClure and Parish, *Memoirs of Eleazar Wheelock*, 242.

42. *Account of the Society*, 16–17. Love states that the Society aided Wheelock "during the twelve years before the 'Trust Fund' was raised," but he does not expand on this point. He also describes the makeup of the board. Love, *Samson Occom*, 13, 99–100. The Connecticut Board of Correspondents served in lieu of a charter for Moor's school, which Wheelock had been unable to obtain. McCallum has argued that Wheelock "was actually the dictator of it." McCallum, *Eleazar Wheelock*, 98.

43. Occom Diary, 1:86, DCA; Love, *Samson Occom*, 100.

44. Love, *Samson Occom*, 99–104; Occom to Wheelock, September 8, 1764, 764508.3, DCA; Wheelock to Whitefield, September 26, 1764, 764526.2, DCA.

45. William Johnson also had three children by Catherine Weissenberg, a German woman who died in 1759. Feister and Pulis, "Molly Brant," 300–301, quote on 301.

46. Love, *Samson Occom*, 106–107. McCallum states that six ushers were approved in addition to the English missionaries. McCallum, *Eleazar Wheelock*, 98–99. During the fall of 1764, Joseph Woolley, a Delaware, and Samuel Kirkland traveled to the Oneidas. Woolley taught school at Onohoquaga for about a year before dying from tuberculosis. Kirkland traveled west to the Seneca, where he went through considerable privation for about eighteen months before he returned to be ordained and was sent by the Connecticut board as a missionary to the Oneidas. "Extract of a Letter of Mr Samuel Kirkland, 1768," 1768 folder, correspondence [original document at the University of Tübingen, Germany], SKP-HCL.

47. Statistic compiled by author and located in author's collection.

48. "Tagawaron Speaker," in "Speech to Chiefs of the Oneida Tribe," February 24, 1772; Wheelock to Kirkland, February 26, 1772, February 1772 folder, correspondence, SKP-HCL.

49. Calvin to Wheelock, August 14, 1767, qtd. in McCallum, *Letters*, 58.

50. Fowler to Wheelock, June 21, 1765, file 765523.5, DCA.

51. March 31, 1765, entry in Pilkington, *Journals of Samuel Kirkland*. Wheelock's concern about the schoolmasters' attire suggests how much they may have looked like the English: "I suppose it will be best for them to be able to appear both in the habit of Indians and English, as occasion shall be. To be sure it will be safest for them, if they should travel through tribes who are not friendly to the English, to go in an Indian habit." Wheelock to Andrew Gifford, July 16, 1764, in McClure and Parish, *Memoirs of Eleazar Wheelock*, 251.

52. Calvin to Wheelock, August 14, 1767, cited in McCallum, *Letters*, 58.

53. Samuel Johnson to David Avery, October 27, 1766, reel 8. David Avery Papers, Speer Library, Princeton Theological Seminary, Princeton, New Jersey.

54. A possible exception to this speculation was the relationship between the Iroquois and the Delawares. Iroquois speakers generally referred to the Delawares as "grandfather."

55. Connell Szasz, *Indian Education*, 244–47.

7. Dugald Buchanan and Samson Occom

1. This argument about the spectrum of positions has long been debated both within and outside indigenous societies. I have tried to avoid the generic concepts of progressive versus traditional because the ambiguities are legion, and the differences among different groups are impossible to generalize. The discussion also leads to the issue of cultural intermediaries and whether those figures emanate from the center or the periphery of a group. On some of these issues, see Connell Szasz, *Between Indian and White Worlds*, 3–20.

2. Lachlan MacBean, *Buchanan: The Sacred Bard of the Scottish Highlands* (London: Simkin, Marshall, Hamilton Kent, 1919), 10.

3. Ian Grumble, *Scottish Clans and Tartans* (London: Hamlyn, 1989), 31.

4. Dodgshon, "Pretense of Blude," 195.

5. A. Sinclair MacLean, *Reminiscences of the Life and Labours of Dugald Buchanan, Formerly Teacher and Evangelist at Rannoch, Perthsire* (Edinburgh: MacLachlan and Steward, 1885), 66.

6. MacKinnon, *Gaelic*, 50.

7. MacBean, *Buchanan*, 15.

8. *Collins Encyclopedia*, 648; Thomson, *Introduction to Gaelic Poetry*, 159.

9. Thomson, *Introduction to Gaelic Poetry*, 157, 205. Also see John Lorne Campbell, *Highland Songs of the Forty-Five* (Edinburgh: Scottish Gaelic Texts Society, 1984), 32–163.

10. Thomson, *Introduction to Gaelic Poetry*, 158.

11. MacBean, *Buchanan*, 16–17; "Dugald Buchanan's Confessions," in MacBean, *Buchanan*, 196.

12. Dugald Buchanan to Mr Ramsay, November 27, 1753, qtd. in ibid.

13. "Dugald Buchanan Confessions," 130.

14. Ibid. In Scotland it was customary for women to retain their birth names after they were married.

15. Ibid., 130–32.

16. A. S. Cowper observes that Nicol Ferguson served as Buchanan's schoolmaster, but Ferguson's tenure at the Braes of Balquidder was 1741–47 and 1751–53. Since Buchanan was born in 1716, he would have attended school in the mid-to-late 1720s. *SSPCK Schoolmasters*, 27.

17. "Dugald Buchanan Confessions," 135.

18. Ibid., 135, 138.

19. Ibid., 143.

20. Ibid.

21. Ibid., 147.

22. In Scots a "wark" is a revival.

23. "Dugald Buchanan Confessions," 171.

24. Ibid., 170–71. Donald E. Meek believes that Whitefield had a profound influence on Buchanan. Meek interview, Edinburgh University, June 14, 2002. Derick Thomson concurred in *Introduction to Gaelic Poetry*, 205. Also see Bruce Lenman, "From the Union of 1707 to the Franchise Reform of 1832," in *The New Penguin History of Scotland*, ed. R. A. Houston and W. W. Knox (Allan Lane: The Penguin Press and National Museums of Scotland, 2002), 333–34.

25. MacBean, *Buchanan* 157; "Dugald Buchanan Confessions," 196.

26. The phrase "religious contentment" is borrowed from Dugald Buchanan, *The Spiritual Songs of Dugald Buchanan*, ed. Donald MacLean (Edinburgh: John Grant, 1913), 87. MacLean employs the phrase in his analysis of Buchanan's "Am Bruader" (The Dream), which expresses the poet's philosophy of life and strongly advocates religious contentment.

27. MacBean, *Buchanan*, 18. Also see "Dugald Buchanan Confessions," 207, for his reference to his "loving wife and pleasant child."

28. Buchanan, *Spiritual Songs*, viii.

29. Rev. A. Sinclair MacLean recorded an individual reminiscence in 1873 that specified locations where Buchanan served as itinerant schoolmaster, including "Strathyre, then in the Braes of Balquhidder, and at another time in Lochearnhead." *Reminiscences*, 63. Also see MacBean, *Buchanan*, 80.

30. A. MacLean, *Reminiscences*; Buchanan, *Spiritual Songs*, viii.

31. Peter G. B. McNeil and Hector L. MacQueen, *Atlas of Scottish History to 1707* (Edinburgh: Scottish Medievalists and Department of Geography, University of Edinburgh, 1996), quote on 426, map on 427.

32. This section is based on Dodgshon, *From Chiefs to Landlords*, 47–48, and John MacInnes, *The Evangelical Movement in the Highlands of Scotland, 1688–1800* (Aberdeen: University Press, 1951), 204. In Daniel Defoe's *Highland Rogue* (1723) the MacGregors' most famous leader was "Rob Roy" MacGregor, renowned as the hero of Sir Walter Scott's novel *Rob Roy* (1818) and the film of the same name, starring Liam Neeson, all of which epitomized in mythic proportions the lot of the "broken men." The Clan MacGregor was outlawed in 1603 by James VI and I, and the clan name was proscribed again after the 1689 Jacobite uprising and probably after the Forty-Five. On Rob Roy, also see Magnussen, *Scotland*, 568–71.

33. Forfeited Estates Papers, Scottish Historical Society *Publications*, 217, qtd. in MacInnes, *Evangelical Movement*, 204.

34. Following the Forty-Five the lands of the Jacobite clan chiefs were forfeited and the heritable jurisdictions of the Highland chiefs abolished. Some of these "lands were 'annexed' to the Crown and the management of the income [about £5,000 per year] was assigned to trustees who were directed to apply it to the promotion of Protestantism, good order, and education in the Highlands. . . . In 1784, the forfeited lands were returned to their former owners upon payment of moderate sums." J.D. Mackie, *A History of Scotland* (London: Penguin Books, 1964), 279–80. The trustees were the "Forfeited Estates Commissioners."

35. M.S. Forfeited Estate (Strowan) Papers, 1753, quoted in MacInnes, *Evangelical Movement*, 205.

36. Forfeited Estates Papers, Scottish Historical Society *Publications*, qtd. in ibid., 222.

37. Dugald Buchanan to Mr. Ramsey, November 27, 1753. Small had evidently sent these accusations in a letter to the Barons of Exchequer. In his assessment of Small, Buchanan described Small's letter as "the false Report of an immoral man when a hundred honest men can attest the contrary." This letter appears in MacBean, *Buchanan*, 215–19, quotes on 217–18.

38. The Gaelic version of "An Gaisgeach" appears in Buchanan, *Spiritual Songs*, 37–39. The English translation by Lachlan MacBean is in *Buchanan*, 102–106. In *An Introduction to Gaelic Poetry*, 205, Derick Thomson notes that in this poem Buchanan "may be reacting to mac Mahigstir Alasdair's glorification of heroic and savage qualities." In *Evangelical Movement in the Highlands*, 282, John MacInnes suggests more broadly that "Buchanan endeavours to give his fellow-Highlanders a juster conception of heroism than that fostered by the secular bards."

39. Buchanan, *Spiritual Songs*, x–xi; A. MacLean, *Reminiscences*, 70–71. Derick

Thomson believes "The Day of Judgement" was Buchanan's "most powerful and imaginative" work. *Introduction to Gaelic Poetry*, 206.

40. MacInnes, *Evangelical Movement*, 280.

41. Ibid., 262.

42. Ibid., 263–64.

43. MacBean, *Buchanan*, 11.

44. Thomson, *Introduction to Gaelic Poetry*, 205.

45. Meek, *Scottish Highlands*, 22.

46. A. MacLean, *Reminiscences*, 66; *The Autobiography of Benjamin Rush*, ed. George W. Comer (Princeton: Published for the American Philosophical Society by Princeton University Press, 1948), 30.

47. Rush, *Autobiography*, 30.

48. Johnson and Boswell, *Journey to the Western Isles*, 389–90; James Boswell, *The Life of Samuel Johnson* (New York: The Modern Library, 1952), 142–44.

49. Durkacz, *Decline of the Celtic Languages*, 67.

50. Meek depicts the publication of the New Testament in Gaelic as "an event of great significance for Scottish Gaelic literature." Surely it was as significant as the earlier translations into Welsh and Irish. He also notes that the publication of the Old Testament, which was not completed until 1801, "proved to be a much larger and more difficult undertaking." Meek, "Gaelic Bible," 15–16.

51. This interpretation is drawn from A. MacLean, *Reminiscences*, 55–56. Also see MacBean, *Buchanan*, 24–25.

52. David Daiches, Peter Jones, and Jean Jones, eds., *The Scottish Enlightenment, 1730–1790: A Hotbed of Genius* (Edinburgh: Saltire Society, 1996), 1. On the beginnings of New Town see James Buchan, *Crowded with Genius: The Scottish Enlightenment: Edinburgh's Moment of the Mind* (New York: Harper Collins, 2003), 173–207.

53. For further studies on the Scottish Enlightenment see Allan, *Scotland in the Eighteenth Century*, esp. 127–64; Arthur Herman, *The Scottish Enlightenment: The Scots Invention of the Modern World* (London: Fourth Estate, 2003), 60–216; James Buchan, *Capital of the Mind: How Edinburgh Changed the World* (London: John Murray, 2004).

54. On Buchanan's famous conversation with David Hume, see A. MacLean, *Reminiscences*, 56–57.

55. A. Sinclair MacLean quotes Eric J. Findlater, pastor of the Free Church Manse, Lochearnhead, on December 18, 1874, who commented on the site of Buchanan's burial: "It is one of the many clan cemeteries common in Perthshire. As they could not agree on earth, they were resolved to offer no temptation when under it." Ibid., 60–61. Also see MacBean, *Buchanan*, 25–26.

56. For a balanced assessment of Uncas see Oberg, *Uncas*. See also, Eric S. Johnson, "Uncas and the Politics of Conflict," in Grumet, *Northeastern Indian Lives*, 29–47.

57. On Occom's lineage see Blodgett, *Samson Occom*, 28; Love, *Samson Occom*, 21–23. Love's account of Occom bears some resemblances to A. MacLean's *Remi-*

niscences. Both were written a few generations after their subjects had passed away, and both relied, at least in part, on oral recollection.

58. Oberg, *Uncas*, 16–18, 70–72. The persistence of the legacy was reinforced by "a Pequot woman who, when asked in the 1970s about the nearby Mohegans, replied that the Pequots had not had much contact 'ever since what they did to us.'" Jack Campisi, "The Emergence of the Mashantucket Pequot Tribe, 1637–1975," in *The Pequots in Southern New England*, ed. Lawrence M. Hauptman and James D. Wherry (Norman: University of Oklahoma Press, 1990), 117. Lawrence M. Hauptman concludes that "modern Pequots cannot completely forget the Sassacus-Uncas rivalry [Sassacus was a leading Pequot sachem], the Mohegan-English alliance in the War of 1637, and the subsequent enslavement of the Pequots." "The Pequot War and Its Legacies," in Hauptman and Wherry, *Pequots in Southern New England*, 80.

59. Simmons, *New England Tribes*, 3.

60. Occom Diary, September 17, 1768, 1:82, DCA.

61. Ibid.

62. Ibid., 82–83. The teacher was probably Jonathan Barber, who served alternately as minister and schoolmaster to the Mohegans from 1733 to 1738. Barber's predecessor, Capt. John Mason, opened a school for the Mohegans in 1727, where he taught the children for about seven years. Love, *Samson Occom*, 27–29. It is unlikely, however, that Occom received any instruction from Barber or Mason.

63. Occom Diary, September 17, 1768, 1:83.

64. Quotes are from Occom Diary, September 17, 1768, 1:83. W. DeLoss Love quotes Wheelock's assessment of Occom's conversion: "Samson Occom was converted, according to the testimony of Doctor Wheelock 'by . . . the labors of Rev. Mr. Davenport.'" *Samson Occom*, 34. In his biography of Wheelock, James Dow McCallum writes that Occom "had been converted during the Great Awakening perhaps by James Davenport." *Eleazar Wheelock*, 80. The port town of New London attracted the New Light ministers of the Great Awakening. Davenport, however, did not preach in New London until 1743. In 1741 Gilbert Tennent visited New London briefly, and it is possible that Occom heard him. That was the year that Occom, by his own admission, was converted. Further clouding the issue, Arnold A. Dallimore observes that Occom was converted "under the ministry of Whitefield and Tennent." Arnold A. Dallimore, *George Whitefield: The Life and Times of the Great Evangelist of the Eighteenth-Century Revival*, vol. 2 (Westchester, Ill.: Cornerstone Books, 1980), 459–60.

65. Occom Diary, September 17, 1768, 1:84. On schooling for the Mohegans during this time, see Connell Szasz, *Indian Education*, 185–87.

66. Occom Diary, September 17, 1768, 1:84. Sarah Ockham may have worked for Wheelock as a servant in the minister's home in order to help pay for her son's tutoring. Blodgett, *Samson Occom*, 31. If this is accurate, it suggests the depth of her commitment.

67. On the Mohegan land controversy, known as the Mason Case, see Kellaway, *New England Company*, 253–55; Love, *Samson Occom*, 119–29; Blodgett, *Samson*

Occom, 74–80, 95; Connell Szasz, "Samson Occom: Mohegan as Spiritual Intermediary," 67–68.

68. Blodgett, *Samson Occom*, 36.

69. The issue of economic disparity is covered in Occom Diary, 1:91, and in Blodgett, *Samson Occom*, 40–44. A more critical appraisal of his position is in Love, *Samson Occom*, 44–45.

70. Occom Diary, 1:90.

71. Occom is described as "the first Indian minister that was ever in Britain." *Scots Magazine* 29 (September 1767): 499.

72. During the fund-raising trip to England, Wales, and Scotland, Occom's faith in Whitefield was reconfirmed. He noted in his diary on February 14, 1766, "Mr Whitefield *takes unwearied* Pains to Introduce us to the *religious Nobility* and others, and to the best men in the City of London—yea he is a *tender father* to us." Occom Diary, 1:69.

73. En route to Oneida, however, during a stopover near New York City, Occom recorded his shock at the Christian profaning of the Sabbath: "Sabbath, June ye 14 [1761]. [T]here Mouths were full of Cursing. . . . I have thought there was no Heathen but the Wild Indians, but I think now there is Some English Heathen . . . yea I believe they are worse than ye Savage Heathens of the Wilderness." Ibid., 1:53.

74. Letter quoted in Blodgett, *Samson Occom*, 73.

75. Ibid. On Mary and Samson's house that was under construction, see Love, *Samson Occom*, 101–102; Connell Szasz, "Samson Occom: Mohegan as Spiritual Intermediary," 61, 65–67. The two-story home, located just east of Norwich, became a landmark in the area, surviving for some years after the Occoms moved to Oneida lands.

76. Blodgett, *Samson Occom*, 73.

8. The Edinburgh Connection

1. Smith to Wheelock, March 30, 1764, published in Leon Burr Richardson, *An Indian Preacher in England* (Hanover: Dartmouth College, 1933), 19–20; a portion of the Smith letter is quoted in Blodgett, *Samson Occom*, 84.

2. Quote from Whitefield letter of 1760 is in Blodgett, *Samson Occom*, 84. On Wheelock's arrangements with the Connecticut board, see Wheelock to Whitefield, July 6, 1764, in McClure and Parish, *Memoirs of Eleazar Wheelock*, 246–47; the full Whitefield to Wheelock letter of August 30, 1760, is in ibid., 223–24.

3. In their anger, the Boston commissioners wrote to the governor of the New England Company in England that Occom had been raised under the Christian influence of the school they had sponsored at Mohegan and was not a pagan when he went to Wheelock. When Occom learned of their accusations, he denied the charges through a brief autobiography, which he never completed. Love, *Samson Occom*, 134–35.

4. Occom qtd. in ibid., 88.

5. On the relationship between the English and Whitaker see Blodgett, *Samson*

Occom, 99–101; Love, *Samson Occom*, 147–48. Love notes that "Mr. Whitaker soon became a mere agent" (147).

6. Love, *Samson* Occom, 139, 142.

7. Whitefield to Wheelock, February 2, 1766, in McClure and Parish, *Memoirs of Eleazar Wheelock*, 267.

8. Love notes that the Anglicans' initial interest in the plan eventually turned to opposition. Love, *Samson Occom*, 143–44.

9. The Earl of Dartmouth requested the portrait of Occom that was painted during his visit, and that is one of the two extant likenesses of the Mohegan. Blodgett quotes Whitefield's assessment of Occom's initial sermons: "Mr. Occom hath preached for me with acceptance." *Samson Occom,* 91; the quote referring to Pepys is on 89.

10. Occom Diary, June 23, 1766, 1:75, DCA.

11. Whitaker to Wheelock, March 7, 1767, qtd. in Richardson, *Indian Preacher in England*, 229.

12. Although they had received more than £100 per week in England, the party collected only £37.19.7 in Liverpool, a town of thirty thousand people. Whitaker to Wheelock, May 2, 1767, quoted in ibid., 248–49. A. L. Drummond contrasts "the emergence of Arminianism, Arianism and Socinianism . . . [and] the individualism of 'the dissenting interest'" in England with "the theological solidarity of 'the standing order' of established Congregationalism in New England." "Scotland and New England in Church History: A Parallel and a Contrast," *Records of the Scottish Church History Society* 7 (1941): 78. Whitaker clearly found this contrast distasteful.

13. Few of the letters in Richardson's collection were penned by Occom. The complaints of the various correspondents suggest that he seldom responded, let alone initiated correspondence with them. At one point, Robert Keen, secretary of the English trust and a faithful supporter of Occom, chided the Mohegan in a letter to Whitaker: "let Mr Occum read or hear you read this, & let him know, if he don't write once a fortnight or thereabouts to me, I'll either not put him in my Will, or cut him off with a Shilling." Keen to Whitaker, December 4, 1766, qtd. in Richardson, *Indian Preacher in England*, 191.

14. SSPCK Records, Minutes of Committee Meetings (MCM/SSPCK), May 22, 1767, 399, GD95/2/8, General Register House, National Archives of Scotland, Edinburgh (NAS).

15. *Caledonian Mercury*, May 16, 1767. Occom and Whitaker had gathered testimonials throughout the region to support the fund-raising. Occom had secured Sir William Johnson's; Whitaker had obtained the endorsements of dozens of prominent religious and political figures who signed a letter written by Wheelock. One member of the board of trustees formed to manage the funds collected in England wrote, "Whitaker's recommendation looked like Ezekiel's scroll, full on both sides from one end to the other." The testimonials were included in *A Brief Narrative of the Indian Charity School*, printed in London in 1766. On this issue see Love, *Samson Occom*, 131–36, quote on 133.

16. Whitaker to Wheelock, May 7, 1767, qtd. in Richardson, *Indian Preacher in England*, 229–30.

17. MCM/SSPCK, May 23, 1767, 399, GD95/2/8, NAS.

18. Ibid., May 27, 1767, 400–401.

19. The meeting attended by Occom and Whitaker was on June 3, 1767; the meeting held a week later was on June 7, 1767, in MCM/SSPCK, 401–402.

20. *Caledonian Mercury*, June 15, 1767.

21. The committee agreed that Whitaker should preach on three consecutive days and that "the Committee should attend upon these occasions to receive Contributions from well disposed Persons for Mr Wheelock's Indian Academy." MCM/SSPCK, July 8, 1767, 404, GD95/2/8, NAS.

22. *The Scots Magazine* 29 (June 1767): 400.

23. John Erskine to Whitaker, June 12, 1767, qtd. in Richardson, *Indian Preacher in England*, 263–64.

24. *Glasgow Journal*, June 11–18, 1767.

25. Webster to Whitaker, June 13, 1767, qtd. in Richardson, *Indian Preacher in England*, 264–65.

26. *Aberdeen Journal*, July 13, 1767.

27. *Glasgow Journal*, June 11–18, 1767.

28. *Aberdeen Journal*, July 6, 1767.

29. Ibid., July 13, 1767.

30. Richardson, *Indian Preacher in England*, 15. Richardson points out that the net proceeds of £11,000 (which excluded the £1,000 for expenses) remained greater than the sum raised by any other American institution in Britain during the colonial era.

31. MCM/SSPCK, October 24, 1764, 273, GD95/2/8, NAS.

32. Ibid., June 1, 1758, 509.

33. Ibid., December 20, 1764, 280, 283.

34. Ibid., June 3, 1765, 305; July 12, 1765, 310; November 21, 1765, 320; January 2, 1766, 332.

35. Ibid., March 4, 1766, 343.

36. Ibid., March 4, 1766, 343; April 3, 1766, 346.

37. Ibid., June 26, 1767; July 2, 1767, 403–404.

38. Wheelock to Whitaker, quoted in Blodgett, *Samson Occom*, 95.

39. After their initial opposition to the removal of Moor's School to New Hampshire, on April 3, 1769, the board of trustees in England finally agreed to the transfer. Love, *Samson Occom*, 157–58. For the Dartmouth College charter, see McClure and Parish, *Memoirs of Eleazar Wheelock*, 180–94.

40. Samson Occom, *A Sermon, Preached at the Execution of Moses Paul, an Indian, Who Was Executed at New Haven on the 2d of September 1772, for the Murder of Mr. Moses Cook* (New Haven: Thomas and Samuel Green, 1772). See Love, *Samson Occom*, 169–175; Blodgett, *Samson Occom*, 138–44.

41. Samson Occom, *A Choice Collection of Hymns and Spiritual Songs, Intended for the Edification of Sincere Christians, of All Denominations* (New London, Conn.: Timothy Green, 1774).

42. Love, *Samson Occom*, 169–87, quotes on 181, 183. Love notes that Occom composed these hymns "during that period of despondency which followed his

return from England. He has wrought his experience into them" (182). Also see Blodgett, *Samson Occom*, 144–46.

43. The most extensive coverage of the migration to Oneida is in Love, *Samson Occom*, 207–46. Also see Blodgett, *Samson Occom*, 146–68.

44. On the Occoms at Brothertown, see ibid., 200–214; Love, *Samson Occom*, 247–98; Connell Szasz, "Samson Occom: Mohegan as Spiritual Intermediary," 75–78.

45. McClure qtd. in Love, *Samson Occom*, 153.

46. Thomson, *Introduction to Gaelic Poetry*, 139.

47. Norman Maclean, *The Former Days* (London: Hodder and Stoughton, 1945), 40.

Conclusion

1. Derick Thomson, "Although Calvin Came," in *Creachadh Na Clàrsaich, Plundering the Harp, Collective Poems, 1940–1980* (Edinburgh: MacDonald, 1982), 172–73.

2. Leon Burr Richardson notes that Mary Occom "is described as 'intelligent, virtuous and comely,' but also as more attached to Indian ways than was entirely pleasing to her husband." *Indian Preacher in England*, 100n1. Excerpts from their letters illustrate the contrast between their experiences. On March 11, 1766, Occom wrote to his wife from London, "Trust in the Lord Jehovah, for in Him is Everlasting Strength." Sixteen months later, on July 15, 1767, Mary Occom wrote in desperation to Wheelock, just as her husband was leaving Scotland, "I am out of Corn, and have no money to buy any with, and am afraid we shall suffer for Want, and Sr. if you will be pleased to help me in my Distress." Qtd. in ibid., 99–100, 279.

Bibliography

Manuscript Collections and Archives

Baker Library, Dartmouth College, Hanover, New Hampshire
    Eleazar Wheelock Papers
    Samson Occom Papers
    Transcript of Samson Occom's Journal [Diary], 3 vols.
    Records of Moor's Indian Charity School
Connecticut Historical Society, Hartford, Connecticut
    Indian Papers
Hamilton College Library, Clinton, New York
    Samuel Kirkland Papers
Inverness Library, Inverness, Scotland
    Transactions of the Gaelic Society of Inverness
National Archives of Scotland
    Church of Scotland General Assembly Papers
        Hyndman-Dick Report, 1760
        William Drummond Report, 1760
        Patrick Butter's Journal, 1824
        John Tawse Journal, 1827
    Records of the SSPCK
National Library of Scotland
Siabost School Museum, Isle of Lewis
    Oral History Collections
Speer Library, Princeton Theological Seminary, Princeton, New Jersey
    David Avery Papers
Ulapool Museum and Visitor Centre, Ulapool, Scotland

Newspapers and Periodicals

The Aberdeen Journal
The Caledonian Mercury
The Edinburgh Evening Courant
The Glasgow Journal
The Guardian Weekly
The Scots Magazine
The Scotsman

Published Sources

Allan, David. *Scotland in the Eighteenth Century*. Edinburgh: Longman, 2002.

An Account of the Society in Scotland for Propagating Christian Knowledge. Edinburgh: A. Murray and J. Cochrane, 1774.

Andrew, Graham. *A Brief Survey of the Society in Scotland*. Edinburgh: C. J. Cousland and Sons, Ltd., 1957.

Axtell, James. *The Invasion Within: The Contest of Cultures in Colonial North America*. New York and Oxford: Oxford University Press, 1985.

Bailyn, Bernard. *Education in the Forming of American Society*. New York: Vintage Books, 1963.

Bailyn, Bernard, and Philip D. Morgan, eds. *Strangers within the Realm: Cultural Margins of the First British Empire*. Chapel Hill: Published for the Institute of Early American History and Culture, Williamsburg, Virginia, by the University of North Carolina Press, 1991.

Bannerman, John. "Literacy in the Highlands." In *The Renaissance and Reformation in Scotland: Essays in Honor of Gordon Donaldson*, eds. Ian B. Coward and Duncan Shaw, 214–35. Edinburgh: Scottish Academic Press, 1983.

———. *Studies in the History of Dalriada*. Edinburgh: Scottish Academic Press, 1974.

Bilharz, Joy. "First among Equals? The Changing Status of Seneca Women." In *Women and Power in Native North America*, eds. Laura F. Klein and Lillian A. Ackerman, 101–12. Norman: University of Oklahoma Press, 1995.

Bingham, Carolyn. *Beyond the Highland Line: Highland History and Culture*. London: Constable, 1991.

Blodgett, Harold. *Samson Occom*. Hanover: Dartmouth College, 1935.

Boswell, James. *The Life of Samuel Johnson*. New York: Modern Library, 1952.

Brainerd, David. "The Life and Diary of the Rev. David Brainerd: With Notes and Reflections." In *The Works of President Edwards*, by Jonathan Edwards. 8 vols. Leeds: Printed by E. Baines, 1806–11.

———. *Memoirs of the Reverend David Brainerd*, eds. Edward Parsons and Edward Williams. In *The Works of President Edwards*, by Jonathan Edwards. 8 vols. 1817. Reprint, New York: Burt Franklin, 1968.

Brainerd, Thomas. *The Life of John Brainerd*. Philadelphia: Presbyterian Publication Committee, 1865.

Brasser, T. J. "Mahican." In *Handbook of Northeastern Indians*, vol. 15, *Northeast*, ed. Bruce J. Trigger, 198–212. Washington, D.C.: Smithsonian Institution, 1978.

Breen, T. H. "An Empire of Goods: The Anglicization of Colonial America, 1690–1776." *Journal of British Studies* 25 (October 1986): 467–99.

Brinton, Daniel G., ed. *The Lenape and Their Legends, with the Complete Text and Symbols of the Walum Olum*. 1884. Reprint, New York: AMS Press, 1969.

Brotherstone, Terry, and David Ditchburn. "1320 and A' That: The Declaration of Arbroath and the Remaking of Scottish History." In *Freedom and Authority, Scotland, 1050–1650: Historical and Historiographical Essays Presented to*

Grant G. Simpson, eds. Terry Brotherstone and David Ditchburn, 10–31. East Linton: Tuckwell Press, 2000.
Buchan, James. *Crowded with Genius: The Scottish Enlightenment: Edinburgh's Moment of the Mind.* New York: Harper Collins Publishers, 2003.
———. *Capital of the Mind, How Edinburgh Changed the World.* London: John Murray, 2004.
Buchanan, Dugald. "Dugald Buchanan's Confessions." In MacBean, *Buchanan,* 130–212.
———. *The Spiritual Songs of Dugald Buchanan,* ed. Donald MacLean. Edinburgh: John Grant, 1913.
Burns, Robert. *Poems and Songs of Robert Burns,* ed. James Banks. 1955. Reprint, London: Harper Collins, 1991.
Burt, Edmund. *Burt's Letters from the North of Scotland.* Edinburgh: Birlinn, 1998. Originally published as *Letters from a Gentleman in the North of Scotland to His Friend in London.* London, 1754.
Calloway, Colin G., ed. *After King Philip's War: Presence and Persistence in Indian New England.* Hanover: Dartmouth College and University Press of New England, 1997.
Campbell, John Lorne. *Highland Songs of the Forty-Five.* Edinburgh: The Scottish Gaelic Texts Society, 1984.
Campbell, Joseph. *The Hero with a Thousand Faces.* New York: World Publishing, 1971.
Campisi, Jack. "The Emergence of the Mashantucket Pequot Tribe, 1637–1975." In *The Pequots in Southern New England,* eds. Lawrence M. Hauptman and James D. Wherry, 117–40. Norman: University of Oklahoma Press, 1990.
Child, Brenda J. *Boarding School Seasons.* Lincoln: University of Nebraska Press, 1998.
"The Church and Education in the Highlands." *Transactions of the Gaelic Society of Inverness* 7 (1877–78): 8–26.
Clive, John. "The Social Background of the Scottish Renaissance." In *Scotland in the Age of Improvement,* eds. N. T. Phillipson and Rosalind Mitchison, 225–44. Edinburgh: Edinburgh University Press, 1996.
Coleman, Michael C. *American Indian Children at School, 1850–1930.* Jackson: University Press of Mississippi, 1993.
Colley, Linda, *Britons, Forging the Nation, 1707–1837.* New Haven: Yale University Press, 1992.
Collins Encyclopedia of Scotland. Eds. John Keay and Julia Keay. London: Harper Collins, 1994.
Connell Szasz, Margaret, ed. *Between Indian and White Worlds: The Cultural Broker.* Norman: University of Oklahoma Press, 2001.
———. *Indian Education in the American Colonies, 1607–1783.* Albuquerque: University of New Mexico Press, 1988.
———. "Native American Children." In *American Childhood: A Research Guide and Historical Handbook,* eds. N. Ray Hiner and Joseph M. Hawes, 311–42. Westport, Conn.: Greenwood Press, 1985.

———. "Native American Children." In *The Chicago Companion to the Child*. Chicago: University of Chicago Press, forthcoming.

———. " 'Poor Richard' Meets the Native American: Young Indian Women at School in Eighteenth-Century Connecticut." *Pacific Historical Review* 49 (May 1980): 215–35.

———. "Samson Occom: Mohegan as Spiritual Intermediary." In *Between Indian and White Worlds: The Cultural Broker*, ed. Margaret Connell Szasz, 61–78. Norman: University of Oklahoma Press, 2001.

———. "Samson Occom: Mohegan Leader and Cultural Broker." In *The Human Tradition in Colonial America*, eds. Ian K. Steele and Nancy L. Rhoden, 237–55. Wilmington, Delaware: Scholarly Resources, Inc., 1999.

Cowper, A. S. *SSPCK Schoolmasters 1709–1872*. Edinburgh: Scottish Record Society, New Series, 1997.

Cowper, H. and W. Pickard. "Education." In Daiches, *Companion to Scottish Culture*, 87–91.

Cremin, Lawrence A. *American Education: The Colonial Experience, 1607–1783*. New York: Harper and Row, 1970.

Cruikshank, Marjorie. *A History of the Training of Teachers in Scotland*. London: University of London, 1970.

Cummings, A. J. G. "The Business Affairs of an Eighteenth-Century Lowland Laird: Sir Archibald Grant of Monymust, 1696–1778." In *Scottish Elites*, ed. Tom M. Devine, 43–61. Edinburgh: John Donald, 1994.

Daiches, David, ed. *The New Companion to Scottish Culture*. Edinburgh: Polygon, 1993.

Daiches, David, Peter Jones, and Jean Jones, eds. *The Scottish Enlightenment, 1730–1790: A Hotbed of Genius*. Edinburgh: The Saltire Society, 1996.

Dallimore, Arnold A. *George Whitefield, The Life and Times of the Great Evangelist of the Eighteenth-Century Revival*, Vol. 2, Westchester, IL: Cornerstone Books, 1979.

Dames, Michael. *Mythic Ireland*. London: Thames and Hudson, 1992.

Daunton, Martin, and Rick Halpern, eds. *Empire and Others: British Encounters with Indigenous Peoples, 1600–1850*. Philadelphia: University of Pennsylvania Press, 1999.

Davids, Dorothy W. "Stockbridge-Munsee." In *Native America in the Twentieth Century*, ed. Mary B. Davis, 619–20. New York: Garland Publishing, Inc., 1994.

———. "Stockbridge-Munsee, (Mohican)." In *Encyclopedia of North American Indians*, ed. Frederick W. Hoxie, 611. Boston: Houghton Mifflin, 1996.

Davies, John. *A History of Wales*. London: Penguin, 1993.

Defoe, Daniel. *A Tour through the Whole Island of Great Britain*, eds. P. N. Furbank and W. R. Onans. New Haven: Yale University Press, 1991. Originally published in three volumes, 1724–26.

Dennis, Matthew. *Cultivating a Landscape of Peace*. Ithaca: Cornell University Press, 1993.

Devine, Tom M. *Clanship to Crofters' War.* Manchester: Manchester University Press, 1996.
———. *The Scottish Nation, 1700–2000.* London: Allen Lane, Penguin Press, 1999.
———. *The Transformation of Rural Scotland.* Edinburgh: University of Edinburgh Press, 1994.
Dickason, Olive Patricia. *Canada's First Nations.* Norman: University of Oklahoma Press, 1992.
Dodgshon, Robert A. *From Chiefs to Landlords.* Edinburgh: Edinburgh University Press, 1998.
———. "'Pretense of Blude' and 'Place of Their Duelling': The Nature of Scottish Clans, 1500–1745." In *Scottish Society: 1500–1800*, eds. Robert Allen Houston and Ian D. White, 169–98. Cambridge: Cambridge University Press, 1989.
———. "West Highland Chiefdons, 1500–1745: A Study in Redistributive Exchange." In Mitchison and Roebuck, *Economy and Society*, 27–37.
Donaldson, Gordon. *The Faith of the Scots.* London: B.T.D. Batsford, 1990.
———, ed. *Scottish Historical Documents.* Glasgow: Neil Wilson, 1999.
Druke, Mary A. "Linking Arms: The Structure of Iroquois Intertribal Diplomacy." In *Beyond the Covenant Chain: The Iroquois and their Neighbors in Indian North America*, eds. Daniel K. Richter and James H. Merrell, 29–39. Syracuse: Syracuse University Press, 1987.
Drummond, A. L. "Scotland and New England in Church History: A Parallel and a Contrast." *Records of the Scottish Church History Society* 7 (1941): 78.
Durkacz, Victor Edward. *The Decline of the Celtic Languages: A Study of Linguistic and Cultural Conflict in Scotland, Wales, and Ireland from the Reformation to the Twentieth Century.* Edinburgh: John Donald Publishers, 1983.
Erdoes, Richard and Alfonso Ortiz, eds. *American Indian Myths and Legends.* New York: Pantheon Books, 1984.
Feister, Lois M., and Bonnie Pulis. "Molly Brant: Her Domestic and Political Roles in Eighteenth-Century New York." In Grumet, *Northeastern Indian Lives*, 295–320.
Fennell, Barbara A. *A History of English: A Sociolinguistic Approach.* Oxford: Blackwell, 2001.
Fenton, William N. *The Great Law and the Longhouse: A Political History of the Iroquois Confederacy.* Norman: University of Oklahoma Press, 1998.
———. "Northern Iroquoian Culture Patterns." In *Handbook of North American Indians*, vol. 15, *Northeast*, ed. Bruce G. Trigger, 296–321. Washington, D.C.: Smithsonian Institution, 1978.
Fraser, Amy Stewart. *Dae Ye Min Lansyne? A Pot-pourri of Games, Rhymes, and Ploys of Scottish Childhood.* London: Routledge and Kegan Paul, 1975.
Frazier, Patrick. *The Mohicans of Stockbridge.* Lincoln: University of Nebraska Press, 1992.
Gaustad, Edwin Scott. *The Great Awakening in New England.* 1957. Reprint, Chicago: Quadrangle Books, 1968.
Goodare, Julian. "The Statutes of Iona in Context." *Scottish Historical Review* 77, no. 203 (1998): 31–57.

Grant, I. F. *Highland Folkways*. London: Routledge and Kegan Paul, 1980.
Grant, I. F., and Hugh Cheape. *Periods in Highland History*. 1987. Reprint, London: Shepheard-Walwyn, 1997.
Green, Miranda. *Animals in Celtic Life and Myth*. London: Routledge, 1998.
Gregory, Donald. *History of the Western Highlands and Isles of Scotland from A.D. 1493 to A.D. 1625*. Edinburgh, 1836. Reprint, Bowie, MO: Heritage Books, 1996.
Grumble, Ian. *Scottish Clans and Tartans*. London: Hamlyn, 1989.
Grumet, Robert S., ed. *Northeastern Indian Lives, 1632–1816*. Amherst: University of Massachusetts Press, 1996.
Haldane, A. R. B. *The Drove Roads of Scotland*. Edinburgh: Birlinn, 1997.
Hauptman, Lawrence M., and James D. Wherry, eds. *The Pequots in Southern New England*. Norman: University of Oklahoma Press, 1990.
Herman, Arthur. *The Scottish Enlightenment: The Scots Invention of the Modern World*. London: Fourth Estate, 2003.
Hewett, J. N. B. "A Constitutional League of Peace in Stone Age America." In *An Iroquois Source Book*. Vol. 1, *Political and Social Organization*, ed. Elisabeth Tooker, 527–45. New York: Garland, 1985.
Hinderaker, Eric. "Translation and Cultural Brokerage." In *A Companion to American Indian History*, eds. Philip J. Deloria and Neal Salisbury, 356–75. Malden, Mass.: Blackwell, 2004.
Houston, Robert Allen. "Scottish Education and Literacy, 1600–1800: An International Perspective." In *Improvement and Enlightenment*, ed. Tom M. Devine, 43–61. Edinburgh: John Donald, 1989.
Humphreys, Rob and Donald Reid. *Scottish Highlands and Islands, the Rough Guide*. London: Penguin Group, 2000.
Hunter, John. *Last of the Free*. Edinburgh: Mainstream Publishing, 2000.
Jenkins, Geraint H. "From Reformation to Methodism 1536–1750." In *The Tempus History of Wales 25,000 B.C.–A.D. 2000*, ed. Prys Morgan, 141–74. Stroud, Gloucestershire: Tempus, 2001.
Johnson, Eric S. "Uncas and the Politics of Conflict." In Grumet, *Northeastern Indian Lives*, 29–47.
Johnson, Samuel, and James Boswell. *A Journey to the Western Isles of Scotland and the Journal of a Tour to the Hebrides*. London: Penguin Books, 1984.
Jones, M. G. *The Charity School Movement*. Cambridge: Cambridge University Press, 1938.
Kartunnen, Francis. *Between Worlds: Interpreters, Guides, and Survivors*. New Brunswick, N.J.: Rutgers University Press, 1994.
Kellaway, William. *The New England Company, 1649–1776*. London: Longman, Green, 1961.
Kerr, John. *Scottish Education, School, and University, from Early Times to 1908*. Cambridge: Cambridge University Press, 1910.
Knox, H. M. *Two Hundred and Fifty Years of Scottish Education, 1696–1946*. Edinburgh: Oliver and Boyd, 1953.

Lenman, Bruce P. "From the Union of 1707 to the Franchise Reform of 1832." In *The New Penguin History of Scotland*, eds. Robert Allen Houston and W. W. Knox, 276–354. Allan Lane: The Penguin Press and National Museums of Scotland, 2002.
———. "Union, Jacobitism, and Enlightenment." In *Why Scottish History Matters*, ed. Rosalind Mitchison, 65–78. Edinburgh: The Saltire Society, 1991.
Lomawaima, K. Tsianina. *They Called It Prairie Light: The Story of Chilocco Indian School*. Lincoln: University of Nebraska Press, 1994.
Love, W. DeLoss. *Samson Occom and the Christian Indians of New England*. 1899. Reprint, Syracuse: Syracuse University Press, 2000.
Lynch, Michael. *Scotland: A New History*. London: Pimlico, 1993.
MacBean, Lachlan. *Buchanan: The Sacred Bard of the Scottish Highlands*. London: Simkin, Marshall, Hamilton, Kent, 1919.
MacDonald, Rev. A. *The Poems of Alexander MacDonald*. Inverness: Northern Counties Newspaper and Printing and Publishing, 1924.
Macinnes, Allan. *Clanship, Commerce, and the House of Stuart, 1603–1788*. East Linton: Tuckwell Press, 1996.
———. "The Impact of the Civil Wars and Interregnum: Political Disruption and Social Change Within Scottish Gaeldom." In Mitchison and Roebuck, 58–69.
MacInnes, John. *The Evangelical Movement in the Highlands of Scotland, 1688–1800*. Aberdeen: The University Press, 1951.
Mackay, William. "Education in the Highlands." *Transactions of the Gaelic Society of Inverness* 27 (1908–11): 250–71.
Mackie, J. D. *A History of Scotland*. London: Penguin Books, 1964.
MacKinnon, Kenneth. *Gaelic: A Past and Future Prospect*. Edinburgh: Saltire Society, 1991.
MacLean, A. Sinclair. *Reminiscences of the Life and Labours of Dugald Buchanan, Formerly Teacher and Evangelist at Rannoch, Perthsire*. Edinburgh: MacLachlan and Steward, 1885.
Maclean, Norman. *The Former Days*. London: Hodder and Stoughton Limited, 1945.
MacLeod, John. *Highlanders: A History of the Gaels*. London: Hodder and Stoughton, 1997.
MacPherson, James. *Fingal, An Acient Epic Poem, Composed by Ossian, the Son of Fingal*. London: N.p. 1765.
———. *Fragments of Ancient Poetry, collected in the Highlands of Scotland*. Edinburgh: N.p., 1760.
———. *The Poems of Ossian*. London: N.p., 1773.
Magnusson, Magnus. *Scotland: The Story of a Nation*. New York: Atlantic Monthly Press, 2000.
Malcolm, Derek. "Mel Takes the High Wood." *Guardian Weekly*. September 17, 1995.
Malone, Henry T. *Cherokees of the Old South*. Athens: University of Georgia Press, 1956.

Martin, Martin. *A Description of the Western Isles of Scotland ca. 1695: A Late Voyage to St. Kilda*. 1703. Reprint, Edinburgh: Birlinn, 1999.

Mason, John. *A History of Scottish Experiments in Rural Education From the Eighteenth Century to the Present Day*. London: University of London Press, 1935.

———. "Scottish Charity Schools of the Eighteenth Century." *The Scottish Historical Review* 33 (April 1954): 1–13.

Matthews, John. *Classic Celtic Fairy Tales*. London: Blandford, 1997.

McBride, Kevin A. "The Legacy of Robin Cassacinamon: Mashantucket Pequot Leadership in the Historic Period." In Grumet, *Northeastern Indian Lives*, 74–92.

McCallum, James Dow. *Eleazar Wheelock, Founder of Dartmouth College*. Hanover: Dartmouth College, 1939.

———, ed. *The Letters of Eleazar Wheelock's Indians*. Hanover: Dartmouth College, 1932.

McClure, David and Elijah Parish. *Memoirs of the Rev. Eleazar Wheelock*. Newburyport, MA: Edward Norris, 1811.

McLoughlin, William G. *Cherokee Renascence in the New Republic*. Princeton: Princeton University Press, 1986.

McLynn, Frank. *The Jacobites*. London and New York: Routledge and Kegan Paul, 1988.

McNeil, Peter G. B., and Hector L. MacQueen, eds. *Atlas of Scottish History to 1707*. Edinburgh: The Scottish Medievalists and Department of Geography, University of Edinburgh, 1996.

Meek, Donald E. "The Gaelic Bible." In *The Bible in Scottish Life and Literature*, ed. David F. Wright, 9–23. Edinburgh: The Saint Andrews Press, 1988.

———. *The Quest for Celtic Christianity*. Edinburgh: The Handsel Press, 2000.

———. "Scottish Highlanders, North American Indians, and the SSPCK: Some Cultural Perspectives." In *Records of the Scottish Church History Society* 23, part 3 (1989): 378–96.

———. *The Scottish Highlands: The Churches and Gaelic Culture*. Gospel and Culture Pamphlet 11. Geneva: World Council of Churches, 1996.

———. "Scottish SPCK." In *Dictionary of Scottish Church History and Theology*, 761–62. Edinburgh: T and T Clark, 1993.

Mitchell, Ian R. "The Whiskey Wars in Scotland." *History Scotland* 5 (November–December 2005): 34–39.

Mitchison, Rosalind, and Peter Roebuck, eds. *Economy and Society in Scotland and Ireland, 1500–1939*. Edinburgh: John Donald, 1988.

Morgan, Philip D. "Encounters between British and Indigenous Peoples. c. 1500–c. 1800." In Daunton and Halpern, *Empire and Others*, 42–78.

Murchison, Rev. Thomas M. "Raining's School, Inverness: A Seedbed of Talent." *Transactions of the Gaelic Society of Inverness* 52 (1980–81): 405–59.

Murray, David. *Forked Tongues: Speech, Writing and Representation in North American Indian Texts*. Bloomington: Indiana University Press, 1991.

Nelson, Dana D. " 'If I Speak Like A Fool, But I am Constrained,' Samson Occom's

Short Narrative and Economies of the Racial Self." In *Early Native American Writing: New Critical Essays*, ed. Helen Jaskoski, 42–65. Cambridge: Cambridge University Press, 1996.

Nicholson, Adam. *Sea Room*. London: Harper Collins Publishers, 2002.

Oberg, Michael Leroy. *Uncas: First of the Mohegans*. Ithaca: Cornell University Press, 2003.

O'Brien, Jean M. "'Divorced' from the Land: Resistance and Survival of Indian Women in Eighteenth-Century New England." In Calloway, *After King Philip's War*, 144–61.

Occum, Samson. *A Choice Collection of Hymns and Spiritual Songs, Intended for the Edification of Sincere Christians, of All Denominations*. New London, Conn.: Timothy Green, 1774.

——. *A Sermon, Preached at the Execution of Moses Paul, an Indian, Who Was Executed at New Haven on the 2d of September 1772, for the Murder of Mr. Moses Cook*. New Haven: Thomas and Samuel Green, 1772.

Pennick, Nigel. *Celtic Sacred Landscapes*. New York: Thames and Hudson, 1996.

Pettitt, George A. *Primitive Education in North America*. Berkeley: University of California Publications in American Ethnology and Archaeology, 1946.

Peyer, Bernd D. *The Tutor'd Mind: Indian Missionary Writers in Antebellum America*. Amherst: University of Massachusetts Press, 1997.

Pilkington, Walter, ed. *The Journals of Samuel Kirkland*. Clinton, NY: Hamilton College, 1980.

Raftery, Barry. *Pagan Celtic Ireland*. London: Thames and Hudson, 1997.

Ramsey, Jarold, ed. *Coyote Was Going There*. Seattle: University of Washington Press, 1999.

Rennie, Frank. *Celtic Culture, Cultar Ceilteach, The Western Isles, Nah Eileanan an Iar*. Isle of Lewis: Western Isles Island Council, Acair, n.d.

Richards, Eric. "Scotland and the Uses of the Atlantic Empire." In Bailyn and Morgan, *Strangers within the Realm*, 67–114.

Richardson, Leon Burr. An Indian Preacher in England. Hanover: Dartmouth College, 1933.

Richter, Daniel K. *The Ordeal of the Longhouse*. Chapel Hill: University of North Carolina Press, 1992.

Riley, Patricia, ed. *Growing Up in Native America: An Anthology*. New York: William Morrow, 1993.

Robertson, James. "Memories of Rannoch." *Transactions of the Gaelic Society of Inverness* 51 (1978–80): 199–206.

Rolleston, T. W. *Celtic Myths and Legends*. New York: Avenal Books, 1986.

Ross, Stewart. *Ancient Scotland*. Moffat: Lochar, 1991.

Rush, Benjamin. *The Autobiography of Benjamin Rush*, ed. George W. Comer. Princeton: Published for the American Philosophical Society by Princeton University Press, 1948.

Salisbury, Neal. *Manitou and Providence: Indians, Europeans, and the Making of New England, 1500–1643*. New York: Oxford University Press, 1982.

Salwen, Bert. "Indians of Southern New England and Long Island: Early Period." In *Handbook of North American Indians*, vol. 15, *Northeast*, ed. Bruce G. Trigger, 160–76. Washington, D.C.: Smithsonian Institution, 1978.

Scherman, Katharine. *The Flowering of Ireland: Saints, Scholars, and Kings*. Boston: Little, Brown, 1981.

Scotland, James. *The History of Scottish Education*, two vols., vol.1, *From the Beginning to 1872*. London: University of London Press, 1969.

Shaw, Francis T. *The Northern and Western Islands of Scotland: Their Economy and Society in the Seventeenth Century*. Edinburgh: John Donald, 1967.

Simmons, William S. *Spirit of the New England Tribes*. Hanover: University Press of New England, 1986.

Simpson, Grant G. "The Declaration of Arboath: What Significance When." Unpublished manuscript.

Sloan, Douglas. *The Scottish Enlightenment and the American College Ideal*. New York: Teachers College Press, Columbia University, 1971.

Smith, Donald. *Storytelling Scotland: A Nation in Narrative*. Edinburgh: Polygon, Edinburgh University Press, 2001.

———. *Scottish Folk-Tales and Legends Retold by Barbara Kerr Wilson*. Oxford: Oxford University Press, 1989.

Smout, T. C. *A Century of the Scottish People, 1830–1950*. New Haven: Yale University Press, 1986.

———. *A History of the Scottish People, 1560–1830*. London: Collins, 1969.

Snow, Dean R. *The Iroquois*. Oxford: Blackwell, 1996.

Speck, Frank G. "Mohegan Traditions of 'Muhkeahweesug' The Little Men." *Papoose* 1.7: 11–14.

Squire, Charles. *Mythology of the Celtic People*. 1912. Reprint, London: Bracken Books, 1996.

"State of the Society in Scotland for Propagating CHRISTIAN Knowledge, in the Year 1769." N.p.: 1769.

Stevenson, David. *The Covenanters: The National Covenant and Scotland*. Edinburgh: The Saltire Society, 1988.

Stevenson, Robert Louis, *Kidnapped*. New York: Tom Doherty Associates, 1991.

Thomson, Derick. "Although Calvin Came." In *Creachadh Na Clàrsaich, Plundering the Harp, Collective poems 1940–1980*, 172–73. Edinburgh: MacDonald Publishers, 1982.

———, ed. *Gaelic Poetry in the Eighteenth Century*. Aberdeen: The University of Aberdeen, 1993.

———. *An Introduction to Gaelic Poetry*. London: Victor Gollancz, 1974.

Tuchman, Barbara. *The Iroquois in the American Revolution*. Syracuse: Syracuse University Press, 1972.

Vickers, Daniel. "The First Whalemen of Nantucket." In Calloway, *After King Philip's War*, 90–113.

Watson, Adam, and R. D. Clement. "Aberdeenshire Gaelic." *Transactions of the Gaelic Society of Inverness* 48 (1980–82): 373–403.

Watson, W. J., ed. *Scottish Verse from the Book of the Dean of Lismore*. Edinburgh: Scottish Gaelic Texts Society, 1937.
"The Waulking Day." *Transactions of the Gaelic Society of Inverness* 13 (1886–87): 201–17.
Weslager, Clifford Alfred. *The Delaware Indians: A History*. New Brunswick, N.J.: Rutgers, 1972.
Wesley, John. *The Journal of the Rev. John Wesley, A.M*, ed. Nehemiah Curnock. 8 vols. London: Epworth Press, 1938.
Wheelock, Eleazar. *A Narrative of the Original Design, Rise, Progress and Present State of the Indian Charity-School in Lebanon*. Boston: Printed by Richard and Samuel Draper, in Newbury-Street, 1763.
White, Richard. *The Middle Ground: Indians, Empires, and Republics in the Great Lakes Region, 1650–1815*. New York: Cambridge University Press, 1991.
Williams, Nicholas. "Literature in Irish." In *The Oxford Companion to Irish History*, ed. S. J. Connelly, 336–39. Oxford: Oxford University Press, 2002.
Williams, Ronald. *The Lords of the Isles: The Clan Donald and the Early Kingdom of the Scots*. London: Chatoo and Windus, the Hogarth Press, 1984.
Williams, Samuel C. "An Account of the Presbyterian Missions to the Cherokee, 1757–1759." *Tennessee Historical Magazine* ser. 2, I (1931): 125–38.
Wilson, Howard McKnight. *The Tinkling Spring Headwater of Freedom*. Fishersville, Va.: Tinkling Spring and Hermitage Presbyterian Church, 1954.
Withrington, Donald J. *Going to School*. Edinburgh: National Museums of Scotland, 1997.
Wyss, Hilary E. *Writing Indians: Literacy, Christianity, and Native Community in Early America*. Amherst: University of Massachusetts Press, 2000.
Youngson, A. J., ed. *Beyond the Highland Line*. London: Collins, St. James Place, 1974.

Index

Page numbers in italics refer to illustrations.

ABCFM (American Board of Commissioners for Foreign Missions), 247n33
Aberdeen, Scotland, 206, 208, 209
Aberdeen Journal, 208
Aberdeenshire, Scotland, 95, 96
Abertarff school, Scottish Highlands, 74, 77, 93
Act of Settlement (Act of Succession), 73
Act of the Security of the Church of Scotland, 70
Act of Union. *See* Union of 1707
Adoption, Iroquois practice of, 22–23
Alasdair, Alasdair mac Mhaighstir (Alexander MacDonald), 99–100, 167–68, 179
Algonquians, 9, 21, 121; appeal for financial aid by, 12–13; bilingual Bible, 122; and Christianity, 125, 221; education of, 132–33; epidemics, 22; and foreign travel, 162; gender roles of, 29, 39, 40; kinship network of, 30; land and climate of, 25, 38; marriage, 35; migration of, 215; and Moor's School, 141, 155, 157; myths and origin stories of, 11, 16, 19, 41; and New England Company, 123; Occom criticized by, 224; schoolmasters and ushers, 154–58; society and culture of, 29, 164–65; and Society in Scotland for the Propagation of Christian Knowledge, 116, 122, 125–26, 162; in southern New England, *139, 156;* storytelling and songs of, 124; traditional education of, 39–40, 41; warfare, 23

American Board of Commissioners for Foreign Missions (ABCFM), 247n33
American Indians. *See* Native Americans
American Revolution, 147
"An Gaisgeach" ("The Hero") (Buchanan), 178–79, 254n38
Anglicanism, 9, 119; Brant and, 149; and Native Americans, 118, 125, 132, 158, 221; Wheelock and, 138
Anglo-Normans, 21
Anne, Queen, 68, 73; and Society in Scotland for the Propagation of Christian Knowledge, 75, 78
Apprenticeship schools, 110–11
Arbroath, Declaration of, 65–66, 97–98, 236n66
Argyll, Scotland, 95
Articles of Union. *See* Union of 1707
Atlantic Ocean, crossings of, 116, 162, 163
Ayonhwathah, 36

Badenoch, Wolf of (Alexander Stewart), 44
Badenoch district, Scottish Highlands, 57
Bailie, Robert, 106
Bailyn, Bernard, 5
Bain, Jean, 97
Balliol (family), 21
Bank of Scotland, 62
Bannerman, John, 49, 50
Barber, Jonathan, 256n62
Bardic traditions, 32, 33, 38, 47, 49
Beaver Wars, 23, 39
Benbecula, Isle of, Scotland, 47; school report from, *103*
Bernard, Francis, 131

273

Bible: Gaelic translations of, 10, 100–101, 179, 182–83, 209, *210*, 211, 218, 223, 255n50; Irish translation of, 100, 101; Massachusett-English, 122; reading of, and education, 112; Welsh translation of, 100, 101

Bilingualism: of Grampian foothills, 242n39; of Raining's School, 109; of schools of Society in Scotland for the Propagation of Christian Knowledge, 101, 102, 104–105, 109; of Scotland, 96

Black Isle, Scotland, 27

Blair, William, 92

Blodgett, Harold, 195, 200, 203

Boswell, James, 63, 88

Brainerd, David, 122, 126, *127*, 128–29, 131, 134, 135, 137, 138, 160, 221, 247n33

Brainerd, John, 131–35, 137, 138, 158, 160, 221

Brant, Joseph (Thayendanegea), 147, *148*, 149

Brant, Molly, 146, 153

Braveheart (film), 46

Breen, T. H., 5

Brotherton, New Jersey, 131

Brothertown, New York, 12, 215, 223

Brown, George, 207

Bruce (family), 21

Buannachan (warriors), 37, 47, 51, 52

Buchan, Alexander, 95

Buchanan, Dugald, 10–11, 13, 94, 209, 222–23; cottage of, *176;* as cultural intermediary, 165, 215–16, 224; culture and society of, 164; death and burial of, 185, *186;* early life and education of, 165–66, 168–70; in Edinburgh, 182–83, 185, 223; and Gaelic New Testament, 182, 209, *210*, 211, 223; and Highlanders' defeat at Carlisle, 168; linguistic abilities of, 181, 183; monuments to, *175, 187;* Occom's similarities to, 192, 212–13, 223–25; religious awakening of, 170–71, 173; residence of, *173;* as schoolmaster, 173–77; and Society for the Propagation of the Gospel in Foreign Parts, 173; as spiritual bard, 178–83

Buchanan, Margaret Brisbane, 173, 185

Burns, Gilbert, 58

Burns, Robert, 58, 60, 61, 110, 237n66

Burt, Edmund, 20, 27, 29–30, 36, 52, 87, *99*, 106

Bute, Isle of, Scotland, 57

Butter, Patrick, 83, 87, 102, 111, 112, 243n57; journal of, *103*, 104

Caithness, Scotland, 180

Caledonian Mercury, 204, 206, 208

Calvin, Hezekiah, 137, 155–56, 158

Calvinism, 125. *See also* Congregationalism; Presbyterianism

Cambuslang Wark, 171, 173

Cameron clan, 177

Cameronians (Covenanters), 63, 65

Campbell clan, 166, 237n3

Carlisle, England, 168, 178

Carlisle Indian School, Pennsylvania, 249n7

Catechism, Presbyterian, 179

Catholicism, 7, 47, 56, 71, 90, 218, 233n14; and Society in Scotland for the Propagation of Christian Knowledge, 72, 84, 97, 98

Caton-Jones, Michael, 46

Cattle raising: in Highlands, 52–54, 56; in Lowlands, 58

Cayugas, 22, 36

Céilidh, 60, 180

Celtic church, 246n19

Celtic Culture, Cultar Ceilteach, The Western Isles, Nah Eileanan an Iar (Rennie), epigraph from, 3

Celtic literature, 18

Celtic people, 20–21; in North American colonies, 117

Central Highlands, Scotland, 24–25

Charity boarding schools, 136, 137, 138. *See also* Moor's Indian Charity School

Charles, Prince. *See* Stewart, Prince Charles Edward

Charles II, 51, 63

Cherokees, 119, 120, 221

Choice Collection of Hymns and Spiritual Songs, A (Occom), 214
Christianity, 6, 7; in North America, 19, 41, 125; of Scotland and Ireland, 18–19. *See also* Great Awakening, First; *and specific Christian denominations*
Church of Ireland, 251n34
Church of Scotland (Presbyterian Church), 46, 56, 62, 63; antiunionist position of, 70; and Buchanan, 174; General Assembly of, 201, 203, 204–205; Schism of 1843, 112; and Shorter Catechism, 179; and Society in Scotland for the Propagation of Christian Knowledge, 74–75, 90
Clan systems: of Highlanders, 20, 30, 31, 33, 34, 35, 37–38, 48, 50–56, 125, 166, 218, 220; of Iroquois, 30, 31, 34, 35, 36
Clark, Donald, 83
Clearances, 93, 166
Clow, John, 99
Cockenoe, 122
College of New Jersey (Princeton), 120, 132, 147, 160
Colley, Linda, 4
Columba, St. (Colm Cille), 19, 32
Company for Propagating the Gospel in New England. *See* New England Company
Company of Scotland, 69
Congregationalism, 9, 223; Kirkland and, 147; at Moor's School, 149; and Native Americans, 117, 119, 120, 122, 125, 132, 160, 190, 221; and Presbyterianism, 136–37, 159; Wheelock and, 135, 136, 138
Connecticut, 124, 186, 188
Connecticut Board of Correspondents, Society in Scotland for the Propagation of Christian Knowledge, 124, 152, 154, 159, 160, 197, 199, 205, 214, 222, 251n42
Cornish (language), 96
Cottars, 58, 59, 62; education of, 89; poverty of, 125
Covenanters (Cameronians), 63, 65
Cradle, Scottish, 41–42

Cradleboard, Native American, 41–42
Craig, James, 119
Cranbury, New Jersey, 131
Creeks, 118, 119, 221
Crofters' Holding Act, 244n68
Cromdale, Battle of, 237n3
Crosswicks (Crossweeksung), New Jersey, 129–30
Cruikshank, Marjorie, 106
Cú Chulainn, 53
Culloden Moor, Battle of, 11, 23, 166, 171, 182, 218
Cultural colonialism, 9, 13, 215; of Society in Scotland for the Propagation of Christian Knowledge, 77, 80, 110, 123, 224
Cultural intermediaries (cultural brokers), 5–6; Brainerd, John, as, 132; monks as, 18; Occom and Buchanan as, 165, 216, 224; Society in Scotland for the Propagation of Christian Knowledge as, 81
Cumberland, Duke of (William Augustus), 241n31
Cuming, Hew, 86

Daiches, David, 185
Dalriada, Scottish, 20, 229n15
Dames, Michael, 32
Danes, 21
Daoine-uaisle, 37
Darien, Panama, 69, 77, 238n7
Dartmouth, Earl of, 198, 258n9
Dartmouth College, 121, 132, 152, 198, 213–14, 222
Daunton, Martin, 5
Davenport, James, 190
Davidson, Ebenezer, 94
Davidson, John, 206
Davies, John, 100
Davies, Samuel, 120, 136
Declaration of Arbroath, 65–66, 97–98, 236n66
Defoe, Daniel, 25, 254n32
Deganawidah, 36
Delaware Indians (Lenni Lenapes), 121, 129, 131–32, 160, 248n35; and Wheelock's school, 137, 138, 140, 141, 221

Dennis, Matthew, 22
Description of the Western Isles (Martin), 90
Devine, Tom M., 20, 35, 46, 48, 59
Disarming Act of 1746, 166–67
Dodgshon, Robert A., 54
Donald clan, 21, 34, 44
Donaldson, Gordon, 65, 66–67
Druids, 18
Drummond, Lewis, 86
Drummond, William, 182
Dumfries, Scotland, 206
Dundee, Viscount (John Graham of Claverhouse), 68, 237n3
Dunkeld, Scotland, 174, 176, 180
Durkacz, Victor, 95
Dutch Reformed Church, 221
Duthchas, 52, 235n30

East Highlands, Scotland, 24
Edinburgh, Scotland, 9, 10, 11, 62–67; Buchanan in, 182–83, 185, 223; conferences in, 48–49, 50; funds raised in, by Occom and Whitaker, 208; Greyfriars Kirk, *184*, 185; Occom in, 203–209, 211–12; professional classes in, 75; and Society for Reformation of Manners, 71; and Society in Scotland for the Propagation of Christian Knowledge, 73–74, 76, 77
Education, 3; Great Awakening and, 135; of Highlanders, 49–50, 56–57, 89–90; importance of, 3; of Lowlanders, 8, 56–58; of Native Americans, 129, 131–33, 135–38; and Society in Scotland for the Propagation of Christian Knowledge, 3–5, 72, 73, 74, 76; Statutes of Iona and, 49–50; traditional patterns of, 38–42
Education Act of 1872, 9, 107, 109, 244n68
Edwards, Jonathan, 131, 135
Eeyamquiltoossuconnuck, New York. *See* Brothertown
Eliot, John, 122, 190
England: fund-raising in, by Occom and Whitaker, 199, 208; union with Scotland, 4, 7–8, 68–71, 238n9, 239n23
English colonists, in North America, 117; in Connecticut, 188–90; perception of Native Americans by, 12, 144
English language: Buchanan's use of, 181; use of, at Moor's School, 143. *See also* Scots
English Trust, 222
Enlightenment, Scottish, 75, 185
Epidemics, among Native Americans, 22
Episcopalianism, 7, 47, 56, 63, 65, 70, 71, 90, 218, 238n10
Erse, 98

Famine (Scotland 1690s), 69
Farming: and famine of 1690s, 69; by Highlanders, 58, 182; by Lowlanders, 58–59, *59*, 62; in Native American societies, 143–44, 156–57
Fenians, 33, 34, 231n49
Fergus Mór, 20
Ferguson, Nicol, 253n16
Feudalism, 21
Fielding, Fidelia, 41
Fife Adventurers, 48
Fine, 37, 47, 48, 51, 55, 56
Fingal, 231n49
Finn Mac Cumhal, 33, 34, 231n49
First Book of Discipline, The, 57
Fir-taca. *See* Tacksman
Fishing, 58, 236n55
Folk tales. *See* Myths, origin stories, and folk tales
Forbes, John, 83
Fordun, John of, 43–44
Forfeited Estates Commissioners, 177, 178, 254n34
Forrest, John, 205
Fort William, in Scottish Highlands, 55, 69
Forty-Five. *See* Jacobite rebellions, of 1745
Fowler, David, 95, 135, 141, 142, 143, 147, 150–54, 156, 157, 159, 195, 196
Fowler, Jacob, 141, 154, 156

Fraser, John, 83
French and Indian War (Seven Years' War), 23–24, 120

Gaelic (language), 7, 9, 32, 43, 44, 49, 50, 71, 95–101, 112; Alasdair and, 167; bardic traditions, 32, 33, 38, 41, 124, 178, 180; Bible translations in, 10, 100–101, 179, 182–83, 209, *210*, 211, 218, 223, 255n50; Buchanan and, 166, 178–81; literacy in, 102; myth cycles, 33, 34, 231n49; Napier Commission and, 107; oral tradition of, 179–81, 218; in Perthshire, 176; and Raining's School, 109; renaissance in, 114; and Society in Scotland for the Propagation of Christian Knowledge, 72, 90, 95, 98–102, 104–105, 218, 219, 243n57; in twenty-first century, 219–20
Gaelic-English vocabulary, 99, 179
Gaels, 20, 21, 32, 46–47; clan system of, 30, 33, 34. *See also* Highlanders
Gàidhealtachd, Scotland, 95–96, 101, 112
Galick and English Vocabulary, 99
Garrett, Hannah, 141
Geddes, Jenny, 63
Gender considerations: of Algonquians, 29, 39, 40; and education of Lowlanders, 58; and education of Native Americans, 132; of Highlanders, 29–30, 38–39; of Iroquois, 29, 36, 39, 40, 156; at Moor's School, 136, 138, 144, 145, 250n22, 250n24; of teachers and pupils in schools of Society in Scotland for the Propagation of Christian Knowledge, 82, 110–11, 217, 244n75
George III, 199
Georgia, 117–19
Gibson, Mel, 46
Glaciers, 16
Glasgow, Scotland, 62, 206–209, 220
Glasgow Journal, 207
Glencoe Massacre, 56, 69, 237n3
Gordon, Duke of, 111
Gow, Niel, *61*

Graham, John, of Claverhouse (Viscount Dundee), 68, 237n3
Grampian Mountains, Scotland, 95, 96, 242n39
Grant, Alexander, 83
Grant, I. F., 52, 54
Grant, John, 83
Grassick, William, 83
Great Awakening, First, 9, 120, 125, 134–35, 138, 160, 225; Occom and, 190; Wheelock and, 149
Great Britain, 4; Native American allies, in American Revolution, 147; Occom's tour of, 196–201, 203–209, 211–13
Great Design, Wheelock's notion of, 136
Great League of Peace and Power. *See* Iroquois League
Greek (language), 143
Greyfriars Kirk, Edinburgh, Scotland, *184*, 185

Hadrian's Wall, *202*
Halpern, Rick, 5
Hancock, John, 198
Hanoverians, 8, 11, 70, 72, 98, 99, 166, 171, 218; and Act of Settlement, 73
Harvard College, and bilingual Bible, 122
Hebrew, 143
Hebrides (Western Isles), Scotland: education in, 49; isolation of, 60; land and climate of, 16, 24, 27; language of, 7, 43, 95, 96, 220; mythology of, 32; religion of, 47; society and culture of, 21, 37, 44; tenants in, 54–55. *See also* Inner Hebrides; Outer Hebrides
"Hero, The" ("An Gaisgeach") (Buchanan), 178–79, 254n38
Heroes of Ulster, 231n49
Hiacoomes (Iacoomes), 123
Highlanders, Scottish: ancestry and lineage of, 29; blended culture of, 23; Buchanan, Dugald, 166, 174, 216; Carlisle, defeat at, 168; clan system of, 20, 30, 31, 33, 34, 35, 37–38, 48,

Highlanders, Scottish (*continued*) 50–56, 125, 166, 218, 220; diaspora of, 128, 166, 219; early history of, 6; economic and financial development of, 50–55, 58–59, 62, 69, 218; in Edinburgh, 183, 185; education of, 56–57; family names of, 29; gender roles of, 29–30, 38–39; homes of, 87–88; isolation of, 60, 62, 220; James VI and, 46, 48; languages of, 43, 49, 50, 90, 95, 96; marriage, 35; as missionaries in North America, 118; music of, 60, 93–94, 124, 219; myths, legends, and stories of, 11, 20, 32, 41, 124; and Native Americans, similarities between, 124–25; and outsiders, 110; population of, 238n21, 241n38; poverty of, 86, 89, 125; religion of, 47, 56, 70, 90–91, 112; society and culture of, 12, 27, 29–30, 36–38, 44, 46–47, 60, 114, 163–64; and Society in Scotland for the Propagation of Christian Knowledge, 72–73, 74, 76, 77, 79–81, 82–83, 85–87, 89–93, 112–14, 115; traditional education of, 38–39, 41, 89–90; and union of Scottish people, 67. *See also* Gaels

Highland Line, Scotland, 7, 43, 46, 56, 58, 220

Highland Rogue (Defoe), 254n32

Highlands, Scotland, 4, 7, *45*; immigrants, 21; land and climate, 16, 24–25, 27, 33, 38; Romanticism of, 46; and Society in Scotland for the Propagation of Christian Knowledge, 5; subregions of, 24–25

Highlands and Islands, University of the (UH), 235n49

Highlands and Islands Education Trust, 244n69

Historians (*seanachaidh*), 47, 51

Hodenosaunee, 22, 36, 40, 121, 125. *See also* Iroquois

Horton, Azariah, 247n26

Hume, David, 185

Huntingdon, Countess of (Selina), 199

Hurons, 22, 23, 125, 221

Iacoomes (Hiacoomes), 123

Indian Preacher in England, An (Richardson), 203

Indian Pride, Wheelock's notion of, 146, 200, 213

Indians, American. *See* Native Americans

Industrial training, by Society in Scotland for the Propagation of Christian Knowledge, 110–11, 217

Ingham, Benjamin, 118, 119

Inner Hebrides, Scotland, 24; education in, 57; language of, 95, 96; religion of, 56

Inverness, Scotland, 27, 36, 107, 110, 206; Raining's School, 105–106, *108*, *109*, 243n61

Inverness-shire, Scotland, 95

Iona, Isle of, Scotland, 32

Iona, Statutes of, 48–50, 90

Ireland, 18–19, 32, 33; myths of, 31–32; Occom and Whitaker in, 213

Irish (language), 90, 95–96, 100, 101

Iroquois, 9, 21, 121, 122; adoption, 22–23; Algonquian schoolmasters and, 155–58, 162; Algonquians' migration to lands of, 215; and American Revolution, 147; and Christianity, 125; clan system of, 30, 31, 34, 35, 36; education of, 132; epidemics, 22; Europeans, interactions with, 221; gender roles of, 29, 36, 39, 40, 156; kinship network of, 30; land and climate of, 25, 38; marriage, 35; myths and origin stories of, 11, 15, 16, 19, 31; orators, 38; population of, 221; society and culture of, 29; and Society in Scotland for the Propagation of Christian Knowledge, 116, 125, 154, 160, 222; in southern New England, *156;* storytelling and songs of, 124; towns, 35–36; traditional education of, 39–40, 41; and Wheelock's school, 140, 150, 151, 153

Iroquois League (Great League of Peace and Power), 22, 36, 158, 221

Islands, Scottish: climate of, 27; culture of, 23, 41; population of, 238n21;

and schools of Society in Scotland for the Propagation of Christian Knowledge, 112. *See also* Hebrides; Orkneys; Shetlands

Jacobite rebellions, 48; of 1689, 55, 68–69, 72; of 1715, 39, 98; of 1745, 11, 23, 39, 71, 72, 98, 166, 167, 168, 171, 180, 182, 220, 254n34
Jacobitism, 8, 70, 71, 72, 99; Dundee, Viscount, and, 237n3; and Society in Scotland for the Propagation of Christian Knowledge, 72, 73, 98–99, 217–18
James VI of Scotland (James I of England), 7, 46, 48–49, 52, 55, 73, 119
James VII of Scotland (James II of England), 55, 63, 69, 73
James VIII of Scotland (James III of England; Old Pretender), 70, 73
Jamieson, George, 84
Jenkins, Geraint H., 100
Jesuits (Society of Jesus), 23, 47, 125, 126, 221
Jewett, David, 190
John XXII, Pope, 65
John of Fordun, 43–44
Johnson, Joseph, 135, 145–46, 149
Johnson, Samuel, 19, 63, 88, 182
Johnson, William (student at Moor's school), 145–46, 149, 250n29
Johnson, William (trader and businessman), 146, 147, 149, 153–54, 204, 252n45
Johnston, James, 98

Kaunaumeek, Massachusetts, 126, 128
Keen, Robert, 258n13
Kelpies, 56
Kidnapped (Stevenson), 13–14
Kildonan, Strath of, 93
Killiecrankie, Battle of, 68
Killing times, 63
King Philip's War, 23
Kinship: and clan system, 54–55; at Moor's School, 141–42
Kirkland, Samuel, 121, 135, 137, 142, 146–47, 154, 157–59, 160, 221, 246n13, 251n31, 252n46
Knox, John, 57, 63, 76

Laing, Sophie, 111
Languages: Native American, 155, 158; of Scotland, 7; teaching of, at Moor's School, 143. *See also* Gaelic; Scots
Laoidhe Spioradail, le Dùghall Bochannan, 179
Latin, 49, 57, 97, 143
Lenman, Bruce, 68
Lenni Lenapes. *See* Delaware Indians
Lewis, Butt of, Scotland, 27
Lewis with Harris, Outer Hebrides, 21, 48, 57, 60; homes on, *88, 91;* language of, 96, 220
Linlithgow, Scotland, *59*
Literacy: Congregationalists' promotion of, 122; of Highlanders, 49–50, 90, 102, 114, 179; of Lowlanders, 58
Liverpool, England, 201, 208, 258n12
Lochaber district, Scottish Highlands, 57
Longhouse, 29, 30, 31, 36
Long Island, North America, 117, 120, 121
Lords of the Isles, 21, 32, 41, 44, 48, 232n72
Lothian, Marquis of, 206
Louis XIV, 73
Love, W. DeLoss, 203, 214
Low, William, 87
Lowlanders, Scottish: as creditors to Highlanders, 51; economy of, 58–59, 62; and education, 3, 8, 56–58, 75–76, 97; historic role of, 67; professional classes of, 75–76; religion of, 46, 56, 65; as schoolmasters, 88–89; society and culture of, 8, 27, 44, 56, 67; and Society in Scotland for the Propagation of Christian Knowledge, 73; tenant-landowner relationship, 59
Lowlands, Scotland, 4, 7; Gaels residing in, 56; immigrants, 21
Lynch, Michael, 20

280   Index

MacCodrum clan, 34
MacDonald, Alexander (Alasdair mac Mhaighstir Alasdair), 99–100, 167–68, 179
MacDonald, Flora, 167
MacDonald, Ronald, 97, 98–99
MacDonald clan, 56, 177, 237n3
MacGregor, "Rob Roy," 254n32
MacGregor clan, 166, 177, 254n32
Macinnes, Allan I., 37, 46, 47, 56, 72
MacInnes, John, 180
Mackay, John, 180, 181
Mackay, William, 94
MacKenzie, Lady, 111
MacLean, A. Sinclair, 181
MacLean, Donald, 178
Maclean, Norman, 106–107, 109–10, 216
MacLeod, John (journalist), 52
MacLeod, John (missionary), 118, 119
MacLeod, Ruarri Mór, 234n24
MacLeod clan, 48
Macleod Stone (Clach Mhic Leonid), Isle of Harris, 79
MacPherson, James, 231n49
Magnus the Lawmender, 21
Mahicans, 121, 126, 128
Mair, John, 44
Manners Society, 71, 72, 73, 76, 93
Manson, Donald, 111
Marshall, John, 198
Martin, Martin, 54–55, 78, 90
Mary, Queen (wife of William of Orange), 63, 68, 69
Mason, John, 95, 256n62
Massachusetts, 124, 126
Massachusetts Board of Correspondents, Society in Scotland for the Propagation of Christian Knowledge, 124
Matoaka (Pocahontas), 162
Mayhew, Thomas, Jr., 123
McGregor, Donald, 86
McLean, Norman, 87
M'Clure, David, 145–46
McWatie, Archibald, 94
Meek, Donald E., 46, 72, 181
Middle Ground, The (White), 129

Missionaries, to Native Americans, 9, 19, 154, 221; in Northern colonies, 121–24; in Southeast colonies, 118–21
Mitchison, Rosalind, 48
Mohawks, 22, 35, 36, 117, 121, 125; Algonquian schoolmasters and, 155, 156, 158; and American Revolution, 147; Brant, Joseph, 147; Johnson and, 153; Occom and, 150; ushers (assistant schoolmasters), 154
Mohegan River (Thames River), Connecticut, 186, 188, *188*
Mohegans, 23, 41, 116, 120, 256n58; English colonists and, 187–90; migration of, 215; Occom, Samson, 135, 186–89; and Pequot War, 187–88; tribe marker, *189*; and Wheelock's school, 141
Monasteries, 19, 32
Moncrieff, Rob Scott, 205
Montauks, 116, 120, 121; migration of, 215; Occom, and, 135, 160, 191–93; and Wheelock's school, 140, 141
Moor's Indian Charity School, 10, 138, 140–46, 160, 222; Algonquian pupils at, 155, 221; amenities at, 157; Brant's enrollment at, 147, 149; chores of students at, 143–44, 150, 156–57; Connecticut Board of Correspondents for, 152; course of learning at, 142–43; daily schedule at, 143; discipline and punishment at, 142, 250n19; enrollment at, 249n9; funding of, 151, 197, 205–208; kinship connections at, 141–42; Occom's recruitment for, 194; race and ethnic issues at, 145–46; religious instruction at, 143, 144, 145; transfer to New Hampshire, 152, 198, 213, 259n39
Moravians, and Native Americans, 118, 119
More, Joshua, 138
Morgan, Philip D., 5
Muhakaneoks, 121, 126, 128
Mull, Isle of, Scotland, 57
Murdoch, John, 58

Murray, James, 87, 104
Music and song: of Buchanan, 178–83; of Highlands, 60, 93–94, 124, 180, 181, 219; of Lowlands, 60; of Native Americans, 124, 129; Occom's hymn collection, 214; religious instruction in, 94–95
Muskogees, 118
Mystic Fort Massacre, 187
Myths, origin stories, and folk tales: of Algonquians, 11, 16, 19, 41, 124; of Ireland, 18, 31–34; of Iroquois, 11, 15, 16, 19, 31, 41, 124; of Scotland, 11, 18, 19, 20, 32, 33, 34, 41, 124, 231n49

Napier Commission, 107, 244n68
Narragansetts, 121; migration of, 215; and Wheelock's school, 140, 141, 150
National Covenant of 1638, Scotland, 63, 65
Native Americans: alcohol and, 125; children at boarding schools, death rates of, 249n7; cultural values of, 124–25; diet of, 157; early history of, 6; education of, 129, 131–33, 135, 136; English colonists' perception of, 12, 144; epidemics among, 22; and Great Awakening, 134–35; Great Britain and, 4; and Highland Gaels, similarities between, 124–25; migrations and displacements of, 128, 129, 215; and Moor's Indian Charity School, 137–38, 140–46; mythology and origin stories of, 15–16, 19, 30–31; of northeastern river valleys, *130;* oral tradition of, 41; poverty of, 125; and Society in Scotland for the Propagation of Christian Knowledge, 3–5, 9, 116–26, 128–29, 131–33, 147, 150, 151, 152, 154, 159–63, 217, 220, 221, 222; of southern New England, *139, 156;* Wheelock and, 153–54, 163. *See also* Algonquians; Iroquois
Nesuton, 122
New England, 121; Algonquians of, *139, 156;* Great Awakening in, 134; Irquois of, *156;* and Society in Scotland for the Propagation of Christian Knowledge, 117, 122; and Wheelock's boarding school, 136
New England Company (Company for Propagating the Gospel in New England), 119, 122, 123, 126, 128; Occom and, 137, 152, 191, 192, 197; Wheelock and, 151
New Jersey, 121, 124, 129–32
New Jersey Board of Correspondents, Society in Scotland for the Propagation of Christian Knowledge, 124
New Lights, 134, 135
New Netherlands, 126
New Stockbridge, New York, 12
New Testament. *See* Bible
New York, 12, 124
New York Board of Correspondents, Society in Scotland for the Propagation of Christian Knowledge, 120, 124, 150
Niantics, 121, 152; migration of, 215
Norsemen, 20–21
North America: immigrants, missionary efforts among, 119; land and climate of, 25; Northern colonies, 121–24; Scots Irish immigrants in, 119; and Society in Scotland for the Propagation of Christian Knowledge, 117; Southeast colonies, 118–21. *See also* Native Americans; New England
Northern and Western Islands of Scotland, The (Shaw), epigraph from, 15
Northern Isles, Scotland, language of, 7
Nova Scotia, Canada, 219

Oberg, Michael Leroy, 22
Occom, Mary Fowler, 141, 152, 192, 215, 216, 224, 260n2
Occom, Samson, 10–13, 95, 116, 120, 121, 135–37, 160, *194, 200,* 252n46; Atlantic voyage of, 163–64; British tour of, 196–201, 203–209, 211–13; Buchanan's similarities to, 192, 212–13, 223–25; conversion of, 190–91, 256n64; as cultural intermediary,

Occom, Samson (*continued*)
165, 224; culture and society of, 164, 215–16; early life and education of, 185–91; in Edinburgh, 203–209, 211–12; funds raised by, 201, 203, 259n30; house of, 195–96, 257n75; hymn collection by, 214, 259n42; last years and death of, 215; and migration of New England Algonquians, 215; at Montauk, 191–93; and New England Company, 137, 152, 191, 192; and Oneidas, 150, 151, 194, 195; printed sermon of, 214; in Scotland, 201, 203–209, 211–13; and Society in Scotland for the Propagation of Christian Knowledge, 150–51, 160, 193–94, 221, 222; and Wheelock, 140, 147, 150–53, 191, 193–96, 213–14

Ockham, Joshua, 185, 186, 189

Ockham, Sarah Wauby, 185, 186, 189, 190, 191, 256n66

Oisin (Ossian), 33, 34, 231n49

Oneidas, 22, 36, 117, 121, 141, 160; Algonquian schoolmasters and, 155, 159; Algonquians' move to lands of, 215; and American Revolution, 147; Fowler and, 157; Kirkland and, 147, 154; Occom and, 150, 151, 194, 195; and Wheelock's school, 250n19

Onondagas, 22, 36

Oral tradition: of Gaels, 11, 179, 180, 181, 218; of Native Americans, 41; of Occom and Buchanan, 212, 223

Origin stories. *See* Myths, origin stories, and folk tales

Oriskany, Battle of, 147

Orkneys, Scotland, 24

Ossian (Oisin), 33, 34, 231n49

Outer Hebrides, Scotland, 24; clan origin in, 34; education in, 57; language of, 95, 96; religion of, 56

Overhill Cherokees, 119, 120

Patrick Highlanders, 220

Peat, 58, 59, 85–86

Pennsylvania, 121, 129

Pequots, 23, 116, 121, 186, 187, 188, 256n58; migration of, 215; and Wheelock's school, 141

Pequot War, 23, 187–88

Perth, Treaty of, 21

Perthshire, Scottish Highlands, 168, 174, 176, *177*, 180, 181

Picts, 19, 20, 229n17

Pocahontas (Matoaka), 162

Poetry: Buchanan's, 174, 178–81; Gaelic, 180, 181

Pole, William, 87

Politeness, 71

Presbyterianism, 7, 8, 9, 47, 56, 63, 65, 71, 90, 218; and Brainerd brothers, 126, 131–33; and Buchanan, 181, 223; and Congregationalism, 136–37, 159; and Gaelic language, 98; and Kirkland, 147; music and, 219; and Native Americans, 117–20, 125, 126, 132, 160, 161, 220, 221; and Occom, 193, 223; and Scots Irish in North America, 119–20; Shorter Catechism, 179; and Society in Scotland for the Propagation of Christian Knowledge, 72, 90–92; Wheelock and, 138. *See also* Church of Scotland

Printer, James (Wowaus), 123

Pritani, 20, 229n17

Pumshire, John, 137

Puritans, 122

Raftery, Barry, 18

Raining, John, 105, 123, 243n61

Raining's School, Inverness, Scotland, 105–106, 107, *108*, 109, *109*, 110, 216, 243n61, 244n69

Ramsay, Donald, 86

Rannoch, district, Scottish Highlands, 10, 87, 104, 168, *173*, 174, *175*, 176, *177*, 178, 180

Redistributive exchange, Dodgshon's notion of, 54

Reformation, Scottish. *See* Scottish Reformation

Religion: of Highlanders, 47, 56, 112, 218; of Lowlanders, 46, 56; of Native Americans, 158, 221; of Scotland,

63–67; and Society in Scotland for the Propagation of Christian Knowledge, 72, 90–93; teaching of, at Moor's School, 143, 144, 145, 149. *See also* Great Awakening, First; *and specific Christian denominations*

Rennie, Frank, epigraph from, 3

Rents: of Highlander tenants, 51, 54, 55, 89; of Lowlander tenants, 59, 62

Rich, Thomas, 86

Richardson, Leon Burr, 203

Richter, Daniel K., 23

Riddell, Sir James, 111

Rising of 1689. *See* Jacobite rebellions, of 1689

Robertson, James, 97

Robert the Bruce, 44

Rob Roy (film), 46

Rob Roy (Scott), 254n32

Roebuck, Peter, 48

Romanticism: of Highlands, 46

Rose, James, 85

Rose, William, 111

Ross, John, 84

Ross and Cromarty, Scotland, 95

Rule, Andrew, 86, 106

Rush, Benjamin, 181, 185

Sabhal Mòr Ostaig, Isle of Skye, 114, *114*

Sage, Kenneth, 111

Salisbury, Neal, 35

Sasannach, 4–5

Schoolmasters, in Native American lands, 154–59

Schoolmasters, in Scottish Highlands, 79–81, 82–92; of apprenticeship schools, 111; assignments of, 89; bilingualism among, 102, 104, 109; Buchanan, Dugald, 174; community support of, 85–86, 112; curriculum of, 93; dwellings and classrooms of, 86–87, 111; Gaelic, instruction in, 94–95, 102, 104; inspectors of, 101, 102, 104; Jacobitism and, 98–99; linguistic restrictions of, 90, 96–97, 101, 102, 104–105, 218; music instruction by, 93–95; religious instruction by, 90–93; textbooks of, 92–93; training of, 106–107, 109; wages of, 85, 86

Scotland, *17*; clan pedigrees of, 20; economic and financial developments, 50–55, 58–59, 62, 69, 218; land and climate of, 16, 18, 33, 43; languages of, 7, 43; Occom in, 201, 203–209, 211–13, 222; origin stories of, 18, 19–20; union with England, 4, 7–8, 68–71, 238n9, 239n23. *See also* Highlands; Jacobite rebellions; Lowlands

Scots (English language), 7, 8, 49, 50, 71; and Society in Scotland for the Propagation of Christian Knowledge, 90–92, 102, 104, 113–14

Scots (people), 20

Scots Irish, in North America, 119, 120

Scots Magazine, 208

Scott, Sir Walter, 46, 254n32

Scotti, 18, 31, 32, 98

Scottish Enlightenment, 75, 185

Scottishness, Simpson's notion of, 66

Scottish Reformation, 46, 47, 63, 65, 66, 76; and Gaelic language, 98

Seanachaidh (historians), 47, 51

Selina, Countess of Huntingdon, 199

Senecas, 22, 36, 121, 157, 160

Sergeant, John, 138

Seven Ill Years, 69, 86

Seven Years' War (French and Indian War), 23–24, 120

Shapeshifting, 30, 34, 56

Shaw, Francis T., 55; epigraph from, 15

Shetlands, Scotland, 24

Simmons, William S., 16, 41

Simon, Daniel, 150

Simons, Sarah, 140

Simpson, Grant G., 66

Sinauky, 118

Skye, Isle of, Scotland, 27, *28*, 57, 96, *114*

Small, Mr. (Rannoch farmer), 178, 254n37

Smallpox, 22, 199

Smith, Charles Jeffrey, 197

Smith, Donald, 11

Smout, T. C., 58

Snow, Dean R., 36

Society for Reformation of Manners, 71, 72, 73, 76, 93
Society for the Propagation of the Gospel in Foreign Parts (SPG), 118, 119
Society in Scotland for the Propagation of Christian Knowledge (SSPCK), 3–5, 7–11, 50, 239n31; bilingual policy of, 101, 102; boards of correspondents of, 120, 124, 150, 151, 152, 154, 159, 160, 221; and Brainerd brothers, 137–38; Brant's connection with, 147; Buchanan and, 168, 169, 173; and cultural colonialism, 224; and Dartmouth College, 222; financing of, 77–78, 81, 111, 115, 121, 123–24, 246n15; founding of, 66–68, 70–75, 217; Fowler and, 151; and Gaelic, 72, 90, 95, 98–102, 104–105, 218, 219, 243n57; and Gaelic New Testament, 182, 209, 211; and General Assembly of Church of Scotland, 205, 217; gentlemen founders of, 75–76; goals of, 76–77, 115–16, 217, 218; Highland society described by, 12; industrial oriented schools, 110–11, 217; legacy of, 112–14, 220; membership qualifications, 84; and Moor's Indian Charity School, 147, 150, 151, 152, 154, 160–61, 205–208; and Native Americans, 3–5, 9, 116–26, 128–29, 131–33, 147, 150, 151, 152, 154, 159–63, 217, 220, 221, 222; Occom and, 150–51, 160, 193–94, 201, 203–206, 221, 222; and Raining's School, 105–107; schools opened by, in Highlands, 112, 113; in Stevenson's *Kidnapped*, 13–14; Wheelock and, 151, 152, 154, 160. *See also* Schoolmasters
Society of Jesus (Jesuits), 23, 47, 125, 126, 221
South Harris, Isle of, Scotland, 16
South Uist, Isle of, Scotland, 47
SPG. *See* Society for the Propagation of the Gospel in Foreign Parts
Spinning schools, 110–11, 112, 217, 245n80
Spiritual colonialism, 189

SSPCK. *See* Society in Scotland for the Propagation of Christian Knowledge
Stamp Act, 197
Statutes of Iona, 32, 48–50, 90
Stevenson, Robert Louis, 13–14
Stewart (Stuart), House of, 7, 21, 44, 47, 65, 68, 72, 73
Stewart, Alexander (schoolmaster), 83
Stewart, Alexander (Wolf of Badenoch), 44
Stewart, James (schoolmaster), 84
Stewart (Stuart), Rev. James (translator), 182, 209, 211
Stewart, John, 89
Stewart, Prince Charles Edward, 167, 182
Stewart, Robert, 87
St. Giles Cathedral, Edinburgh, Scotland, 63, *64*
St. Kilda, isles, Outer Hebrides, 78–79, 80, 95, 217, 222, 239n32
Stockbridge Indians, 128, 138, 248n35
Stockbridge-Munsee Band (Mohicans), 128
Storytelling, 124
Stuart, House of, 7. *See also* Stewart, House of
Stuart (Stewart), Rev. James, 182, 209, 211
"Sunways" circle, 47
Sutherland, Scotland, 95, 180, 181, 217
Syncretism, of Occom and Buchanan, 216

Tacksman (*fir-taca*), 37, 47, 51, 54, 56, 57, 89, 125, 218; and support of schoolmasters, 85, 111, 112
"Táin Bó Chuailagné" (Irish myth), 31–32
Tause, Arthur, 106
Tause, Charles, 106
Tawse, John, 87
Tay Bridge, Aberfeldy, Scotland, *99*
Tenants: and Crofters' Holding Act, 244n68; and education of Highlanders, 89, 111, 112; Highlander, 51, 54, 55, 56, 125; Lowlander, 58, 59, 62
Tennent, Gilbert, 256n64

Tennessee, 117, 119
Thames River (Mohegan River), Connecticut, 186, 188, *188*
Thayendanegea (Joseph Brant), 147, *148*, 149
Thomson, Derick, 12, 167–68, 181, 216, 224
Thomson, James, 181
Tiree, Isle of, Scotland, 12, 27
Tolboth Kirk, Edinburgh, Scotland, 207
Tomochichi, 118, 162
Tomockham, 186
Trial of an Interest in Christ (Guthrie), 93
Tuatha Dé Danann, 231n49
Tunxis, 121, 215
Tuscaroras, 121

Uncas, 186, 187
Union of 1707, 4, 7, 8, 68–71, 238n9, 239n23
Union of the Crowns (1603), 7, 8, 48
Universities, Scottish, 75–76
University of the Highlands and Islands (UH), 114, *114*, 235n49
Ushers (assistant schoolmasters), 154–55

Virginia, 117, 119–20
Vision quests, 30–31

Wade, George, *99*, 241n31
Wadsetting, 51, 54
"Wak'd by the Gospel's Pow'rful Sound" (Occom), 214
Wales, Occom's funding-raising in, 208
Wallace, Arch, 205
Wampanoags, 23
Warriors (*buannachan*), 37, 47, 51, 52

Watts, Isaac, 181, 214
Webster, Alexander, 205, 207
Welsh (language), 96, 100, 101
Wesley, Charles, 118, 119
Wesley, John, 118, 119, 245n8
Western Isles, Scotland. *See* Hebrides
West Highlands, Scotland, 24–25
Westminster Confession, 65
Wheelock, Eleazar, 10, 120, 135–38, 146, 149–54, 158, 163; and Dartmouth College, 198, 213–14, 222; fund-raising by, 198; and Great Awakening, 149, 190; Occom and, 140, 147, 150–53, 191, 193–96, 213–14; and Society in Scotland for the Propagation of Christian Knowledge, 151, 152, 154, 160. *See also* Moor's Indian Charity School
Wheelock, John, 145–46
Whigs (Scotland), 70, 71, 72, 167
Whitaker, Nathaniel, 197, 198, 199, 201, 203–207, 222
White, Richard, 128–29
Whitefield, George, 138, 152, 160, 163, *172*, 190; at Cambuslang Wark, 171, 173; and fund-raising in Britain, 197; Occom and, 193, 198, 199, 258n9
William Augustus (Duke of Cumberland), 241n31
William III (William of Orange), 47, 55–56, 63, 65, 68, 69, 237nn3–4
Williams, Daniel, 123
Willingboro, New Jersey, 131
Withrington, Donald J., 57
Wood, Seymour, 115
Woolley, Joseph, 137, 252n46
Wowaus (James Printer), 122
Wright, Francis, 86

Yamacraws, 118, 119
Young, Edward, 181